Peter H

the columba press

First published in 2002 by
the columba press
55A Spruce Avenue, Stillorgan Industrial Park,
Blackrock, Co Dublin

Cover by Bill Bolger
Origination by The Columba Press
Printed in Ireland by Colour Books Ltd, Dublin

ISBN 1 85607 346 7

Contents

Introduction

day is breaking.' But Jacob said, 'I will not let you go, ᵘᵘⁱᵉˢˢ ʸ bless me.' So he said to him, 'What is your name?' And he said, 'Jacob.' Then the man said, 'You shall no longer be called Jacob, but Israel, for you have striven with God and with humans, and have prevailed.' Then Jacob asked him, 'Please tell me your name.' But he said, 'Why is it that you ask my name?' And there he blessed him. So Jacob called the place Peniel, saying, 'For I have seen God face to face, and yet my life is preserved.' The sun rose upon him as he passed Peniel, limping because of his hip. (Gen 32:24-31)

Three key facts
This story about Jacob emphasises three interesting facts. It emphasises the fact that Jacob saw God face to face or that he came to know God in an intimate way. The story also emphasises how much Jacob desired this experience of intimacy when it says that he sought to know God's name. This was something Jacob was willing to wrestle with or to employ all his energy and every muscle to attain. Finally the passage tells us that even though Jacob attained his deepest longing he left the scene limping. In encountering the Holy One 'face to face' he also encountered his own woundedness, the weakness and waywardness that are a feature of Jacob's story as they are of ours.

To see God face to face

This book is based on the basic fact that the three persons of the Trinity *want to reveal themselves to us* and thus to satisfy our deepest longing, *the hunger we are* for their love. This, according to the prophet Jeremiah, is the purpose of the New Covenant that each person, 'the least no less than the greatest' should 'know God'. (Jer 31:34) The passionate pursuit of this purpose is what motivates Jesus throughout the gospel.

> I have made your name known to them and will continue to make it known so that the love you have for me may be in them and that I too may be in them. (Jn 17:26)

To know God in the way Jesus wants us to requires a disciplined effort to reflect and to pray that is comparable to wrestling. This effort, in which we employ as much ingenuity and energy as we would when we wrestle, is required if we are to enter fully into the relationships the persons of the Trinity initiate when they reveal themselves to us. In other words, to become intimate we must learn how to engage in the combat of dialogue.

The combat of dialogue

The film *The Horse Whisperer,* in its portrayal of the struggle required if we are to develop and maintain our relationships, provides us with a symbol similar to that of Jacob wrestling with God. The film tells the story of Tom and how he uses his ability to relate with horses to help a young girl overcome the effects of a traumatic event in her life. She had been involved in a horrific accident when a lorry crashed into the horse she was riding.

While Tom is employed to deal with the effect of the accident on the horse, with its refusal to let anyone come near it, he finds himself drawn into coping with the after-effects of the accident on the young girl. She is struggling to deal with the shock of the accident, with having her leg amputated and with what has happened to her horse. Tom has also to wrestle with the girl's parents who are too preoccupied with their work to make their relationship with their daughter and with each other a priority.

The wrestling involved in relating

The way Tom wrestles with these problems is a symbol of our

lifelong struggle to establish and maintain our relationships. We come to these with our own unique traumas which events from the past have generated. These traumas, like that of the horse, cause us to keep others at a distance for fear that they might open up old wounds again.

In depicting Tom's efforts to establish a relationship with the horse there is a marvellously symbolic scene in the film when the horse manages to escape into a large field. Rather than try-

horse is like a dialogue he goes to great rounds to initiate. However, it is not just the horse that he engages in this dialogue but the mother and her daughter as well. By drawing them into this dialogue Tom helps them to overcome their fear of intimacy so that they gradually draw near to him. Yet we know that what he has begun with them will be a life-long struggle that will continue to engage and exercise every fibre of their being.

Prayer as conversation

The central role that conversation plays in Tom's relationships is highlighted by the saying that *a relationship is as good as the communication going on within it.* This saying is as true of our relationship with God as it is of all our other relationships. However, our relationship with God is the central one, for on it all others depend. This is because the vision of ourselves that we see in God's eyes when we pray determines the way we see and relate with others and with everything around us.

Jesus' commandment that we love others and all things as he has loved us is more a statement of fact than a command. If we believe that Jesus loves us, we are not only led to see and feel about ourselves in a new way but about others and all things as well. Therefore, prayer as a conversation which the Father, Jesus and the Spirit initiate when they reveal themselves to us is essentially a struggle to establish and sustain all our relationships. This is why Jesus spends much of his life engaging people in conversation for he sees their ability to listen and respond to him as 'the one thing necessary'. (Lk 10:38-42)

Two Traditions

In a book called, *The Love of Learning and the Desire for God,* Jean Leclercq gives us the fruit of his study of two traditions concerning prayer that we are heir to. The earlier of these was a monastic tradition and its aim was wisdom, or an intimate knowledge of God. This tradition, which deeply influenced people from the 4th to the 13th century, was rooted in personal experience of reflecting on and praying with the Word of God. The later tradition of the Scholastics, which has predominated since the middle ages, aims at what is a more exterior knowledge which is achieved through rational analysis or speculation.

Four steps of Jacob's ladder

To attain its interior knowledge the monastic tradition employs what is known as the Benedictine method of prayer. It uses the symbol of the ladder in Jacob's dream to emphasise the nature of prayer as a conversation. There are four stages or steps in this conversation at which we:

1) focus our attention on some piece of the Word of God we want to pray with,

2) listen to this,

3) respond to what we have heard,

4) and contemplate what God opens up for us in the first three steps to gain an interior knowledge of it.

The Spiritual Exercises

The Spiritual Exercises are a practical way St Ignatius of Loyola devised of sharing with us his experience of what the persons of the Trinity revealed to him. To do this Ignatius adopted the Benedictine method of prayer as a way of savouring and assimilating all that the Father, Jesus and the Holy Spirit plan to share with us. Central to this plan is the Incarnation through which they want to give us *an interior knowledge of Jesus Christ our Lord who became a human being out of love for each of us.* Coming to know Jesus in this way is, for Ignatius, at the heart of his book of exercises for we are thus drawn into the love of the Father which Jesus expresses in human terms and which the Holy Spirit leads us into an interior knowledge of. In the quest for this interior knowledge the Spiritual Exercises add two important dimensions to the Benedictine view of prayer.

Firstly, the Spiritual Exercises seek *to involve our whole person in*

to him as a spiritual pilgrim, Ignatius invites us to learn from our own experiences by doing exercises. He says to us in effect, 'Do these exercises and I feel sure that you will be given the intimate knowledge of the love of Jesus that I was given.'

The role of reflection

Reflection is central to the Spiritual Exercises as it is to this book. The reason is that, if the persons of the Trinity are to reveal themselves to us when we pray, it is essential that we learn to reflect on our experience of how they do this. It is essential to notice, to articulate and to keep coming back to the way the Father, Jesus and the Spirit reveal themselves to us by gently and gradually enlightening and attracting us. This enlightenment and attraction is like the 'gentle whisper' in which Elisha was led to recognise the voice of God. (1 Kgs 19:12) It is easy to miss this 'gentle whisper' unless we develop our ability to notice it, to understand the way we are enlightened and to respond to the way we are attracted to make our own of it. By means of reflection we become aware of and take responsibility for the way the Spirit 'leads us into all the truth' or into an interior knowledge of 'how long and broad, how high and deep is the love of Christ'. (Jn 16:13, Eph 3:17-19)

The twofold purpose of this book

Learning how to pray and reflect

This book has a twofold aim. The main one is to enter into the fullness of the Christian life by gaining an intimate knowledge of the love of Jesus, and the other is to learn the basic ways of gaining this interior knowledge through prayer and reflection. These basic ways people have learned to pray and reflect over the centuries are essential to the growth not only of our relationship with God but to the growth of all the relationships which constitute our inner world. The following is an outline of the eight parts of the book, through which we hope to develop our ability to pray and reflect:

Part 1 (Exs 1-3) deals with how basic to all our relationships is our *desire to pray*. Making space in our life to pray is essential if we are to develop the relationship with *the three persons of the Trinity* on which all others depend.

Part 2 (Exs 4-8) deals with how we get *our whole person*, 'heart, soul, mind and strength' involved in getting *an interior knowledge of the love of God* 'poured into our heart by the Holy Spirit'.

Part 3 (Ex 9) deals with how we can draw on our *imagination* to increase our involvement in prayer.

Part 4 (Exs 10-13) deals with a way of *praying with the Word of God* and with how we can use *reflection* to become more sensitive and responsive to the way God enlightens and attracts us in prayer.

Part 5 (Exs 14-15) deals with how we *come to know Jesus* in the gospels.

Part 6 (Exs 16-18) deals with what is involved in *answering Jesus' call to know, love and follow him*.

Part 7 (Exs 19-20) deals with how we can *enter into the suffering and death of Jesus* and grow in our appreciation of the passionate love which led him to undergo all of this.

Part 8 (Exs 21-22) deals with how we can enter into *the glory and joy of Jesus' resurrection* and how we let this glory and joy pervade our lives.

'All I want is to know Christ'

The main aim of this book is to learn how we can use prayer and reflection as a means of gaining an intimate knowledge of the love of Jesus and thus to be 'filled with the utter fullness of God'. (Eph

3:16-21) We will seek this intimate knowledge with the help of the Spiritual Exercises, hoping that they will provide a way of attaining this knowledge working within the context of our daily routine. To do the Exercises in this way requires that we set aside an hour for prayer each day. It will also help greatly if we can get someone who knows us and the Spiritual Exercises to accompany us on our journey through these Exercises. For the person wanting to do the

Spiritual Exercises in the context of an ordinary day, Exercises 1-22

At *the second stage* we look at the story of how we have failed to make God the Lord of our life. We examine the nature of this failure or of our sinfulness and its seriousness so that we might appreciate how faithful God is to us.

At *the third stage* we seek an intimate knowledge of Jesus Christ our Lord who become a human being out of love for each of us.

At *the fourth stage* we look at how Jesus calls us to be his companions and at what is involved in being with him in this way.

At *the fifth stage* we look at how as Jesus' companions we are called to share in his sufferings so that we may realise how much he loves us.

At *the sixth stage* we focus on how we are called to enter into the glory and joy of Jesus and into the way he wants to make our lives glorious and joyful.

PART 1

Prayer as the basis of all our relationships

In Part 1 we will examine the true significance of *our desire to pray* springing as it does from our dream or deepest longing. This longing is to enter fully into the relationships which make up our inner world but especially into the relationship which the three persons of the Trinity initiate by revealing themselves to us.

In this context prayer is primarily a *listening* to this revelation but it is also a *response* of the heart to what we have listened to. Thus, prayer is essentially a *conversation* in which God engages each person 'face to face as a friend'. (Ex 33:11) Through this conversation we seek to establish and maintain our relationship with the Father, with Jesus and with the Spirit, because on the health of our relationship with them all our other relationships depend.

If we are to meet this basic need we have to pray, we must make a fundamental decision which is to *make the space* that prayer requires.

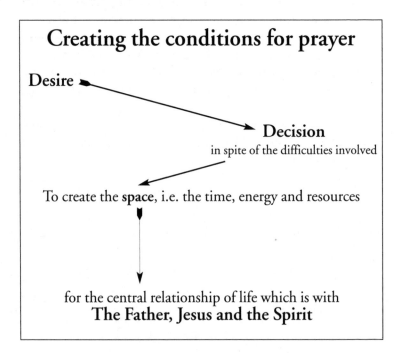

Creating the conditions for prayer

Desire

Decision
in spite of the difficulties involved

To create the **space**, i.e. the time, energy and resources

for the central relationship of life which is with
The Father, Jesus and the Spirit

EXERCISE 1

The fundamental nature of our desire to pray

The deep desires of our inner world seek to emerge
when those of our outer world are satisfied.
Blocking their emergence deadens us.

to God's own

This conversation provides the foundation
on which rests all our other relationships.

*'The contemplative act
is the permanently basic act of all external action:
it is active and effective, fruitful and missionary
beyond all external undertakings of the Church.'*
Hans Urs von Balthasar

Our need to pray springs from our deep desire

to converse with God in prayer.

On the fulfilment of this desire

rests the health of all our relationships.

The Second Journey

In the film *Shall We Dance?* we have the story of a man who is happily married, has a child, a steady job as an accountant and has just moved into a fine new house. He seems to have fulfilled his life's ambitions and yet there is a heaviness about him at home and at work. One evening as he travels home from work by train he notices a beautiful young woman standing at an open window and he is entranced by her. Each evening after that the glimpse he gets of her brings him alive. When he discovers that the woman is a teacher of ballroom dancing he decides to take dancing lessons in the hope that he might meet her. Even though this does not work out, as beginners have a more mature lady instructing them, a whole new world surrounding dancing opens up for him. All that surrounds this world is outside the bounds of propriety and would be frowned on by his wife and those with whom he works. In spite of the risks involved he continues his lessons as it meets some deep need in his life and the enlivening effects on him become obvious as the film proceeds.

Our deeper longings

At a certain stage in life we reach a point when, like the man in the story above, we have satisfied most of the needs of our outer world. For example, when we have become successful at the work we do or when we have married and reared a family, we may feel the need to meet the deeper needs of our inner, spiritual world or to realise a deeper dream. This emerging desire to focus more of our energy on meeting the needs of our inner world centres around our relationships. These are chiefly the ones we seek to develop with our inner self and with a circle of people who play a significant role in our life. These key relationships also include ones we develop with a wider range of people and with the world around us. If we do not take responsibility for deepening these relationships we will feel frustrated even though we may not know why.

Opening up our relationships through conversation

The main way we develop the relationships which are at the centre of our inner world is by developing the communication that goes on within them. These relationships will be as good, healthy or intimate as this communication. The reason why this communication, or our ability to listen and respond, is so central to our inner world is that it is the most effective way we receive and return the

that with the signi...

like our parents whose love has given us life and like our friends whose love sustains us. The most important of these people and the ones with whom we have the deepest need to communicate are the three persons of the Trinity. They are always seeking to make themselves known to us in new ways so that they might extend and deepen their relationship with us. If they are to be able to do this it is necessary that we listen and respond to what they wish to say to us. This ability to converse with the Father, with Jesus and with the Spirit 'face to face as with a friend' is what we mean by prayer.

Contemplative prayer is nothing else than
the close sharing between friends.
Teresa of Avila

The Exercise

To understand your deeper longings and how central a life of prayer is to satisfying them you may find some of the following suggestions helpful.

1) Look through a magazine you are familiar with and see do any of the advertisements in it make use of our deeper aspirations to increase the appeal of some product. In any of the articles in the magazine is there a reference to our deeper longings?

2) What way do you notice deeper human concerns surfacing in the life of one person you know well? In a story you have read or seen acted out in a play or in a film describe an aspiration of one character that you identified with. What did it say to you about your own deep desires? Write down one deep desire that has been surfacing in your life of late and describe it. Say, for example, when and how it emerges and what feeling you associate with it.

3) When you reflect on your own deep longings or those of others do you associate prayer with meeting any of these longings? Is there a view of prayer which you have inherited that makes it seem an unrealistic way of meeting your deeper needs? Say what prayer has meant for you at one time in the past and compare this with how you see it now. What idea about prayer appealed to you most in the introduction to this exercise?

4) List some of the ways you pray formally or informally during the day. What do you want to do about giving prayer a more important place in your life? What is your main reason for doing this? Describe a difficulty you foresee if you are to take your desire to pray seriously?

Various ways of praying

Some of the ways people pray are more active while others are more contemplative. The active approach is seen in people's preference for vocal prayers such as the rosary or in their use of mental prayer to reflect on the meaning of the Word of God and on its implications for their lives. People who use a conversational form of prayer often begin in an active way but their conversation may gradually

God's Word on what emerges from the exercise.)

The story of prayer in the Bible begins with God opening up a dialogue or conversation with people like Abraham. This conversation is initiated when God reveals a plan for Abraham's future and when Abraham responds by revealing how he feels about this plan. (Gen 12:1-5). This dialogue is continued with Moses with whom God 'spoke face to face as with a friend'. (Ex 33:11) The Psalms are a heartfelt response to God's revelation and to our longing for God. (Ps 42 & 43) Through the prophet Jeremiah we learn that God wishes to initiate a dialogue with each person. (Jer 31:34) Like Samuel we need to learn to discern through reflection what God wants us to listen and respond to in prayer. (1 Sam 3:1-21) Jesus seeks to satisfy our deepest longings by making the Father's love known to us in the intimate way that he knows it. (Jn 7:37-39, Jn 6:35, Jn 10:14-15, 17:26) Jesus makes it clear that this intimate knowledge is attained through listening and responding to the Word (Lk 8:19-21) and he appreciates the difficulty we have in making space to do this. (Lk 8:11-15)

EXERCISE 2

The space we need to pray

We tend to make time for what is urgent
and neglect what is important.

If we are to make the space or the time, energy and resources
we need for prayer,
we must keep clarifying the importance of prayer
within all our relationships.

Preparing the immediate space we need for prayer involves
choosing a suitable time, place and posture,
as well as creating the right atmosphere within which
we can quieten our body and focus our spirit.

*'Things that matter most must never be at the mercy
of things that matter least.'*
Stephen Covey

If the growth of all our relationships

depend on our ability

to converse with God in prayer

then the space it requires must be a priority.

Taking time to sharpen the saw

At the end of his book, *Seven Habits of Highly Effective People*, Stephen Covey gives the following illustration of a choice that is always confronting us. He asks us to imagine ourselves walking in a forest and coming across a forester culling trees. After watching him for some time we become aware that his saw is not very sharp for even though he is working hard he is not

of time, energy and resources that is available to us each day. Often we meet pressing or urgent needs and postpone or neglect more important ones. We become so busy that we have no time to sharpen the saw. For example, in our work or relationships we may spend most of our energies meeting urgent or immediate needs and have little left for clarifying our priorities and defining the goal of each of these and the means we need to take to attain it. If this situation continues, the way we relate and the way we work becomes, like the blunt saw, ineffective.

Creating space for prayer

We have seen in Exercise 1 how important prayer is to all our relationships. This is so because our relationships are as good as the
communication going on within them and prayer is the communication that goes on within the relationship on which all others
depend. Now it is a fact that we make space in our day for what is
important, provided its importance remains clear or defined.
Therefore, we need to keep clarifying for ourselves the nature and
importance of prayer if we are to make the space that it requires.

The time, energy and resources prayer needs

Making space to pray involves making available the time, the energy
and the resources it requires. In other words, prayer requires prime
time when our energy level is high. It also requires us to be as re-
sourceful when we pray as we are when we engage in any activity
that is a priority for us. Our reluctance to make space for inner
work, such as the exercises in this book, is due in part to the fact
that we are not as accountable for its quality as we are for that of
our outer work. There is a lot more tangible pressure on us to use
all our resources in our work situation than when we come to do
the inner work of prayer.

Preparing the immediate space prayer requires

There is another kind of space we need to create when we pray.
Creating it involves choosing a suitable time and place to pray as
well as cultivating a suitable atmosphere and adopting a helpful
posture. The most important preparation for prayer is to quieten
our body and to centre our spirit. Some suggestions for doing this
are provided on the final page of this exercise.

The Exercise

Some of the following questions and suggestions may help you to clarify the need you have to make space in your life for prayer.

1) What does the world of advertising or that of TV want us to make a priority or to give the lion's share of our time and attention to? As you listen to people's stories on the radio or on TV do you find that your priorities differ much from those of others?

in your day.

3) What do you plan to do about establishing a time, a place and the right atmosphere in which to pray? What might you do to create this prayerful atmosphere in the place where you intend to pray? As you begin your prayer choose a way to slow down, to let go of your preoccupations and to relax. There are some suggestions as to how you might do this on the following page. When you have become quiet and relaxed, shift your attention to a phrase or short sentence which expresses an idea or a sentiment that is important for you. You may take the words or the phrase you use from scripture or from your own experience. Repeat these words slowly until you become quiet and focused.

Ways of quietening yourself

1) Become aware of the sounds you hear around you, the more obvious ones first and then the more subtle ones.
2) Spend a short time noticing how your face feels and then do this with your hands, arms, chest, back, legs and feet.
3) Focus on the sensations you experience in one part of your body.
4) Relax each part of your body in turn, letting any tension you notice there drain away.
5) Become aware of your breathing as you notice it in your nose or in your stomach.
6) Become aware of your heartbeat and let this sensation grow till it pervades your whole person.
7) Become aware of how you feel just now. As soon as some feeling surfaces stay with it to let it expand and be owned.

Scripture: 'Be still and know that I am God'
(Choose any of the following passages of scripture that help you to stay with any enlightenment you received while doing the exercise)

The need to make space in our lives for what is important or a priority is stressed in the parable about the guests invited to a wedding feast. (Lk 14:16-24) In the parable of the rich fool, (Lk 12:16-34) and in the parable of Dives and Lazarus, (Lk 16:19-31) Jesus urges us to free ourselves from a preoccupation with many things so that we make space for what he terms 'the one thing necessary'. (Lk 10:38-42) This consists in the relationships with God, ourselves and others that Jesus calls us to come apart and make space for. (Mk 6:31) What is central to all these relationships, as it gives us the ultimate proof of our own significance and that of others, is Jesus' love of us. (Jn 15:12) This love is what we remember and celebrate at Mass. (Lk 22:19) We have a deep need to calm the storm of outer events if we are to find the stillness Jesus wants to reign in our lives. (Mk 4:35-39)

EXERCISE 3

The relationships we make space for

The main thing we want to make space for
is to foster our relationships and especially that
which the Father, Jesus and the Spirit initiate
~~when they reveal themselves to us~~

'And the Catholic Faith is this:
That we worship one God in Trinity, and Trinity in Unity;
neither confounding the Persons, nor dividing the Substance.'
Athanasian Creed

The key relationship

we make space for when we pray

is that which the three persons of the Trinity

initiate when they reveal themselves

to each of us

Prayer as a conversation
with the three persons of the Trinity

What we need to make space for in our lives is to foster the relationships which form the basis of our inner world. Chief among these relationships is that which is initiated by the persons of the Trinity when they reveal themselves to us. One of the most striking efforts to portray this relationship is the icon painted by the monk Andrea Rublev in 1425.

The Rublev Icon, one of the great masterpieces of Russian art, is based on an incident in the book of Genesis. 'The Lord appeared to Abraham by the oaks of Mamre, as he sat at the entrance of his tent in the heat of the day. He looked up and saw three men standing near him. When he saw them, he ran from the tent entrance to meet them, and bowed down to the ground'. (Gen 18:1-2)

In the centre of the Rublev Icon is the Eucharistic cup, and the three youthful figures, as much women in their appearance as men, are a picture of serenity as they contemplate lovingly the plan of Redemption. It has been stated 'that nowhere does there exist anything similar with regard to strength of theological synthesis, the richness of symbolism, and artistic beauty'. It is generally accepted that the person on the right represents the Holy Spirit, that the person in the centre represents the Son and that the person on the left represents the Father. The aim of the artist, however, was not to lead us to one person or another of the Trinity but to help us contemplate the relationship they wish to establish with us as they reveal themselves to us especially in the Eucharist.

A Vision Always the Same Always New

The fundamental purpose of prayer is to build up and to maintain the relationships which the persons of the Trinity initiate by revealing themselves to us. We enter this relationship when we listen and respond in prayer to the Father's self-revelation as love, to how Jesus expresses this in human terms and to the intimate knowledge the Spirit gives us of it. Listening and responding to their love in prayer

for relationships for it initiates a new

this love more real it will help to think of it, for example, in terms of the way they acknowledge, accept, appreciate and are concerned for us. To recall their love it is better to work with one significant memory of it at a time. As we dwell with these memories we will get glimpses of who each of the persons is for us now.

Capturing the vision in words

By putting words on what arises as we tell the story of our relationship with each of the three persons, a picture of the Father, of Jesus and of the Spirit will emerge. By using a word or phrase that captures some aspect of this picture as it emerges, and then repeatedly listening and responding to this word or phrase, our relationship with each of the three persons will become more clearly defined, personal and authentic.

The Exercise

Some of the following suggestions may help you to clarify how you see, feel about and relate to each of the persons of the Trinity.

Telling the story

Begin by recalling a key moment in the development of your relationship with each of the three persons. There may be other experiences triggered off by this key one that you feel drawn to dwell with. As you recall these experiences, pause from time to time to notice and to express any feelings that these experiences awaken.

Clarifying the picture that emerges

If any of these feelings aroused by telling the story of how you see the Father, Jesus or the Spirit are strong it will indicate that something significant is being said to you about the way you see this person. Express what is being said to you in a phrase or image drawn from the Word or God, from a prayer or from your experience of someone who has given you a glimpse of this kind of love. Listen to this word or phrase a number of times and then express any feeling it arouses.

Conversing with the Trinity

Since a conversation is what is called for by the self-revelation of the three persons of the Trinity, it is fitting to conclude your prayer by spending some time with the Father, with Jesus and with the Spirit. What you talk about depends on what struck you during the prayer.

Four Aspects of the Holy Trinity's Love

The following scripture passages may help you to become more aware of how the Father, Jesus and the Spirit acknowledge, accept, appreciate and are concerned for you.

1) They *acknowledge* us by their sensitivity to and respect for us. 'I have called you by name, you are mine. (Is 43:1) Zacchaeus is a

gives us the Spirit who reconciles us. (John 20:22)

3) They *appreciate* us, 'Your fame spread among the nations on account of your beauty, for it was perfect because of my splendour that I had bestowed on you'. (Ezek 16:14) 'Therefore, I tell you, her sins, which were many, have been forgiven; hence she has shown great love.' (Lk 7:44-50) 'And all of us, with unveiled faces, seeing the glory of the Lord as though reflected in a mirror, are being transformed into the same image from one degree of glory to another; for this comes from the Lord, the Spirit.' (2 Cor 3:7-18)

4) They are *concerned* for our welfare, 'I know the plans I have for you, says the LORD, plans for your welfare and not for harm, to give you a future with hope.' (Jer 29:11) 'I came that they may have life, and have it abundantly. I am the good shepherd who lays down his life for the sheep.' (Jn 10:10-11) '... the Spirit of truth will guide you into all the truth.' (Jn 16:13)

PART 2

Our main resource for prayer

In Part 1 we looked at our need to make space in our lives to pray if the three persons of the Trinity are to reveal themselves to us and thus to satisfy our deepest desire. In Part 2 we look at the way we are led into this revelation or into *an interior knowledge of the love of God* which the Holy Spirit 'pours into our hearts'. (Rom 5:5)

Who is the Holy Spirit for you?
In Part 2 we will concentrate on our relationship with the Holy Spirit. We will ask ourselves, Who is the Holy Spirit for me and what role do I see this third person of the Trinity playing in my prayer? We will see how the Holy Spirit leads us into 'all the truth' or into the love of God Jesus makes tangible for us. This love is made tangible not just in Jesus' own person but through all those who give us a glimpse of what his love is like. They give us this glimpse in the way they relate with us at the four levels at which we carry on all our relationships.

Our stream of inner wisdom
From a lifetime of relating at these four levels we have stored up in our memory a vast amount of experience of *the sensate events* of our story, of the *feelings* these events arouse, of *intuitive glimpses* of ourselves and others we glean from the events of our story and of the deep *convictions* of what is true and of value which these glimpses put us in touch with. Unfortunately, we may be unaware of much of this experience so that it runs like a stream of inner wisdom well below the surface of our lives. Part 2 will, therefore, be devoted to developing a way of arousing these dormant experiences so that we get an intimate knowledge of the love which the Spirit guides us into. (Jn 16:13)

Digging our well
to draw on four levels of experience

Sensate

These four feed our
underground stream of inner wisdom

EXERCISE 4

The Holy Spirit

The best part of life passes us by
when we remain unaware of the precious Jewel
that is ours in the Spirit's gift of love.

Our interior knowledge of this gift remains dormant
because it is dominated by an exterior knowledge
that is easier to attain and seems more real.

To arouse our interior knowledge of the Spirit's love
we need to get involved in
four levels of experience we have of it.

*'Let us hang upon the lips of all the faithful
for the Spirit of God is upon every one of them'.
Paulinus of Nola*

The story of how the Holy Spirit

has led us into the love of God

is written in our senses, heart, soul and mind.

It is tragic if we fail to remember this story

of all the love we have received and returned

The Spirit's essential gift of love

The journey in search of the jewel

There was once a man on a journey who came across a cave in which to his amazement he discovered a priceless jewel. This jewel was to be the inspiration of the rest of his life. However, all he could do was gaze at the jewel for it was held firmly in the grasp of a ferocious beast. During the years that followed, even

take the jewel away with him. As he made his way back home he gradually realised the meaning of what had happened.

This experience the man had in the cave unfortunately became largely dormant after he left the cave. This was because he busied himself with his external world and allowed his inner one which the jewel symbolised to remain untended. He missed out on so much enjoyment that could have been his if he had taken the trouble to remain aware of the jewel and the way he was gradually being led to take possession of it.

Our jewel is *the gift of love the Spirit gives us at our baptism*. Because of this gift we have always access to 'an experience of the love of God flooding through our hearts' (Rom 5:5) It is tragic if for most of our lives we remain unaware of and do not gradually take possession of the gift that is the realisation of all our dreams.

> The greatest sin is to remain unaware
> of the inner eventfulness of our lives.
> *Carl Jung*

The Spirit teaches you all things

Throughout our lives the Spirit seeks to 'lead us into all the truth' (Jn 16:13) or into the 'length and breadth and height and depth of the love of Christ' that the word 'truth' stands for. (Eph 3:14-21) We have as a result a huge body of experience of being loved and of being loving. It is, however, experience we are largely unaware of as it has become dormant. The reason for this is that the exterior knowledge we have of our outer world is so tangible and real for us that it makes the interior knowledge we have of our inner world seem unreal and unimportant by comparison. If we allow this situation to continue we will be greatly impoverished by being cut off from the world where our real riches are.

How we gain this interior knowledge

To arouse the vast amount of interior knowledge of the love which the Spirit has led us into we need to look at four aspects of it.

1) We need to *relive experiences* we have had of this love in our personal experience and in the Word of God.
2) Reliving important experiences arouses *feelings* that need our attention as they play a vital role in our relationships.
3) Feelings often indicate where something important is said to us so we need to capture these *glimpses* we get of ourselves and others by putting words on them.
4) These glimpses are the basic material out of which the *convictions* that shape our lives are formed.

Drawing on these four levels of experience is extremely important for it is what makes the love which the Spirit 'pours into our hearts' real and engaging.

The Exercise

The aim of this and the next four exercises is to help you to become more aware of who the Holy Spirit is for you now and how your life has been influenced by the four levels at which you have experienced the Spirit's gift of love throughout your life.

Who is the Holy Spirit for you?

After quietening yourself for some time, recall an experience in

Four loves

There are four aspects of the love the Holy Spirit gives you a gift of and constantly leads you into. These are: 1) the love God has for you, 2) the love you have for God, 3) the love significant people in your life have for you and 4) the love you have for these people. Taking each of these four loves in turn, recall a time when you experienced it. Let the Spirit say to you a number of times how you were loved or how you loved in the incident you have recalled.

How the Spirit looks on you lovingly

Imagine that you are on your way to meet the Spirit in some quiet place. When you meet the Spirit mention something about your relationship that concerns you and then listen to the Spirit's reply. Ask how the Spirit views your life and spend time with the way *the one who is love* accepts and affirms you.

Our relationship with the Holy Spirit

How the Spirit influences us

We are given seven gifts by the Spirit through which we are led into the love which is God's essential gift. Three of the seven (Wisdom, Understanding and Knowledge) help us to *listen to our experience* of this love and four (Counsel, Fortitude, Piety and Fear of the Lord) help us to *respond to it.* By teaching us to listen and respond to the love of God in this way the Spirit draws us into a union or 'fellowship'. This is the friendship the Father and Jesus initiate by revealing their love for us and which the Spirit's seven gifts help us to develop and maintain. (Jn *15:15*)

Scripture: Our experience of LIFE-GIVING LOVE

In the story of creation and in that of the dry bones, as well as in the baptism of each Christian, it is the Spirit who gives life. (Gen 1:1, Ezek 37:14, Jn 3:5) Jesus tells us that this life he has come to give us in abundance (Jn 10:10) consists in coming to know the Father and himself and especially their love for us. (Jn 17:3) The Spirit gradually leads us into this life-giving love throughout our lives. (Jn 16:13) If this love the Spirit opens up for us is to be really life-giving it is not sufficient that it be known in an intellectual way. It must be experienced at the four levels at which we receive and return all love, i.e. with our 'whole heart, soul, mind and strength'. (Lk 10:25-28)

EXERCISE 5

The sensate dimension of love

Through our senses we can re-enter
the events of our story and listen to
'the music of what happens'.

but there is a life-giving love awaiting us there.

*'Love makes an entry through our senses
and always depends on them.'*
Captain Corelli's Mandolin

Our senses activate and engage us

in the story of how the Spirit had led us

into all the love

we have received and given

The sensate level of our experience

One day the Irish mythic warrior Fionn was resting for a while when he and his companions were out hunting. A question arose about what was the most beautiful music in the world. Oisin said it was the cuckoo calling while Oscar said that in his opinion it was the ring of a spear on a shield. Other companions said that the finest sound was the belling of a stag, the baying of hounds heard in the distance, the song of a lark, the laughter of a gleeful girl or the whisper of a moved one. When they eventually turned to Fionn and said, 'Tell us, chief, what you think,' he answered, 'The music of what happens, that is the finest music in the world'

There is a music in the stories people tell about what has happened to them in their lives that we never seem to tire of. Each person's story can be compared to a tapestry for it is woven with the threads of events which form a distinctive pattern. This pattern becomes obvious in hindsight when we recall the events of our story, the places we have been, the people we have met, and the significance of these. When we become aware of this pattern of events that is like the design of a tapestry or like the artful arrangement of notes in a piece of music, it arrests the eye and the ear like any work of art does.

It was St Patrick's desire to show us the tapestry that he sees woven around his belief in the Trinity that urged him to write his *Confession*. He wrote it in spite of all the difficulties and dangers he knew this self-disclosure involved.

> Although I am imperfect in many ways I want my brethren and relatives to know what kind of man I am, so that they may understand the aspiration of my life ... My decision to write must be made, then, in the light of our faith in the Trinity. The gift of God and his eternal consolation must be made known regardless of danger.

The music of what happens

The most basic level at which we experience the Spirit's gift of love is through our senses. All our experience begins with the sensate aspect of the events of our story as 'There is nothing in our mind that was not first of all in our senses'. (St Thomas Aquinas) This experience of love which our senses provide comes mainly from reflecting on the major events of our story but also from reflecting on the

Because of the emphasis on our mind in the way we are educated, we tend to think about the events of our story rather than relive them. However, if we start with our memory of the way people relate with us in the events of our story our whole person, and not just our mind, gets involved. This is because reliving events puts us in touch with our feelings, with engaging glimpses which can trigger off deep convictions about what means most to us.

'Take care that you do not forget!'

Our reluctance to re-live the events of our story is partly due to the disciplined effort this requires but it is also due to painful memories of our limitations and those of others we encounter in our story. However, if we take the trouble to re-live those events of our story, in which people loved us in very real, even if limited ways, we will find ourselves nourished by our memories. We will understand why God urges us not to forget the good things that have happened to us. (Deut 6:4-14)

The Exercise

Some of the following suggestions may help you to become more aware of the importance of your senses in the way the Spirit leads you to receive love and to return it.

1) Choose a picture from a magazine or paper that says something to you and then notice one way it appeals to your senses to do this. Recall an advertisement you have seen on TV and notice how many of your senses it appeals to. Recall a story and notice some of the ways it depends on your senses to get you involved in it.

2) Recall an incident in your life where love entered through your senses and has always remained dependent on them. Notice how many of your senses were involved in the way love entered your life in this incident and in the way it has been sustained. Tell the story of a significant event in your life and, after writing down why it was significant, describe how dependent you were and are on your senses to remember the event.

3) Relive an incident in which you experienced the love of someone. As you do so, write down who was involved, what was said and what was done. Allow yourself time to savour the atmosphere, to be touched by and to resonate with 'the music of what happens'.

4) Let one of your senses tell you the story of its relationship with you. Then let it describe where that relationship is now. Write out one thing this sense wants to say to you and then your reply to this. If you wish you could continue writing down this dialogue until you both are satisfied you have said all you want to say to each other.

Listening to four stories

There are four stories we need to keep telling. The first of these is about what happens each day, the events which have something important to say if we but listen. Then there is the story of the significant events of our life in the light of which we need to see the events of each day. There is a third story we need to keep listening to as it talks to and highlights aspects of our own story, whose meaning and value we might not otherwise notice. This story is one we hear

more than in any other way

are the supreme moment of revelation in the Old Testament just as the events of the death and resurrection of Jesus are the supreme moment of revelation in the New Testament. These events are a revelation of the provident love of God which pervades our life in the sense that all the events of our lives fall within the circle of this providence. (Deut 1:29-33) When seen against the background of God's providence every event in our lives can be constructive, (Rom 8:28) provided we strive to find its true significance against this background. (Deut 6:10-12) Everything that happens is ultimately a manifestation of God's care (Deut 7:7-9) and it is this care, when it is appreciated, that makes and sustains us. (Deut 32:6-9). It is easy to lose touch with this wider context that a sense of providence provides and in this way to get 'cut off from God's kindness'. (Wis 16:11) There is always this danger of letting the deeper significance of what happens 'slip from our hearts' (Deut 4:9) and of becoming deaf to 'the music of what happens'.

EXERCISE 6

Feelings are central to all our relationships

The belief that 'feelings don't count'
or that they hinder rather than help us relate
has left us largely illiterate emotionally.

Feelings are aroused when we tell our story
as they are central to the love
we receive and give in all our relationships.

Feelings are positive and negative,
a movement into or out of relationship,
a measure of our involvement in them.

By noticing, naming and sharing our feelings
we deepen and extend the range of our positive ones
and free ourselves from negative ones.

'We are governed more by our feelings than by reason.
Events that excite those feeling will produce wonderful effects.'
S. Adams

Feelings are central

to how we receive and return

the love of God which the Spirit gives us as gift.

We need to learn how

to notice, name and share

both our positive and negative feelings.

Becoming emotionally literate

In one of Woody Allen's films called *Another Woman* we have the unfolding of the story of a woman's attitude to her feelings. At the beginning of the story we meet her as a successful lecturer in philosophy. She is very intellectual and controlled and seems to be devoid of passion, showing little or no feeling, apart from being embarrassed when her friends talk openly about their sex lives. It is when she tries to move further into her intellectual

her by what is happening next door. She gradually realises how she has stifled her feelings, for the sake of intellectual pursuits, and how this has led her to a loss of intimacy in her relationships. Through going back to the memory of someone who had fallen in love with her, she learns to believe again in her capacity to feel deeply and to live more passionately. As a result she experiences a sense of peace for the first time in many years and she finds that the creativity to write her book is released.

We have been deeply influenced by the belief which used to be expressed in the statement, 'Feelings don't count'. Feelings were seen to be too subjective and it was believed that by clouding our vision they made us unreasonable. The result of underrating our feelings in this way is that we find it difficult to be emotionally honest or, to put it more strongly, we have become to a large degree emotionally illiterate.

The important role feelings play in relationships

Our feelings are aroused when we tell our story or relive important events from it. These feelings are aroused both at the level of emotion and of conviction. The level of emotion is what we normally think of as feelings but we also experience them at a deeper level in the form of convictions we have developed about what is worthwhile or of value. Whether they emerge as emotions or convictions, feelings are essentially a movement towards or away from the people and things we come across in the events of our story or of our daily experience. Feelings are thus a movement into relationship or away from it and they are at the heart of the love which the Spirit gives us as a gift, the love we receive and return within all our relationships.

Enlivening relationships

When we communicate with others we know how engaging this is by the amount of feeling that surrounds it. A lot of the colour, intensity or passion we experience in our conversation depends on whether we and the other person are aware of and are willing to share our feelings. Conversations where little feeling is allowed to surface and be shared are often formal or lifeless.

Positive and negative feelings

If feelings are to be allowed to enliven our relationships by being part of the way we communicate we need to allow both our positive and our negative feelings to surface and be expressed. If we cultivate our positive feelings by noticing, naming and sharing them they will be intensified by being expressed and the range of feeling that we are sensitive and responsive to will be extended. We will experience a similar beneficial effect if instead of trying to bury our negative feelings we notice, name and share them. We will be freed from the way they tend to dominate and deaden our relationships. Sharing these feelings can also lead to a new level of intimacy.

The Exercise

Some of the following suggestions may help you to improve your way of dealing with positive and negative feelings so that they become a constructive influence in the way you relate.

1) Think of someone who represses his or her feelings, and then someone who releases them too readily, and finally someone who expresses them when the occasion calls for this. After re-

have you adopted? When you look at the picture the gospels paint of Jesus do you see a person who keeps his feelings under strict control or do you see a person who expresses them with passion? Read a few stories from the gospels and note down what feelings Jesus expresses in them.

3) Taking a positive feeling and then a negative one, follow any of these steps that you find helps you. Recall an incident in which you experienced this feeling and dwell with the circumstances in which it arose. Allow the Spirit who is familiar with all the movements within you to sit with you as your most intimate friend. The Spirit asks you to talk about this feeling and so you mention any of the circumstances surrounding it that you find it helpful to mention. Ask the Spirit how she feels about what you have said and then let your weaknesses be accepted and your goodness be affirmed.

Cultivating good feeling

What is negative in our experience has a tendency to colour the way we see and feel about ourselves. As a result we easily lose touch with the predominantly positive feelings that surround the gift of love which the Spirit has given us (Rom 5:5) and encourages us to cultivate throughout our lives. (Jn 16:13, Gal 5:22) If these positive feelings are to flourish, we need to work with the negative ones. Otherwise they tend to dominate our experience and colour the way we see ourselves. Even more important than dealing with our negative feelings is the cultivation of positive ones that are ranged around the Spirit's essential gift of love. On one side of this love is *faith* which is an intimate knowledge of being loved. Our deepest and most lasting *joy* springs from the conviction of being loved that faith gives us. (Jn 15:9-11) On the other side of love is *hope* which urges us to realise the dream which the Spirit has planted in us. From faith and hope an array of positive feeling springs up within us such as, reverence, gratitude, compassion, enthusiasm and a sense of wonder.

Scripture: Loving with your whole heart

Feeling is central to the gift of love which the Spirit 'pours into our hearts'. (Rom 5:5) This gift of love empowers us to keep the Great Commandment which calls us to love others as we are loved, with our whole heart or with our immense capacity for feeling which our heart symbolises. The Spirit inspires in us feelings of love, joy, peace, patience, kindness, goodness faithfulness, gentleness and self control. (Gal 5:22, 1 Cor 13:4-7) Other feelings that the scripture associates with love are appreciation and wonder, (Ps 8:4-8) praise and gratitude (Ps 9:1-2, Ps 103) and celebration. (Lk 15, Jn 15:11)

EXERCISE 7

Glimpses of love the Spirit inspires

People who give us a glimpse of what love
and thus what God is like
are truly significant people.

*'Although our view of the most sublime things is limited and weak,
it is a great pleasure to catch even a glimpse of them.'*
St Thomas Aquinas

Intuitive glimpses

of being loved and loving

become central to the story of how

the Spirit has led us 'into all truth'

if we can capture them.

Capturing glimpses of glory

A young peasant lad was summoned by a great king to appear before him. When he arrived at the palace, the king said to him, 'My kingdom is so large that I cannot meet all my people and touch their lives as I would want to. My wish is that you would give the people you meet each day an impression of who I am.' As symbols of the new role he was to play, the king gave the youth a sceptre, a robe and a crown.

Now, since he did not know the king, the peasant lad was very confused about what he was being sent to do. He was too awe-struck to ask the king what he meant, so he went to consult a wise person he knew. He was told to go back to his little farm and just be himself. As time went on, many people came to visit him for they found in him a sympathetic ear and a compassionate heart. Gradually he realised that this was what the great king had sent him to do. This was the way he was to give people an impression of what the Great King was like.

People who give us an impression of what goodness is like, and especially of our own goodness, are truly significant people. It is not only that the sense they give us of our own goodness sustains us at a human level, but their love also acts as a bridge to the life-giving power of the love of God. Their love is indispensable for releasing this power because the intimations they give us of love are so concrete and real that without them the love of God can remain too abstract and spiritual to exert much influence on us.

It is worth noticing that we more readily intuit other people than ourselves, and what is negative more than what is positive. This fact challenges us to develop our ability to capture the positive glimpses others give us of our true selves in the way they, for example, accept and affirm us.

Our gift of intuition

A third level of experience is called into play when we ask the central question, as we frequently do, 'Am I important in this situation?' or 'Am I significant for this person?' The intimations, insights, impressions or glimpses of being worthwhile which we receive from the way people treat us can provide a constant sense of significance that builds us up and sustain us. However, the ultimate importance

important to notice and clarify these glimpses of love we get on a regular basis so that we might cherish and make our own of them. If we do not develop a way of capturing these glimpses we will lose the valuable insight which they can give us into some aspect of the love of God which the Spirit leads us into. (Jn 16:13)

One way of capturing these glimpses we are given of God's love is to cultivate the difficult art of expressing them in a brief mantra-like statement. For this statement to be really effective it should have three characteristics. It should be *a statement of fact* we allow another to say to us rather than be just an idea we think about. *It should be addressed to us personally* using our name, and the words used should be challenging in that they are *creative* or imaginative. If we repeat this statement as we would a mantra it challenges us to change the way we see ourselves so that we might move closer to believing in the good news it expresses.

The Exercise

The following suggestions may help you to be more sensitive and responsive to the way the Spirit enlightens and attracts you.

Capture the glimpse you get in a mantra ...
Recall to mind someone who has given you a good impression of yourself though he or she may have done this in limited and in subtle ways. Choose an incident in which this person gave you a glimpse of how significant you are in his or her eyes. Notice who was present, what was said, what was done and how you feel as you walk around in this experience again. Turn your attention now to what was said in effect to you in the incident, by the way someone looked at you or by some gesture. Try to capture what was said to you in a mantra-like statement that has three characteristics:

... that is creative
It should be *creative* or an imaginative expression of what in effect you heard being said to you. This means that you will have to employ the poet in you to capture the experience in words that engage your imagination and feelings.

... factual
We tend to express something significant that is said to us as an idea rather than as a *factual statement.* So we report an impression we get of ourselves in a statement like, 'John seems to like talking to me' rather than letting John say, 'I really enjoy talking to you.'

... and personal
Let what was said to you be expressed in a *personal* way or face to face by the person involved in the incident. Let this person address you by name.

Four aspects of love of which we regularly catch a glimpse

We glimpse people's love for us in a very concrete way when they *acknowledge* us or tune into and respect our essential goodness as Jesus did with the woman in Simon's house. (Lk 7:44-47) We glimpse love too in the way that others *accept* us with all our limitations. They thus encourage us, as Jesus encouraged Zacchaeus, to see our human poverty in perspective. (Lk 19:5-6) People who ap-

Scripture: Discerning the glimpses of God's love we get

At the end of the Exodus Moses sought to express a glimpse of God he had received during this forty year journey on which God accompanied him. (Ex 34:6-7) The people as a whole were slow to recognise the hand of God in these events, (Hos 11:3-4) and that it was God who led them 'all along the way they travelled'. (Deut 1:29-33) Jesus is conscious of how slow we are to see the point of his miracles as signs of his love and providence. (Mk 8:1-10, 14-21) Healing our blindness (Mk 8:22-26) and opening our eyes to the deeper significance of what is going on around us is central to what Jesus came for. (Lk 4:18) There are signs of love and providence in the most unlikely places if we open our eyes to them and cultivate a sense of wonder and gratitude. (Gen 28:15-19, Ps 139). Even though what we see of God in this world is but a dim reflection of the divinity, (1 Cor 13:12) it is a very real glimpse of his glory. (2 Cor 4:6) Each of us is 'a letter from Christ' written by the Spirit. (2 Cor 3:3) Jesus is sensitive to the glimpses he receives of people's goodness and expresses these in colourful ways. (Mk 14:3-9, Mk 12:41-44)

EXERCISE 8

The conviction that we are loved

Our dream of being loved and cared for
is realised only when we learn how to
convert glimpses of this love into convictions.

This conversion is an answer to Jesus' call
to repent and believe the good news.

The most effective way to reach this conviction
that we are loved is by listening and responding
to the evidence of it which we receive
from the other levels of our experience.

*To be convinced that we are loved, to believe it,
is so much more than just to feel or glimpse it.*

The climax of the other three levels

at which we experience the Spirit's love

is *the conviction* that we are loved.

We reach this through listening

to the glimpses of this love which we are given.

From Glimpses to Convictions

The film, *You Can Count On Me,* is about a brother and sister called Terry and Sammy who were orphaned when young. Sammy is divorced and lives her well ordered life with her son Rudy. Her brother's life is not so tidy as he is a wanderer and comes to visit his sister at the beginning of the film apparently because he is unemployed and short of money. She welcomes

ations, can be counted on to open up the wider world Rudy needs to live in. Even though before the end of the film Terry decides to leave, Rudy is sufficiently convinced of his uncle's concern for him that he can live content in his new found faith in himself and in the care of those around him.

Our dream is to be sure that we are loved and cared for. We strive to be certain of our significance and to gradually build up our convictions that we are accepted and appreciated in spite of our weakness. Ultimately, it is up to each of us, as it was to Rudy, to weigh the evidence which would allow us to convert intimations of this acceptance and appreciation into convictions. Developing these convictions is difficult for we have to deal with a lot of evidence to the contrary. However, developing these convictions is worth the effort for on them depends how alive and happy we are going to be.

The supreme happiness is the conviction of being loved.
Victor Hugo

Developing Our Convictions

In this exercise we focus on the fourth and deepest level at which we experience love, the level at which we learn to believe that we are loved. Learning to believe this involves developing a way of converting the glimpses of love we are given into convictions. This is what Jesus invites us to do when he calls us to 'repent and believe the good news' that we are loved and cared for by God. Developing this conviction, which faith is, involves letting go of all the illusions about ourselves that make it difficult or impossible for Jesus to convince us that we are loved.

The key role that conviction plays

We can see how important our ability to reach the conviction that we are loved is from the example of two young people who are thinking of getting married. They both have to ask themselves whether they are sufficiently convinced of each other's love to commit themselves permanently to each other. So much rests on their answer to the question, 'Does he/she love me?' It is not sufficient that they get the odd glimpse of this love. They need to arrive at a solid conviction of it, one that rests on concrete evidence.

How we arrive at this conviction

Listening and responding to the glimpses people give us of their love is the most practical and effective way of converting these glimpses into convictions. By listening we become receptive and gradually adjust to what they intimate to us about ourselves. By responding to what we have listened to them saying we allow the positive feelings this stirs up to develop, to expand and deepen. When we allow our feelings of resistance to what they say to be voiced we gradually free ourselves from this resistance.

The Exercise

Use any of the following suggestions you find helpful to learn how to convert the glimpses you get of being loved into the conviction that you are loved.

What conviction expressed in a play, a film or a novel you have found moving recently do you identify with? Recall an event which stirred some deep conviction in you and then express this convic-

was said to you in the glimpse you were given of yourself. Let the way you express this be brief and as creative, factual and personal as you can make it.

... involves listening

Now *listen* to this mantra-like statement repeatedly to allow yourself time to savour and absorb it. As you repeat this statement it may help to emphasise one word and then another.

... and then responding frankly to it

Notice what feelings are aroused as you listen repeatedly to what was said to you. These feelings will most likely be a mixture of positive and negative ones, for one part of you may welcome what is said while another may resist it. Take one of the positive feelings and after putting words on it repeat these a number of times. Make sure that the words you choose are as expressive as possible. Next do the same with a feeling of resistance.

The Christian Vision

Throughout these five Exercises of Part 2 we have been building up an intimate knowledge of the love which the Holy Spirit is constantly leading us into. We have sought this intimate knowledge by examining the four levels at which we receive and share this love. To understand and appreciate the knowledge we derive from the four levels at which we relate, it may help to look at two ways we come to know others. The first way involves getting an *intellectual* grasp of who people are by getting to know a lot about them. The second, more *experiential* way we can come to know people is by piecing together an image of them from the way they relate with us. Where we rely on our mind mainly to get an intellectual grasp of who they are, we attain a more intimate knowledge of them through the convictions we derive from the evidence of our senses, our feelings and our intuitions.

Scripture: Faith as an intimate knowledge of being loved

Jesus invites us, as he did his first disciples, to come to know him by meeting and being with him. (Jn 1:39) He calls us to accompany him as his companions (Mk 3:13-15) and ultimately as his friends. (Jn 15:9-15) To prepare us for this friendship Jesus spent his life sharing an intimate knowledge of himself with us and fostering our faith in his love. (Jn 17:26) This faith is 'a conviction of things not seen' (Heb 11:2) and it has its basis not in intellectual ideas but in the way he shows his love for us in the events of his life, death and resurrection. (Jn 3:15-16) By remembering and celebrating these events in the Eucharist we maintain this conviction. (Lk 22:19) Jesus gives us glimpses of the meaning of the events of his life by means of his word. (Lk 24) He invites us to listen and respond to these glimpses so that they become deeply held convictions or ones that we 'hold fast to with a noble and generous heart'. (Lk 8:15) The intimacy of our knowledge of Jesus will depend on our willingness to maintain our conversation with him in prayer. (Lk 8:21)

PART 3

The role of our imagination in prayer

In Part 2 we looked at how we can use our memory to get our whole person, 'heart, soul, mind and strength' involved in the way God's love is revealed to us by the Spirit in our prayer. In Part 3 we

on and get more engaged in our own personal experience. The Word of God also benefits from the experience our imagination gives us access to, as a good story or the use of fantasy opens up areas of experience which the Word of God can then speak to in an engaging way.

Who is God the Father for me?

In Part 3 and 4 we focus on our relationship with God the Father. In Exercise 9 we begin to examine this relationship by discerning with the help of our imagination as well as our memory how in actual fact we relate with the Father. We seek to discern whether the way we see and feel about God is healthy or unhealthy. We will judge this on the basis of the images and feelings that surface when we tell the story of this relationship and when we enter into a fantasy in which the Father is involved.

IMAGINATION
through fantasy and imagery accesses

the depth dimension of our experience,
in our underground stream
of inner wisdom

EXERCISE 9

Imagination and the discernment of relationships

Story and fantasy make use of our imagination
to question how we see God the Father.
We need to discern and evaluate
the images of God the Father we inherit

'Though our brother is on the rack,
as long as we ourselves are at our ease,
our senses will never inform us of what he suffers ....
It is by imagination that we can form any conception
of what are his sensations.'
Adam Smith

Our imagination

using the four levels of experience

fantasy and story can stimulate

help us to discern

what images of God the Father

help or hinder our belief in the good news

Discerning how we relate with God our Father

The Master Craftsman

The tapestry maker weaves his work of art on a piece of gauze stretched across the centre of a room. He is on one side of this while on the other are a number of small boys, each with his own colour of thread from which the tapestry is woven. The tapestry maker indicates where he requires the particular colour he wants to be pushed through the gauze and the little boy with that colour follows his instruction. But from time to time one of the boys loses concentration and pushes through the wrong colour or not at the place indicated. Instead of reprimanding the one who made the mistake and asking him to undo it the master craftsman, being so skilled, graciously and ingeniously incorporates this mistake into his plan and even makes it a feature of the tapestry.

Growing awareness of God the Father

We can make use of stories to discern, with the help of our imagination, how we see God and ourselves. For example, the story above challenges us to believe that God, as the master craftsman, is gracious in *accepting* our failings and ingenious at transforming them so that they become a feature of the beautiful tapestry our life is constantly becoming. The story can also help us to discern how we feel about the Father as one who *appreciates* us as his work of art, a work of art in which he delights. The image of the tapestry maker not only speaks to our personal experience but it opens up and gives us an engaging insight into the image of God we find expressed at the end of the Exodus story, Ex 34:6-7.

Discerning our relationships with God

We inherit a lot of ideas, images and feelings about God which we change, consolidate or add to as we go through life. Some of these ideas and images are true and are accompanied by positive feelings while others are false and are accompanied by negative feelings. We need to evaluate these ideas, images and feelings and decide which ones help and which ones hinder our relationship with our Father.

own splendour and celebrates our conversion is a fulfilment of the patient, compassionate, kind and forgiving image of God which emerged from the Exodus story. (Ex 34:6) There are also images we have inherited that are unhealthy in the sense that they are distorted and lead to feelings that are negative and deadening. For example, if we imagine God the Father as demanding, critical or judgmental, these images will cause fear, guilt or anxiety. Jesus urges us to 'repent' or change the distorted way we see and feel about God and to cultivate belief in healthy images of God and the positive or constructive feelings these give rise to.

God's work of art

Life can be seen as a journey we undertake in response to Jesus' call to repent and believe the good news. On this journey we not only discover, explore and make our own of Jesus' revelation of his Father but of who we are in our Father's eyes. This journey into who we are may begin with an image of ourselves as failing to live up to God's expectations that gradually gives way to an image of ourselves as a work of art in which God delights. (Eph 2:10)

The Exercise

Some of the following suggestions may help you to clarify your relationship with God the Father and the role your imagination can play in the development of this relationship.

Is God as good as good people?

When you reflect on your relationship with your parents, family and friends what qualities of their concern for you do you find yourself attracted to. Write down a few of these qualities and then enter the conversation you will initiate by asking God is he and she as good as any one of these people. Next select the quality of someone's love for you that you find most attractive and after putting words on how this person has expressed this love let God say these words to you a number of times.

Entering a dialogue

Recall a time in your life when your relationship with God the Father changed. Describe or use an image to represent what God was like before and after this change. What image of God do you now have? In the light of this image say to God what your relationship means to you at present and then start a short dialogue after which you write down what is the main thing you want to say to God and then write down God's reply.

The Tapestry Fantasy

Begin the following fantasy by quietening and centring yourself and then imagine that you are in your inner room where you are invited to 'pray to your Father in secret'. (Mt 6:6) All that is in this room tells your story but what is central to this story is symbolised by a beautiful tapestry. Notice its design and how it uses all the colours you find most attractive. There are areas of bright colours and areas of dark ones but notice how the dark areas act as a foil for the silver and gold threads that run through them. When you ask God how the tapestry of your life can be so beautiful in spite all your limitations and weakness, God uses the story of the master craftsman at the beginning of this exercise to answer you. Conclude by writing down the main thing God wants to say to you, and your reply to this.

Is God as good as the best people we know?

If the bible images of God the Father are to be real for us we need to build a bridge between them and our personal experience. Within this personal experience it is most likely that there will be positive images surrounding our idea of fatherhood as well as negative ones. We need to bring both to consciousness or the negative images will block our belief in the fact that *God is love.* (1 Jn 4:8) We need to build on the positive images of the loving people we have known if

Scripture: The LOVING-KIND nature of LOVE

The opening statement of the Nicean creed, *'I believe in God the Father almighty',* expresses the basic Christian belief that God the Father is more loving and provident than anyone we know. This is because God is not just loving but *is love* (1 Jn 4:8-10) The image of God as 'tender, compassionate and constant' emerged at the end of the Exodus. (Ex 34:6-7) It is an image which captures what is best in parental *affection.* (Hos 11:1-4) This image was extended and deepened by the prophets as they articulated what was revealed to them of a God who *acknowledges* our essential dignity, (Is 43:1-5, Jer 31:31-34) who *appreciates* us to the point of delighting in us, (Is 62:2-5) and who *accepts* our limitations and sinfulness not allowing them to block or diminish this delight. (Hos 2) God our Father is always *concerned* for our welfare, (Jer 29:11, Is 41:8-10, 13-14, 49:14-16) down to the minutest detail. (Lk 12:22-28)

The Spiritual Exercises
An Introduction

The Spiritual Exercises present you with a way of answering the essential call of the gospel. This call is to deepen your faith in the good news of God's love and providence or to attain an intimate knowledge of 'how wide and deep and long and high is the love of Christ'. (Eph 3:19) This is what the three persons of the Trinity want to reveal to you if you are willing to listen and respond to it in an ever fuller way by learning how to pray and reflect.

The purpose of Exercises 1-22 is to help you to learn some of the most basic ways of praying and reflection which have been devised in order to satisfy your hunger for the love God wants to reveal to you. Even though these 22 exercises as well as the Spiritual Exercises present you with ways of believing more deeply in the love of God, the Spiritual Exercises highlight different aspects of this love while the 22 exercises highlight how you can grow in your belief in this love through prayer and reflection.

The love these exercises provide you with a way of discovering, exploring and assimilating is opened up in the six stages of the Spiritual Exercises. At the first stage you seek to deepen your belief in the loving-kindness of God and at the second stage to deepen your faith in the permanence of this love. At the third stage you look at how personal this love is in the way Jesus calls you to be with him, and at the fourth stage you look at how provident Jesus' love is in his plan to give you an abundance of life and happiness. At the fifth stage when you seek to be with him in his passion and death you want to discover how intense or passionate his love for you is. At the sixth stage when you seek to enter into the joy and glory of his resurrection you want to discover how profound and joyful the love of Jesus is as he leads you into a love of friendship by sharing with you 'everything' he has heard from his Father. (Jn 15:15)

The First Stage
of
The Spiritual Exercises

The Loving-kindness of our God

As you begin the Spiritual Exercises there are three terms that you

you are invited to look at your image of God as one who loves you
and in the third cycle you are invited to look at God as one who is
your Lord.

Cycles 1-2: Clarifying your image of God

In these first two cycles focus your prayer on getting in touch with
your basic image of God's goodness to you. You will find help to do
this if you go back to the exercises you have done so far and notice
what images of God appealed to you most.

Recall a peak time in the story of your relationship with God. Write
a sentence describing what way you were led to see God at that time
and another sentence describing how that experience influences the
way you see God at present. What are some of the images of God
you feel comfortable with now? What pieces of scripture express
your image of God most appealingly?

Spend some time with one of these pieces of scripture, letting God
express for you the kind of love that is revealed to you in it. Let the
way God expresses this love for you be as personal and as challenging as you can make it. The aim here is *to listen to God telling you of
his love for you.* After you have spent time listening, talk to God
about how you feel about this expression of his and her love. As

well as saying how positively this love makes you feel, share as honestly as you can any resistance you may notice in yourself to this love.

Cycle 3: The way God as my lover becomes my Lord
Spend the five periods of prayer in this cycle with the reality that God is your Lord as well as being the one who loves you more than anyone else in your life. This means that as well as being one who is close and walks with you (Deut 1:31) God is also utterly holy and awesome. (Ex 20:1-3) Dwell for some time with any experience that gives you a sense of awe. Your experience of how awesome stars are or how wondrous a newborn baby is may help you be in touch with how awesome God is. Psalm 8 or 139 or the hymn *Oh Lord, my God* may help to intensify this sense of wonder.

Focus on one or both of the following Bible experiences of God's holiness. In Exodus 3:1-6 a sense of reverence is expressed while a sense of the moral consequences of God being Lord is expressed in Deut 6:1-13. Liturgical prayers such as the Gloria, the Prefaces, the 'Through him, with him ...' may help you to give expression to your response to God's holiness while baptismal, marriage or religious vows may help you grasp the implications of God being your Lord.

'I am the Lord your God'
During the five periods of prayer in this cycle incorporate into your prayer the following considerations.

In the story of the Fall described in the book of Genesis things fell apart when God was no longer seen to be central to people's lives. The Song of Songs describes the reversal of this movement away from God when it tells us what happens when we realise that we are God's beloved or the centre of God's concern and that God is the one we want to be at the centre of ours.

Built into this image of our being God's beloved, is the belief that God wants to become the Lord of our lives by gradually winning our hearts through the growth of his and her attractiveness for us.

In other words, what God wants to happen is similar to what occurs when we fall in love, when someone wins our heart and becomes the centre of our universe. This experience effects all our relationships, that with the person with whom we fall in love, that with ourselves, with others and with everything around us.

In this cycle you are asked, What would be the effect on your life if you were to make God your central concern, as you are urged to do

The three persons of the Trinity plan to reveal themselves to you, and this revelation is of an overwhelming love that you not just desire but are a hunger for. To realise their plan and satisfy this hunger or deepest longing, you need to listen and respond to their revelation of themselves to you.

All else in the universe is created to help you to attain this purpose. Therefore, you need to strive to be free enough to use all that helps you to attain this purpose and to leave aside all that would hinder its attainment. Your one desire and choice should be what is more conducive to the purpose for which you are created.

PART 4

Praying with the Word of God

The role of prayer
In Part 4 we will look at how the Word of God invites us to pray, or to *listen* and *respond* to the Word as God's self-revelation. To get us fully involved in this conversation the Word needs to speak, not just to our mind, but to the full range of our experience that we looked at in Exercises 5-9.

The role of reflection
We can savour and assimilate only a small piece of God's Word or self-revelation at a time. It is through reflection we become more *sensitive* and *responsive* to the piece of this revelation which God wants to open up for us in prayer.

The role of repetition
If we are to make our own of the piece of revelation reflection tells us is important for us, we need to listen and respond to it repeatedly.

to that part of the Word of God

which *reflection* discerns we are ripe

to assimulate through *repetition*

EXERCISE 10

Prayer as conversation

The divorce of the Word of God
from our personal experience
means that the Word has become unreal and irrelevant
and that our personal experience has lost its meaning.
To unite the word and our personal experience again
we need to initiate a dialogue
or a conversational form of prayer in which we:
* listen rather than think,
* listen to 'good news' rather than to 'good advice'
* and respond honestly to what we have listened to.

*'Anyone who's not prepared to listen to God in the first place
has nothing to say to the world.'*
Hans Urs von Balthasar

The Word of God engages our whole person

in a conversation initiated by

God our Father's self-revelation as love

Prayer as an engaging conversation

In the 1960s Ronald Goldman did some very influential research on the religious thinking of young people which he described in his book *Religious Thinking from Childhood to Adolescence.* He noticed that these young people's experience of the Word of God had become divorced from their personal experience in a way that was unhealthy for both. The Word of God separated from their personal experience became unreal as it lacked rele-

to the Word making it more real, tangible and engaging, while the Word clarifies, confirms and deepens our personal experience.

Reintegrating three levels of our experience

What Ronald Goldman found to be true about young people is equally true of adults in that we need to re-integrate our personal experience and that of the Word. With a view to doing this we examined in Exercises 4-9 our *personal experience* and how it emerges from our own story. We also looked at how the more *universal experience* which is expressed in other people's stories speaks to our story and gives it a deeper meaning. In this exercise we will look at how the three persons of the Trinity want to reveal themselves to us in the Word of God. But they want to address their Word to our personal and universal experience to make sure that what they say to us is real and that it involves not just our mind but our whole person.

Listening and responding to the Word of God

For the Word of God to be relevant and to engage our whole person in prayer, it must speak to the fund of experience we sought to become more conscious of in Exercises 5-9. If the Word is allowed to involve our whole heart, soul, mind and all our senses in this way it will initiate an engaging conversation in which we listen and respond to the wondrous nature of God's self-revelation as love. There are a number of aspects of how God wants to engage us in this conversation that are worth noting.

1]   The Word is primarily a revelation of some facet of God's love we are invited to listen to. Therefore, thinking through the meaning and the message of the Word is not our main concern when we pray. If we *think,* we are *active,* moving from one idea to another, working out their meaning and implications. On the other hand, when we *listen* to the Word we are *receptive* and absorb the fact that we are loved in the way the Word reveals.

2]   If in prayer we think through the meaning and the message of a passage of scripture we will get what we might term *'good advice'.* If we constantly get advice from the Word of God we will feel diminished by it. On the other hand, if when we listen to the Word we meet someone who loves and affirms us, we will be enlivened by the experience.

3]   Having listened to the word of God we need *to respond to it in an emotionally honest way.* We may expect to feel positively if what we hear is affirming but we may also resist this as too good to be true. Both kinds of feeling need to be noticed, named and shared if the positive feelings are to grow and if we are to become free from feelings of resistance that block this growth.

The Exercise

Some of the following suggestions may help you to develop your capacity to pray with the Word of God or to listen and respond to God's ongoing self-revelation to you.

After quietening and centring yourself in some way you find helpful, read a piece of God's Word until a phrase that expresses something about *God's love* emerges. Repeat this phrase to savour what it

When you have found the words that express this love let God say to you 'Am I as good as this person? May I say my love for you in the words this person used?' Finally, return to the words of scripture that struck you and allow God to address them to you in the way they have been coloured by the experience you have relived.

Responding to the Word

As you listen to God speaking to you in this way, it is likely that your feelings will be aroused. Single out one feeling and express it as frankly as you can a number of times. So you might say, 'I love to hear what you are saying to me' or 'I find what you are saying to me too good to be true'. Conclude the prayer by spending some time talking to the Father, to Jesus, to the Spirit and to Mary about anything that struck you during the prayer.

Three traditions

The approach to prayer we have adopted in this exercise is sometimes called the Benedictine method. It is more contemplative than mental prayer and more active than the quieter forms of prayer that many people use today.

Jacob's ladder

Compared to the mental prayer that characterised the Scholastic tradition that followed it, the Benedictine tradition focuses on listening as opposed to thinking. It sees prayer as *a conversation* in which we seek to savour and assimilate the Word of God. It took as the symbol of this exchange between God and ourselves the ladder which Jacob saw in his dream stretching between heaven and earth. (Gen 28:10-22) This ladder on which God descends to us in self-revelation is also the means by which we ascend to God in our heartfelt response to this revelation.

The four steps of the ladder

There are four steps on this ladder. The first step at which we read the Word intensively is called *lectio divina*, the second one at which we listen to a word or phrase that strikes us is called *reflectio*. A third step at which we respond to what we have listened to is called *oratio* and this may be followed by a step called *contemplatio,* at which we gaze in a quiet way at some aspect of God's love which emerges from the first three steps.

Scripture: Prayer as a conversation with God

The ladder in Jacob's dream (Gen 28:10-12) symbolises the two movements of prayer, a downward one of God's revelation to which we listen and an upward movement of our heart in response to this revelation. Prayer is thus a conversation like that which Moses has with God. (Ex 33:11) The revelation in the Word and in the Eucharist which initiates this conversation is so rich that Jesus compares it to a banquet. (Jn 6:1-55) This conversation is the condition of our growth in intimacy with Jesus, (Lk 8:19-21, Lk 10:38-42) of our happiness, (Lk 11:27-28) and of living life to the full. (Lk 8:15, Jn 10:10)

EXERCISE 11

The role of reflection in prayer

Through reflection we seek to become
more sensitive and responsive
to God's ongoing self-revelation

*the power to tell the good from the bad,
the genuine from the counterfeit,
and to prefer the good and the genuine
to the bad and the counterfeit.*
Samuel Johnson

Through reflection we become

sensitive and responsive

to God's ongoing revelation,

in the form of enlightenment and attraction,

we need to notice, understand and respond to

Attuning ourselves to God's ongoing revelation

Jacob came to a certain place and stayed there for the night, because the sun had set. Taking one of the stones of the place, he put it under his head and lay down in that place. And he dreamed that there was a ladder set up on the earth, the top of it reaching to heaven; and the angels of God were ascending and descending on it. And the Lord stood beside him and said, ... 'Know that I am with you and will keep you wherever you go, and ... I will not leave you until I have done what I have promised you.' Then Jacob woke from his sleep and said, 'Surely the Lord is in this place and I did not know it!' And he was afraid, and said, 'How awesome is this place! This is none other than the house of God, and this is the gate of heaven.' So Jacob rose early in the morning, and he took the stone that he had put under his head and set it up for a pillar and poured oil on the top of it. He called that place Bethel. (Gen 28:10-19)

Jacob's dream provides us with one of the most basic images of prayer and reflection in the Bible. The vision of the ladder, with the angels ascending and descending it, represents as we have seen the two movements of prayer. In reflecting on this experience Jacob does three things. He *notices* God's self-revelation and *understands* not only the meaning of this revelation but that it is God who is speaking to him face to face. He then *responds* by setting up a monument to make sure he does not forget what he has come to know about God.

The elements of reflection

Reflection, in the sense we are using it here, means becoming sensitive and responsive to the way God's self-disclosure takes place especially when we pray. This self-disclosure takes the form of an *enlightenment* we are invited to become sensitive to and an *attraction* we are drawn to respond to.

attraction or follow it, as the loving thing that is said to us by God or others is often resisted, and therefore passed by and unnoticed. It is important to take responsibility for this attraction for it indicates a part of our dream we are ready to realise, something we are being invited to savour and assimilate.

The Spirit 'will lead you into all the truth'

The way God enlightens and attracts us rests on the reality that we learn best *bit by bit according as we are ripe to be taught.* There is always a bit of God's self-revelation as love that we are ripe for or ready to learn and we will be made aware of what this is by the enlightenment and the attraction we experience. It is important that we *notice* the way we are enlightened in prayer, that we seek to *understand* or clarify what is said to us about God's love by putting words on it and that we *respond* by making our own of this love.

The Exercise

The following suggestions may help you to develop a practical way of reflecting on your prayer or of *noticing, understanding* and *responding* to the way the Spirit enlightens and attracts you during it.

Noticing

The first movement of reflection involves *noticing* what happened in the prayer. So, immediately after or even during your prayer notice what surfaced, what you were given a glimpse of, what you made space for, what you became aware of, remained attentive to, focused on or listened to. In doing this you are seeking to become aware of the enlightenment and attraction of the Spirit that is so easily missed.

Understanding

The second movement of reflection takes place in your effort to *understand* what you have noticed by putting words on it or by writing it down. In this way you clarify and define the way you have been enlightened by the Holy Spirit. It is important to remember that this enlightenment is not an idea but the way you see God or others looking at you lovingly in the piece of God's Word you are praying with. By attempting to express this way you are loved you clarify some aspect of the love of God or of 'the truth' the Spirit seeks to lead you into. (Jn 16:13)

Responding

The third movement of reflection is *a response* you feel drawn to make to the attractiveness of the love which the Spirit has led you to see. The effect of this attraction is that you want to savour and assimilate this love and you can do this most effectively by listening and responding to it in prayer. Thus reflection that leads into prayer in this way becomes a most basic and practical way of answering the call of the gospel to 'repent and believe the good news'. (Mk 1:15)

Reflecting on our difficulties in prayer

At times our experience of prayer can be discouraging when we find ourselves distracted, dry and uninvolved. But this experience may become a constructive one if we learn how to notice, understand and respond to its potential for growth.

When we are distracted in prayer we need *to notice how we feel.* For

ment or joy that Jesus says belongs to those who adopt this attitude to life.

Scripture: Fostering the reflective spirit

Jacob is in awe of the intimate way God's self-revelation takes place in the midst of the ordinary events of his story. (Gen 28:15-17) Eli helps Samuel to discern how God is speaking to him. (1 Sam 3:1-21) This revelation is intimate and inconspicuous (1 Kings 19:9-13) and is made to each person, to 'the least no less than the greatest'. (Jer 31:34) Jesus seeks to cultivate a reflective spirit in us by opening our eyes to the signs of this revelation. (Mk 8:1-26) This reflective spirit is necessary if we are to notice, understand and respond to the way the Father, Jesus and the Spirit make themselves known to us. (Jn 17:26, 16:13)

EXERCISE 12

Repetition as a way of assimilating the Word

Repetition is necessary
if we are to assimilate
the bit of revelation or of God's Word
reflection indicates we are ripe for.

To believe in God's on-going revelation
calls for a change of mind and heart
effected by repeatedly
listening and responding to it.

'If anybody enters the path of repentance
it is sufficient
to advance a step every day.
Do not wish to be like a charioteer.'
The rule of St Comgall (AD 559)

By repeatedly listening and responding

to the bit of God's self-revelation

reflection tells us we are ripe for

we can savour and assimilate it

Repetition is the mother of learning

When I was a student of theology we had a teacher who stressed two outstanding characteristics of the Christian God. One was that God is three persons and the second he initially called X. Over a period of a couple of months he gradually opened up for us what X stood for. It turned out to be an elaboration of Jesus' claim that he is our 'teacher' (Jn 13:13) It was

The first of these is that the Spirit will be able to teach us only if we *remain long enough with* what we are being invited to assimilate. This is difficult, for we like novelty and easily lose interest when we have to go over the same ground repeatedly. However, repetition is the mother of learning.

The second reality we need to face if the Spirit is to teach us is that we learn *bit by bit and only what we are ripe for.* The bit of revelation that the Spirit finds us ready to listen to and make our own of will be indicated to us by the areas of enlightenment and attraction that emerge when we reflect on our prayer.

Savouring and assimilating on-going revelation

Rather than staying with an area of light which the Spirit opens up for us, there is a temptation to opt instead for something new that satisfies our intellectual curiosity. However, if we succumb to this temptation the seed, which represents the Word of God, 'will not mature'. (Lk 8:14) The Spirit who 'teaches us everything' (Jn 14:26) can do so only with those who 'hear the Word of God and take it to themselves and yield a harvest through their perseverance'. (Lk 8:15)

Repetition and changing our mind and heart

Repetition is a key way of assimilating the light we receive but it takes time and effort to do this, especially if what we are being led to see is new or contrary to what we believe. If we have developed a distorted image of ourselves and of God we will have to go to great rounds to change this way we see and feel. The change of mind and heart that God's revelation calls for is not achieved by a single exposure to the truth but by repeatedly coming back to the area of light the Spirit has opened up for us. This repetition is essential to learning to believe in the good news, for by listening and responding to it over and over again we develop that conviction about it in which faith consists.

Resistance to repetition

We may expect to find a lot of resistance to repetition. This may arise from a fear of boredom or from our reluctance to face the difficult task of changing deeply ingrained ways of seeing and of feeling about ourselves and others. Repetition will also put us in touch with our limitations because when we repeat what we wish to assimilate we leave ourselves open to more distractions than usual.

The Exercise

The following suggestions may help you to develop a way of savouring and assimilating what the Spirit has enlightened you about and attracted you to.

This exercise is best done over a number of days during which you use the same subject matter for your prayer. As you return to this

resist returning to it. You may also find it is worthwhile returning to some important point that resisted your efforts to grasp it.

Getting your whole person involved

If you wish to savour and assimilate the light you receive or what attracts you in prayer, you need to develop your capacity to remain focused. To help your concentration, keep in touch with the scene in the gospel where you got the enlightenment and with any personal experience that makes what you have seen real for you. Keep to hand as well any image you associate with what you are focusing on and express any feeling aroused by all of this.

Handling your resistance to repetition

When you still your mind in an effort to focus on a small part of your experience, you leave yourself open to more distractions than usual. Handling these in a constructive way will involve learning to see them as an invitation to live with the reality of your human limitations. This will involve adopting a gentle approach to yourself when you get distracted so that you do not allow yourself to become frustrated by this.

'I want you to change your mind and heart'
The conversion Jesus calls for when he invites us to repent and to believe the gospels involves a change of mind and heart and not just of behaviour. It is difficult enough to change the way we act but to change our vision and our values, the deeply ingrained ways we see and feel, is extremely difficult. The fact that old habits die hard seems to be the point Jesus emphasises in his parable of the seven evil spirits. (Lk 11:24-26) The most effective way to bring about this change, by listening and responding to the Word of God, is the point that the parable of the sower makes. The reason given in the parable why the Word does not bear fruit is that those who hear it do not give it the conditions it needs to take root and to grow.

Scripture: The PERMANENT nature of LOVE
The erratic nature of the way the gods of Israel's past acted contrasts with the rock-like constancy or permanence of the God of Abraham, Isaac and Jacob. (Deut 32:4) The promise to be with us 'all along the way we travel' first made to Abraham reaches into the future. (Deut 1:29-32) Faithfulness becomes a major attribute of God as a result of Israel's experience of the Exodus. (Ex 34:6) In the prophets, God's fidelity is contrasted with our infidelity, (Hos 2) and has all the warmth of parental love which never allows us to be forgotten. (Is 49:14-16). In Ezekiel the permanence of God's devotion to us is expressed in a covenant that is eternal. (Ezek 16) Jesus highlights the permanence of his Father's love in the parable of the prodigal son and he gives this love its fullest expression in the way he relates with sinners (Lk 7:36-50, 19:1-13) and with the disloyalty and betrayal of those closest to him. (Jn 21:15-17)

The Second Stage
of
The Spiritual Exercises

How our infidelity highlights God's fidelity

In the second stage of the Spiritual Exercises we concentrate on
~~God's acceptance of us as limited and sinful and on a resulting sense~~

as the injustice we see in the world today.

2)   We also ask to grow in a sense of *our involvement* in sin, in a
     sense of our basic sinfulness.

3)   Finally, we seek to grow in a sense of *the extraordinary response
     of God to our sinfulness*. We will get the clearest picture of the
     extent of God's fidelity to us by exploring the full extent of our
     infidelity to God.

Images of sin in the Bible

The sense of sin we find in the Bible centres on the image of *separation*. (Lk 15 & Gen 3-12) It is through sin that we separate ourselves
from God, from ourselves, from others and from the whole of creation. Sin is thus seen as a loss of intimacy resulting from 'what we
do or fail to do' (sins of commission or omission).

What brings about this separation may be our *unbelief*. For example, what distances us from God may be a poor image of ourselves
which blocks our belief in the fact that God loves us and that we are
lovable. Again, the separation may be caused by *infidelity* or going
after 'false gods', (Hos 2 and Ezek 16) by our *ingratitude* to God,
due to our failure to appreciate all the gifts we have received, (Lk
17:16-19, Rom 1:16-32) or it may be due to *our failure to listen* to
God's Word. (Lk 8:4-15)

We need to discover the sin behind our sins or the most basic way we are involved in sin. For example, traditionally pride is seen to be the root of all our sins because it involves putting something other than God at the centre of our lives. What people put at the centre, instead of God, is something different for each person. For example, one person may make having a good time central while another may give a central place to becoming a success. What we put at the centre of our life and seek with a passion may be the false god that is the object of one of the three temptations that Jesus experienced in the desert.

Three temptations

In the three temptations of Jesus we have a description of three ways that we are tempted to put someone or something other than God at the centre of our life. When we succumb to the first of these temptations we allow our lives to be governed by what Sigmund Freud called 'the pleasure principle'. For example, we may make a priority of life being exciting, action packed, pleasurable or it may be that we give our comfort and convenience precedence over all else. The second temptation is to allow our lives to be ruled by 'the power principle'. This happens when, for example, we decide that what matters most is having influence, being a success in our career or being popular. The third temptation is to laziness when we allow ourselves to drift or fail to take responsibility for meeting our deeper needs such as our need to reflect and pray.

Procedure for cycles 1-5

As in the first stage of the Spiritual Exercises this one is divided into cycles each of which has five exercises or periods of prayer. For the first period of prayer in the following five cycles we focus on *the nature and seriousness of sin*. The parable of the prodigal son (Lk 15:12-32) is the main passage we will take for this first period of prayer in each of these five cycles. Other pieces of scripture will be suggested as we go along which may help you to expand or deepen what you discover while praying with this parable.

The Colloquy

At the end of each period of prayer it is recommended that you pray in 'the way that one friend speaks to another', talking very sincerely about what you have been led to see or about how you feel. This conversation or colloquy is with Christ on the cross asking him how it is that though he is the creator of all things he has stooped to become one like us so that he might die for our sins. Then ask yourself the following three questions: What have I done for Christ? What am I doing for Christ? What do I want to do for Christ? (These questions are meant to elicit feelings rather than de-

a) To develop *a true sense of your limitations* as a human being consider how small you are before the number and the magnificence of the stars or compared to the billions of people on earth. In the light of this greatness of God's creation be aware of how limited you are compared to the creator of the universe.

b) Sin means drifting out of relationship with God, oneself and others. This *tendency to drift* manifests itself in our unwillingness to take the time to establish intimate relationships and to maintain them by cultivating the ability to communicate that good relationships requires. (LK 15:11-32, Lk 10:38-42, Mk 4:13-20, Lk 14:16-24)

c) Sin means *being unfaithful to the true God* because we chase after false ones. In other words, we are seduced by superficial desires and as a result miss 'the one thing necessary'. (Hos 2, Ezek. 16, Lk 12:16-21, Lk 8:14, Jas 1:13-18, 1 Jn 2:12-17) We become enslaved by the world's pleasures and riches. (Lk 12:16-21)

d) Sin is also seen as *becoming separated* from God, from our deeper selves and from others. When we get cut off from our essential relationships we become lonely, sad and dehumanised by the fact that we make something superficial all-important.

Thus the 'one thing necessary' becomes secondary. (Gen 3:1-24 & 4:1-16, Lk 10:38-42, Rom 1:16-32)

e)   A sign of our sinfulness appears in our tendency to allow the 10% of life that is negative to dominate our thoughts and feelings and so we become impoverished by neglecting the 90% that is life-giving. *We fail to make the time and space to believe the Good News* and to appreciate and be grateful for the 90% of life that is symbolised in scripture by the banquet God urges us to come to. (Lk 14:16-24, Rev 3:16-32)

When you repeat this second exercise in each of the next four cycles, use the texts in brackets to open up the descriptions and images of your sinfulness you identified with in a-e above.

The third exercise in each cycle is *a repetition,* the nature of which is explained in Exercise 12. The purpose of a repetition is to make your own of what has struck you most deeply in the first two exercises. Work with the principle that 'It is not a multiplicity of ideas which will satisfy the human spirit but to taste a little interiorly'. (St Ignatius)

What to repeat: Return to where something struck you, or to where you saw something that attracted you. You might also return to important points you had not time to look at in your prayer or you might return to significant images or ideas you felt resistance to or you might visit again something you felt was important for you but that has so far resisted your efforts to savour and assimilate it.

The second colloquy
In this second way of making the colloquy at the end of each period of prayer, talk to each of the persons of the Trinity and Mary concerning any or all of the following petitions:

1) Ask for a deep realisation of what sin is in your life and that you may not become permissive but firmly resist it.

2) Ask for an understanding of the circumstances in which you tend to sin so that you might resist these firmly.

The fourth exercise in each cycle is *a summary*. This is similar to a repetition but it is simpler. This is because there will most likely be less material you will feel drawn to return to and what you do return to will, being more affective or deeply felt, occupy more of your prayer time.

The fifth exercise in each cycle is aimed at facing two basic facts about sin: 1) that *you are free to choose* the way to 'destruction' as well as the way to 'life'. (Mt 7:13-14) and 2) that *you must take responsibility for your choice* and its consequences. There is a healthy abhorrence or fear of choosing 'the way that leads to destruction' that is consistent with a sane view of life.

The first time you do this fifth period of prayer, focus on the Christian experience of hell. For example, take the fact that Jesus mentions 'hell' 17 times in the gospels. Stay with what this reality means for you. Do not get involved in issues which cause intellectual problems such as whether hell exists or what it means in the Bible.

When you come back to this fifth exercise again take the same subject matter or take scenes from the gospels such as the following:

Luke 16:19-31 about Dives and Lazarus, Matthew 25:31-46 about the last judgment, John 3:16-21 about the fact that we judge ourselves rather than that God judges us, and Mark 8:36-37 'What does it profit...?'

The colloquy for this fifth exercise is with Jesus and it is about the reality of your choice of the two ways and the consequences of this choice.

The final cycle
The final cycle of this stage of the Spiritual Exercises will be devoted to savouring how faithful, permanent and enduring is God's love for you. Return to experiences, feelings, images and pieces of scripture in the exercises so far about how faithful God is to you. Alternatively you might use some of the following pieces of scripture to experience more deeply how constant or steadfast God is in your life: Lk 15:4-7, 20-24, Hos 2:21-22, Ezek 16:8-14, Lk 7:36-50, 19:1-10.

PART 5

Praying with the gospels

In Part 5 we turn our attention to the way we pray with the gospels
or to the way Jesus engages us in conversation by making himself

Getting an interior knowledge of Jesus' love
When we have become aware of the images of Jesus we have adopted
over the years which are consistent with what Jesus calls 'the good
news' we need to find the best way of getting an interior knowledge
of them. To get this we need to do three things:

*   We need to contemplate the gospel stories as portraying so
    many facets of the love of Jesus rather than thinking about
    what is the meaning and the message of each story.
*   We also need to integrate into our contemplation of the gospel
    stories our experience of people who make the love of Jesus
    portrayed in each story real for us.
*   Finally, we need to get our whole person 'heart, soul, mind
    and senses' involved in our prayer.

Savouring a little to assimilate it
In practice attaining interior knowledge of some aspect of Jesus'
love involves developing a way of remaining with it long enough to
savour and eventually to assimilate it.

*'We would love to meet Jesus
in the way we did'*

John came to know Jesus intimately

People asked him, 'Who is Jesus?'

John told the story of Jesus

By listening to this story

we come to know Jesus
just as John did

EXERCISE 13

Discerning our images of Jesus

We answer the central question
Jesus asks each of us in the gospels,
'And you, who do you say that I am?'

*Praise be to you, Lord Jesus Christ,
for all the benefits and blessings you have bestowed upon me,
for all the insults and injuries you have borne for me.
O most merciful friend, brother and redeemer,
may I know you more clearly,
love you more dearly
and follow you more closely. Amen*
Prayer of St Richard

'Who do you say that I am'?

We need to discern the images

we use to answer Jesus' question

to see which help and which hinder

our belief in him.

Images of love we are all heir to

There is a well known prayer attributed to St Patrick that portrays Christ's love or care for us as a breastplate. It expresses the belief that Jesus' love envelops us in the way a parent's love envelops an infant:

Christ be beside me, Christ be before me,
Christ be behind me, King of my heart.
Christ be within me, Christ be below me,
Christ be above me, never to part.

There are nine aspects of the love with which Jesus envelops us like a 'breastplate'. These nine gradually emerge in each person's life. The most striking one is the love that more than anything else *gives us life*, nurtures and sustains it. Basic to Jesus' love also are the four essential characteristics of *affection*. We experience these, especially as children, from those who acknowledge, accept, appreciate and are concerned for us. When we go to school we experience a *personal* love from those who choose us to be their companions. When we move away from home and begin to fend for ourselves we very often become aware of a *provident* love. This makes itself felt in the absence of our parents who until then have met all our needs especially the most practical ones of feeding, clothing and putting a roof over our heads. At some stage we experience the dramatic effects of *falling in love*. But this intense kind of love can go as quickly as it comes so we have to struggle to make it *permanent* and to deepen it so that it becomes *profound*. When we experience how broad and long, how high and deep love can become we experience how *joyful* it can be. The fruit of all these experiences of love, and especially of the passionate kind which has become permanent and profound, is the love of *friendship* in which people give us a gift of themselves in self-disclosure.

Who do you say that I am?

Having contemplated our relationship with the Holy Spirit in Exercises 4-8 and that with God our Father in Exercises 9-12 we now turn to our relationship with Jesus. To get a sense of who he is for us we need to let him ask us the question he asks his disciples after they have had time to get to know him. *'And you, who do you say that I am?'* In answering this question we are challenged to eval-

our life, it is likely that we see Jesus in a corrective role or as one who gives advice about how we should live. On the other hand, if we see the gospels as depicting one who is the love of God made visible (Rom 8:39) then it is likely we see Jesus in an affirming role or as one who loves us in the rich variety of ways that the gospel stories illustrate.

In the first part of the exercise to follow we look at the story of our relationship with Jesus. If in telling this story we become aware of the images of Jesus we have adopted, a picture will emerge of who he is for us. We will find this appeal to memory an easier way to answer Jesus' question about who he is for us than analysing our idea of Jesus in an abstract way. As well as using our memory to uncover the images of Jesus we have inherited from the past we will use fantasy to clarify what image of Jesus we live with at present.

The Exercise

The following suggestions may help you to clarify the nature of your relationship with Jesus and the fantasy may give you an insight into how you actually relate with him.

Telling the story of your relationship

Remember an event which influenced your image of Jesus and describe how it effected your relationship with him. Talk to him about this image and then write down the main thing he says to you about it. Tell him how you feel about what he says.

The fantasy of the inner room

Imagine yourself in your inner room where the events of your story are represented by the photographs and images displayed around the walls of this most intimate place. When you have quietened yourself let Jesus join you. He reflects with you on some key moments in your story as told by the pictures and images around the walls. Listen to what he says to you about one of these key moments in your story and tell him how you feel about what he says. Allow him to reflect with you on a central event in the present period of your story. Once again, notice what he says to you and tell him how you feel about this. Finally, talk about your hopes for the future and about what kind of relationship he wants with you and you want with him.

Reflection on the fantasy

As you reflect on your meeting with Jesus notice what image of him emerges from your time together. Was he serious or lighthearted, solemn or joyful, enthusiastic or tired? Did you get a sense that he was happy with your life or did he focus more on the way things might be? What was your impression of Jesus at the end of the fantasy and what image do you now have of yourself as a result of it?

Discerning the image of Jesus you live with

When you reflect on your relationship with Jesus, do you feel that he acknowledges you? Is he sensitive to the unique quality of your life and does he respect this? Do you get a sense of his acceptance of your limitations and weakness, of his appreciation of your strengths and of his concern for you? Notice how you feel when you are with him, whether you are as comfortable with him as you are with a

portrait of the *personal love* of Jesus as he chooses disciples and calls each of them by name to be his companion. (Mk 3:13-15) In the second half of the gospels Jesus reveals his *provident love* in a plan he has that we would live life to the full. (Jn 10:10) In the story of his passion and death we see a portrait of the *passionate love* of Jesus who loves us with great intensity or 'to the utmost extent'. (Jn 13:1) Then in the resurrection scenes we have a picture of a *joyful Jesus* who desires our complete and constant happiness. (Jn 15:11) In these resurrection scenes, especially as they are interpreted in John chapters 14-17, we have a portrait of *how profound and permanent* the passionate love of Jesus is. Finally, he calls us his *friends* because he has shared with us 'everything he has heard from his Father'. (Jn 15:15)

EXERCISE 14

Contemplating the gospels

The attractiveness of Jesus in the gospel stories grows
if we see them as portraying
the many aspects of his love.

This vision of the gospel challenges us
to contemplate the love of Jesus in each scene
rather than look for its meaning and message.

We need to filter our contemplation of Jesus' love
through that of significant people
if his love is to become real
and to engage our whole person.

If you accept the gospel and become Christ's,
you will stumble on wonder upon wonder, and every wonder true.
Brendan to King Brude

The gospel stories paint portraits

of Jesus' love which significant people

can make real and engaging for us.

The growing attractiveness of Jesus

There is a scene in a book called *Captain Corelli's Mandolin* where Dr Janis the local doctor speaks to his daughter when he realises she has fallen in love with Captain Corelli.

> Love is a temporary madness, it erupts like volcanoes and then subsides. And when it subsides you have to make a decision.
>
> when all the pretty blossoms had fallen from our branches we found that we were one tree and not two. But sometimes the petals fall away and the roots have not entwined. Imagine giving up your home and your people, only to discover after six months, a year, three years, that the trees had no roots and have fallen over. Imagine the desolation. Imagine the imprisonment.

As we read the gospels it becomes obvious that Jesus exercises a growing attractiveness for those who come to know him. Very early on in the gospel story we realise that a volcano has erupted in the lives of his disciples. We are told that Jesus had become so attractive for them that they 'left everything and followed him'. What happened to them as they come to know Jesus is like what happens when we fall in love. There is an experience of the intense attractiveness of someone on whom we centre our whole self in a way that can transform us. However, if we are to grow in this relationship we have, as Dr Janis says, to make a decision. The choice love puts before us is whether or not we are willing to take the steps involved in becoming intimate.

'All I want is to know Christ'

In this exercise we seek an intimate knowledge of Jesus who became a human being out of love for each one of us. This love is what Jesus wants to reveal to us in each gospel story. It is the love of the Father which he became incarnate to express in a human way. Our primary interest as we read each gospel story is not the meaning and implications of what is described there but the love of Jesus of which each story portrays some aspect. This is what the writers of the four gospels want for us when they say in effect, 'We met Jesus and came to know him intimately. Our hope is that in contemplating the picture of Jesus we present in the gospel stories you too will come to know him in the intimate way that we have.' The gospels can thus be seen as a series of stories that paint portraits of Jesus, portraits whose attractiveness engages our whole person.

Making love real and engaging

However, if the love portrayed in the gospels is to be real and to engage our whole person we need to draw on our experience of the people who have given us a concrete experience of what love is like. Without this concrete experience the love of Jesus can remain too spiritual and fail to become incarnate or to involve more than our minds. Jesus' ideal in becoming human is to engage our 'whole heart and soul, mind and strength' in the way we come to know and love him.

Two challenges

The challenge that faces us as we contemplate the gospels is twofold. We are challenged to contemplate the gospel stories as portraits of various aspects of the love of Jesus and to let the attractiveness of this love grow. The second challenge is to let this love involve our whole person by filtering it through our personal experience of people who have given us an intimate knowledge of what love is like and who have made love real and colourful for us.

The Exercise

The aim of this exercise is to help you to develop a way of coming to an intimate knowledge of Jesus' love for you.

People who make love real for us

Divide a page into three columns. In the first of these, write the

~~[text obscured]~~ people who have given you a glimpse of what love is

Next, take one of these ~~scenes~~ quality of Jesus, which you have chosen the scene to illustrate, emerges as you read the story a few times. Give yourself time to be attracted by this quality in Jesus. Now write down briefly what in effect Jesus is saying to the person in the scene. Since this is the most difficult part of the exercise you may need to go back to Exercise 7 to see how to express what Jesus is saying in effect in the gospel scene you are looking at. Finally, let Jesus say to you the words you have chosen a number of times and then tell him how you feel about what he says.

An intimate knowledge of Jesus' love

A way to make the love of Jesus in a gospel story more real and engaging is to spend some time with an incident in which someone gave you an impression of what this kind of love is like. After recalling this incident express in a phrase or short sentence what in effect was said to you in the incident. Listen to this being said to you a few times and then express how you feel about this. Now let Jesus say these words to you a number of times and then tell him how you appreciate what he says to you but tell him too if you experience some resistance to what he says.

The intimately personal nature of Jesus' love

As we contemplate Jesus in the gospels we become aware of his growing attractiveness. We see how he exercises this attractiveness in the gospels when he exerts such a magnetic influence over his disciples that they 'leave everything' to be with him. This attractiveness reaches its climax when, 'lifted up' on the cross and in glory, he 'draws all' to himself. What he draws us into is his own profound friendship with his Father. (Jn 15:15) The gospels can, therefore, be described as painting a picture of Jesus going around making friends and drawing all into his own relationship with his Father.

Scripture: The PERSONAL nature of LOVE

The personal dimension of how Jesus relates with us is seen in the way he calls his first disciples. He invites us as he invited them with the words, 'Come and see' as he wants us to come to know him person to person. (Jn 1:39) Jesus chooses his disciples and makes himself known to them. (Mt 10:1-4) He chooses them to be with him as his companions (Mk 3:13-15) and as his friends. (Jn 15:15) As this friendship develops and his disciples come to know him he calls 'his own by name'. (Jn 10:3-4) This means that he appeals to something unique in each person, something that makes his relationship with that person different from his relationship with anyone else. We see this personal way he relates in the way he acknowledges the Samaritan woman. He shows himself to be highly sensitive to her unique circumstances and he respects her freedom. (Jn 4:26-30)

EXERCISE 15

An intimate knowledge of Jesus

To gain an intimate knowledge
of the love Jesus reveals to us
we need to taste and savour it.

Our greatest experiences are our quietest moments.
Nietzsche

We seek an intimate knowledge

of some aspect of Jesus' love by:

* listening to what he says.

* watching what he does,

* tasting and savouring this love

* to touch and be touched by it.

The application of the senses

Psyche's third task

In the Greek story of Psyche's relationship with Eros we have a description of what a woman must do if she wishes to go on her inner journey. Basically she needs to involve her animus or the male side of herself in this endeavour. When Psyche seeks to do this by examining the face of Eros while he is asleep she disregards their agreement when they married that she must never attempt to see his face. As a result Eros goes back to live with his mother, Aphrodite. In order to get him back Psyche has to perform three very difficult tasks. These tasks symbolise Psyche's need firstly to be aware of and to distinguish the different areas of her experience. Secondly she needs to understand the relationship between these areas of her experience as well as how they are related to what is central to them. It then remains for her to take a small piece of her experience at a time to savour and digest it.

The three tasks Psyche is given illustrate the three stages of reflection we examined in Exercise 11. Psyche's third task, in which she is invited to make her own of the experience she has become aware of and understood, is difficult, for our mind dislikes being stilled so that it can focus on a small piece of experience at a time. Yet we need to focus all our attention on this piece of our experience if we wish to absorb it. The mind according to St Teresa of Avila is like a little child who is told to remain still while her mother gets on with her knitting. The child may obey for a time but soon grows restless and starts pulling the thread or playing with the ball of wool. The mind like the child cannot bear to remain still for long but keeps interfering as it reaches out for some new image or idea. However, unless we remain still and in the one place long enough to listen to and to savour a small piece of our experience, we will not be able to get the intimate knowledge of it that we seek.

Tasting a little interiorly

'It is not a multiplicity of ideas that will satisfy the soul but to taste a little interiorly.' (St Ignatius Loyola)

For the Father, Jesus and the Spirit to realise their plan to give us an interior knowledge of their love we need to learn how to rest with what they reveal. The most effective way of doing this is to focus on

of the Trinity gradually opens up for us. With the help of these senses we can also *listen to* some part of this vision that we find expressed in the Word of God or in a mantra that we create to capture some personal experience. We can then *taste and savour* the bit of revelation we have captured in this way. By means of these spiritual senses we allow our whole person to be *touched* by the aspect of God's love which we have incorporated in our mantra.

Getting our whole person involved

When we try to still the mind and use our spiritual senses to savour a small area of our experience, we leave ourselves open to more distractions than usual. To remain attentive or focused it may help to create a mantra that captures the bit of experience we want to stay with. We may find it helpful to enlist the support of a personal experience, an image, a feeling or a few words from scripture to help the mantra we have chosen to hold our attention.

The Exercise

The following suggestions may help you to improve your capacity to get an intimate knowledge of the love of Jesus by savouring it as it emerges bit by bit in prayer.

Begin the exercise by taking the time it needs to quieten and centre yourself and then focus on some experience that you wish to savour. You might recall a scene in the gospel or in your own story where you caught a glimpse of something you want to make your own of. Listen to and look at the situation in which you got this glimpse so that your whole person is drawn into the circumstances which surround it. For example, if you want to savour the reality that the little child in the manger is God, you might let Mary give you Jesus to hold. *Listen* to the child breathing and *look* with your inner eye at the reality that this baby is your Lord. Allow yourself to *savour* what is happening in this scene and to *be touched* by this overwhelming reality.

The use of a mantra

Create a mantra that captures the reality you want to assimilate. This mantra may be an expression of the enlightenment you have noticed and articulated in your times of reflection on your prayer or it may be an expression of a feeling aroused by the attractiveness of some aspect of the love of Jesus for you. It helps greatly if the mantra you choose is brief, personal, factual and creative in the way explained in Exercise 7.

Facing the difficulties inherent in this exercise

It can be difficult to create the right atmosphere for this exercise. For example, you may find it difficult to still your mind sufficiently to adopt the contemplative approach to reality that this exercise requires. We are used to being intellectually active so that when we try to still the mind we may find distractions difficult to avoid. It is important that you face this experience of your limitations and not allow yourself to be frustrated by the difficulty of remaining focused.

Interior knowledge

The aim of the three persons of the Trinity is to make themselves known to us in the way our heart pines for. (Ps 42:1-2) This revelation is the aim of the New Covenant announced by Jeremiah (Jer 31:31-34) and the main objective of Jesus' life. (Jn 17:26) It is his hope that we would come to know him and his Father in the intimate way they know each other. (Jn 10:14-15)

message conveyed by all of this was that God loves us. (Deut 4:37) The response this love called for is that we should get our whole person, our 'whole heart, soul, mind and strength' involved in receiving and returning it. (Deut 6:4-7, Mt 22:34-40) In the prophets the extent and depth of God's love is drawn out. For example, Hosea reveals how intense and deep it is when he compares it to married love (Hos 2:16-22) while Jeremiah reveals God's desire to speak with each person, as with Moses, 'face to face'. (Ex 33:11, Jer 31:34)

A knowledge beyond all understanding

This involvement of our whole person in knowing God is what Jesus makes possible by becoming incarnate (1 Jn 1:1-4) and what he encourages us to do when he says to each of us, 'Come and see!' (Jn 1:39) Jesus wishes us to come to know the full range of his love in a way that surpasses all human knowing. (Eph 3:14-19) What makes this possible is his gift of the Holy Spirit who gives us an experience of 'the love of God flooding through our hearts' (Rom 5:5) and leads us into all the ways in which Jesus expresses this love in human terms. (Jn 16:13-15)

The Third Stage
of
The Spiritual Exercises

An intimate knowledge of Jesus

What we seek at this third stage of the Spiritual Exercises is '*an intimate knowledge of Jesus the Lord who became a human being for me, that I may love him more and follow him more closely*'. We have taken a detailed look at how we might obtain this intimate knowledge in Exercises 13-15. This is the evangelists' wish for us in writing the gospels. We could imagine John saying to us, 'I met Jesus and I was charmed by him, so much so that I left everything and followed him. Now I would love you to meet and come to know him in the way that I did.'

Procedure

In this as in the previous stages of the Exercises there are a number of cycles in each of which there are five exercises or periods of prayer. At this third stage of the Spiritual Exercises the first two exercises in each cycle are devoted to contemplating two scenes from the gospels. The third and fourth exercises are repetitions and the guidelines for these are the same as those used at the second stage of the Spiritual Exercises. The fifth period in each cycle is *an application of the senses* and for this we follow the procedure we had in Exercise 15. In brief, we *look at* what is happening in the scene from the gospel we are praying with, we *listen to* what is said to us in it so that we may *taste and savour* the glimpse of Jesus' love we get and *allow ourselves to be touched* by this. You will probably find it easier to use some of these spiritual senses than others but use as many as you find helpful. Keep in mind the purpose of the application of the senses as it is expressed in the words of the Spiritual Exercises, 'It is not a multiplicity of ideas which will satisfy the soul but *to taste a little interiorly*'.

Cycle 1: Contemplating the Incarnation and the Nativity

For the first two exercises in this cycle take the *Incarnation* and the *Nativity*. These two scenes are part of the infancy narratives in which belief in the reality of Jesus being the Lord or God is very clearly stated. The aim of all the periods of prayer at this stage of the Spiritual Exercises is to get 'an interior knowledge of our Lord who became a human being for me'. There are three extraordinary realities we seek to come face to face with in all the cycles of this stage of the Exercises:

1) Jesus the Lord or God 2) become a human being 3) for me.

mate knowledge of the extraordinary

The Nativity

Read the description of the Nativity in Luke's gospel (2:1-20) but this time, rather than contemplating it from the perspective of the persons of the Trinity, enter the scene by listening to what is said and watching what is going on. Here the emphasis is on the persons acting out God's plan but especially on Jesus who is the Lord becoming a poor helpless child for us. To grasp this reality more fully get as involved as you can in what is going on, in how you feel and in savouring any glimpse of the mystery you are given. For example, you might ask Mary if you could hold the child for a while and as you do notice how you feel and what glimpse you are given of the three aspects of the mystery we noted above.

Cycles 2 and 3

In cycles 2 and 3 keep in mind that you are looking for *an interior knowledge* of the fact that *Jesus who is your Lord and God becomes a human being for you.* To attain this interior knowledge of Jesus' love for you *keep drawing on your experience of people* who have given you a glimpse of the love of Jesus revealed in each scene from the gospels you contemplate. This will help you to avoid looking at the following scenes from the gospels in a way that is too intellectual or spiritual.

Cycle 2

In this cycle contemplate the Presentation of Jesus in the Temple (Lk 2:22-39) and the Flight into Exile in Egypt (Mt 2:13-23). Follow the same procedure you used in contemplating the Nativity.

Cycle 3

In this cycle contemplate the Finding of the child Jesus in the Temple, (Lk 2:41-50) and the life of Jesus at Nazareth from the age of twelve till he was thirty. (Lk 2:51-52)

PART 6

The two ways

We frequently ask ourselves the question, 'Am I significant for this or that person or in this or that situation?' The answer we give depends on who and what we choose to believe. We can choose to be-

doubt and anxiety that are never far below the surface. This self-doubt gradually erodes our image of ourselves and makes it difficult for us to hear or believe in those who believe in us. In the parable of the two ways Jesus tells us that many people drift down this road to 'destruction'. (Mt 7:13-14)

The mass of men lead lives of quiet desperation. — *H Thoreau*

Owning the significance Jesus gives us
For Jesus our significance is a gift. It is seen in the eyes of one who loves us with a love that has not got to be earned. In the presence of this love we are acknowledged as being essentially lovable and worthwhile. This essential and deep significance is gradually revealed to us each day by all who acknowledge, accept and affirm us. Whether we take 'the narrow way that leads to life' depends on whether we make the effort to notice, name and believe the fact that before God we are 'beautiful, lovable and attractive'.

God has not only delivered us from sin but has made us beautiful, lovable and attractive. — *St John Chrysostom*

Who do you believe?

There are two versions of ourselves put before us:
one that leads to 'life'
the other to 'destruction'

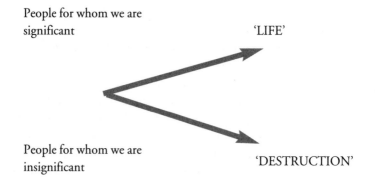

People for whom we are
significant

'LIFE'

People for whom we are
insignificant

'DESTRUCTION'

The way to life is through faith
and that to destruction through unbelief

The choice on which all rests

In the second half of the gospels
Jesus challenges us
with a momentous choice between two ways.

We are not permitted to choose the frame of our destiny.
But what we put into it is ours.
Dag Hamnnarskjold

Jesus challenges us

to choose between two ways:

* the way to life
through belief in his love

* or the way to destruction
through our failure to believe.

Who do you believe?

The film *Character* tells the story of a child called Katadreuffe growing up in Holland in the early nineteen hundreds. His father is a dour and aggressive city bailiff whom his mother refused to marry as he had forced himself on her when she was in his employ. She is burdened by providing for herself and her child and gradually becomes more and more uncommunicative. Katadreuffe, cut off from both parents, seeks to make his own way in life. He is fired by two ambitions, to succeed in life and to revenge the wrong his father has done to him and to his mother.

While Katadreuffe studies to become a lawyer he becomes enthralled by a young woman as she gives him a vision of a love he has always lacked. For some time he follows the way to life and happiness which her love opens up for him but then, consumed by his ambitions to make a name for himself and to avenge his father's cruelty, he ceases to respond to her love.

At the end of the film, while sitting with his mother in a park, Katadreuffe meets the young woman again. He discovers that she is now happily married to a book-keeper and has a child. His mother, sensing his sadness at having missed the love of his life, cannot help remarking on how foolish he has been.

Choosing between life and death

The choice that confronts Katadreuffe is that which confronts each person. It is a choice about who and what we decide to believe, a choice between two visions or images of ourselves. We are asked to believe in a life-giving vision or image of ourselves and others by Jesus and by those who love us. However, if we allow ourselves to be dominated by images of our insignificance we will, like Katadreuffe, spend most of our lives earning a sense of significance that is limited, fragile and fleeting.

The vision Jesus opens up for us

In the first half of the gospels Jesus makes himself known to his disciples and calls them to be with him as his companions. Then in the second half he explains to them what is involved in becoming his companions on his journey to Jerusalem. This is a journey on ⸻ we are invited to die and rise with him by wrestling with the ⸻ and heart involved in believing in

poverty ⸻
11:29) Poverty leads to a reliance on and ⸻
essential worth rather than relying on our own resources for ⸻
Humility leads us to face the reality that in spite of our human limitations we are supremely 'beautiful, lovable and attractive' in God's eyes. (Eph 1:3-14)

The way that leads to destruction

What blocks belief in Jesus' love and in our lovableness in his eyes is primarily the distorted image of our insignificance that we have accepted. Since being significant and worthwhile is so important for us we seek to earn it if we do not own the gift of it that Jesus gives us. Into this effort to earn our worth we channel most of our time and energy with the result that we have little left for the main relationships of our life. God and the significant people in our lives become secondary so that we become spiritually impoverished and take the road to 'destruction'.

The Exercise

The following suggestions may help you to understand the plan Jesus has that you be fully alive and happy and the way you can participate in it. This exercise also seeks to clarify what may block your participation in Jesus' plan for you.

Culture and counter culture

When you are watching television, a play or a film is there a view of life or a value that you regularly find yourself identifying with. In a film like *The Horse Whisperer,* which we examined in the introduction, is there something about Tom's view of life or a priority he has that appeals to you? What are the views and the values you hear expressed in the media that make you feel that you belong to a different world than the people who express these views? Collect a few pictures from a paper or magazine that express a cultural view you identify with and a few that represent areas of the consumer culture that you feel at odds with.

The two ways

In the following reference read about the choice you must make between the way that leads to life and that which leads to death. (Deut 30:15-20) Think of someone you know whom you feel has chosen a healthy way of life, whose view of life and whose values makes him or her happy. How does this person differ from someone you know whose life does not seem to be so healthy or happy? Read Psalm 1 and notice what you identify with in it.

Read the parable of the two ways (Mt 7:13-14) and say what is your initial understanding of it. After reflecting on the parable in the light of the introduction to this exercise, see do you wish to add anything to your initial understanding of it. What does the film *Character* say to you about these two ways? In a sentence or two express what is the 'life' Jesus says is the object of your journey and what means he suggests you adopt to reach it. Do the same for what Jesus says about the way that leads to 'destruction'.

The provident love of Jesus

Scripture: The PROVIDENT nature of LOVE

The pervasive nature of Jesus' care for each of us can be seen most clearly against the backdrop of God's provident love in the Old Testament. It is this love which inspires God to lead the Israelites out of slavery in Egypt and into the Promised Land. (Ex 3:7-10) There the plan for their 'peace' or 'welfare' is worked out. (Jer 29:11)

Being fully alive and happy

We see the provident nature of Jesus' love in his plan to give us the fullness of life and happiness, a plan he spends his life working out. (Jn 10:10, 15:11) The life Jesus plans for us consists in coming to know and to believe in his love for us (Jn 17:3) and so he constantly fosters our faith in this love. (Jn 17:26) He tells us that if we are to believe in this love we need to repent (Mk 1:14-15) or let go of our distorted images of him and of ourselves.

A sensitive and deferential providence

We see how sensitive and deferential the provident love of Jesus is in his concern for the Samaritan woman. He is sensitive to how she sees things, respects where she is coming from and very gradually leads her to a vision of herself that is so affirming that it fills her with the desire to get others to meet him. (Jn 4:28-30)

EXERCISE 17

Facing the dark side of our daily experience

We know from our daily experience
when we are on the road to 'destruction'
by the strong negative feelings which arise
when we allow the 10% of life that is limited
to put us in touch with:
- a sense of insignificance
- the illusion of our poor self image
- what erodes or blocks belief in the good news.

Strong negative feelings such as fear or frustration
can be constructive as they indicate where we need to
- accept Jesus acceptance of our limitations.
- appreciate all the goodness he finds in us.

Christianity is about acceptance,
and if God accepts me as I am,
then I had better do the same.
Hugh Montifiore

Our daily experience of limitations

can diminish us and erode our belief

but it can also stimulate our belief

in Jesus' acceptance of this side of us.

The pillar of fire by night

In Exercise 11 we reflected on the way the persons of the Trinity reveal themselves to us in prayer. In this and in the next exercise we will reflect on how they reveal themselves to us in our daily experience. In this present exercise we will look at how they lead us through our daily experience of darkness or with 'the pillar of fire by night' and in the next exercise we will look at how they lead us

was worthless and ugly stood out and grew even worse. At a certain point in the story the mirror disintegrates into a billion pieces and tiny particles of it, like specks of dust, lodge in people's eyes. Each speck has the same effect on people as the whole mirror 'so that everyone has eyes only for what is bad'.

The eye for what is bad

We have a tendency to focus on what is defective and to let this small part of reality dominate the whole picture of it. 10% of what happens in our daily experience can easily obscure our view of the other 90%. If we do not notice this damaging tendency and do something about it, we can find ourselves drifting down what Jesus calls the way that leads to destruction. (Mt 7:13-14) We get an indication that we are moving in this unhealthy direction when we notice the presence of strong negative feelings. These are feelings like anger, guilt, fear and anxiety that are prolonged or excessive. They are highly significant as they tell us when and where we are under the influenced of the illusion of our insignificance.

The illusion of our insignificance

The daily experience we have of our insignificance can arise out of people's failure to affirm us or it can arise out of our inability to hear their affirmation. If we are not watchful, we can become the victims of the illusion of our insignificance. There are three levels of this illusion and noticing how this illusion begins and how it develops is important if we are to guard against taking the unhealthy direction in which it tends to lead us.

Three levels of illusion

At the first level we will notice how a negative feeling such as anger can make a whole day appear bad when in fact it was largely good. If we do not deal with this anger, it colours not just the way we see our day but the way we see ourselves as well. It feeds a second level of illusion which is that of the poor self-image we are prone to adopt. A third level of this illusion becomes operative when our poor self-image erodes or blocks our belief in those who constantly invite us to believe in how significant we are for them.

To name the demon is to slay him

In the exercise to follow we focus on a constructive way of dealing with our negative feelings and with the illusion which they indicate is operative. There are three stages in the exercise. First we notice, name and share our feelings so that we gradually free ourselves from their dominance. Then we seek to accept our limitations so that what led to a poor self-image may lead to a contented self-acceptance, to the joy Jesus says belongs to the poor in spirit. (Lk 6:20) Finally, we seek to view the 10% of us that is limited against the background of the 90% that is positive and that Jesus wants us to appreciate. This balanced view that accepts what is limited in the light of all that needs to be appreciated is the essence of the humility Jesus invites us to learn from him. (Mt 11:29)

The Exercise

The following suggestions may help you to cultivate a healthy way of dealing with those experiences of your limitations and sinfulness which tend to drag you down.

The Emmaus road walk

Before you begin this fantasy, choose some area of your life, or a

is troubling you and about how it makes you feel. Next, ask him how he feels about you and listen to his acceptance of you. This may take the form of his being comfortable with you in your weakness, forgiving you for the wrong you have done and wanting you to forgive yourself. (Jn 20:22-23) Jesus' acceptance could also take the form of identifying with you in your weaknesses and temptations (Heb 4:14-15) or of his desire to get you to see your weakness in perspective – that it is only 5% or 10% of you. (Lk 19:1-13)

Appreciating where you are most heroic

Jesus not only wants to accept you but to affirm you and to delight in your life. Notice how he did this with the woman in Simon's house (Lk 7:36-50) and when he finds the lost sheep. (Lk 15:1-7) He asks you to notice how heroic you are in the way you struggle with your weakness and how you show courage, patience and humility in living with your own weakness and with that of others. Jesus also wants to highlight your goodness by asking you to pick out three of your best qualities and then he talks to you about how much he appreciates these. End the fantasy by telling Jesus how you feel about his acceptance and about his appreciation of you.

The growth of self-acceptance

In dealing with areas of our lives where we experience a lot of negative feeling Jesus will want to be with us in the way he was with the two disciples on the road to Emmaus. Like a good friend he will seek to share our experiences of desolation by inviting us to tell him about these experiences and how they make us feel. Conscious of what these areas of strong negative feeling do to our image of ourselves Jesus will be anxious to teach us an acceptance of ourselves by his acceptance of us. Jesus will also want to say how much he appreciates how we have struggled over the years with these areas of weakness. He will want us to appreciate the fact that in wrestling with our weakness we are at our most heroic.

Scripture: Being led into the joy of the poor of spirit

There are a number of ways Jesus loves the sinner in each person. The first of these ways is where Jesus accepts and is content to be with us in our weakness. We see how he wishes to cultivate this attitude in his giving us the sacrament of reconciliation. (Jn 20:19-23) In it he asks us to accept his forgiveness, acceptance and the fact that he is happy to be with us as we are. He also invites us to forgive, accept and be content to walk with this side of ourselves. Another way Jesus wants to be with us in our weakness is by identifying with us there since he 'is familiar with all our weakness and was tempted in every way that we are'. (Heb 4:14-15) He wishes to be with us in all life's messiness rather than being above all this. Jesus in the story about the woman in Simon's house seeks to make it clear to us that he sees and wants us to see our weakness in perspective. (Lk 7:36-50) He does this by highlighting all the goodness that surrounds areas of our weakness so that we see ourselves in a positive light. In the parable Jesus told about the lost sheep he portrays himself as a person who goes out in search of parts of our shadow side that we have repressed and tried to get rid of. (Lk 15:1-7) He brings these back to us as the object of his delight for it is in our struggle with our weakness that we have become truly heroic.

EXERCISE 18

Reaping the harvest of daily experience

In our daily experience we are offered a vision
seen in the way people look at us lovingly.
This can add a new dimension to Jesus' love,

or to notice, name and make our own of it.

All our life is a celebration for us, that God is always everywhere.
Clement of Alexandria

An ongoing revelation of love

is available in our daily experience

if we reflect on the subtle signs of it we get

in the way people look on us lovingly.

Reflection on our daily experience

In her book, *Angel and Me,* Sarah Maitland tells a story about a woman who used to go for a walk each day while her four children were at school. On these walks she would often talk to her angel about what concerned him most at the time. One day when she was feeling bored she asked her angel if she could arrange for her to have a vision, perhaps, like Jacob's vision of the ladder stretching between heaven and earth. The angel said that that would be difficult but she promised to do what she could. As a result of this engaging conversation with her angel the woman lost her way and when she arrived home much later than usual she found that her children had prepared tea and scones for her. She was delighted with their thoughtfulness even though there were a lot of jam stains about especially on the hands of her youngest child.

When the woman was preparing for bed the angel appeared to her all excited and asked, 'Did you see the vision?' When she looked puzzled the angel chided her for her lack of perceptiveness. That night, however, the woman had a dream about four angels running up and down a ladder. She noticed to her surprise that they were all keeping away from the smallest of these angels, one with jammy hands.

Listening to the music of what happens

There is a vision of himself and of ourselves that Jesus reveals to us in our daily experience. This vision, which can be seen in the eyes of significant people and heard in the music of what happens, is easily missed unless we learn to reflect on it.

Do you see the vision?

There is a way that Jesus reveals himself to us in our daily experience that is distinct from and adds to the way he reveals himself to us in the Word of God and in the Eucharist. In our daily experience we are given a vision that gradually unfolds in the way people look at us or in the way they acknowledge, accept and affirm us. This form of revelation adds a very concrete dimension to the rev-

ciation of us in each

voice. But not to notice and take in what these signs are saying to us is to miss one of the main manifestations of God's love. To avail of this form of revelation we need to notice, name and own it.

Noticing, understanding and responding to the signs
Noticing our experience means making space to become aware of what happened, what was said and what was done and how we feel about this. *Understanding* comes with the effort to put words on what happened, what events say to us and how we feel about this. This effort to clarify and define what an experience is saying to us is helped by expressing this in a mantra that captures the experience in a colourful way. *Responding* to what we have noticed and understood involves returning to the experience so that by repeatedly listening and responding to what it says to us we may make our own of this.

The Exercise

The following suggestions may help you to notice, understand and respond to the moments of revelation that occur in your daily experience.

Notice what happened

Recall a good experience you had recently and after you have re-lived what happened notice a positive feeling it arouses. Express this feeling for yourself and then share it with the person involved in the incident you have re-lived. Notice if expressing how you feel helps you to expand and deepen your experience of what happened.

Understand what the event says to you

If you remember an event and there are strong feelings aroused by doing so it is a sign that the event has something important to say to you. Understanding what is being said to you may be difficult as the positive things you hear are often said in effect or in gestures. Express what the event you recalled above is saying to you sketchily at first and then express this in a mantra which, as you saw in Exercise 7, needs to be as personal, factual and creative as you can make it.

Respond by making your own of your experience

It is important, once you have noticed and expressed what was said to you in the incident you have relived, to make your own of this. The most effective way to do this is to say the mantra you have created a number of times to savour and assimilate the wisdom it reveals to you. Finally, let Jesus say the words of the mantra to you and then express any feelings that hearing him saying this gives rise to.

'Take care you do not forget'

Remembering

One of the major preoccupations of the Bible is with remembering the significant events of our past. It warns us, 'Take care that you do not forget Yahweh who brought you out of the land of Egypt.' (Deut 6:12) This concern comes out of the belief that to forget what these events are saying to us about God's love and providence

what happens when we lose touch through forgetfulness with the love that is at the core of life. As a result of forgetting and being out of touch with God we forget our own true meaning, that of others and of all of creation.

Do this in memory of me

Remembering becomes a really important activity when it is a concrete way of keeping alive the love which is latent in the events recalled. The supreme act of remembering in the New Testament is the Eucharist, just as that of the Old Testament is the Passover meal. (Lk 22:7-20) In both of these meals we remember the main events of the Exodus and of the death and resurrection of Jesus in order to savour the love and providence which these events are the deepest expression of. (Jn 15:13) It is in the light of these events that all others reveal their true significance in the glimpses they give us of God's extraordinary love in the ordinary love of the people around us. (Jn 15:12)

The Fourth Stage
of
The Spiritual Exercises

'I am the way'

Cycle 1: Two visions and value systems

For an introduction to this stage of the Spiritual Exercises go to the explanation of it given in Part 6 and in Exercise 16. What we seek and pray for here is to become *sensitive and responsive* to the way we are being influenced in life by two visions and value systems. Jesus wants us to believe in a vision that gives us life and happiness. It is a vision of what he calls the good news that God loves each person and that Jesus expresses this love in human terms. So Jesus calls us to come to know this love, to return it and follow him along the road which leads to 'life'. (Mt 7:13-14) There are three attitudes which we need to adopt if we are to follow Jesus along this road.

1) An attitude of *poverty* which leads us to trust in and to depend on God rather than on our own resources,

2) An attitude of *surrender* to life's limitations, hardships and humiliations. These can then become a most effective way we learn that it is God's love and not our own achievements that make us worthwhile.

3) An attitude of *humility* by which we face the truth about ourselves by accepting our limitations and sinfulness as Jesus does and by learning to appreciate the reality that God's love or Grace is the source of our true worth.

There are also three attitudes which lead us down what Jesus calls the road to 'destruction':

1) An *attachment to 'riches'* through which we seek to earn our worth rather than accept it in humility as a gift from God. 'Riches' is the term St Ignatius uses for that through which we compulsively seek to earn our worth and it can take many forms and even assume

a noble disguise. (Lk 10:38-42) For example, we may tend to set our heart on something like success and seek it with a passion. If this happens everything else including the essential relationships of life have to take second place.

2) An attachment to *'honour'* which is the term St Ignatius uses for the sense of significance or worth we wish to earn or buy with our

Procedure

Spend two periods of prayer reflecting on the parable of the two ways (Mt 7:13-14) and on the meaning of this given in Exercise 16 and in the introduction to this stage of the Spiritual Exercises given above. Spend the following two periods repeating this material.

The main focus of our attention in this fourth stage of the Spiritual Exercises is to continue to grow in *an interior knowledge of our Lord who has become a human being for each one of us so that we might know, love and follow him.* We seek to become more sensitive and responsive to the attitudes we need to adopt if we want to follow Jesus. We also seek to become more sensitive and responsive to *the various ways we are seduced* by 'riches and honour' to follow another way than that of Jesus.

Give most of your time in prayer to letting Jesus attract you and win your heart with the way he expresses his personal love and concern for you. To help you to do this there are in each cycle some suggestions about what qualities of Jesus's love for you you might focus on. There are also some suggestions as to how you can become more aware of the way you are tempted to follow the road that leads to 'destruction'.

In each cycle there are two scripture passages recommended to you and these will be numbered 1) and 2).

Cycle 2: Jesus leaves Nazareth and is baptised by John

In contemplating how Jesus left Nazareth to begin his public life and how he was baptised you might, for example, focus on the attractiveness of his *single-mindedness* and *dedication.* He gives himself wholeheartedly to the accomplishment of his Father's will in spite of the difficulties this involves for him. There are other qualities of Jesus you might like to focus on such as those of the 'Suffering Servant' listed in the first contemplation below.

In this cycle we will focus on the form of *seduction* we see in *the first temptation of Jesus.* This is the temptation to weigh up everything on the basis of whether it is satisfying or feels good. As soon as our relationships or our prayer become difficult or dry we seek to escape and we do not take responsibility for staying with life's hardships.

1) *Jesus leaves Nazareth* (Mt 3:13)

Jesus lived in obscurity in Nazareth for thirty years. There he did the routine job of helping Joseph in his work as the local handyman. Jesus experienced the insignificance and the uneventfulness that characterised the life of someone who lived in an out-of-the-way place like Nazareth. All this time, however, he was `growing in wisdom, age and grace', gradually becoming aware of his identity as the Suffering Servant. This was a role he had already become aware of and accepted by the time of his baptism.

The 'Servant' personifies Israel's experience of itself, especially of its suffering. This person with whom Jesus identifies is depicted for us in the four 'Servant songs' of Is 42:1-4, 49:1-6, 50:4-9, 52:13-53:12. In these the Servant *is led by the Spirit* and is *joyful* and *gentle,* yet *firm* and *courageous.* He is *a light to guide others* as well as *a healer.* He *sets people free and brings them peace.* He achieves this through suffering which he bears *patiently,* trusting *confidently* in God.

Be with Jesus at Nazareth and focus on some characteristic of his that is manifest to you in his years of obscurity and of waiting, He keeps alive his deep aspirations in spite of 'the years and years of world without event' (Hopkins) Be with Jesus as he leaves Nazareth and in your prayer focus mainly on what attracts you about him.

2) *The Baptism of Jesus* (Mt 3:13-17)
In his baptism Jesus accepts his role as the Servant or 'Son' and all ᵗʰᵃᵗ ᵗʰⁱˢ ⁱⁿᵛᵒˡᵛᵉˢ (Is 42:1-4) He puts aside his own pleasure and

Jesus is, seeing 'he was tempted in every way that we are'. (Heb 4:15) Notice too how *compassionate* he is since 'he is familiar with all our weakness'. (Heb 2:16-18) No matter what you go through Jesus can say, 'I know how you feel, I understand what you are going through for I have been there.' There is in the temptation of Jesus a *detachment* and a *freedom* from all that would divert him from what his Father wants him to do. (Lk 9:57-62)

In this cycle we will focus on *the seduction* we are prone to which is illustrated in *the second temptation of Jesus.* This is the temptation to earn our own worth rather than owning that which is inherent in the good news of God's love. This is the worth Jesus finds in us and that he asks us to believe in. Our 'riches' or that through which we seek to earn our worth takes different forms for each of us. It is usually an over-preoccupation with something that is good, such as our work, career or talents.

1) *Jesus is tempted in the desert* (Lk 4:1-13, Mt 4:1-11)
The temptation of Jesus described by Luke and Matthew is an expression of the great temptation of Israel (Deut 8 & 10) and of each Christian. Jesus was led by the Spirit into the desert, a place where people seek to meet God but where they also come face to face with their limitations and waywardness. (Heb 4:14-15) From the charac-

teristics of Jesus described above in the introduction to this cycle, or from any that may emerge for you as you read the story of the temptation, choose one to contemplate here. Stay with the attractiveness of this characteristic of Jesus rather than analyse the meaning of the temptation. When you come to look at what form of 'riches' you are tempted by, take something simple and obvious to stay with.

2) *The Rich Young man* (Lk 18:18-30) or *The Rich Fool* (Lk 12:16-21) Even though these two pieces of scripture highlight the riches by which you are seduced, your primary concern must be what they reveal about Jesus and his attractiveness. Many of the qualities noticed in the introduction to this cycle are to be found in the scripture recommended here.

Cycle 4: The call to be with Jesus as his companions

As you contemplate the attractiveness of Jesus calling you to be with him as his companion (Mark 3:13-14) you might notice the *respect* Jesus has for his disciples. He *trusts* them as his companions and is *intimate* with them in 'calling each by name'. (Jn 10:4) Jesus honours his disciples, sharing his own life and work with them. He *lays down his life* for them so that they might have life in coming to an intimate knowledge of how passionately he loves them. (Jn 13:1)

In this cycle the main seduction we look at is found in *the third temptation of Jesus*. This is a temptation not to take responsibility for adopting the means necessary if we are to enter the banquet Jesus has prepared for us. (Lk 14:16-24) We all experience a tendency to laziness or to drift. We do not want to take responsibility for the immense discipline demanded by the change of mind and heart involved in believing the good news. (Mk 1:15) We avoid the effort involved in listening and reflecting and take things for granted and become complacent. The result is that we live on a subsistence diet instead of taking the trouble to come to the banquet Jesus invites us to.

1) *Jesus calls those he wants to be with him as his companions* (Lk 5:1-11, Mk 3:13-19)

Jesus calls us to be with him as his companions and leads us into a profoundly intimate relationship with him. He enthrals those he calls so that they 'leave all' and follow him. Thereafter he is the 'Lord' for them. (Lk 5:8) He chooses 'those he wants' to share his work.

is unique to each of us. He is willing to pay the ultimate price his concern for us calls for when he lays down his life for us. This love of us 'to the end' (Jn 13:1) is what he wants us to keep in touch with when we celebrate the Eucharist. Laying down his life for each person establishes a friendship which is like that which he has with his Father. (Jn 15:13-15)

Cycle 5: The one who 'consoles' and encourages us

When Jesus puts before us the implications of following him he knows how daunting it sounds so he takes us aside to comfort and encourage us. He does this by giving us a vision in which he seeks to help us to clarify, articulate and own the interior knowledge he has been giving us of his love. He invites us to remember the transformation this interior knowledge is bringing about in us, one that is symbolised in the Transfiguration and in the raising of Lazarus to life. This is the transformation Paul refers to when he writes. 'We are transfigured in ever-increasing splendour into his own image and the transformation comes from the Lord who is the Spirit.' (2 Cor 3:18)

An alternative passage of scripture is given for the first and for the second period of prayer in case you want to extend your prayer into a sixth cycle.

In this cycle *the seduction* that is highlighted is our tendency *to neglect Jesus' call to listen to the Word of God* or to fail to take responsibility for the growth of our belief in the good news of God's self-revelation to us in Jesus. The results of listening to the Word of God as the fourth group of people in the parable of the sower do are symbolised by Mary sitting at the feet of Jesus listening to him. The way we are tempted not to listen and respond to the Word of God is also illustrated in a challenging way by the parable of the Sower and by the story of Martha and Mary.

1) *The Transfiguration* (Lk 9:18-36)
In the Transfiguration Jesus gives us a vision of himself in which he offers us a glimpse of his glory. This glory consists in the fact that Jesus is 'full of grace and truth' (Jn 1:14) or full of the loving-kind and faithful love of God that we got a glimpse of in the first and second stages of the Exercises. Part of this vision too is the love we have seen in his nativity and in his personal love and concern for us in his public life. He also lifts the veil on his glory as it is seen in the love he gives us a glimpse of in his death and resurrection.

In contemplating Jesus' transfiguration it may help to recall how Jesus has revealed himself to us in the Exercises so far and how attractive we find this. If we are to realise the possibilities for intimacy and joy this vision opens up for us we will need to devote ourselves to listen and respond to the Word of God. (Lk 8:19-21, Lk 11:27-28)

Or *Lazarus is raised to life* (Jn 11:1-44)
This story of the raising of Lazarus is one of the major signs Jesus gives us of his glory or of the radiance of his love. It is a glimpse of the life Jesus wishes to give us in abundance (Jn 10:10) by giving us an intimate knowledge of his love. We have seen the loving-kind and faithful nature of this love in stages one and two (Jn 1:14) and we have seen how personal and all-pervasive it is in stages three and four. This love is also seen to be one of friendship as Lazarus is referred to as the friend of Jesus. (vs 3, 11) When Jesus wept at Lazarus' tomb people remarked on how much Jesus loved his friend Lazarus.

2) *The parable of the Sower* (Mk 4:1-44)
The parable of the sower has been called Mark's 'Sermon on the Mount' as it is so central to his gospel. This parable highlights the importance of hearing the Word as God's self-revelation and of accepting it as such. (Mk 4:20) Our failure to listen is illustrated by those who:
a) fail to give the Word their attention, time or effort,

him. The subtle seduction we all experience is that of the good person who lets a life of service become so absorbing that the one thing necessary, time spent listening to Jesus in prayer and reflection, is no longer given the place it deserves.

Three kinds of humility
The exercise called *Three Kinds of Humility* in the Spiritual Exercises is meant to help us to discern how intimate we want our relationship with Jesus to be. Do we want an intimacy:
1) which is based on being faithful to someone so that we do nothing seriously wrong to jeopardise this relationship?
2) which is based on the desire to live peacefully and in harmony with another so that we do not get involved in anything that would be offensive or in bad taste?
3) which is based on such a high degree of sensitivity and responsiveness to another person that we want to enter fully into his or her sorrows as well as joys?

A time for decision
At this point in the Spiritual Exercises the vision Jesus has opened up of his love and its attractiveness gives us a lot of freedom and perspective. He has taken us up the mountain of Tabor where he has given us a vision in which we can see everything in the light of

his love. It is a vision which invites us to live consistently with what we have seen. Therefore, it is important that you articulate for yourself what you think you need to do if you are to walk in the light you have been led to see.

Suggestions about making your decision
Spend time with Jesus' desire that you would enjoy *the fullness of life* he came to make available for you. (Jn 10:10) Then make a list of all the things which might constitute this fullness of life for you. Include every area of your life and not just the more spiritual ones. At this stage do not censor your desires, excluding for example what is not possible at present or what you do not feel you can commit yourself to just now.

Next prioritise your desires by underlining some of them or by putting the more important ones closer to the centre of a page and the less important ones closer to the periphery. Now, select from your list of desires *a basic minimum* you want to do something about. Remember that your objective is a small number of things that at present *you really want to commit yourself to.* Write these out, being as specific as you can about what you want to do. It may help to put this down spontaneously first of all and then to refine what you want to commit yourself to during the remainder of the Spiritual Exercises.

Finally, write down *what exactly you want to do* about each of the things you have chosen to commit yourself to. It may help you to outline some suggestions as you would for someone who might seek your advice. From these suggestions select what is essential. It is very important to be specific as to what you want to do. One of our favourite escapes from our responsibilities is to leave things very general and not be specific.

PART 7

Being with Jesus in his suffering and death

In Part 7 we look at the important role suffering plays in the growth of all our relationships but especially in our relationship with Jesus. Our sufferings from birth to death cause a crisis for they can be ei-

Entering our own sufferings to enter his

In our efforts to share in Jesus' suffering and sorrow it is best to enter our own first for without becoming familiar with our own experience that of Jesus remains unreal and we may find it difficult to identify with or be involved in what he went through. In sharing Jesus' sufferings we will also focus on how similar they are to our own. In doing this we avoid focusing on the physical sufferings of Jesus as these are largely outside our experience and may distract us from entering where most of his suffering lay. It is in experiences like fear, loneliness and sadness that his 'hour of heartbreak' mainly consists. (Jn 12:27)

'He sacrificed himself for me'

The ultimate objective of all our efforts to share Jesus' sufferings is to grasp something of the love which inspired him to undertake them, not just for us as a group but for each person. Facing the personal nature of this overwhelming reality will help us to enter a dialogue with Jesus in which we will get a more intimate knowledge of his love than we would through thinking about it.

'He loved me to the utmost extent'

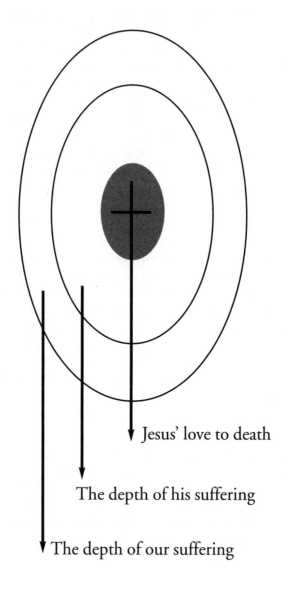

Jesus' love to death

The depth of his suffering

The depth of our suffering

CHAPTER 19

How he laid down his life for his friends

The passion and death of Jesus
is the supreme revelation of his love for me.
I get an intimate knowledge of this love

A pity beyond telling is hid in the heart of love.
W. B. Yeats

The passionate nature of Jesus' love for me

is revealed in the extent of his sufferings

which are entered most effectively

through my own

The Agony and the Ecstasy

The most striking piece of sculpture I have ever seen portrays
the crucified Christ, with Mary standing on one side of the
cross and John the evangelist on the other. Mary is wrapped in
pain as she shares all that her son is going through. In contrast,
John is portrayed in a state of ecstasy, his face aglow and his
hands raised in an expression of utter exhilaration at this ultimate manifestation of Christ's love for him. John knows in that
moment what became for him the central theme of his description of the sufferings and death of Jesus, *that he, John, is loved by
Jesus 'to the utmost extent'.* (Jn 13:1)

A fantasy

Before you begin the following fantasy spend some time recalling a
painful incident from the past. Do not take an experience where
your feelings may overwhelm you and block your progress through
the fantasy. When you have reflected on the incident you have
chosen and have written down what happened and how you feel
about this, begin the fantasy.

Imagine yourself in a quiet place and after being still for some time
let Jesus join you as a friend who wants to share your experience
with you. Tell him about what happened and how you feel about
this. Ask him how he feels about what you are going through and
notice how sensitive and compassionate he is. Next let him talk to
you about how similar your suffering is to what he experienced
throughout the gospels but especially at the time of his passion and
death. Finally, listen to how appreciative he is of your wanting to
share his sufferings and sorrow with him.

Contemplation of the passion and death of Jesus

The suffering and death of Jesus is the supreme revelation of his love. (Jn 13:1, 15:13) Though we may accept this in theory it may be difficult for us to get an intimate knowledge of the fact that he underwent all this out of love, not just for us as a group but for each of us personally. This was Paul's experience when he wrote, 'He loved
_____ f for me'. (Gal 2:20) By striving to enter as

sufferings. Once we get an intimate _____
ings, especially by walking around inside in them with Jesus, we are in a better position to get an intimate knowledge of all he went through.

'Beyond all understanding'

When we get involved in Jesus' suffering and sorrow in this way we are in a position to glimpse the extent and depth of the love which inspired him to suffer and die for each of us. This effort to gain an intimate knowledge of the extent and depth of his love will stimulate a conversation and the listening and responding involved in this conversation is the most effective way of absorbing this love.

The Exercise

The following suggestions may help you to enter Jesus' suffering
with him so that you might get an intimate knowledge of his passionate love for you.

Entering your own suffering
List the main sources of suffering in your life and then underline a
few that are most painful. Areas of suffering might include: getting
old, failing to realise your ideals, the painful sense of insignificance
caused by the lack of appreciation of your gifts and the suffering
caused by your neglect of the main relationships of your life. Spend
time with an experience of one of these sufferings. Recall what happened, how you felt and what it was about the experience that
caused you most pain.

Allowing Jesus to share your suffering ...
Allow Jesus to walk around with you in this experience of suffering.
Notice how he listens to what has happened to you and how he
draws you out, wanting to share your suffering and identifying
with your experience of it. Notice how he makes much of your sufferings rather than making you feel that they are insignificant when
compared to his.

... so that you might share his and the love that inspired them
Take a scene from the passion of Jesus and notice some way he suffers in it that you can easily identify with. Ask him to tell you how
he experienced it. Let him invite you to remember a similar experience to his that you had and allow him to ask you to tell him how
you feel as you remember the way you suffered. Ask Jesus for the
grace of compassion so that you may be able to enter into his sufferings and his sorrow in the way that he has entered into yours. Next,
ask him to tell you about why he entered into his sufferings on your
behalf and about the love that he now wishes to express for you in
this way. (Jn 15:13, Gal 2:20) Conclude by telling him how you feel
about this and then talk to him about how you want to return his
love.

A sense of limitation, darkness and suffering

Jesus sees suffering and death as an essential part of life. He says that if new life is to emerge from the seed it must first die. (Jn 12:24) The life Jesus speaks about here is found through faith in his love (Jn 3:15-16) and in the happiness and consolation that accompanies faith. (Jn 15:11) However, faith or the acceptance of Jesus' ~~way of seeing~~ reality requires that we let go of our own distorted

~~flection and prayer~~

the essential call of Jesus to repent and believe the good news. (Mk 1:14-15)

Scripture: The PASSIONATE nature of LOVE

The passionate love of Jesus has its roots in the Old Testament. There God is portrayed as the lover and each person as the beloved. (Hos 2, Ezek 16, Song 2:16). Four aspects of passionate love characterise the way Jesus relates with us in the gospels. The most striking of these is the *intensity* with which Jesus loves us. He compares his love to a fire (Lk 12:49) and reveals its intensity by laying down his life for us. (Jn 13:1, 3:15-16, 10:11, 15:13) The intensity of his love is like a magnetic force that *attracts all to him* so strongly that he becomes the centre of our world. (Jn 11:52, 12:19, 12:32, Gal 2:20) This reverses the disintegrating effect of the Fall, (Gen 3-12) as it leads us to leave all to be with him. (Lk 5:11) His passionate love has also a transforming effect giving us the courage to *change our minds and hearts.* Finally, his passionate love *gets our whole person involved,* our heart, soul, mind and all our senses in the way that the passionate nature of any falling in love does. (Jn 15:9-10, Lk 10:25-28)

EXERCISE 20

Can our sufferings be constructive?

Suffering causes a crisis
as it can be an invitation or a frustration.
It can be an invitation to grow when it leads to
poverty of spirit, faith, hope and love
and to the joy that is the fruit of these.
Suffering can also frustrate our growth
when it leads to a loss of belief
in ourselves and in God
and a resulting sense of sorrow.

'The tragedy of life is not so much what men suffer,
but rather what they miss.'
Thomas Carlyle

Suffering causes a crisis

as it can make us cynical and sad

or it can refine our faith, hope and love

and the joy these bring

Reflection on our dark times

We are like plants that are initially raised in the ideal conditions of the glasshouse. However, if they are to mature they need to be 'hardened off' or gradually exposed to the harsher conditions outside the glasshouse. This exposure may cause the plants to die back for some time but the overall effect of this hardship is a healthy one. The drier and colder conditions outside the root sys-

separated from our

hours we were at school. But this experience also challenged us to make her present in a new way. We may have gradually learned to rely on our memory of her physical presence to assure us that she had not abandoned us. So we were challenged by this time of separation to find her present in a deeper and more permanent way. We learned our first lesson in how times of difficulty and darkness can foster belief as well as erode it.

The pattern of experience by which we are invited to find that those we love are present in new and deeper ways, despite their apparent absence, keeps repeating itself. The form this absence takes may differ as those we love may not just be absent physically but emotionally as well when, for example, we have a row with someone we love. However the most painful experiences of the absence of others or 'the dark night of the soul' may occur when glimpses and even convictions of their love for us, and of ours for them, are questioned or seem to dry up. This absence of any feeling leads us to question our basic beliefs.

Grace grows best in Winter

Times of hardship in life cause a crisis in that they confront us with a choice between two roads. One of these roads leads to 'life' and the other to 'destruction'. (Mt 7:13-14) Which road we take is determined by how we see, think about or discern the difficulty we are confronted with. So, for example, distractions in prayer might be seen as a frustration of our plans to be with God when we pray but they might also be seen as an invitation to bring our real self to prayer and to live contentedly with all its limitations.

The way of truth

Besides looking at our hardships or sufferings as an invitation to accept our human poverty, we can also see them as an invitation to faith, to hope and to charity. So our distractions in prayer, for example, can become an invitation to find our worth not in how well we perform in life but in the *belief* that we are loved deeply independently of how well we perform. Coming up against our limitations when we pray can also invite us to *trust,* not just in our own resources but in God's ability to draw good from all that happens. (Rom 8:28) Finally, living with our limitations and weakness may invite us to realise that our *charity* or love is proved in the sacrifice that facing these limitations asks of us.

The way of illusion

Life's hardships may easily lead us down a destructive way in that something like distractions may result in feelings of frustration or guilt. If these feelings are not dealt with they can colour not just our day but our way of seeing ourselves. This diminishment of our self-image makes it more difficult to believe that God is happy with our faltering efforts to pray.

The Exercise

The following suggestions may help you to notice, understand and respond to the difficult experiences that are our constant companions so that they become a constructive rather than a destructive influence.

Understand

In the second movement of reflection you are invited to understand your reaction to the difficult experience you described above. You need to work with the principle that it was not the people or the circumstances that caused you to feel the way you did but it was the way you saw, thought about or interpreted the experience. In the light of this principle go back to the experience you described above and see can you discover how you interpreted what happened to you. For example, did you find yourself diminished or belittled by the experience or did it lead you to a more realistic view of your limitations?

Respond

The most constructive response to suffering is that which Jesus led his two disciples towards on the road to Emmaus. (Lk 24) There are three ways we must allow him to help us as he,
1) encourages us to talk to him about our experience,
2) accepts our limitations which the experience reveals,
3) appreciates the way we struggle with our difficulties.

Constructive or destructive suffering

Our lives centre on our relationships and on the periods of involvement and of separation that characterise them. Much of our suffering has its source in events in which we feel separated from others
and especially from those we love and who love us. One of the main
ways that this kind of suffering can become constructive is when it
leads to a deepening of our belief that in spite of appearances we are
loved. As adults our conviction that we are loved is constantly being
questioned by events which separate us from others physically and
emotionally. This happens when the love of God and that of others
is no longer tangible or dries up. In such difficult times, when those
who love us seem to be absent, we have an invitation to find them
present in a more profound and permanent way. This new kind of
presence is cultivated by going back to times when we got glimpses
of their love for us and ours for them. These glimpses can in turn
put us in touch with convictions of our being loved in which faith
consists. It is often only suffering that forces us to draw on these
profound resources we all have.

Scripture: The constructive power of suffering

In Psalm 130 and in Psalm 25 we find an expression of the belief that
suffering can foster faith. From the time of his baptism Jesus adopts
the attitude of the Suffering Servant towards his sufferings which is
one of dependence, trust and surrender to God. Jesus invites us to
learn this attitude of poverty of spirit from him as a way of dealing
with life's burdens. (Mt 11:28) St James considers suffering a privilege as it can foster faith (Jas 1:3-5) while St Paul sees suffering as a
powerful source of hope in God's promises and of patience and perseverance in our pursuit of the goal hope sets before us. (Rom 5:3-5)
It is in the sufferings of Jesus that we find the supreme revelation of
his love for us. (Jn 15:12-15, 3:15-16) In the Acts of the Apostles Jesus'
disciples consider it a privilege to suffer on his behalf. (Acts 5:41)
The joy they experience is the result of hardship accepted in the
light of faith, hope and love. (2 Cor 7:4, 1:3-7)

The Fifth Stage
of
The Spiritual Exercises

Being with Jesus in his sufferings

~~of this fifth stage~~ of the Spiritual Exercises is to enter into

1) Spend a period of two of ~~prayer~~
stances in which Jesus gave us the Eucharist. (Lk 22:19-20) This will
provide a good context in which to begin this stage of the Spiritual
Exercises. In the Eucharist Jesus leaves you a powerful way to keep
alive the memory of his love of you 'to the end'. (Jn 13:1) You might
begin this exercise by listing people in your life, like your parents or
other significant people, who in different ways have sacrificed
themselves for you. Then with the help of Jn 15:13 you might listen
to what Jesus wants you to remember as you begin to focus on how
much he loves you in being willing to die for you. (Gal 2:20)

2) In the second introductory exercise spend a period or two of
prayer listing the kinds of darkness or suffering you are familiar
with. When you have made as comprehensive a list as you can,
notice places in his passion and death where Jesus experienced the
kinds of suffering you are familiar with. Let Jesus ask you about
your sufferings and then talk to him about his.

Procedure
There are five cycles and a review cycle at this fifth stage of the
Spiritual Exercises. As usual there are five periods of prayer in each
cycle and for these take a new scene for each period of prayer or follow the pattern you have been using of taking two passages for the
first two periods, two repetitions for periods three and four and an

application of the senses for the fifth period. The subject matter of your prayer may be:

1) the story of the passion of Jesus in one gospel or

2) the scenes from the story of the passion that appeal to you from any of the gospels or

3) use the following division of the main events of Jesus' passion and death.

Cycle 1: The agony in the garden (Jn 12:23-33)

In St John's version of the agony of Jesus we find a description of Jesus' 'hour of heartbreak'. We see the extreme mental and emotional anguish of Jesus at the prospect of his suffering and death. Like us he wants to escape death when he is faced with the imminent prospect of it. (v 27). He is bewildered, torn by conflicting emotions, moved almost beyond endurance as he faces the ultimate implication of being the Suffering Servant.

His agony is described in the following words by Matthew, Mark and Luke: '... sadness came over him and great distress. My soul is sorrowful to the point of death ... he fell on his face and prayed ... And a sudden fear came over him and great distress ... he threw himself on the ground and prayed ... His sweat fell on the ground like great drops of blood.' (Mt 26, Mk 14, Lk 22)

The colloquy

The colloquy you use when contemplating Jesus' sufferings can take a number of forms. It may be an expression of deep feelings of compassion or love or it may be about what you felt in prayer, depending on whether the prayer was consoling or hard going. The colloquy might also be about what you wish to do for Christ or it may take the form of petition for something you desire or really want. The colloquy can be with each of the persons of the Trinity or with Jesus.

Cycle 2: How his apostles reacted to his passion and death

1) *Peter's denial*: Lk 22:54-62

Peter was accepted into a position of great intimacy with Jesus and was entrusted with great responsibility. In spite of the fact that Jesus knew beforehand of Peter's betrayal it did not prevent him from entrusting Peter with his own work. 'I have prayed for you that you may not lose your faith. Yes, when you have turned back to me you must strengthen these brothers of yours.' Lk 22:32-34. When Peter denies Jesus he does so with an oath – something a Jew did not do lightly. 'He started calling down curses on himself and swearing, I ____ ___ ___ man you speak of.' (Mk 14:71-72) 'The Lord

lonely hours from those closest

Cycle 3: Jesus before the religious leaders

Lk 22:47-53 and 63-71: Jesus from the start is a 'standard which many will attack for he will expose the thoughts of many hearts'. (Lk 2:35) Right at the beginning of Jesus' public life Mark describes in Chapters 2 and 3 of his gospel a series of events which indicate a growing hostility to Jesus to the point where the religious leaders plot to kill him. (Mk 3:6) Jesus gives expression to this hardening of opposition to him in a parable that is in all three synoptic gospels. (Lk 20:9-16) These same leaders who were culpably blind (Jn 9:38) were the ones who were meant to help the people understand what God had been saying over the 2,000 years they were being prepared for the coming of Jesus. Contemplate what Jesus felt as he stood before them, when what he said was treated with contempt, when he was the object of their hatred and malice, when they cried 'Crucify him!'.

Cycle 4: Jesus before the secular leaders

Lk 23:1-25: 'He humbled himself ... even to the extent of dying, and the death he died was the death of a common criminal' (Phil 2:6-8) 'Herod and his guards treated him with contempt and insult, after which they put a magnificent cloak on him.' Jesus is utterly alone and defenceless. 'Pilot then had Jesus taken away and scourged and after this, the soldiers twisted some thorns into a crown and put them on his head.' Share with Jesus the humiliation, gross injustice and the other sufferings he undergoes in silence at the hands of Pilot, Herod and the soldiers.

Cycle 5: The way of the cross

Lk 23:26-49: We can imagine how much Jesus suffers from being alone in his 'hour of heartbreak'. He is aware of the deep pain his suffering is causing his mother and his disciples. He also experiences great sadness when he thinks of what Judas has done. Jesus suffers because of the way the leaders are frustrating God's plan. He experiences disappointment at the failure in human terms of his work and at the failure of his disciples to understand that 'the Son of Man must suffer'. The humiliations, the abuse and contempt he has to bear cause him great pain.

The lack of self pity of Jesus in all these sufferings is remarkable. He is constantly going out to others, e.g. to Malchus and to the women on the way to Calvary. In spite of all he is going through, Jesus' concern is for others and for the accomplishment of his Father's will. His words 'My God, my God, why have you forsaken me' are part of a psalm of confidence in his Father. When he says 'It is finished' he is preoccupied with the completion of his Father's plan. When he says, 'Into your hands, Father …', his concern is for others, just as it is when he says, 'Father, forgive them …', 'Son, behold your mother …', 'This day you will be with me …'

'I will draw all to myself'

By his passion and death Jesus gives us the greatest sign of his love (Jn 13:1) and thereby 'draws all people/things to himself'. (Jn 12:32) Where sin separates us from him, the love revealed by his suffering and death 'brings together into one family all the children of God scattered throughout the world'. (Jn 11:52) The attractiveness of his love causes 'the whole world to run after him' (Jn 12:19) just as it causes his disciples to leave everything in order to be with him. (Lk 5:11)

The Review Cycle

During the final cycle, devoted to contemplating the sufferings and death of Jesus, be with all that you have experienced during cycle 1-5. You might find it helpful to be with Mary under the cross or at the tomb and to go over with her all that she saw and heard. After two periods of prayer leave the rest of the day free to review in an ᵢₓₓₓₗ ₓₓₓ your whole experience of all that Jesus suffered for

PART 8

Being with Jesus in his resurrection

The resurrection scenes in the gospels invite us to rejoice in the joy and the glory of Jesus. They also invite us to become more aware of how Jesus wants to share his joy and his glory with us. This glory is the radiance, the splendour or the beauty of the love Jesus reveals to us. (Jn 1:14) Jesus says that his joy springs from his consciousness of the immense love he, his Father and the Spirit share. (Jn 15:9-11)

We have seen Jesus' glory gradually emerging in the growing attractiveness of the many dimensions of his love we have looked at in the gospel story. It is a glory he wishes to share with us if we are willing to change our minds and hearts so that we may believe in the many facets of his love and of our own lovableness which we see in his eyes. (2 Cor 3:18)

All things become signs of his love
The growing attractiveness of Jesus' love reaches its climax in his death and resurrection when his being 'lifted up' in glory draws all things together and to himself. He describes what he draws us into as a friendship in which everyone and everything is incorporated. Jesus invites us to become aware of the deep significance this gives to everyone and everything as a manifestation of his love.

Immortal Diamond

'This Jack, poor potsherd, matchwood, immortal diamond
is immortal diamond' *G. M. Hopkins*

...ide and deep and long and high is the
of God'

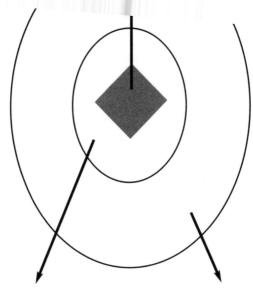

Facets of the diamond or of
Jesus' love in the Word, the
Eucharist, in significant
people, etc.

Finding God in all,
in people, in trees,
in 'the music of what
happens'

EXERCISE 21

The glory and joy of the risen Lord

In his resurrection Jesus realises
with an intense joy,
how wonderful or glorious his life is.
His glory is the radiance of the love
he shares with his Father
and through their Spirit with us.

The glory and joy of the risen Jesus
is the ultimate expression
of the growing attractiveness of Jesus' love
seen in all the gospel stories.

Christ has turned all our sunsets into dawns.
St Clement of Alexandria

The radiance of Jesus' love

seen in his growing attractiveness

in the gospel stories

reaches its climax

in the glory and joy of his resurrection

Contemplating the Resurrection

The film, *It's A Wonderful Life* tells the story of a young man called George Baily who has dreams of greatness. However, he has to sacrifice his dreams when his father dies, leaving him to look after their small business and those who depend on it for employment. Due to the carelessness of one of these employees [illegible] George, feeling himself a failure, con-[illegible]

remember[illegible]

A glimpse of greatness

What made George Baily so joyful was the glimpse of how wonderful his life was when he was led to remember how good he had been to others during the whole course of his life. We can get a similar glimpse of how wonderful or glorious is the love we have received and given from a fantasy like the following. This in turn may give us an insight into the joy and glory Jesus experienced in his resurrection.

Imagine that those who mean most to you in life have gathered for a celebration in your honour. After the meal there are a number of speeches in which your praises are sung by a member of your family, a friend, someone you have worked with for many years and a person you were very good to. After listening to each person, make a note of what they say and after reflecting on this, paint a portrait of the person you see in their eyes. What features of this portrait please you most? Are there features in it that you are surprised that people noticed?

Exploring the joy and glory of Jesus

In contemplating the resurrection scenes in the gospels we will be seeking primarily *to rejoice with Jesus in his joy and in his glory.* The *joy* which Jesus experiences in the resurrection, like that of George Baily, springs from his memory of how he has loved his Father and us 'to the end' but even more so from his memory of his Father's love of him. (Jn 15:9-11) This joy pervades his whole life, his coming, (Lk 2:8-14) his public life (Lk 10:21-22) and most strikingly his resurrection. (Jn 20:19-20) The *glory* of Jesus which we contemplate in the resurrection scenes consists in the radiance or splendour of his love. (Jn 1:14) We see this glory in the gentle way he acknowledges, accepts and affirms people. (Jn 2:11) It is above all in the radiance of his Father's love for him and of their love for us – seen in his passion and death – that Jesus' glory is revealed in its most spectacular form. (Jn 3:15-16)

The splendour of Jesus' love

The glory of the risen Jesus is the ultimate expression of the radiance of his love we have seen in all the gospel stories. The loving-kind and affectionate nature of his love is seen in the way he relates with Mary Magdalene, (Jn 20:11-19, Jn 14:15-26) its permanence is seen in his acceptance of the infidelity of his disciples whom he never abandons even though they abandon him, (Jn 21:15-18, 14:1-3) its personal quality is seen in the way he calls his disciples by name to an ever new level of intimacy. (Jn 20:16-17, Jn 15:9, 16) The provident nature of Jesus' love is manifest in the all-pervasive nature of his concern for us (Jn 21:9-12, 17:20-26) and its passionate quality is manifest in the way he loves us 'to the end' or to death. (Jn 13:1, 15:13, Lk 22:19-22, 24:30-35). We see how profound Jesus' love is in the way he shares 'everything' with us, even the depth of his own relationship with his Father. (Jn 15:9-15, 20:16-17) In disclosing himself to us in this way Jesus seeks to become our friend, (Jn 15:15) one who is always with us rejoicing in our joy and consoling us in our times of darkness. (Lk 24:1-35)

The Exercise

The following suggestions may help you to enter into the glory and
the joy of Jesus and into the way he wishes to share his glory and joy
with you.

Sharing Jesus' joy

most joy in life, from the most spiritual

the time

what impresses you most about what y
own joy.

Images of glory

What images does the word glory arouse in your mind? List some
words that express this notion of glory in a way that makes it attractive for you. What makes people glorious or resplendent in the ordinary circumstances of life and what aspects of your own life give
you a glimpse of glory? To get a sense of the way 'you have been
clothed with God's own splendour' (Ezek 16:9-14) read Mary's
Magnificat (Lk 1:46-55) and then see what you would include in
your own Magnificat.

Contemplating a resurrection scene

Read a resurrection scene. Notice the picture of Jesus' love that
emerges from what you see him doing, hear him saying and from
the way he relates with people. When you have identified what
characterises Jesus' love, spend time with the attractiveness of this
and notice how it reveals his glory or the radiance of his love.
Assuming that the joy Jesus experiences most deeply centres on the
love he receives and gives, talk to him about what gives him most
joy in the resurrection scene you are contemplating.

A profound and joyful love

Scripture: The PROFOUND nature of LOVE

How profoundly Jesus loves each one of us is revealed in the events of his death and resurrection. (Jn 13:1, Rom 5:6-8, 1 Jn 3:16 Gal 2:21) These events are the climax of the Bible story and the depth of the love they express is described for us in chapters 14-17 of John's gospel. In these chapters Jesus makes known the depth of his own relationship with his Father and the Spirit. He tells us that his love for us is as deep as his Father's love for him. (Jn 15:9) He invites us to abide in this love by letting it pervade all our experience. (Jn 15:10) We are constantly being led deeper and deeper into 'all the truth' (Jn 16:13) or into the love of which the Spirit has given us a gift. (Rom 5:5) This sharing of 'everything' about the relationship which the Father, Jesus and the Spirit enjoy with each other opens up for us the possibility of a profound friendship with them. (Jn 15:15)

Scripture: The JOYFUL nature of LOVE

In the Old Testament it is revealed that God has a plan for our peace. (Jer 29:11) Jesus seeks to fulfill this plan by sharing his own peace with us. (Jn 14:27) The Jerusalem Bible defines this peace as the 'perfect happiness and fulfilment' Jesus comes to establish. (Lk 2:10-14, Jn 15:11). This happiness pervades Jesus' whole life (Lk 10:21) and is most obvious in the resurrection scenes. (Lk 24:36-41) It has its roots in our faith or in the conviction that we are loved. (Jn 15:9-11) Therefore, in promoting faith throughout the gospel story Jesus is laying the foundation of our happiness. He wants us to find joy in our dark times (Lk 24:13-35, Jn 16:19-24) just as he wants us to find it in a growing sense of our limitation and sinfulness that he calls poverty of spirit. (Mt 5:1-12) For Jesus all things are a cause for celebration, from the most material such as what we eat and drink (Jn 2:1-11, Jn 6:1-11)) to the most spiritual. (Jn 6:35, 51)

EXERCISE 22

Reconciling all things in Christ

Redemption can be seen as reconciliation,
a befriending of all estranged by sin.

and thus as a sign of his presence and p
is a revelation of his beauty,
and draws us to him.

God's gifts put man's best dreams to shame.
E. B. Browning

Everything

is a revelation of the risen Lord

and can put us in touch with

the glory and joy of his love

The all-inclusive nature of love

The work of our redemption can be seen as one of reconciliation, which means befriending all those areas of our lives from which we have become estranged. The source of this estrangement is described for us in the story of the Fall (Gen 3-12) where we are told that when the love of God ceases to be the centre of our lives, what binds all creation together loses its hold on us and we disintegrate or fall apart. 'The centre no longer holds and things fall apart.' (W. B. Yeats)

Creating a magnetic field

When I was studying science at school there was an experiment we did to demonstrate the power a magnet has to create a magnetic field. The experiment involved putting iron filings on a sheet of paper and then moving a magnet around underneath the paper. The filings that were a disorganised mass when we placed them on the paper began to form a pattern. The power of the magnet created a field of influence drawing the filings into a relationship with the magnet and with each other.

'I will draw all things to myself'

One of the major themes in St John's gospel is expressed in the words of Jesus when he says, 'If I am lifted up from the earth, I will draw all things to myself'. (Jn 12:32) The words 'lifted up' refer to the death and resurrection of Jesus as the ultimate expression of his love. This love, that can be compared in its transforming power to falling in love, creates a new order in which our world centres on our Beloved. What was scattered is drawn back together again into an intimate union with Jesus. (Jn 11:52) One of the effects of this intimacy, as with that created by falling in love, is that everything is bathed in its light and can put us in touch with the one who through his passionate love of us 'to the end' becomes our Lord or the centre of our lives.

Finding God in all things

When we experience the supreme attractiveness of Jesus' love of us 'to the utmost extent' he not only becomes our Lord but everything tends to be seen in a new light. Even the most ordinary things can put us in touch with the love Jesus asks us to remember at Mass. Making this connection, so that we find in all things a manifest-

second is the significance everything ...

on when seen as a gift of God. (1 Cor 4:7) As a gift it is a sign or has a built-in message of another's love. If we adopt this vision, everything has a built-in message of God's love or is a revelation of it. Everything becomes part of a loving providence in which everyone we meet, everything we receive, everything that happens can put us in touch with the love that sustains us in life. Three dimensions of everything as gift will help it to fulfill its most profound role as a wayside sacrament that puts us in touch with the love of Jesus.

Three dimensions of all things as gift

Everything, as for example our body, is *a natural gift* which helps us in many ways as well as being *a source of wonder*. Our body is also *a personal gift* in its role of life-long companion. Finally, our body is *a spiritual gift* as it is a *sign of God's love and providence*. Seen in this way everything around us becomes part of a simple abundance calling us to live life in a spirit of wonder and appreciation, of celebration and gratitude.

The Exercise

The following suggestions may help you to gain an intimate knowledge of the deep significance of all things as so many signs of God's
love inviting us to find God in all things.

Begin the exercise by making a list of three kinds of gifts:
Natural gifts such as the gift of hearing. (Jas 1:17)
Personal gifts unique to your own story. (Deut 1:29-33)
Spiritual gifts like God's love for you. (Rom 5:5)
After making each list reflect on it in the light of the piece of God's
Word suggested.

The three dimension of every gift.
1) Explore the natural dimension of a gift like hearing by noticing
   the various ways your hearing helps you to enjoy life. Then
   imagine what life would be like without it, Allow time for a
   sense of wonder to develop at how effectively your hearing
   works and how for example it opens up to you the world of
   music and conversation.

2) Next, reflect on the personal dimension of your gift of hearing
   by concentrating on the story of your relationship with it. It has
   been your life-long companion, in times when you neglected or
   abused it and in times when you appreciated it and were concerned for it. After appreciating its years of devoted service to
   you, enter a dialogue with it in which you listen and respond to
   each other as life-long friends. Write down the main thing you
   want to say to each other.

3) Finally, become aware of the spiritual dimension of your gift of
   hearing as a gift of God. As such it is a sign of God's love and
   providence putting you in touch with the ultimate expression of
   this love which you remember at Mass. Conclude by expressing
   how you feel about your hearing as a gift of God and a wayside
   sacrament.

'I have called you friends'

'To the Ancients, friendship seemed the happiest and most fully human of all loves; the crown of life and the school of virtue. The modern world, in comparison, ignores it.' (C. S. Lewis) For Christians the love of friendship is, with passionate love, the main symbol of what it means to be a Christian. In seeing it like this they ~~follow~~ing the lead of scripture in its belief that like Abraham

Stage). Falling in love or pass...

comes permanent, finds its fulfilment in friendship especially if what we share is our inmost selves in self-disclosure. When love becomes permanent and profound in this way it leads to a friendship that is a source of deep joy (Sixth Stage).

Scripture: The LOVE of FRIENDSHIP

The friendship that God establishes with Abraham (Gen 18:17) and Moses (Ex 33:11) is shared in the New Covenant with everyone, since 'they will all know God the least no less than the greatest'. (Jer 31:31-34) Jesus comes among us as one making friends and drawing us into his own relationship with his Father. (Mk 3:13-15) The core of this friendship is his sharing with us the love he has for his Father and which his Father has for him. (Jn 10:14-15, 15:15) This self-disclosure is what initiates the friendship but for it to be established we must respond to God's initiative by 'abiding in' this love. (Jn 15:9-10) To maintain this friendship we need to listen and respond to God's ongoing self-revelation as our relationship will be as intimate as this communication is. (Lk 8:19-21)

The Sixth Stage
of
The Spiritual Exercises

Sharing in the glory and joy of Jesus

Having shared the sorrow of Jesus in his passion and death we now wish to share his joy and his glory in the way explained in Exercise 21. Our aim, therefore, in this sixth stage of the Spiritual Exercises is *to be glad and to rejoice intensely because of the great joy and glory of Christ our Lord.* While making the joy and the glory of Jesus your main concern it is important to allow Jesus to share his joy and his glory with you. (Jn 17:13-23) In the resurrection scenes Jesus acts as a 'consoler', opening up to you his own relationship with his Father. He also wishes to share with you the life, friendship and happiness which knowing the Father 'just as' he does makes possible for you. (Jn 10:14-15, 15:9-15, 17:21-23, 17:26)

The Contemplatio

Closely connected with Jesus' desire to share his risen life with us is the way the love he expressed in his death and resurrection draws all things to himself and to each other. St Ignatius in his Spiritual Exercises aims to help us further this reintegration of all things in Jesus by asking us to do an exercise he calls, *The Contemplation to Attain the Love of God,* and which we will call *the Contemplatio* for brevity sake. There is an introduction to this in Exercise 22 where it is explained how the love of God is to be found in all things. Cultivating this vision involves developing our ability to see everything in the following four ways.

1) Everything is *a gift* from God, whether that gift is natural, personal or supernatural. (Jas 1:17)
2) Because everything as a gift is a *sign* of the giver's love everything is a wayside sacrament or a powerful sign of God's love and *presence.*
3) Everything that happens is a sign of God's *providence* in that 'by turning everything to their good God cooperates with all those who love him'. (Rom 8:28)

4) An appreciation of God's gifts leads to an appreciation of *their giver*. (Eph 1:1-14)

This experience of God giving us all things and sharing even himself with us evokes a desire to love and serve God in all things. *The colloquy* as an expression of this desire to respond may be with Jesus or with the three persons of the Trinity.

1) A survey of gifts

Survey the many *natural, personal and supernatural gifts* you have received:

1) There are *natural gifts* such as your eyesight. To become more aware of the value of your eyes spend some time imagining what life would be like without your eyes.
2) Then there are *personal gifts* that are unique to your story. Notice, for example, a person who has had a unique influence on your life.
3) Finally, there are *supernatural gifts* such as your relationship with each of the persons of the Trinity. You have been given many gifts such as the sacraments, the Word of God and especially the Eucharist to help you enter into and maintain this relationship.

When you have reflected on these gifts and their abundance prayerfully, ponder these words from the Spiritual Exercises:

'I will ponder with great affection how much God our Lord has done for me and how much he has given me of what he possesses, and finally, how much, so far as he can, the same Lord desires to give himself to me according to his divine decrees. Then I will reflect upon myself and consider, according to all reason and justice, what I ought to offer the divine majesty, that is all I possess and myself with it. Thus as one would do who is moved with great feeling, I will make this offering of myself.'

'Take, Lord, and receive all my liberty, my memory, my understanding, and my entire will, all that I have and possess. You have given all to me. To you, O Lord, I return it. All this is yours, dispose of it wholly according to your will. Give me your love and your grace, for this is sufficient for me.'

2) *A survey of what gives you joy*
Survey your 'joyful mysteries' or all the things in life that give you joy and make you feel alive. Make as comprehensive a list as possible and note the ones that keep recurring and give you most happiness.

Next, spend time with the reality that God is intent on your peace, (Jer 29:11) that Jesus wants to share his happiness with you (Jn 15:11) and that the Spirit would have you 'always rejoice in his consolation'. Finally, respond to how you feel about all this in the words given above: 'I will ponder …'

Combining the resurrection and the Contemplatio
In each of the cycles that follow, spend the first period of prayer with the resurrection scene suggested and the second with the aspect of the *Contemplatio* outlined after it. Spend two periods repeating what you find helpful from these first two periods of prayer and then in the fifth period do the application of the senses.

The connection between the resurrection scene and the *Contemplatio* can be seen in the diagram for Part 8. There you have three circles. In the centre circle you have Grace or the love of Jesus symbolised by the diamond. This is the love you have being growing in an interior knowledge of and that reaches its climax in the death and resurrection of Jesus, in his love of you 'to the utmost extent'. There is an outline of how this love has developed at the end of Exercise 22. In the middle circle you have the various facets of the diamond or facets of the love of Jesus that the various resurrection scenes highlight. In the outer circle you have all the gifts that the Triune

God has surrounded you with. All these created things as gifts reveal and lead you to the centre circle or to the love of God which Jesus makes visible and of which the Spirit gives you an interior knowledge. Thus all things can put you in touch with the love of God and especially with that which we see a vision of in the death and resurrection of Jesus and which we celebrate at Mass.

develop a vision of all things you

* To make the glory and joy of Jesus more real for yourself notice that this *glory* is the radiance or splendour of Jesus' love and that his *joy* springs from his conviction that he is loved by and loves his Father, the people in these resurrection scenes and you.

* In these resurrection scenes the kinds of love that are prominent at the different stages of the Exercises are revealed to us again but in a quiet or unobtrusive way. For example, in the lakeside scene in John 21 the faithful love of Jesus that we contemplated at the second stage is highlighted as is the personal and provident love that we focused on at the third and fourth stages.

* To enter fully into Jesus' glory, or into the radiance of his love and the joy this gives rise to, it is worthwhile to first invite him to enter into and talk to you about your experience of these kinds of love.

* Finally, remember that 'it is not a multiplicity of ideas that satisfies the soul but to taste and savour a little interiorly'. This is the principle that governs the movement of your prayer towards simplicity and quietness as you make your way in each cycle towards the application of the senses.

Cycle 1: Jesus appears to Mary

1) There is a long-standing belief that after Jesus rose from the dead he appeared first to his mother. Be with Mary as she waits in hope. The predictions of his resurrection must have meant much to her. She had shared the depths of his suffering and now she enters fully into his joy and his glory. 'I shall see you again and your heart will rejoice ...' (Jn 16:19-24) You may find the words of the *Magnificat* or of the *Regina Caeli* helpful.

2) *The Contemplatio: The contemplation of gifts*

What you are seeking in the *Contemplatio* is *an interior knowledge of God's gifts, so that filled with gratitude for them you may in all things serve the Lord.*

For the second period of prayer go back again to some aspects of the two introductory exercises above that you found helpful. Dwell with the way everything in your life is a gift and thus a sign that can put you in touch with the love of Jesus which you have been contemplating in the resurrection scene where Jesus meets his mother.

Cycle 2: Jesus as consoler and friend

1) *Jesus appears to Magdalene:* (Jn 20:11-18)
The following are some aspects of the story of how Jesus appeared to Mary Magdalene that you might choose from:

The intimacy Jesus seeks

In this scene Jesus displays an intimacy which is not so obvious in his public life. He calls Mary by name, like the Good Shepherd calling each person in a unique way. (Jn 10:3) The way Jesus relates with her in a deeply personal manner is a fulfilment of the promise of the New Covenant in which 'each person will know God, the least no less than the greatest' (Jer 31:34). She is chosen by Jesus to announce the fulfilment of this covenant to his followers.

Brother and friend

Jesus speaks of himself as your 'brother' and speaks of God as 'your Father and my Father'. He thus expresses his desire to share with you his own intimate relationship with his Father. (Jn 10:14-15)

Jesus describes this relationship as *knowing* which is a deep personal experience of another person in which a mutual knowing and loving is involved. This is the friendship Jesus wishes to enter into with you, one that is based on the reality of sharing with you 'everything he has heard from his Father'. (Jn 15:15)

A joy no one will take from you

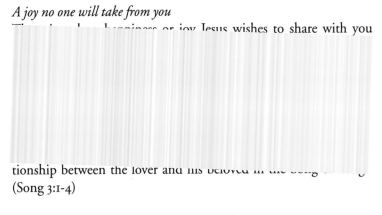

tionship between the lover and his beloved in the Song
(Song 3:1-4)

2) *The Contemplatio: Gifts as signs of God's presence*
Keep in mind that what you are seeking in the *Contemplatio* is an interior knowledge of God's gifts, so that filled with gratitude for them you may in all things serve the Lord.

To dispose yourself to receive this intimate knowledge consider how *a gift is a sign* we give another, how a present we receive has a built-in message. When we give a gift of flowers, we say in effect, 'I thought of you, I love you.' It is the thought that matters when the little child brings his or her mother a gift of a dandelion from the garden. A letter can call up the love that exists between two people even if they are half a world apart. Thus the presence of people to each other depends not so much on their physical presence as on the degree to which they know and love each other and are willing to communicate this.

Everything around us is a sign of God's love and invites us to become aware of, to savour and assimilate this reality. *God's presence becomes pervasive* if we are prepared to let everything put us in touch with all the love that we have gained an interior knowledge of in the exercises we have been engaged in so far. The Eucharist is the supreme expression of this love which we constantly seek to tease out and savour by praying with the word of God. If the memory of this love of Jesus is kept alive in this way, many aspects of our daily experience can put us in touch with it.

Cycle 3: Restoring the lost intimacy of friendship

Keep in mind that in contemplating the resurrection our primary interest is to share the glory and the joy of Jesus and then to let him share this glory and joy with us. His glory, as we have seen, is revealed in the splendour of his love that we see in a resurrection scene like the following one and that his joy is in the giving and the receiving of this love.

1) *Jesus appears at the lakeside* (Jn 21:1-14)

There is a noticeable familiarity and intimacy in the way Jesus relates with his disciples after the resurrection. This is especially apparent in the scene where Jesus appears to his disciples at the lakeside. He addresses them as 'lads' or as 'friends' and reveals how deep this friendship is in his sensitivity to and practical concern for them. He shows this in the way he has breakfast ready for them and in the fact that he serves it. There is a deep significance in the fact that he serves them bread and fish. This brings us back to the Eucharistic implications of the feeding of the multitude (Jn 6) and the table fellowship of the messianic banquet that it symbolises.

We notice how Jesus leads the disciples out of their desolation and into the consolation he enjoys with his Father. He also acts as reconciler, befriending Peter who had estranged himself from Jesus by his denial. Jesus restores him not just to his former intimacy but to an even greater one. It is significant that he asks Peter three times, 'Are you my friend?' This triple restoration of the bond of friendship corresponds in a very touching way to Peter's triple denial.

2) *The Contemplatio: The providence of God in all things*

For the exercise on the *Contemplatio* consider how the provident love of the three persons of the Trinity reaches into every corner of your life. Begin the exercise by praying for an interior knowledge of

God's gifts, especially for how God's provident care for you is manifest in them. Allow a sense of gratitude for this provident love to grow and find expression in your desire to love and serve your risen Lord in all things.

One or two of the following aspects of the lakeside scene you contemplated above may help deepen your sense of how pervasive the ~~idence of the Father, of Jesus and of the Spirit is in your life. In~~

The Holy Spirit is always teaching and guiding us into all the truth'. (Jn 14:26, 16:13)

Cycle 4: The essential gift of the spirit

In contemplating the scene in John's gospel where Jesus gives us the gift of the Holy Spirit, one or two of the following aspects of it may help you to focus on Jesus' glory and his joy.

1) Jesus appears in the upper room (Jn 20:19-29)

What is stressed in this story from John's gospel is the transforming effect of the gift Jesus gives us of *the Holy Spirit*. It is a transformation brought about particularly by *the sacrament of reconciliation*. Through this sacrament of Jesus' acceptance of the sinful side of us we are empowered to befriend all those areas of our lives from which we have become estranged because of sin.

The Holy Spirit is portrayed here by Jesus as the one who brings *a new creation* into being. This new order is the result of our living out Jesus' commandment that we love others and all things as he loves us. This is not so much a command to imitate him as a statement of what will happen if we believe in his love. If we accept his love, we accept our lovableness, that of others and of all things. If we view ourselves, others and all creation in this way we will feel an inner constraint to walk in its light, to live consistently with it and to treat everyone and everything with the respect due them.

We are empowered to keep Jesus' command by the love of God which the Spirit 'pours into our hearts'. (Rom 5:5) We are empowered to see all as 'transfigured in ever increasing splendour ...' (2 Cor 3:18)

2) *The Contemplatio: The giver of all good things*
In this exercise *we move from the gifts to the giver.* (Jas 1:17) We seek to go beyond God's gifts and how God is present and provident in them to contemplate their giver. God is the source of all things and the one whose beauty they all reflect. All things are from above and mirror their Source, the fountain of Light and Life. (Jn 8:12, Jn 7:37-39)

There is a movement here from a love that inspires gratitude to one that inspires an appreciation of the goodness of the giver. (Wis 13:1-5) It might help to re-live an incident in which you experienced the goodness of another person in the gift he or she gave you. In Eph 1:1-23 there is a refrain that runs through the whole passage as a response to the seven blessings it describes God lavishing on us. Each gift or blessing inspires us to '... praise the glory of God's grace.' You may find it helpful to return to the reflection, 'I will ponder with great affection ...' and to the prayer 'Take and receive ....' Prayers such as the Gloria, the prefaces, the Through Him, with Him ... may help you to express how you feel.

Cycle 5: Jesus is with us all along the way we travel
1) *On the road to Emmaus* (Lk 24:13-35)
Jesus' glory is seen in the way he meets two people on the road to Emmaus. They are in despair and he leads them out of this desolation to share his hope and joy. To do this he uses the *Word* to help them to interpret *their experience* in the light his story as the Suffering Servant but especially in the light of his love of them 'to the utmost extent' embodied in the *Eucharist* or in what is here called 'the breaking of bread'. Through these three tables of his banquet he makes the abundance of his Father's love 'known' to us

in all its splendour. (Jn 17:26) What happened on the road to Emmaus is a symbol of what the risen Jesus wants to do in each person's life.

2) *The Contemplatio: The four points of it*

For your second contemplation recall briefly the four points of *The Contemplation to Attain the Love of God* and spend time with any aspect of it that you find helpful. As you do so keep in mind the in-

A BOY OF
GOOD

MIRIAM TOEWS

ISIS
LARGE PRINT
Oxford

First published in Great Britain 2006
by
Faber and Faber Limited

Published in Large Print 2007 by ISIS Publishing Ltd.,
7 Centremead, Osney Mead, Oxford OX2 0ES
by arrangement with
Faber and Faber Limited

British Library Cataloguing in Publication Data
Toews, Miriam, 1964–
    A boy of good breeding. – Large print ed.
    1. Single mothers – Fiction
    2. City and town life – Canada – Fiction
    3. Large type books
    I. Title
    813.5'4 [F]

ISBN 978–0–7531–7860–7 (hb)
ISBN 978–0–7531–7861–4 (pb)

Printed and bound in Great Britain by
T. J. International Ltd., Padstow, Cornwall

For Neal

CHAPTER
ONE

need for a town. And that's what g......
one less it would be a village and if it had just one more
it would be a bigger town. Like all the rest of the small
towns. Being the smallest was its claim to fame.

Knute had come to Algren, from the city of
Winnipeg, to look after her dad who'd had a heart
attack. And to relieve her mom who said if she spent
one more day in the house she'd go insane.

She was twenty-four years old. Her mother, Dory,
had intended her name to be pronounced "Noot uh,"
but nobody got it so it became just Knute, like "Noot."
Even her mom had given up on the "uh" part but did
from time to time call her Knutie or sometimes, and
she hated this, Knuter.

Knute had a daughter, Summer Feelin', and
Summer Feelin' had a strange way of shaking when she
was excited. She flapped her arms, and her fingers
moved quickly as though she were typing to save her

life, and sometimes her head went back and her mouth opened wide and sounds like *aaah* and *uh-uh-uh* came out of it.

When she first started doing it, Knute thought it was cute. Summer Feelin' looked like she'd lift right off the ground. But then Knute started worrying about it and decided to take her to a specialist, a pediatric neurologist. He did a number of tests, including an encephalogram. Summer Feelin' liked the wires and enjoyed the attention but told the doctor that flapping was just something she was born to do.

Eventually after all the results came in and the charts had been read and analyzed, he agreed with her. She was born to flap. There was no sign of strange electrical activity in her brain, no reason to do a CAT scan, and all accounts of her birth indicated no trauma had occurred, nothing untoward as she had made her way through Knute's birth canal and into this world.

Every night Knute lay down with Summer Feelin'. That was the time S.F. told Knute stories and let her in on her big plans and Knute could feel her daughter's body tremble with excitement. It quivered. It shook. It was out of her control. Knute would hold Summer Feelin' until she stopped shaking, maybe a twitch or two or a shudder, and fell asleep. The specialist said S.F.'s condition, which wasn't really a condition, was very rare but nothing to worry about. Then he'd added, in a thoughtful way, that the condition or lack of condition might be the precipitator to that rare phenomenon known as spontaneous combustion. So Knute worried, from time to time, about S.F. bursting into flames for no apparent reason. And that was the type of concern she couldn't really explain to people, even close friends, without them asking her if she needed a nap or what she'd been reading lately or just plain laughing at her.

March was the month that Knute and Summer Feelin'

were still finding tiny pine needles in his hair and in the many creases of his skin. He picked up a nasty infection called septicemia in the hospital and, as a result, his lungs malfunctioned and he was put on a respirator. Of course, he couldn't talk, but in his more lucid, pain-free moments he could write. Sort of. All he ever wrote, in a barely legible scrawl either stretched out over the whole page or sometimes scrunched up in the bottom corner, was "How is the tree?" Or "Is the tree okay?" Or "Is the tree up?" Or "I'm sorry about the tree."

One day in the hospital Dory told him, "Tom, it's Christmas Day today. Merry Christmas, sweetheart."

His eyes were closed but he squeezed her hand. She said, "Do you remember Christmas, darling?"

And he opened his eyes and looked up at her and shook his head. Yet the next day, again, he wrote about the tree. He couldn't remember Christmas, but he

3

knew a tree should, for some reason, be erected in his living room.

Gradually he could remember a bit more and he could spell "world" backwards and count by sevens and all those things they'd asked him to do in the hospital when he was off the respirator and out of intensive care, but still he had a strange scattered memory, like, for instance, he knew he must, absolutely *must*, shave every morning, but he was unsure why. He reminded Dory to check the battery in the smoke detector, but when she said, "Oh, Tom, what's the worst that can happen if our battery is dead for a day or two?" he didn't have an answer. So he was caught in a bind where he was committed to doing what he'd always done but he couldn't remember why he was doing it. His life, some might have said, had no purpose.

Neither did Knute's, really. Summer Feelin' was in a day care that she hated and Knute was working full time as a hostess in a busy downtown restaurant where everybody was used to seating themselves. She wasn't aggressive enough to say, "Hey, can't you read the sign? It says 'wait to be seated,' " and so, pretty much, she just stood there all day smiling and feeling stupid. From time to time she moved the sign right in front of the door, but people would walk into it and then move it back out of their way. Sometimes the waitresses got mad at her because she wasn't seating anybody in their sections or because everybody was sitting in their section and they were run off their feet trying to keep up with the orders. Then, for a while, Knute would try to keep people from walking past her and she'd say

4

things like, "Please follow me," or "A table will be ready in a minute," or "How many of you are there?" Usually there would be two and when she asked how many of them there were, they'd look at each other like she was nuts, then they'd hold up two fingers or point at each other and say, "one, two," in a loud voice.

"Two!" Knute would say, "okay, two, hmmm . . . two, you say," like she was trying to figure out how to

dishwasher and the two cooks kept telling him to fire her, but her boss kept giving her more chances. He told Knute she'd get the hang of it in a while, just get in their faces and make them wait. "They're like pigs at the trough," he said. "You gotta keep 'em under control."

On her first day Knute had actually managed to lead an old couple to a table. But somehow they got their wires crossed, and Knute pulled a chair away from the table just as the man was going to sit on it. In slow motion he fell to the ground while Knute and his wife stared, horrified. As he fell, he knocked over the fake flower arrangement and the vase shattered.

Knute's boss came running out and picked the old man up, cleaned up the glass and told them lunch was on the house. Then he took Knute into the kitchen, made her a salami sandwich on a bagel, sat her down on a lettuce crate and told her not to worry, not to worry, this was her first day, she'd work out the kinks. But she never did. Anyway, it was a lot better than pumping gas. The one time Knute tried that she accidentally filled up a motor home with gas — not the gas tank, but the interior of the motor home itself. She had stuck the nozzle into the water-spout hole instead of the gas tank hole. The woman driving the van hadn't noticed until she lit up a cigarette and her motor home exploded, partially, and her leg ended up needing plastic surgery. Her husband sued the gas station and won a bunch of money, of course. Knute was let go and told, by her supervisor, that she should get tested for brain damage.

On her way home from the restaurant, Knute would pick up Summer Feelin' and listen to her tell lies about the day care. How Esther, one of the workers, had punched her six times in the face, how Justin, one of the twins, had made her put her tongue on the cold swing set and it had stuck and they left her out there all alone all day, how a terrible man with purple skin and horse feet had come and killed seven of the kids.

"Summer Feelin'," Knute would say, "I know how much you hate it, but for now you have to try to find something good about it. It can't be that bad."

Knute was tired from standing around stupidly all day. But she felt she had to make it up to Summer Feelin', so for an hour or two before bedtime the two of them would play in the park or get an ice cream, maybe rent a movie or walk to the library. And that wore Knute out even more. Her favourite days were when

Summer Feelin' would relax and they could just sit at their little table and talk. Summer Feelin' would tell her funny stories and shake with excitement and then, in the evening, they'd curl up together with Summer Feelin's soft head under Knute's chin. Knute would try not to fall asleep because that would mean that was it, the day. If she didn't fall asleep she'd get up very quietly and make herself a cup of coffee and phone

When Dory called

Summer Feelin' come back to Algren and live with her and Tom for a while, Knute felt like someone had just injected her with a warm, fast-acting tranquilizer. It felt like she had just put her head on a soft feather pillow and been told to go to sleep, everything would be fine. Dory made it sound like she needed Knute desperately to help with Tom, to protect her sanity, and it's true she did. But Dory also had a sense that Knute was tired, really tired. That all she was doing was spinning her wheels. It took Knute about fifteen minutes to quit her job, cancel Summer Feelin's spot at the day care, tell her landlord she was moving, and pack their stuff. When she told Summer Feelin' that she could kiss her awful day care good-bye, she flapped like crazy, and Knute had to put her in a nice, warm bath to calm her down. She told Marilyn she was going to her mom and dad's for a while and Marilyn asked if she could go, too. The next day Summer Feelin' and Knute were on the road.

Not for long, though, because Algren was only about forty miles away from Winnipeg. Knute and Summer Feelin' peered out the car windows at the clumps of dirt and piles of melting snow and S.F. said it reminded her of the moon.

When they got to the outskirts of Algren, which was really the same thing as the town, they saw Hosea Funk, the mayor, standing in a ditch of water with hip waders, gazing soulfully at the billboard that said, Welcome to Algren, Canada's Smallest Town. Of course there's not a lot to be done when people die or when they're born. They come and go. They move away. They disappear. They *reappear*. But more or less, give or take a person or two, Algren was the reigning champ of small towns. Well, there was another famous thing about Algren but it wasn't as impressive (if you can call being a town whose population consistently hovers around fifteen hundred people *impressive*): Algren was also the original home of the Algren cockroach. The Algren cockroach was one of only three types of North American cockroaches. Apparently it was first brought to Algren on a plant or a sack of potatoes or something a hundred years ago from Europe and the rest was history. In the encyclopedia under "cockroach" it listed the Algren cockroach and mentioned Algren as a small town in southern Manitoba. No mention of its being *the* smallest town in Canada, much to Hosea Funk's chagrin.

As they passed Hosea standing in the ditch, Knute honked the horn and waved. "Who's that?" S.F. asked.

"The mayor," said Knute. "He's an old friend of Grandpa's."

The horn startled him out of his reverie and Hosea straightened his golf cap and started up the side of his ditch. He didn't wave back. He tugged for a second at the front of his jacket and then nodded his head, once.

just sorting it out in his head

it. In the playground and at the skating rink he was very cautious. He would creep around the rink clinging to the boards, not caring what the other boys and girls thought. He was keeping himself alive, saving himself for something big. He wanted to make sure he was okay down the road because he knew he had things to do. And because he was all that his mother had.

Hosea Funk was born in the middle of a heat wave on June 11, 1943, in a machinery shed belonging to his mother's parents. The shed was long gone by now and in its place was a large rectangular-shaped patch of dead grass, discoloured and flattened and strewn with rocks and scraps of metal. Euphemia was eighteen years old when Hosea was born and sure her father would kill her, quite literally, if he found out she had had a baby. Getting pregnant in September was a lucky thing for her because all winter she was able to hide her body away in big coats and sweaters. But it was a good thing that Hosea was born when he was because if she'd had to have worn that huge woollen coat a day longer in that heat wave, she would have died for sure. As it was, her parents were so concerned about her health, thinking she must be very ill to need so many clothes in that heat, that they forbade her to leave the house and had a neighbour or a relative watching her just about every minute of the day. Getting to the machine shed to have her baby had not been easy.

Euphemia had had nothing to prepare her for Hosea's birth. Well, almost nothing. Once, as a girl, she had wandered into the barn where her father was helping a mare give birth to her foal. Just about his entire right arm was stuck inside the horse. His left arm he used to brace himself against the horse's buttocks. The mare was kicking him and screeching and her father was purple in the face, cursing the horse and the reluctant foal. Euphemia stood and stared in horror. Would it be possible to stick her own arm inside herself and pull the baby out? There was nobody else to help her, after all. Hadn't some of her father's mares given birth without any help? And hadn't she heard her friends talking about walking out to the field and finding a new calf or piglet or whatever happily sucking milk from its mother and nobody had even known the cow or the sow was pregnant? So, it could be done, Euphemia thought.

Euphemia lay in her bed, in the heat, in her sweaters and coats. She stared at the dark wood and flowered wallpaper of her bedroom. She could smell chicken noodle soup. She could hear her brothers hollering in the yard and things clanking. Her sisters had gone to town and her mother was rummaging around downstairs. Things were as they usually were and it all would have been comforting except for the sticky circle of blood staining Euphemia's cotton underwear. That evening she went into labour.

The pain had started after supper. By now

no, if anything she was feeling ...... to be alone. One after another, her brothers and sisters came to her room and left again, shrugging their shoulders, going back to their business.

By nine o'clock the pain was almost unbearable. Euphemia's lower back, pelvis, stomach, and uterus together had turned into a rigid two-thousand-pound stick of dynamite going off at first intermittently and then continuously. Iron cannonballs were rocketing around inside her body, pounding and bashing, desperate for a way out. If anything, the dull warning pain that preceded each explosion terrified Euphemia the most. She whimpered and moaned. She dug her fingernails into her thighs and almost passed out holding her breath. She cried and prayed to God to help her survive. Beside her, in another twin bed, lay her younger sister, Minty, still asleep, but tossing and turning a bit more with each of Euphemia's muffled moans. Euphemia knew that somehow she had to get out of the house.

By this time it was ten-thirty. Her parents and her other brothers and sisters would be in bed, if not asleep, and if she was stealthy enough she could creep down the hall, down the stairs, and out the back door. If she had time she could make it to the machinery shed.

Euphemia managed to get out of her bed and tiptoe to the door, hunched over, in agony, in tears, but on her way. Just as she crossed the threshold, her little sister woke up. "Phemie?"

"Minty," said Euphemia, "I'm going to the john, go back to sleep. I'm coming right back."

But Minty said, "Wait, Phemie, take me with you. I gotta go, too."

Oh God, thought Euphemia. If she said no, Minty would start to cry and wake up her mother and her life would be over. But she couldn't bring her with her. Of course not. Euphemia clutched the door frame, trying not to cry. "Listen, Minty, if you promise to go back to sleep right now, tomorrow morning I will give you the best present in the whole wide world. Okay?"

Minty stared at Euphemia and asked excitedly, "What is it, what is it, Phemie?"

Euphemia put her finger to her lips. "Shhh, Minty, it's the best thing in the world, I told you, but I can't bring it to you until you go to sleep. Please, Minty?"

"You promise?" said Minty. "Yes, Minty, yes, I promise."

12

Euphemia made it out of the house. In the darkness she stumbled and lurched, cupping her belly with one hand, in an attempt to keep the baby in, until she could make it to the machine shed, to the little bundle of hay she had tossed in one corner months ago, before being confined to her bedroom. The effort of opening the heavy shed door helped to break her water. Inside the shed, Euphemia ripped off her coat, her two

CHAPTER
TWO

When Knute and Summer Feelin' drove up to the house they could see Tom and Dory standing in the living room, staring out the picture window. Next to them were small bronze statues and clay busts that Tom had bought, and he and Dory seemed to blend in with these things. As soon as they saw Knute's beater pull up in the driveway, though, they came to life. Dory zipped to the front door and Tom smiled and waved. These days he stayed away from the doors when they were being opened. He couldn't afford to get a chill and get sick all over again. S.F. ran up to the picture window, flapping like crazy, and Tom gave her a high-five against the glass, smudging it up a bit. Dory came running out of the house saying, "Welcome, welcome, oh I'm sooooo glad you're both here." And she scooped up S.F. even though her heart wasn't in much better shape than Tom's and then, with her other free arm, wrapped herself around Knute. Tom beamed through the glass.

Dory had prepared a large meal. It consisted of boneless chicken breasts with a black bean sauce, steamed broccoli, slices of cucumbers, tomatoes, and carrots, brown rice, and a fruit salad. Knute could just barely pick out the grimace on Tom's face when he sat down at the table, rather ashamed and annoyed that all this dull stuff constituted a celebratory meal. And that it was all made especially for him and his fragile heart. He would have preferred a big piece of red meat with lots of salt, some potatoes and thick gravy, cheese sauce to accompany his steamed broccoli, great slabs of bread with real butter to soak up the gravy and juice from the meat, a large wedge of apple pie and ice cream, and

the chicken and steamed vegetables
they had hardly any taste made S.F., at least, happy.

After lunch Tom did a bit of walking up and down the hall, S.F. went down to the basement to play with the toys, and Dory and Knute had a cryptic conversation about Tom.

"So?" said Knute, and jerked her head in the direction of Tom and the hallway.

"Well," said Dory, "you know . . ."

"Mmmmm . . ."

And then Dory said, "One day at a time . . ." and Knute nodded and said, "Yup . . ."

They sat there and stared at their coffee cups for a bit and Dory added in a very hushed tone, "A bit more," she tapped at her chest, "these days."

Knute tapped her own chest. "Pain?" she asked.

Dory nodded and pursed her lips.

"Hmmm . . . well, what does the doctor say?"

"OH TOM, YOU'RE DONE?" Tom had finished his walk and Dory had been timing him. He had walked for eight minutes. Dory was trying to be extremely upbeat about the eight minutes. "Well, Tom, yesterday it was only seven," and that sort of thing. Tom went over to the picture window and stood with his back to Dory and Knute. He punched his fist into his palm once and then after about thirty seconds he did it again. He slowly walked back to the couch and lay down with a heavy sigh.

After supper (of leftovers), Dory and Knute played Scrabble. For weeks Dory had been playing with "Marie," a phantom Scrabble opponent whom she had given her own middle name to. Knute asked Dory how she felt when "Marie" won, and she said, "Divided." Summer Feelin' had wandered over to the neighbours' house to play with the little girl, Madison, who lived there. Dory could never remember Madison's name. "Montana?" she'd say. "Manhattan?" Which got them onto the subject of names, and Dory wondered if Knute had, perhaps, considered calling S.F. just "Summer" instead of "Summer Feelin'"? Knute knew Dory wasn't altogether enthusiastic about her grand-daughter's name and she told her she'd think about it, although she wondered if Dory was really any authority on girls' names considering the choice she'd made when her own daughter was born.

"Summer," Dory said over and over. "If you say it enough times, you know, Knutie, you *get* that summer feeling. You don't have to actually *say* it. The Feelin' part becomes rather redundant, don't you think? Or maybe you could change the spelling of Feelin' to something, oh, I don't know, Irish, maybe, like Phaelan, or . . ."

Just then the doorbell rang. Tom woke up from his nap on the couch and Dory answered the door. A large man with a pale yellow golf cap tugged twice at the front of his coat before greeting Dory and stepping

William Shatner in the Enterpri

his hair, which had become mussed from lying down. Dory said she'd make a fresh pot of coffee and told Hosea to have a seat.

"Hose, do you remember our Knutie?" Dory asked him, putting her arm around Knute's shoulder and grinning. Hosea's thumb and index finger went for the front of his shirt, but then, through some act of will on his part, he adjusted his golf hat instead and replied, "Why sure, Dory, I remember Knutie." Everybody smiled and nodded and finally Hosea broke the awkward silence. "So, are you here for a visit, Knutie, or . . ."

Knute was just about to answer when Dory said, "No, she and Summer Feelin' have moved back, for the time being."

"Oh, well," said Hosea, "that's great! Welcome back to Algren."

"Tha —" Knute was cut off by Hosea, who had suddenly sprung to life. "You still barrel-racin', Knute?"

Barrel-racing! thought Knute. The one time she had barrel-raced, badly, was in a 4-H rodeo and Hosea Funk had happened to be her timer. That was years ago, before he became the mayor. Back then he got involved in every event in town. If there was a parade, Hosea walked along throwing out candy to the kids. If there was a flood, Hosea organized a sandbag crew. If the hockey team made it to the play-offs in the city, Hosea offered to drive. Once, at a fall supper in a church basement, he was given a trophy by the main street businesses and it said, Hosea Funk, Algren's Number One Booster.

"Nah, I've given it up," said Knute. And she kind of buckled her knees to look bow-legged and horsey. Hosea Funk nodded and Knute could tell he was thinking of something else to say. She waited. A few seconds more. There. This time he couldn't help it. His fingers went to his shirt and tugged, not twice but three times. He was ready to speak.

"But that palomino could turn on a dime, couldn't he? He was something else. Now whose was he? Art Lemke, that's right, he was Art's. Wasn't he, Tom? You know the one I'm talking about? The palomino?"

"Yup, yup, I think you're right, Hose. Wait a minute, no, yeah, he would have had to have been Art's. Well . . . hang on, I'm trying to remember. Nope, he would have been Lenny's. Remember, Hose? Art sold the palomino to Lenny after his accident and Lenny

18

couldn't keep the palomino from jumping the fence and hightailing it back to Art's barn. If I remember correctly . . . it's hard to say. I don't recall how it all turned out exactly, but I do know that horse loved Art all right. Never really took to Lenny . . ."

Hosea leaned back in his chair with his legs stretched out in front of him, his palms pushed against each other as if in prayer, his fingertips against puckered lips. He

age who has never done anything
hate him or love him. They might as well be friendly, although Hosea visited Tom's house more often than Tom visited his. And, since his heart attack, Tom didn't go anywhere except to his doctor's appointments and those visits exhausted him.

Tom had been a veterinarian and knew about animals and that might have been one of the reasons Hosea brought up the subject of the palomino. Hosea might have felt inferior to Tom, being a professional, having a wife and a daughter and even a granddaughter, but Tom didn't think enough about Hosea to feel much of anything towards him other than a simple affection and a certain type of sympathy and from time to time, especially these days, a pang of nostalgia when he remembered himself and Hosea as boys. During all those years while Tom was busy working as a vet and living with Dory and Knute, and while Hosea was

19

living with his mother and looking after just about everything in Algren, their paths had kind of veered away from each other.

Of course, now, with Tom's heart attack, the balance might have shifted. Tom was feeling fragile, while Hosea was still running around town taking care of business. Knute thought Tom was kind of uncomfortable with Hosea showing up like that, unannounced. He probably would have liked to have changed out of his polo pajamas at least and maybe shaved. But Hosea always just showed up. Making his rounds, enjoying a cup of coffee, passing the time. He liked to know what was going on in his town. People were used to Hosea dropping by for a visit.

"So, Hose, what are you up to these days?" asked Tom. Knute could hear him from the kitchen.

"Well, to tell you the truth, I've got a lot on the go right now. I've, uh . . . well, you could say I'm working on a major project, Tom."

"Good for you, good for you," said Tom, and Knute imagined him grimacing, wishing he had a major project besides staying alive, and Hosea tugging, wishing he had something more to say and quickly, too, like a great conversationalist, a real charismatic public figure.

Tom had begun to say something else, though. "Are you ready to divulge the nature of your major project, Hose, or —" But just then, Summer Feelin' came barrelling in through the front door, made a beeline for Tom's lap, leapt, and landed square on her target, knocking off Tom's glasses. Tom let out a big "oooph" and Dory came running from the kitchen thinking it was another heart attack, and Hosea stood there all nervous, tugging, tugging, tugging, until everyone realized what had happened and they began to laugh and S.F. tried on Tom's glasses and coffee was served and the conversation turned to gossip and did you know that so-and-so was let go at the bank, after thirty years? No one's saying why, and did you know that

what Tom and Dory always did when they wondered why Dory didn't serve another couple rounds of coffee or why they didn't just sit down there on the floor in the front entrance area. Coats would be done up, then undone slightly, undone completely, sweat would form on the upper lip, the coats would be taken off and slung over their arms, then a hand on the door-knob, the coats would be on again, all the way, then undone an inch, mittens would be slapped together purposefully, then removed, bodies would stand erect, close to the door, then one leg would buckle and they would slouch against the wall. "Well", the visitor would say like he or she meant it this time, "I'm outta here," and then, "Oh! Did I tell you . . . ?"

Summer Feelin' fell asleep in the hallway on the floor between Dory's legs.

"Excuse me," said Knute, "I'm gonna take her to her bed."

And with that, the three of them, Tom, Dory, and Hosea, began to flutter, and Hosea said, "Okay, yes, the poor kid, here I am keeping her up, keeping you all up, really, I should go." This time Tom and Dory didn't say, "Oh, Hosea, there's no hurry." Tom reached for the door and opened it, not caring at this point whether he got a chill and risked his life.

But just before Tom could close the door gently on him, Hosea turned around and said, "Say, Knutie, if you need any part-time work while you're in town, let me know, I may be able to set you up with something." And then he was gone. Tom and Dory went running for Tom's evening medication, and Knute watched through the large picture window in the living room as Hosea walked away, into the night, through the few empty streets of his town, Canada's smallest.

The baby. Naturally Euphemia had a plan. She had had nine months to figure out elaborate plots, twists and turns, casts of characters, acts of God, all to explain the sudden arrival of this baby. In the end, however, she didn't use any of her fancy stories to explain the baby. Her family had always shrugged off any changes in their lives. If there was no explanation offered they couldn't be bothered to hunt it down or make one up. Of course, the mysterious arrival of a baby in the household was not a small deal. But Euphemia decided to take a chance. A chance on simplicity. Instead of coming up with a thousand details, which could be forgotten or repeated in the wrong order and arouse suspicion, she decided to give her family only one.

The beauty of it, too, was that it wasn't even really a lie.

"I went out late in the evening to use the outhouse and a mysterious man on a horse gave me his baby. All he said was 'Thank-you.' Then he was gone."

Well, that was more or less the situation that had occurred nine months earlier at the harvest dance at the Algren Community Dance Hall.

allowed herself to be taken by the hand to the edge of the canola field behind the dance hall.

Euphemia was the last, well, maybe not the very last, girl in the area anyone would have called immoral. She did her chores, obeyed her parents, had lots of friends, and was pretty, a good runner, and playful. She won spelling bees and quilting bees, and had never even had a boyfriend in her life. In the forties girls like Euphemia Funk did not allow themselves to be led by the hand to dark fields behind dance halls.

She had stepped outside to use the outhouse. The little building was a ways from the dance hall, down a dirt path, towards the canola field. The stranger had been leaning against a tree, smoking a cigarette, and before she could even get to the outhouse, he had wandered over to her and put out his hand. She knew he had been at the dance. She and her friends had seen him and wondered who he was. Probably a relative of someone around there or a farm hand. He had nice eyes and a beautifully shaped back, they thought. "It tapers, it really does," said Euphemia's friend Lou. And he obviously bought his shoes in the city. No, he couldn't have been a farm hand. Not with shoes like that. Euphemia had seen him talking to Leander Hamm, so maybe he was a horse breeder or a horse buyer or maybe he owned racehorses in America. But he looked so young, just a few years older than she was. Euphemia liked the way his thighs filled out the tops of his pants and the way his legs were shaped, vaguely, like parentheses. There was a bit of a curl to his hair at the bottom and it was longer than the hair of any of the boys from around there. Euphemia liked those curls, at the bottom, the ones that rested against his neck.

She just hadn't said no. Nobody had come along to discover them. The night was very dark and warm. The stranger was handsome and sure of himself. Euphemia couldn't think of any reason not to take his hand. She had tried to come up with a reason, but couldn't. Afterwards, he retied the bow in Euphemia's hair and wiped the grass and leaves off of her skirt. It had hurt, but she hadn't cried. She hadn't made a sound. And neither had he. She had kept one hand cupped firmly around the curls on his neck and her other hand beside her, on the ground. Afterwards they sat together, and Euphemia said, "well," and turned and smiled at him. And the stranger smiled back and squeezed her hand and said, "Thank-you." Then he walked over to where his horse was tied up, just on the other side of the dance hall, and rode away.

Euphemia hadn't told a soul about what happened. She hadn't felt a second of guilt. She was thrilled with herself.

"He said 'Thank-you,' and that's all, that was it?" asked Euphemia's mother, as she and Euphemia and .... peered down at the

is barely a day old, Phemie, are you sure he didn't say who he was or why he was giving you this child?"

"Yes, Mother."

Euphemia had successfully been delivered of the baby's placenta and had taken it and the clothes that had blood on them and buried them behind the machine shed. With trembling fingers she had tied a knot in the baby's umbilical cord and wrapped him in one of the sweaters she had been wearing just before he was born. The baby hadn't cried, not really. He had made a few creaking sounds, but nothing that could be called a real wail. By the light of the barn lantern, Euphemia saw the baby open one eye. The other wouldn't open for a few hours. The fingers on his hands moved almost constantly and his head, too, swivelled from left to right, back and forth, towards the lantern's light and away again.

Euphemia put her face to his. She breathed on him and felt his tiny puff of breath in return. She put her index finger against his lips and he tried for a moment to get it into his mouth. She moved her lips and her cheek against his damp head and prayed to God to keep him from all harm. Still, she was not afraid. She would protect him. At the time Euphemia hadn't noticed the baby's black hair curl on his neck and hadn't thought for a second about the stranger, the baby's father, at the dance hall. For the second time in a year she was thrilled with herself.

Euphemia knew that she could not breastfeed the baby. She would have to find a way to wrap her breasts and get rid of her milk. The postpartum bleeding could be explained as normal menstrual blood, if it was explained at all. Bleeding, women's bleeding, was another thing the Funk family shrugged off as one of those things, which it was.

For now she would wrap her breasts in strips of gunny sack and cotton and pray to God they wouldn't start to leak as she sat at the supper table with her family. She would, inconspicuously, drink a lot of black currant tea and if the pressure grew too great, she would squeeze the milk out herself in the john. Maybe she could even save some of it and mix it in with the formula when nobody was looking. Over time she would squeeze out less and less milk as though she were weaning a baby. Euphemia hoped her breasts could be fooled. When Flora Marsden's baby was born dead, she had drunk huge amounts of black currant tea to stem the flow of her milk. Euphemia remembered her mother talking about it to a friend of hers. Her mother and her mother's friend had been outraged that a neighbour of Flora's had suggested she hire herself out as a wet nurse to mothers too busy farming to feed their babies. "I know I was never too busy to feed my own baby, that's for sure," Euphemia's mother had said in a rather convoluted, self-serving indictment of

big book. It opened at Hosea. "There," she shrugged, "Welcome to the world, Hosea." And she stuck the bobby pin back into her hair.

Hosea Funk lay in his bed in his house on First Street, watching the sun come up over Algren. Thank God that health food store hadn't worked out, he thought. If the couple running it hadn't packed up their rice cakes and moved back to Vancouver Island last week, the recent arrival of Knute and her daughter would have put Algren's population at fifteen hundred and two, and that would have been two too many. Hosea closed his eyes and thought about his letter, the one from the Prime Minister. Well, okay, it wasn't a personal letter, it was a form letter, but Hosea's name was on it, and so was a photocopied signature of the Prime Minister's name, John Baert.

The Prime Minister had promised to visit Canada's smallest town on July first, and Algren, the letter had noted, was one of the preliminary qualifiers in the contest. Everybody in Algren knew it had been short-listed, why wouldn't it be? After all, check out the sign on the edge of town. Even the Winnipeg daily paper had mentioned, in one line, on a back page, that Algren had been picked as a nominee for the Prime Minister's visit. But the people in Algren went about their business with very little thought of July first, other than looking forward to the holiday from work, and the rides and the fireworks. If Algren had the smallest population at the time of the count, great. If not, who really cared? After all, they thought, the Prime Minister had made promises before. Of course, they knew Hosea Funk was extremely proud of Algren's smallest-town status, he was proud of everything about Algren. Good for him, they thought, usually with a smile or a raised eyebrow. Might as well be. But nobody in Algren knew what Hosea knew, or what he thought he knew, or just how determined he was to be the winner.

Hosea wanted to relax, to savour the early morning calm, to stretch out in bed, enjoy his nakedness, and happily welcome the new day. A small part of him wished his mornings resembled those in the orange juice commercials where healthy clean families bustle around making lunches and checking busy schedules, kissing and hugging and wishing each other well. But he was alone. And he hated orange juice. It stung his throat.

So Hosea lay quietly in his huge bed. For the last year or so he had been working on his panic attacks. Mornings were the worst time for them. And for heart attacks. His buddy Tom had had his in the morning just about an hour after waking up. Hosea suspected, however, that his determination to stay calm was a bit like overeating to stay thin and so he tried not to think ████████████ Instead he tried to relax his entire

cry, and Hosea thought, Ah Emmylou Harris, a voice as pure as the driven snow, a real class act, all that hair and those cowboy boots with the hand-painted roses . . .

Hosea lay naked in his bed and whispered Emmylou, Emmylou a few times and closed his eyes and mumbled along with her, Heaven only ever sees why love's made a fool of me, I guess that's how it's meant to be . . . He thought of Lorna and the last time they'd made love and then tallied up the days, and the weeks. Almost two months.

He tried to leap out of bed, just as his own personal joke, but ended up getting tangled in the sheet, knocking the radio off the bedside table, and yanking the cord out of the outlet, so that Emmylou Harris was cut off and fifty-two-year-old Hosea Funk, mayor of Algren, was left alone again and aching.

But not for long because by now the sun was up and he had work to do. Fifteen minutes on his exercise bike, a piece of whole wheat toast with honey, black coffee, half a grapefruit, a freshly ironed shirt, and a shave, and Hosea was out the door of his modest bungalow and driving down First Street in his Chevy Impala, humming the Emmylou tune on his way to the Charlie Orson Memorial Hospital.

The town of Algren had four long streets running north-south, one of them being Main Street, and ten short avenues running perpendicular to the streets. It was possible to walk anywhere in town in less than fifteen minutes, but Hosea almost always drove.

Driving down First Street towards Hospital Avenue, Hosea continued to think about Lorna. She had been his girlfriend for about three and a half years. About the same length of time it had been since Euphemia Funk had died. They had met at an auctioneers' convention in Denver. Auctioneering had been another thing Hosea was involved in, following Euphemia's death, but had since abandoned. For a guy who had trouble finding the right words to say hello, auctioneering wasn't the best hobby. Lorna had been wearing a name tag that had said, "Hi, my name's . . ." then nothing — she hadn't filled it in and Hosea was smitten by her for this reason. He looked at everybody else's properly filled-out name tags and thought how ridiculous they all were. And his, too, Hosea Funk, how absurd. Who was this mysterious Mona Lisa with the blank name tag, anyway?

Throughout the convention, Hosea stumbled about hoping to catch a glimpse of her, tugging fiendishly at his shirts and not giving a hoot about cattle calls or estate auctioneering protocol. He had been forty-nine at the time, but he felt like a sixteen-year-old-kid, creating impossible scenarios in his mind whereby he could prove himself worthy of this mysterious woman

children, worked as a medical secretary, and dabbled in auctioneering. The name-tag thing had been an oversight on her part. But Hosea was in love and Lorna thought he wasn't too bad and the rest is history.

"And my relationship with her may be history, too," thought Hosea, "if I don't get my act together."

Hosea couldn't make up his mind, it seemed. Did he want her to move out to Algren and live with him or not? He knew Lorna wanted to, but now, with Hosea's hemming and hawing, Lorna was starting to play it cool. "Whatever," she'd said the last time they'd talked about it. Hosea hated that word. Whatever. All through his childhood on the Funk farm and then in town living with his mother he had heard it being used, oh, almost daily. Whatever, Euphemia would say if Hosea asked if he could have ten cents. Whatever, she'd say if he told her the U.S. had invaded Korea.

It wasn't a question of damaging his public reputation, having Lorna live with him. The townspeople of Algren would have been happy for Hosea to have a woman living with him. And it wasn't a question of room or money. Hosea had enough of both. And it certainly wasn't a question of wavering commitment. He loved Lorna with all his heart. It was just . . . well, would she have been one person too many for Algren? For Algren's status as Canada's smallest town.

And soon Lorna might just give up on him, thought Hosea as he pulled into the parking lot of the hospital. But what could he do?

Hosea focused on the task at hand. He had a question to ask Veronica Epp — just one and he'd leave her alone. Veronica Epp was expecting her fifth child. This fact alone irked Hosea. But now there was some talk around town that she was expecting twins. If she had two babies instead of one, which he had figured on, Hosea would have to do some fancy footwork.

"Good morning, Jean Bonsoir," said Hosea, with one slight tug at his front, to the hospital's only doctor, an import from Quebec. His name was Jean François, but Hosea like to think his alternative pronunciation was funny and helped to break the ice.

"Hosea," the doctor returned with a nod. He was counting the days until he could leave Algren for Montreal, where he could do something other than minor surgery and routine obstetrics and where people would pronounce his name correctly. It still peeved him to think of Hosea Funk calling his girlfriend,

32

Genvieve, who remained in Montreal, Jenny Quelque Chose.

"Uh, listen, Doctor, I need to talk to Mrs. Epp for a minute, tops. Then I'll be out of your hair. Fair enough?"

Jean François had understood the Mrs. Epp part and shrugged Hosea down the hall. "Room four, Hosea, but be quick because she needs to rest."

unfortunately for Hosea, ...

come untied, exposing her buttocks and lower back. Before turning away, Hosea thought to himself how a woman could look, well, like normal, from the back, even while she was ballooning out in the front, and he wondered if he himself looked thinner from behind. It was something to consider. But now, he grabbed at his shirt and took three steps backwards, returning to the hallway and standing on the other side of the doorway.

This was the type of situation that completely unnerved Hosea. Was Veronica sleeping? Should he wake her up? How? Just then he heard a godawful moan coming from across the hall. A tiny tuft of white hair and an atrophied face poked out from beneath a blue sheet. The body attached to it looked like that of an eight-year-old girl. Hosea looked closer. Oh my God, he thought, it's Leander Hamm, Lawrence's dad. Nobody had told him old Mr. Hamm was in the hospital, and, from the sounds of it, he wasn't long for this world. Well, thought Hosea, it could be a good thing. Not that he invited death upon his townspeople regularly, but, after all, Leander Hamm would have had to have been almost ninety-five; and that's a good long life. If he were to buy the farm sometime soon, then Veronica Epp's alleged twins might not be as big a problem. Though it didn't bode well for having Lorna move in with him.

Which reminded him. He cleared his throat and stretched out his arm to knock on Veronica's door, keeping the rest of his body safely behind the wall. He had to find out from Veronica what the story was and he didn't want the doctor coming around and wondering what his problem was.

"Come in?" Veronica called out to the empty doorway. Hosea had quickly pulled back his arm after the knock and was still standing behind the wall next to her door.

"Uh, Mrs. Epp, it's, uh . . . Hosea Funk."

Dead silence then except for the swishing of stiff sheets.

"Oh, Mr. Funk? Well, come in."

Hosea had thought that Veronica Epp would have recognized the name right off the bat. He was the mayor, after all, but then again, she had just woken up and was in a somewhat groggy condition. He wouldn't let it bother him. And besides, as he stood there, far from her actual bed, a look of recognition came over her face and she smiled warmly.

34

She rolled over, on her back now, and Hosea was truly alarmed at how enormous her belly was. Darnit, he thought. That's gotta be twins.

"How are you feeling, Mrs. Epp?" Hosea planted his gaze on her face to avoid having to look at her stomach.

"Fine, thanks. The doctor just thought it would be a good idea to come in a bit before I go into labour,

"Yes, Dr. Jean is very attentive, very good. And, love 'em dearly though I do, it's rather a nice break from my other kids, you know."

No, Hosea did not know. And what was this business with calling Dr. François Dr. Jean? That was rather personal, wasn't it? He knew he would have balked to be called Mayor Hosea instead of Mayor Funk, but then again that wasn't usually a problem in Algren as most people just called him Hosea or Hose. The few times someone like Tom had called him Mayor Funk he had detected just the slightest hint of sarcasm. But, of course, that might have been because Tom was his friend and why would friends be formal? But still.

"Hmmm . . ." Hosea nodded, trying to smile. He stepped towards Veronica and put his hand briefly on top of the mysterious machine making beeping noises and showing various squiggly lines on its screen.

35

"Handy contraption, this, eh?" Hosea stared at the lines in deep concentration as if he knew what they meant. What he was trying to do was figure out how he could best ask the question without appearing to be prying, that is, inappropriately curious about what was so obviously none of his business.

Veronica strained to turn her enormous body towards the machine to get a better look. The sight of her shifting startled Hosea and he stared, wide-eyed, hoping her gown would not slip off and expose her privates.

Hosea was beginning to feel very warm. Veronica looked uncomfortable. She grimaced slightly, then scratched her stomach. As she did so her gown shifted over a bit, and what was revealed to Hosea was just about the most gruesome thing he had ever seen. He thought he would be sick. What was it, he wondered, a scar? A birth defect? A smallish, round, bluish disk of smooth skin with what looked like lips in the centre of it stretched across the middle of her stomach. It wasn't a tiny head pushing through, was it? Hosea knew it couldn't be. He knew, of course, that babies did not just poke through the abdominal skin of their mothers for a look around or a bit of air. However, it looked like it would burst any second and Hosea did not want to be around when it did.

"Ha, would you look at that?" Veronica laughed. "Wouldn't know it was a belly button, would you?"

A belly button! thought Hosea. Of course! And suddenly Hosea felt very lonely. Something so simple, so tender and common as a belly button and he had not been able to identify it. He had been scared of Veronica Epp's belly button. He was fifty-two years old. He should know about these simple things by now. Old Leander Hamm, all shrivelled up and dying, he had a belly button, too. And Lorna Garden and Tom and Dory and Jean François. For some reason the thought made him sad, momentarily. He had to get on with the job here. He would have to get directly to the question,

well, they think it's maybe

beamed up at Hosea. For her it was like winning the lottery. Hosea's gaze moved down to her mountain of a stomach and then out the window towards the tiny trickle that was Algren's Main Street. Lawrence Hamm's dad moaned from across the hall. Hosea felt like he had just been kicked in the groin.

"You mean three?" he whispered.

CHAPTER
THREE

"Knutie!" Dory had said after a week of Knute's hanging around the house trying to help. "Didn't Hosea mention some kind of part-time job or something or other?"

"Ick," said Knute. She wasn't so resistant to the idea of working for Hosea Funk as to the idea of working, period. She was still licking her wounds from the awful experiences of her last two part-time jobs. And, of course, she was working. She was taking care of Summer Feelin', getting her acquainted with the few kids in the neighbourhood, organizing tea parties, trips to the park down the street, keeping her amused in her relatively new environment. Also, she was helping out around the house. She helped Tom with things like changing the oil in the car. He knew it needed to be changed but had forgotten why. She tried to explain as best she could. She helped him set a trap for a skunk that had been lurking around the back door. She hacked away all the ice on the sidewalk so he wouldn't slip when he went outside. She took him grocery shopping in the hope that they could find something healthy and delicious for him to eat. She experimented with new chicken and fish recipes and tried to spruce meals up for him with wine and candlelight and a red-and-white checkered tablecloth. And she was teaching him how to juggle.

He loved to juggle. So far he had two balls mastered. Summer Feelin' would scurry around picking up dropped balls and throw them back at Tom and he'd try again. "Remember, Dad," Knute would say, "one and then the other. The right goes over to the left, and

when he was busy. Usually she'd go out to her friends or to her office where she did some part-time bookkeeping for the farm labour pool. Or she'd shop at the Do-It Centre in Whithers for wallpaper and carpets and flooring and cupboard fixtures and curtains. She was re-doing the entire house, one room at a time. It had been twenty-five years since anything had been changed and now suddenly she was attacking every square inch of her house. She was getting rid of everything that was beige, brown, avocado, or moss green (which was everything) and replacing it with light sunny colours or pastels or white.

She had vowed she would not stop until the entire house was done. When she was tearing wallpaper off walls she'd wear an old pair of Tom's sweatpants, cut off at the bottom or rolled up, and a T-shirt that said SoHo, New York, on it. Tom would take a floor heater and down-filled sleeping bag and the paper or sometimes one of his veterinarian manuals and go and read in the garage while she worked. He hated the noise and mess but he loved Dory, and if Dory wanted to change the house around he wasn't about to stop her. He'd sit in the garage and wait until he heard the washing machine go on, which meant Dory was washing the sweatpants and SoHo shirt and all the rags and things she used and her work for the day was over.

Often, after Dory had removed the easier sheets of wallpaper and moved on to the next room, Knute would stay behind and finish off the tougher bits, steaming and soaking and, finally, scraping them off. Dory would yell to her from the next room, "Hey, Knutie, do you remember Mr. Pagliotti?" And Knute would say, "Uh, yeah . . ." just knowing something awful had happened to him because Dory seemed to be in a morbid mood these days and was constantly telling Knute about somebody or other who had died or been diagnosed with terminal cancer or had a leg amputated or lost her baby.

"His grandson found him dead in his car," she'd holler from the other room, from up on her ladder or stretched out on the floor with a hammer.

"Hmmm . . ." Knute would say bracing herself.

"Yeah, he and his grandson were taking a look at the field and apparently he had told his grandson that he was a bit tired and he was going to go and have a little nap in the car."

"Oh oh," Knute would say. She knew what was coming.

"The grandson came back to the car, found Mr. Pagliotti, well, you know, his grandpa, and then ran back to the house telling everyone Grandpa won't get up. He's sleeping and he won't get up."

"Yikes," was about all that Knute could muster. And she could imagine Dory in the other room sucking in her breath or shaking her head. Knute thought, maybe, that Dory was trying to prepare herself for Tom's death,

these morbid anecdotes was somehow related to home renovations. And as soon as she'd positioned herself on the stepladder, holding a steaming kettle in one hand and a scraper in the other, she could expect Dory's "Hey, Knutie, do you remember so-and-so, something terrible's happened" stories to come floating over from the other rooms.

So, Knute was working. But then again she wasn't making any money. Not that she had a lot of expenses. No rent, no food, no utilities. Tom and Dory would never have thought to charge their own daughter room and board. But at her age, she figured, a little contribution to the general management of affairs might be in order.

She wondered just what Hosea Funk would pay her to do. It couldn't be that complicated being the mayor of a town with fifteen hundred people. Besides, nothing ever really changed in Algren. About the only thing she remembered Dory telling her was that Johnny Dranger's farm kept being rezoned. One week it would be in the town limits of Algren, the next it was, well, sort of in limbo. Somewhere in the municipality of Libreville, but not actually in any town. Which makes sense, Knute thought. What's a farm doing in a town? Last time she checked farms were in the country, not next to a 7 Eleven or a credit union. But she didn't think it was Hosea doing the rezoning anyway because mayors didn't have that privilege. It was a provincial government thing. She thought.

So after Johnny Dranger's being in and then out and then in again, the only other change in Algren was the new indoor arena and curling rink. Hosea had battled long and hard to get that built. None of the older people in Algren thought it was a good idea. They had always played hockey outdoors — why shouldn't their grandchildren? They would have liked to have seen the money spent on another doctor, an English one preferably, though nobody would have said it, or maybe new blacktop on some of the roads. In Algren the oldies lived for new blacktop. But, in the end, Hosea had managed to convince them. He promised that during the summer he would air-condition the indoor arena and curling rink and hold auctions and quilting bees and bake sales and have inspirational speakers and car shows and you name it, he'd get it. So that, in the summer, the seniors of Algren would have a sort of retirement club of their own.

Hosea had also managed to convince the townspeople to name it The Euphemia Funk Memorial Arena,

Curling Club, and Recreational Complex. Of course, nobody called it that, they called it the rink, but it had raised a few eyebrows at the time. Mrs. Funk, as the kids of Algren knew her even though she wasn't married, had this aura of mystery about her. They all found out, at a certain age, that she wasn't really Hosea's mom, and different stories about how she got Hosea were always circulating. According to Tom and

[illegible]

Euphemia, had done anything wrong, considered, by many people in Algren, a bit weird and maybe not entirely healthy for a single unmarried woman to suddenly become a boy's mother. And many people would have preferred Hosea and the arena committee to come up with a different name for the complex, a name that wouldn't have them shifting in their chairs, staring at the ceiling, or changing the subject every time one of their kids asked them who Euphemia Funk was.

But that's what it was called and that was the big news in Algren.

"There it is," thought Hosea. The scribbler was always there, in fact, in the top drawer of his desk, but Hosea would always repeat these words to himself, not so much as an obvious affirmation of what was there but as a sort of mantra, preparing him for his work, a simple prelude to the more complicated nature of his obsession. The scribbler was an orange Hilroy, the kind still available on dusty drugstore shelves in places like Algren. On the front of it, at the bottom, were spaces to fill in personal information. Hosea had filled in each space. Name: Mayor Funk. Subject: 1500. Classroom No.: Mayor's office, town of Algren, Canada's Smallest!

Hosea preferred to take out his scribbler when no one was around. Usually that wasn't a problem as there were only two very part-time employees working in the place. The old renovated house was a municipal government project. It contained the Mayor's Office, the Arts Council Office for Algren and the surrounding areas, the Recreation District Office, the Weed Control District, and the Cemetery Board. Two women, sisters, in fact, shuffled around between the various responsibilities. Hosea's Aunt Minty, Euphemia's younger sister, used to work in the office, but years ago she and her husband, Bert Seeger, had moved to Fresno, California, and Hosea didn't hear much from her anymore. She and Bert had come out for Euphemia's funeral, but most of their time had been taken up with the Seeger in-laws.

Hosea had enjoyed working with his Aunt Minty. Every time he came into work she'd have the coffee made and sometimes fresh pastry, and she'd smile and say to Hosea, "Good morning, sweetie, you're looking well." From time to time Hosea murmured those words to himself under his breath as he stomped the snow from his boots or took off his coat, hoping the sisters

44

working behind the counter wouldn't hear him and look at each other in that way.

But now he was alone. And that was just fine because he needed to make a pertinent entry in his scribbler. Under the Dying and Potentially Dead column, he carefully printed the name Leander Hamm. Then he turned to the very back of the scribbler and, under the Newly Born and Rumoured to be Born he printed

same dog he had seen on his way

Veronica Epp. A woman had been crouching down and holding the dog by its collar and had asked Hosea if he knew whose dog it was. Hosea had been concerned that the dog was not on a leash but running freely, unsupervised, all over Algren. He asked the woman if she would call the pound, or actually Phil Whryahha, the man in Algren who, proudly appointed by Hosea himself, was responsible for stray pets. And that's when John Funk (no relation to Hosea), the caretaker of St. Bartholomew's Church, had walked up and suggested to the woman that she simply let the dog go. That the dog would surely find its way home. There was hardly a car on Algren's streets that would run the risk of hitting it, he'd said, and the dog seemed friendly enough. Let it go, he'd said. It'll be fine.

Hosea had stood there, dumbfounded. Why hadn't he thought of that? Such a simple and obvious solution.

The woman let go of the collar, the caretaker strolled back to St. Bart's, and the dog slowly walked away, towards the edge of town. Hosea stood there. He had said something. Something like "very good." Or "there you go." But he had felt unsure of himself. This dog business had jarred him.

He focussed on his plan to bring the Prime Minister to Algren. It could be a good thing for everybody in Algren, he thought. It would be an exciting day, a coup for a small prairie town, a psychological boost, and a surefire guarantee that Hosea would be re-elected, when the time came, as Algren's mayor.

Hosea whipped open the second drawer from the top of his desk and pulled out the letter from the House of Commons, dated February 12, 1996. "Dear Mayor," it began. Hosea had read and reread, folded and unfolded this letter so often that it had become slightly torn down the middle. He had carefully fixed it with a piece of Scotch tape so the tear was hardly noticeable. Hosea moved his finger across the photocopied signature, John Baert, Prime Minister. The contents of the letter were by now so familiar to him that he could sit back in his chair, close his eyes, and recite it from memory:

Dear Mayor,

As part of the federal government's commitment to rural growth, I have promised to visit Canada's smallest town for 24 hours, on July 1, 1996. Algren may be one of our candidates. We will inform you of further plans at a later date, providing you are interested in participating in the aforementioned event.

Sincerely, John Baert, Prime Minister

Hosea sat at his desk and imagined the day the Prime Minister would come to Algren. Hosea would be there _____ _____ with Lorne at his side. He'd have bought

announcing Algren to the world would be repainted and so would some of the storefronts along Main Street. He and the Prime Minister would shake hands warmly and the Prime Minister would pat him on the back and congratulate him, would take him into his confidence, and they would exchange jokes and leadership tips and anecdotes and discuss crisis management and possibly even correspond after the visit. At dinner, prepared by the Elks or the Kinettes and served in the Euphemia Funk Memorial Arena, Curling Club, and Recreational Complex, Hosea and the Prime Minister would raise their glasses for the photographers and toast to hmmm, whatever, rural prosperity, perhaps. There would be stories written in the papers and pictures taken, bearing eternal witness to the event and to Hosea's and Algren's victory, to their reigning status as Canada's smallest town.

It would be a day like no other. Hosea now sat way back in his chair, his legs up on his desk, his hands clasped behind his head, his thumbs making circles on the nape of his neck. So lost in thought was he that he didn't notice his pen roll off his desk and onto the shiny hardwood floor. Even Hosea's sexual fantasies couldn't hold a candle to his fantasy of meeting the Prime Minister and having Algren shown off to the world. Yes, it would be a day like no other, that's for sure, thought Hosea and leaned back even farther so that his swivel chair almost fell over backwards and he had to lurch forward and grip the hard wooden edge of his desk to keep his balance. He must have slammed the palm of his right hand hard against the wood, because that pain triggered a flood of memories and now Hosea pictured another day that was full of pomp and circumstance and nervousness and . . . what? What was it about that day, anyway? Hosea wondered.

He had been outside playing in the small yard behind the house on First Street. He hadn't had a jacket on, or was it shoes he hadn't had on? Had it been March or July? Well, he had picked flowers later that day, so it must have been July. But hadn't he just come home from school? Yes, of course, he had walked home with Tom who had lived across the street. Well, actually they had run home because two older fellows were chasing them and one of them had taken Hosea's jacket. That was it. He wasn't wearing his jacket, because the older boy had taken it, and it must have been a day in May or June. Sometime when flowers could grow in Manitoba.

48

Roses. He was sure they were roses because they had pricked the palm of his hand when he held them.

"Run, Hosea! Run!" Tom had already been caught as usual and managed to yell out the simple instructions to Hosea before a big hand was clamped over his mouth and he was taken away for his session. These sessions consisted of various activities. Tom and Hosea, ~~f~~ ~~y~~~~ear in~~ ~~particular,~~ were the whipping boys for a

Anyway, on this day they had ~~~~ jacket but not him. Hosea didn't want to go inside his house, he remembered, because Euphemia might get mad at him for losing his jacket. He would never have told her what had really happened. Even now, at age fifty-two, Hosea shuddered to think of his mother marching over to the home of one of the big boys and telling his parents what he had done and demanding that her son's jacket be returned immediately. But Euphemia wouldn't have been angry, really, thought Hosea. She would have shrugged and said something like, "Well, easy come, easy go." And then she would have gone to the hall closet and pulled out one of her old curling sweaters and rolled up the sleeves and made Hosea try it on for size. "There you go, pumpkin, a new jacket."

She wouldn't have gotten into a flap over a jacket. She wouldn't have run over to the school to look for it, or asked Hosea to think back or retrace his steps. She wouldn't have asked why this was the third jacket he had lost in as many months or why his jackets always had grass stains and leaves and twigs and dirt on the back of them as though he'd been rolling around on the ground like a crazed horse with a bad case of ringworm. Why, thought Hosea, did he possess none of her insouciance? Why, Hosea thought further, did her laissez-faire attitude towards just about everything irritate him so?

Finally Hosea went inside the house. He remembered hoping his mother would act normally and be upset about the jacket, and yet knowing she wouldn't be upset comforted him. What Hosea got from his mother was what he wanted but what he didn't get was what he felt he needed. Euphemia would have disagreed with this, he knew. "Why shouldn't I do my best to make you happy, Hose?" And he would have said something like, "Well, it's just that maybe I need more discipline or maybe you should get mad at me more." And he'd tug at his shirt and stare at the ground and Euphemia would look at him and then pull his head to her bosom and rub her lips in his hair and laugh. "Oh, Hose. Don't make it harder than it has to be." He remembered the song she always sang exuberantly at full volume. "Man's life's a vapour, full of woes . . ."

Anyway, that day Hosea tiptoed inside hoping to make a silent detour of the kitchen and go directly to his bedroom. But Euphemia was right there, standing at the stove, her back to Hosea. He changed his mind and decided to surprise her instead. He crept up behind her and said "hello," clear as a bell, and Euphemia, startled by the sudden greeting, twirled around and knocked him against the stove. Hosea put his hand out, against the red-hot element, to break his fall and would up with a large oval-shaped burn on his right palm. Euphemia had apologized profusely and rushed around getting butter and ice and ointment for Hosea's burn. Afterwards Euphemia and Hosea had sat

Because Hosea remembered the thorns pricking the burn on his palm, even after Euphemia had tied around it a beige piece of cotton from one of her aprons. Hosea even remembered thinking that he deserved the pain, that it was a token of his allegiance to Tom who had been caught by the big boys when Hosea hadn't and who was probably experiencing some pain right then, too.

This was the memory that had been triggered when he had banged his right palm against his desk, trying to keep himself from falling over backwards in his chair. Hosea looked at his right palm. There was a very faint trace of scar tissue. Unless it was bumped in a certain way, and it never had been until now, he felt no pain there. He brought his palm up towards his face. He stared at it. He moved his lips over it. Nothing. He couldn't remember anything else of that day. The roses had pricked his palm, so therefore he had picked them.

And he would only have picked them if his mother had asked him to. And she would only have asked him to pick roses if they had been going to see someone very special. Like, for example, the future Prime Minister. "Your father," Hosea recalled the words Euphemia had spoken on her deathbed, "is the Prime Minister of Canada."

But why couldn't he remember what happened that day he picked the roses? Hosea sat at his desk now and slammed his fist against his thigh.

Who was the special person? Had Euphemia told him or hadn't she? Had he asked? Had he wanted to know then? Had the special person been the man who was now Prime Minister of Canada? Why had Euphemia, on her deathbed, told Hosea that his father was John Baert, the Prime Minister of Canada? Surely she had been hallucinating. She must have been crackers, substituting reality with good intentions. She had always wanted the best for Hosea, after all, and knowing Hosea's penchant for public office, his respect for politicians, and especially successful leaders, people who didn't shrug their lives away but made decisions and tried to change the world, she had made up this one final ridiculous story. This was her parting gift to Hosea, the words, "Your father, your father, is John Baert." And then, "Come back . . ." The words not spoken to Hosea or to Dory or to a doctor or to the Lord, but to John Baert, the stranger on the horse, the young man from long ago with the dark curls on his neck, her only lover, the father of her beloved Hosea.

But had she made it up? Hosea wondered. Or was it true? In any case, if he had met his father on that day, perhaps his father would see, in Hosea, a resemblance to himself? Hosea had, since the day Euphemia told him his father was the Prime Minister, stared long and hard at any photograph, any news footage of the Prime Minister trying to see some similarities. They both had blue eyes and dark hair, but then so did millions of

ha. But what if what Euphemia had said was simply morphine-induced rambling? Hosea didn't want to think about that. He had the letter, the form letter with the photocopied copy of the Prime Minister's signature promising to visit Canada's smallest town. Hosea had always been interested in maintaining Algren's status as smallest town. It had kept the town on the map and given the folks in Algren a dose of civic pride, of recognition beyond being the birthplace of the Algren cockroach.

But now, since the arrival of the letter three months ago, Hosea's job became clear. It was more than a job, though: it was his mission in life and his only dream. He must bring the Prime Minister to Algren. He must. "John Baert." Hosea murmured the name quietly, his eyes tightly closed, his mind trying to batter down the door that blocked his memory of that day he burned his hand and picked the roses.

CHAPTER
FOUR

"I think he's dead," Summer Feelin' whispered.

"I doubt it. His lips are moving," Knute whispered back.

"Say something, Mom."

Knute cleared her throat. "Excuse me?"

Hosea, for the second time that afternoon, lurched forward in his chair and banged his scarred palm against the edge of his desk, sending a few paper clips skittering off the side.

"Caught you sleeping on the job, eh? Ha ha," Knute said. Summer Feelin' stood beside Knute, holding her hand and staring at Hosea, who was now tugging at his shirt with one hand and smoothing the already smooth surface of his desk with the other.

"Oh no, oh no, I wasn't sleeping. I was just, thinking, so how are you, Knutie? Hi there, uh . . . Autumn . . . uh, May?"

"Summer Feelin'. Say hi, S.F."

"Hi, S.F."

"Ha, ha, that's her little joke."

"Oh yes, that's, uh . . ." Hosea felt his hand go to his shirt again but this time he stopped himself from

54

tugging by lunging towards the floor and picking up the fallen paper clips.

"Well, I just thought I'd take you up on that job offer, remember, when you came by to visit my folks you mentioned that —"

"Yes. Yes, I remember. I do, well, I will have work for you. Quite a bit of work, actually, very soon. Well, what I'll need you to do, mainly, is, you know, answer

himself for not being prepared. He needed a young, attractive woman at his side, plain and simple, if he was going to impress the Prime Minister. Look at all the politicians. They all had attractive aides and writers and handlers, not to mention young, beautiful wives. Lorna would do just fine as the wife, Hosea figured. Granted, she wasn't that young, and she did stoop slightly and forget to do little things like lay down her collar or straighten her necklace so that the diamond Hosea had given her was often draped over her shoulder instead of hanging down towards her cleavage, but Hosea loved her and was confident she would pass muster with the Prime Minister. Who knows, by then she might even be living with him in Algren? And Knute would be his lovely and capable assistant, provided she wore something other than torn jeans and police boots. Hosea could picture it now. There he'd be with Lorna on one side and Knute on the other, waiting for John Baert to emerge from the limousine, to offer Hosea his hand and —

"So when do I start?" asked Knute. She could sense Hosea was nervous about this whole thing. Summer Feelin' was trying to drag her out of the room so she was trying to get it over with as fast as she could.

"Start. Well. Tomorrow. Tomorrow morning. Say about ten o'clock."

"Okay," said Knute. "Sounds good."

"Oh, Knute?"

"Yeah?"

"How's your father's health?"

"Oh, comme ci comme ça, you know . . ."

"Hmmm . . . Do you think his heart is getting stronger?"

"I think so, yeah. He's learning to juggle."

"Juggle? Really?" For a brief moment Hosea was nine again and he heard Tom's voice. "Run, Hosea, run!" It seemed like just the other day. "Juggling, well, what do you know?" said Hosea.

By then Summer Feelin' had dragged Knute out of the room and halfway down the hall. Knute managed to yell over her shoulder to Hosea who was still sitting at his desk tapping a paper clip against his teeth, "See ya tomorrow!"

The snow was melting and the sun was hot, so Knute and Summer Feelin' walked home with their jackets tied around their waists and this was enough to make S.F. flap. Normally when she flapped in public Knute tried to calm her down. She'd take her hand or rub her back or say her name or get S.F. to look at her and tell her what she was so excited about. But this time Knute thought she'd just let S.F. get it out of her system. They stood right in front of the big windows of the Wagon Wheel Café and S.F. stood on one spot, her head back, mouth open, and flapped like she was about to lift right off the ground. Knute was excited, too. The world is full

at her and stared for a while and then went back to their coffee.

When she and S.F. got back to the house they saw Combine Jo lying on the ground in front of the front door. Tom was sitting in a lawn chair beside her wearing a tuque and a downfilled jacket and reading a Dick Francis novel.

"Hello, ladies, how'd the interview go?" asked Tom.

"What the hell is she doing here?" said Knute.

"Do you mean what the hell is *she* doing here?" said Tom, "or what the hell is she doing *here*?"

S.F. crawled onto Tom's lap and peered down at Combine Jo. "Is she dead?" she asked Tom, who looked at Knute and winked.

"No, she's just resting." Tom put his head back and swallowed a couple of times for the benefit of S.F. who had, recently, become intrigued with his Adam's apple and liked to follow its course with her fingertips. "Aack, not so hard, S.F. I'll choke." He bulged his eyes and Summer Feelin' giggled.

"This is ridiculous," Knute said and went inside the house. She had to step over Combine Jo's right arm, which was stretched out as a pillow for her head. She had almost made it into the house. Her bloated fingers grazed the sill of the door and, as Knute stepped over her, lifted slightly as if she were waving.

Knute stormed into the house and flung her jacket onto the floor.

"Why the hell is Combine Jo here and what the hell is she doing lying on the ground?" she yelled in the general direction of the den, where Dory had been painting for the past few days.

"Oh, Knutie?" came Dory's reply. "I'm glad you're here. Jo fainted and she's too heavy for Tom and me to move so I just sent Tom out to sit beside her and keep an eye on her 'til she woke up. You know, it's warm enough out there today for her to lie there, and anyway he'd likely have another heart attack if he tried to lift her, you know, and my back isn't —"

"She did not faint, Mother, she passed out. She's drunk. I'm not a child. I know when somebody is drunk. You know, I've been drunk myself, I realize when something like this is happening."

By now Dory had come out to the kitchen. She was covered in paint and wearing her SoHo T-shirt. Knute was sitting on the counter, swinging her legs like a kid and drinking milk directly from the carton.

58

"I'm not hauling her inside if that's what you think," she sputtered through a mouthful of milk. "Forget it."

"Okay, okay, Knutie, calm down, okay? Just calm down." Dory put her hands on Knute's thighs and looked at her imploringly in very much the same way Knute looked at S.F. when she flapped.

Just then Combine Jo came thrashing through the door holding S.F. in her arms with Tom behind her,

it right on, sending bits of glass and plaster flying. Tom, still in his tuque, started doing a sort of jig to avoid stepping on it, saying, "Dory? Dory? Dory, you gotta help me here."

"Goddamn it!" Combine Jo slurred as one of her feet involuntarily slid out in front of her like Fred Astaire and then began to plow her way to the living room couch. "Christ, girl, hang on! We're almost there!" she told S.F., who answered meekly, "I am. I am." By this time Tom and Dory were flanking her like two tugs bringing in the *Queen Mary*, and Knute was frozen to the spot, livid.

"Ho!" Combine Jo belched out as she fell onto the couch. S.F. kind of dropped beside her and then attempted to climb off the couch, but before she could escape Combine Jo grabbed her by the shirt and said, "Not so fast, you little devil. I want to have a good look at you."

At this point Knute intervened. "Leave her alone, Jo. S.F., come here, sweetie."

"S.F., come here, sweetie," Combine Jo mimicked, moving her head back and forth. "Jesus, Knuter, I'm not gonna kill the kid. When the hell are you gonna bury the hatchet, eh, Knute? I've apologized until I'm fucking blue in the face."

"Coffee, Jo?" Dory asked.

"Thanks, honey." Combine Jo sat on the couch. She was wearing giant Hush Puppies and a tent dress with tiny anchors all over it. She stared at S.F. "God, she's an angel, Knute. She's an angel made in heaven. Aw c'mon, let me have her. Let her sit with me for a second. Doncha want to, eh, Summer Feelin'?"

"No." S.F. tightened her grip on Knute's hand. Tom was busy sweeping up the broken glass in the hallway. He asked S.F. if she would like to do a puzzle with him in the den and she nodded and flew out of the room.

"Lookit her go. Runnin' like the goddamn dickens. How old is she, anyway, Knuter? Five, six?"

"Four."

Combine Jo sighed heavily. "I heard you two were in town, Knute. I had to come and see you. See her. You know I've got no way of getting to the city to see you. How was I gonna see you and S.F.?"

"Nobody invited you."

At this Combine Jo slapped her thigh and barked, "Ha! You haven't changed at all, Knute. Not one iota. Still a spark plug, you crazy kid. You and I should have a drink together some day. But, you know I like your spunk. I've always loved your spunk. And you know

60

what? So did Max. Of all Max's girlfriends you were my goddamn favourite and that's no lie. The rest were pffhh . . . In fact, that's another reason why I'm here."

Dory handed Combine Jo her coffee and immediately Jo spilled a few drops on her anchor dress. "Whoops. Shit." Then Jo did it again. "I'll be goddamned!" she said. Dory attempted a tortured smile. Knute stood a ~~with her arms folded across her chest. The~~

wouldn't be? He's coming back, Knuter. And he wants to see his goddamned daughter!"

"Are you serious?" Marilyn muttered over the phone later that evening. "That's what she said? Just like that?"

"Yeah. Can you believe it?" Knute was soaking in a tub of hot water and talking to Marilyn on Tom's new cordless phone. Tom and Dory and S.F. were all in bed together eating popcorn and watching TV. She could hear an occasional laugh track through the bathroom wall.

"I can believe that he's broke," said Marilyn.

"Some things never change," Knute answered.

"What are you gonna do?" she asked.

"I don't know. What can I do? I can't keep him from coming back. I'm not gonna leave just because he's coming back. And besides, he's not a terrible person or anything, he's just completely hopeless. I don't know."

"Well, he's an asshole, Knute. He knew you were pregnant and he took off."

"Well, I kind of told him to get lost."

"Yeah, but that doesn't mean get lost, *get lost* like for five years. It means just fuck off for a while and don't bug you."

"Yeah, but he might have figured that out himself if he wasn't such a slave to his mother. She's the one who told him his life would be ruined forever if he became a father and stayed in Algren."

"Well, that's probably true."

"Thanks, Marilyn."

"Well, for Christ's sake. He'd have to be a total moron to believe her."

"Yeah, shhh, I know. I know. Actually I think he just wanted to leave. He couldn't deal with it. I don't think he ever listened to his mom."

"Oh, so he's Leonard Cohen all of a sudden, moping around Europe in a big black coat all grim and sad-faced because it's what he has to do? Gimme a break. So now you're just gonna forgive him and let him see S.F. and waltz right back into your life, just like that? Have some self-respect, for Pete's sake, Knute."

"Yeah, but what about S.F.? He is her father, after all. If he wants to see her, shouldn't I let him? Just because he's a moron doesn't mean she wouldn't want to see him, right? She knows about him and everything. I mean, she can decide later if she hates him enough

62

never to see him again. I can't really decide that for her, you know."

"Why not? Lots of parents do that. If you think she's better off without him in her life, then that's that. You decide."

"Well, you let Ron see Josh even though Ron's an idiot."

"Yeah, but he pays me, Knute. You know child

"Well, Marilyn, that doesn't make any sense. He *is* his father. *You're* the one who could have done better than him for a boyfriend. There's nothing you can do about him being Josh's dad. And just because he's a twit doesn't mean Josh doesn't like him."

"Hmm, I don't know, Knute. You know what I think? I think you're still hot for Max."

"Wrong-o."

"You are! I can tell. I can always tell. You definitely are still hot for Mighty Max."

"Oh God, Marilyn. I don't even *know* him anymore."

"Yeah? So what's your point? Welcome to —"

S.F. came into the bathroom and asked if she could join Knute in the tub. Marilyn heard S.F. asking and said, "Oh God, don't you hate that?"

"Yeah. I have to add more cold. Okay, I gotta go."

"You know what you have to do, Knute?" said Marilyn.

"What."

"You have to learn how to make pudding. It says on the box you have to stir constantly, *constantly*, and it takes a good twenty or thirty minutes before the stuff boils. So if S.F. is bugging you, you know, asking for this and that, you say, Sorry ma'am, do you want pudding or not? I cannot leave this pudding for a second."

"Yeah?" said Knute.

"Yeah," said Marilyn, "it's great. I make tons of pudding, and while I stir I read. Thin, light books 'cause you only have one hand to hold 'em. Josh can't do a thing about it, so he actually amuses himself and I get a decent break. All hell can break loose around me. I don't care, I'm making pudding."

"That's a great idea, Marilyn," said Knute. "What happens when he gets sick of pudding?"

"I don't know, I hadn't thought of that. I'll think of something when that time comes, though. Something less fattening."

"Yeah. Marilyn, you have to come and visit me here soon, okay?"

"Definitely," said Marilyn, and they put off saying good-bye for a while and then eventually hung up.

That night just before Knute went to bed she watched S.F. sleep. A strand of hair was stuck in her mouth. Knute removed it. S.F. put it back in. She was beautiful. An angel made in heaven, as Combine Jo had

64

said. God, thought Knute, that woman was S.F.'s paternal grandmother! Not that it mattered. In Knute's opinion, Combine Jo was more interested in her next drink and her piles of money than she was in S.F. Or even Max.

Dory had told Knute, when she was pregnant with S.F., that Combine Jo hadn't always been the way she was now. Years and years ago, she had been the wife of

[illegible] back to Algren. The next day she returned *[illegible]*

Max, her baby, just about frozen to death, lying unconscious and bruised on the kitchen floor — her husband beside him, dead and covered with logs. Apparently he had had an epileptic seizure while trying to fire up the woodstove, dropped Max, whom he had been carrying in one arm, fallen down and died right there. After that Combine Jo started eating and drinking and swearing and generally raising hell all over Algren, until she became too fat and alcoholic to easily make her way out of her house.

With all the money left to her and Max in her husband's will, and by selling most of the farm, Combine Jo was able to hire enough people to look after Max when he was little, and bring her food and booze. She got the name Combine Jo not because she was as big as one, but because each spring she would take her husband's old combine out of the barn and drive it up and down

Algren's Main Street as a personal spring-seeding celebration. Dory thought that Combine Jo might carry a sawed-off rifle in the cab of the combine, but nobody knew for sure. She would career down the street, one hand on the wheel, the other clamped around her bottle of Wild Turkey. She would then drive the combine to her husband's grave, often right up over it, and enjoy a toast with him. She'd pour half a bottle of bourbon into the grass on top of his grave, light a cigarette and prop it up, as best she could, in the grass around where his head would have been, six feet under, and then she'd lie there beside him, where she felt she belonged.

Combine Jo had loved her husband deeply. The affair had been a stupid distraction, a way to pass the time while her husband farmed night and day. Knute wondered if Jo had ever given Max any advice on love. Maybe she'd told Max to leave town when she found out Knute was pregnant. Maybe it wasn't his idea at all. Maybe Jo gave Max a million bucks to leave. Maybe I'm a complete idiot, thought Knute.

If she thought he had left because Jo had told him to, she was fooling herself. And her telling him to get lost the day that she found out she was pregnant and he hadn't seemed happy enough — happy at all, really — wouldn't have been enough for him to leave, either. Knute was always telling him to get lost, knowing he'd come back.

No, Max had left because he'd wanted to leave. And now he was coming back because he wanted to come back, and he wanted to see his "goddamned daughter."

"Well," Knute concluded, "Fuck him."

66

★ ★ ★

That same evening, Lorna had come out to Algren on the bus to visit Hosea. When Hosea got home from work he had listened to her message on the machine. And then he had listened to it again, sitting on his couch, still in his coat and dripping water from his boots on to the living room carpet. "Hi, Hose,"

used to, at the beginning of their relationship, but after a while she had told him he always sounded distracted at work and she didn't need to call long distance to get the cold shoulder. Hosea had pleaded with her to understand. He was the mayor, after all, of Canada's smallest town. He had work to do. He loved her more than life itself but . . . But no, Lorna was unmoved. And since then had called him only at home. "Our office is closed tomorrow so I thought I'd come on the bus and stay over and you could take me home the next day or the next, or I'll just take the bus again. Okay. Whatever. You're really not there, are you? Hmmm. Okay, call me, but if you get this message after six o'clock, don't bother because I'll be on the bus. I should —"

Damn, thought Hosea. He still hadn't installed one of those endless-tape answering machines. She should what? he thought. She always seemed to forget about the length of the tape. Sometimes she'd call back — sometimes two or three times — and just carry on with her monologue, entirely unruffled by the fact that she'd been abruptly cut off. This time she hadn't called back to continue. Why not? Details like this could give Hosea chest pain. Did it mean she was angry at being cut off? Or if not angry, then (and this was worse), oh God, offended? Had she been suddenly incapacitated by an aneurism? Or was she simply in a hurry to get on the bus to see her sugarbaby, her man, Hosea? Hosea would just have to wait and see. But oh, how he hated to wait. Why hadn't old Granny Funk stuck her bobby pin in the book of Job when they were naming him, instead of at Hosea? Hosea! Could Lorna really love a man she called Hose? He glanced at his watch, a Christmas present from Lorna before she knew him well enough to know that he was never late for anything, and in fact already owned five working watches. Okay, if she takes the 6:15 bus, thought Hosea, she'll be here at 7:15. That gave him exactly half an hour to get things ready, maybe call the doctor and still make it to the bus depot to pick Lorna up. Hosea decided to make the call first.

"Dr. Bonsoir?"

"Hosea?"

"Yes, Doctor, Hosea Funk here. Yes, I know. Well then, okay. Any news over there?"

"News?" said the doctor.

"Yes, news. Has Mrs. Epp —"

"No, she has not. Hosea, I'm a busy man. I'm sure you understand."

"Why yes, yes, indeed I do, but then, quickly, before I go, how's, uh . . . Leander?"

"Do you mean Mr. Hamm?"

"Yes, yes, that's the one. How's he doing? Not good. I see. Any prognosis or —"

"No, I do not have a prognosis, nor would I be giving

"Of course, well then, thank-you, Doctor."

"Mmmmm," said the doctor in reply.

"Au revoir, Doctor," said Hosea cheerfully.

"Good-bye, Hosea."

Well, of course he was busy, he was a doctor, thought Hosea. No problem. He'd go back to the hospital and see for himself how things were. Hosea checked his watch. Lorna would be pulling up in front of the pool hall, which doubled as a bus depot, in a few minutes. He grabbed two old tablecloths of Euphemia's. One he threw over the dining room table and the other he draped over his shoulder. He lugged his exercise bike downstairs and put it into its usual hiding place, behind the furnace next to the hot water tank. He yanked the tablecloth that was on his shoulder and threw it over the bike. One time Lorna had said, "You know, Hosea, you're in great shape for a man your age and you don't even care. That's what I like about you."

Since then, Hosea had pedalled furiously every morning on his bicycle to nowhere — as Euphemia had called it — and had hid it in the basement each time Lorna came to visit.

Hosea checked his watch. Damn, he thought. The tape!

"You're late," said Lorna.

"I know. I'm sorry," said Hosea. He couldn't tell Lorna the real reason he was late, and he hadn't had time to make one up, so he stood there, thumping his breast with his big green Thinsulate glove (because he couldn't get a proper pincer grip to tug), and hoping her love for him would sweep this latest infraction right under the rug. It had taken Hosea twenty minutes to set his new Emmylou Harris tape to exactly the right song. Fast forward, oops too far — rewind. Too far, fast forward again. Darn! Too far *again*! He had planned to rush into the house ahead of Lorna and push play on his tape deck so that as she entered the house she would hear Emmylou singing "Two More Bottles of Wine," at which point Hosea would produce two bottles of wine, red for the heart, one in each hand, and they would sit down and have a drink.

None of this happened. The tape hadn't played when he'd pushed play because he had, in his haste, unplugged the tape deck to plug in his tri-light desk lamp to create more of a mood. He hadn't been able to find his corkscrew for the wine and so, while Lorna roamed around the house switching lights on and wondering out loud why it was so dark in there, he had rammed the cork down the neck of one of the bottles with his ballpoint pen and then spilled the wine all over himself when it splurched out around the cork. He used the tea towel hanging on the fridge handle to wipe up the wine and then, pushing the cork way down with his pen, managed to pour two glasses without much spillage.

He brought the wine to Lorna and sat down beside

machine. "Well, because of your message. You didn't call back to finish it. Usually you do."

Lorna put her wine down and took Hosea's hand in hers. She slung one of her legs over his and stroked the top of his hand with her thumb. "Hosea," she said, "you really are something, you know that?"

Hosea used his remaining free hand to flatten her hand over his and stop her from stroking. He longed for his glass of wine, but now his hands were busy. He smiled at Lorna. "You're something, too," he said.

"I suppose I am," said Lorna.

Hosea shifted slightly and smiled again. He stared at their hands, tangled together and resting on Lorna's thigh. He noticed that the middle knuckles on Lorna's fingers were wider than the other parts of her fingers, whereas his own fingers tapered to a point. He wished his fingers were more like Lorna's.

"Hmmmm," murmured Lorna.

71

"Lorna?" said Hosea.

"Yeah?"

"Are you mad at me?"

"No, Hosea, I am not mad at you. Look at me here. I'm trying to get closer to you. Jesus, Hose, can't you figure it out?"

"But what about the message on the —"

"I was in a hurry, okay? I love you, I'm not mad at you. I love you."

"Well, what were you going to say, I should what, you should what? You know, you were going to say you should do something and I . . ."

"I was going to say, 'I should go if I'm gonna make the bus.' That's what I should do, go. Okay? Go so I could make the bus to get to *you!*"

Lorna sighed, removed her hands from Hosea's, and used one of them to reach for her glass of wine.

"Well, now you're mad then, aren't you?" asked Hosea.

"Hosea, what the hell is your problem? Why do you have to derail every romantic moment in our lives with your paranoid worrying? Do you do it on purpose? Maybe you don't love me, maybe you're mad at *me* and you don't know how to tell me, and you turn it around to make it look like I'm mad at you and then you won't feel so bad, and you'll be the martyr. Great. Now I *am* mad at you."

"I knew it," said Hosea. "And I do love you." He looked at his hands, at his tapered fingers. They were pudgy, he thought. Why? The rest of him wasn't fat. Could he lose weight in his fingers? They looked childish to him. He slipped them under his thighs for a few seconds, then pulled them up and folded them behind his head. Just a minute ago Lorna had been stroking one of his hands and he had wanted her to quit. Now he wanted her to continue, more than anything. He reached for his glass of wine.

"No, you do not know it, Hose, I'm not really mad at you. Can't we just have a normal time together?"

"Oh God, Lorna, I've missed you," said Hosea.

"Yeah?" said Lorna.

"You know, I've missed you, too, Hose," sighed Lorna about thirty minutes later.

Hosea hated lying around and talking after having sex. He preferred to go outside, flushed and happy, and feel the earth and the sky, and himself sandwiched between them, and know that as things go in the universe, he had just been blessed. But he knew from experience this was not Lorna's first choice. One time he had dragged her outside in the dark, naked and sweaty, and she had started to cough and complain about mosquitoes, and had not said she felt blessed when Hosea had asked her. And so this time he decided he would just get up and get that Emmylou Harris song playing, finally. He brought the tape box back to the floor with him and lay down beside Lorna so that his head was right under the coffee table. Together they listened to the music and looked at the box, at the picture of Emmylou folded up inside it.

"God, does she have long toes, eh?" said Hosea.

"Wow. They're kinda creepy-looking, don't you think?" asked Lorna. Hosea didn't think so. He imagined Emmylou's toes contained in her painted cowboy boots, slightly splayed, planting her body onstage while she belted out "Born to Run."

"Yeah they are, aren't they?" said Hosea.

"Hmmm," said Lorna. "Is this song about heartbreak?" Lorna put her head on Hosea's chest. He patted her head and stared up at the underside of the coffee table. Made in Manitoba, it had stamped on it.

CHAPTER
FIVE

"Cross my heart and hope to die," he'd said and moved his tapered little index finger in the shape of an X over the general vicinity of his heart on the outside of his sweater.

"Okay," said Minty. "Good boy."

They were sitting together in the back seat of a rusted-out car that somebody had abandoned on the edge of Grandpa Funk's alfalfa field.

Minty looked out the windows on each side of the car to make sure nobody was watching. Hosea did the same.

"Lookie," said Minty.

Hosea stared. Minty spread her skinny bare legs, making sure her dress didn't ride up and thumped on her flat stomach a couple of times with the bottom of her fist like she was checking a soccer ball for air. Hosea's eyes widened and Minty nodded.

"Yessir," she said. "But not me. Euphemia. You came right out of her . . ." Minty thumped her belly again.

"You're lying," said Hosea.

And then Minty panicked and saw her chance at redemption at the same time.

"Yeah, I am," she said. She smiled, relieved.

"Are you?" said Hosea.

"Yeah, I am," she said.

"Are you sure?" said Hosea.

"Yeah, I'm sure," said Minty.

"Good," said Hosea.

They were both relieved. They smiled and giggled and Hosea thumped lightly on his stomach, too, just to try it out.

"Punch me as hard as you can," said Minty.

"No," said Hosea.

"C'mon, Hose, just do it. I've tightened it up so it won't hurt." She put her chin down to her chest and moved her arms behind her back.

"No," said Hosea. He started kicking the back of the dusty seat in front of him.

"Don't you want to?" asked Minty.

"I don't want to," he said. He was four years old.

The next evening at the supper table Hosea sat on Euphemia's lap finishing off his potatoes. From time to time he would thump on Euphemia's stomach and she, irritated and trying to finish her own potatoes, would tell him to stop. Minty noticed this and tried to get Hosea's attention. Hosea ignored Minty. He was grinning and he continued to thump Euphemia's stomach. Minty was afraid Hosea was going to say something to get her in trouble, so she suggested that they go outside and play catch.

"Uh-uh," said Hosea. Finally, Euphemia had had enough.

"Hosea!" she said. "Stop it, you're hurting me!" By now all the Funks were looking at Hosea and Euphemia, sternly, curiously, amusedly, in a number of ways. There were a lot of them.

Hosea on her hip. But not without first noticing the look on her father's face and the way his head swivelled ever so slowly to meet her mother's own incredulous stare.

The Funks had, actually, considered the possibility of Euphemia being Hosea's natural mother before this (five months of sickness, huge coats in the summertime, a man on a horse? The Funks might have been complacent but they weren't stupid), but hadn't wanted to make the situation worse. They had decided, without speaking about it or agreeing to it, to leave well enough alone. Euphemia's honour would remain intact, and so would their reputation as decent people. But now, for some reason, Euphemia's father broke their unspoken pact and opened a can of worms. Had he kept his mouth shut and his eyes on his plate and allowed Euphemia and Hosea to leave the table without further ado, they would have gone on for another four or ten or fifty years, swallowing their suspicions and not rocking the boat. Maybe Euphemia's father wanted some drama in his life. Maybe he was tired of shrugging everything off. Maybe he wanted to get angry at something. Who knows? His gaze said it all. His wife knew it. She panicked. The jig was up.

Euphemia flung Hosea onto his bed upstairs and asked him just what the heck he was talking about, wanting to get back in? Just then Minty came flying through the door, white as a sheet, and said, "Phemie, Phemie, I didn't tell him anything. I was just joking." Hosea lay on his back in his bed.

"She said I came out of your stomach," he said, starting to cry.

"But I said I was lying, you little shit. You know I did," said Minty. Now she began to cry.

"Shut up, Mint, and lock the door," said Euphemia. She knew her parents and her other brothers and sisters would be upstairs and in the room in no time.

"You promised me, Minty, you fat liar," said Euphemia. She shoved Minty onto the bed next to Hosea.

"Let us in, Phemie!" Euphemia's father roared from the hallway. Her mother was begging him to calm down. Euphemia stared at Hosea. He had put his pillow over his head to muffle his sobs. The back of his neck poked out, soft and very narrow. It looks like somebody's wrist, thought Euphemia. Two brown curls framed the tiny nape of Hosea's neck. Euphemia kicked Minty's leg, gently. She didn't care. Not really. It was probably a good thing. She walked over to the door and let the rest of her family in.

"What's this all about, Euphemia? What does Minty have to do with this? What the hell is going on?" Euphemia's father looked from one girl to the other, barely acknowledging the small, heaving lump on the bed.

Euphemia couldn't believe it. Her parents had

even Minty for keeping the secret. She'd had to tell Minty. She'd had to tell someone. She had been thrilled. And still was.

Euphemia sat down on the bed beside Hosea. She stroked his back. She didn't try to remove the pillow. She moved her thumb up and down the back of his neck, dipping in and out of its soft hollow and feeling his hairline begin just above it. She put her mouth to his curls and kissed them.

"C'mon, Hosea," she whispered, "we're going."

Euphemia's parents had tried, in the end, to get them to stay. They had been angry and shocked and hurt and embarrassed, but they weren't the kind of people to throw their daughter and grandson out on to the street. Why hadn't she told them the truth? they asked Euphemia, to which she responded with a shrug. Euphemia's father had told her she was a tramp, but had then apologized. Minty had been grounded for two weeks, which, after a day, was modified to one week, and had told Euphemia a thousand times she was sorry. Euphemia's mother had asked her who the father was and Euphemia said she had no idea, a man on a horse. "Oh, Phemie, not that old cock and bull story," her mother would say. "Your mother's right, Phemie, that dog won't hunt," her father would echo, and Euphemia said calmly, "It's true, that part of it is true." Euphemia's father would rise from the table and slam his fist down and curse Euphemia up one side and down the other and would then lie on the couch, spent and despondent.

But all the while Euphemia was packing her bags. In her mind she had already moved on. She had left. She had locked up this part of her life and thrown away the key. She had turned the page. The next morning she and Hosea were standing on the side of the road, hitching a ride to town.

Hosea would miss the farm. He'd miss Minty. He had planned to marry her when he was older. He was sorry he hadn't punched her in the stomach when she had begged him to. But he didn't really know why they had to go. He had crossed his heart and hoped to die in that old car, in the field with Minty. He had bothered his mother at the supper table. He had pretended to crawl into her stomach. He had thought it was funny but his grandpa and grandma were very angry and Minty was crying and now he and his mother were moving to town. He had heard his grandpa yell, "She's his mother, for God's sake," and he hadn't known why that was suddenly a problem. She had always been his mother and Grandpa had been happy. He had offered to play catch with Minty, thinking that might be it, but she said it was no use, it didn't matter anymore.

Hosea stood at the side of the road and tugged at his shirt.

"Please," said Euphemia and straightened out his

They walked together towards town. Euphemia asked Hosea if his boots were pinching his toes yet, and he said no.

"That's good," she said. Hosea asked Euphemia if she'd give him a piggyback ride. She hoisted him up onto her back, and reminded him every twenty yards or so to put his arms around her shoulders and not her neck. After about half an hour they stopped and walked into the ditch and through it and up the other side and sat in the grass and leaned against a farmer's fence.

"Hosea," said Euphemia.

"What?" said Hosea.

"You did come from me, from inside me, inside my stomach."

"Oh," said Hosea. He pulled out some grass and started to make a pile.

"I'm your mother, Hosea, your real honest-to-goodness mother."

Hosea looked up at her briefly and smiled and nodded.

"Do I got a dad?"

"He's a cowboy."

"Where is he?"

"Well, I suppose he's riding the range. Cowboy's can't stay put, Hose."

"That's good," said Hosea. He threw a piece of grass into Euphemia's lap. And then another and another until he had made himself a pillow, and he put his head down on it and had a little nap.

"Why can't I come along?" Summer Feelin' wanted to go with Knute to work. Every time Knute made a move to get dressed, brush her teeth, eat breakfast, Summer Feelin' made exactly the same move. She wasn't letting Knute out of her sight.

"Because. I'll be working."

"So?"

"Well, I'm working for the mayor."

"So?"

"So, it's . . . detailed work."

Summer Feelin' was quiet for about ten seconds. Dory gave Knute a look (raised eyebrows, chin on chest) from the sink indicating she could have done better with the explanation.

"Grandma and Grandpa are boring," said S.F. finally.

"Summer Feelin'!"

"Well, goodness, Knutie, it's true, isn't it?" said Dory, staring directly at Tom.

82

"No, no," Knute began to say, glaring at S.F. and wondering if the question was actually intended for Tom. Dory was still staring at him.

"Well, I don't know," he said. "Boring? I suppose we are."

"I suppose we are," said Dory. She slammed down the milk in front of Tom and got up for her toast.

Tom and Knute looked at each other and shrugged

She left the room then, and Tom and S.F. and Knute sat in silence for a while. One half of Dory's toast had fallen off the plate and onto the table when she slammed it down. Tom put the toast back on her plate, lining it up perfectly alongside the other half. S.F. went over to the fridge and tried to open the door as fast as she could to catch the light coming on. Then, when that didn't work, she opened it slowly, slowly, slowly. Tom and Knute watched, curious to know if it would work.

"C'mon, Summer Feelin'," sighed Tom. "Let's do some juggling. Your mom's gotta go. Hosea's a stickler for punctuality."

Knute walked along Third Avenue towards Hosea's office. She knew she had to make some other kind of babysitting arrangements for S.F. Dory had been getting more work, lately, at the farm labour pool and Tom couldn't look after S.F. all day, every day, by himself. Later on, she might be able to bring S.F. to work with her occasionally, but not right then at the beginning. Her old friend Judy Klampp from high school had a couple of little kids, but Knute didn't think she'd want to look after Summer Feelin' as well. And about a hundred years ago Knute had gone to a party with Judy Klampp's husband, before he was her husband, and had left with his brother and . . . no. Forget Judy Klampp.

Knute told herself she would not think of Max. As far as she was concerned, he was yesterday's news. S.F. thought it was cool that he was coming back to Algren. She thought he would be very happy to see her do her cartwheels and spell her name. She wondered if he'd have a present for her.

"Not bloody likely," Knute thought. She moved the hair out of S.F.'s eyes and said, "Of course he will, sweetie." Max, she supposed, could take care of S.F. while she worked. But no, he couldn't, because he'd be living with Combine Jo and she would maul S.F. every chance she got and who knows? thought Knute, S.F. might hate Max.

Well, she thought, she'd have a cigarette and worry about all that later. She walked along Third Avenue and a dog in a hurry passed by without glancing up at her. She heard the sound of someone practising a violin. Must be spring, she thought.

When she got to the office Hosea was sitting in his chair with his hands folded on his desk in front of him as if he were waiting for a cue from the director to spring into action. His chin jutted out slightly and his face was flushed. His hair was fluffier than usual.

"Ho! You scared me. How are you, Knute?"

"Fine, thank-you. How are you?"

"Whoosh, whoosh, whoosh, very busy," said Hosea, making chopping motions with his hands. "All over town. In fact, I've gotta fly."

"Okay . . ." said Knute. She wasn't sure what she

flowers along Main Street, new lettering on the water tower, some new blacktop, maybe check into the price of a new Zamboni, that sort of thing. Okey-dokey? At about noon you can go and get my mail from the post office. Just tell 'em who you are. Fair enough?"

"Okay," she said again. She nodded and smiled. She was about to ask Hosea if she could smoke in his office, in their office, in the office, but he was gone.

Hosea Funk hurried up the steps of the Charlie Orson Memorial Hospital. The hospital was perched on top of a small hill, and from its front doors Hosea could just see the smoke coming out of the chimney of his house, a block away. Man's life's a vapour, full of woes, he thought, seeing the smoke twist in the sky and disappear. He cuts a caper and down he goes. But then he remembered his beloved Lorna, probably still asleep, warm and soft, her hands curled up like a baby's beside her head, her dark eyelashes . . . and Hosea's thoughts flip-flopped from one end of the spectrum to the other in a matter of seconds: from life's woes to passion's throes. Then, looking once again at the smoke escaping from the chimney, his thoughts tumbled back towards the woes, lodging themselves somewhere in the humdrum middle of the spectrum with thoughts of Knute and his work, and Knute's ripped jeans in conjunction with his mayoral status, and would it all work out — should he mention the jeans, should he not?

"Ello, Hosea, you're looking . . . sound."

"Good morning, Dr. Bonsoir, I'm feeling . . . sound." Hosea smiled.

"Well then," said the doctor. "If you are so sound, what can I possibly do for you? I am a physician. Wait. Don't tell me. You're here to check up on my patients. On my quality of care? Perhaps you could check Mr. Hamm's IV levels, or inspect Mrs. Epp for signs of dilation, or maybe you would like to discuss the radical new treatment for enlarged polyps recently making its debut in the *New England Journal of Medicine*, eh? Mr. Hosea Funk, why do you feel you have the right to 'check in' as you call it, on my patients? You are not a priest or a funeral home director. You are not family. You are not an intern practising for the real thing, you are not a hospital administrator or the CMA. You are not even a florist or a pizza delivery person, not that our patients order pizza every day. So, what do you want? Mayors do not, as far as I know, make hospital rounds every few days. It is not part of their job and you are irritating the hell out of me, do you know that?"

"Well, Dr. Bonsoir, I —"

"And my name is not Bonsoir, it's François. Bon soir, for your information, means good evening. Dr. Good Evening? Have you ever heard of anything so ridiculous? Think about it. Would you like me to call you Mayor . . . Hello? Hello, Mayor Hello. Or Mayor

tugging he flattened his hand over his heart.

"What? Are you having chest pain, Hosea? Sit down there, in that chair. Come on. I'm sorry. Clearly I've upset you. I apologize. Here now, let's loosen your coat."

"Dr. François, I'm sorry, I —"

"Shhhh, I'm taking your pulse. I need to count. Please, shhh." The doctor bent over Hosea, holding his wrist between his thumb and forefinger, looking sternly at the second hand of his watch. Hosea sat there, feeling foolish. His heart was fine. How could he tell the doctor he had a nervous condition, not a heart condition? Hosea felt bad for the doctor, who was feeling bad for Hosea. He looked at the curved back of the doctor, at his dark brown hair just grazing the back of his collar. Such care, such professionalism. For a moment Hosea wished the doctor was his own son. Lorna would have a delicious lunch prepared. He and the doctor would enter the warm kitchen slapping each other on the back, each kindly ribbing the other and gazing at Lorna with mutual tenderness.

The doctor let go of Hosea's wrist and stood up.

"You've got the pulse of a nine-year-old girl, Hosea. Nothing to worry about."

"Thank-you, Dr. François. I'm sorry I irritate you."

"Oh, it's nothing. I realize there isn't that much for you to do, a small town like Algren isn't exactly —"

"But that's not true, Doctor," said Hosea. He stood up.

"I have a lot of work to do. Algren isn't just a small town, it's *the* smallest. You know, just today I've hired a girl — a woman — Tom McCloud's daughter, Knute, to take care of some of the details so I can work on the bigger projects. I'm sure your work is never done even though you work in a small hospital and not one in the city."

"Well, I suppose so. I didn't mean to offend you, Hosea, I was simply trying to shed some light on the subject. Listen, everything is very much as it was three days ago when you were last here. Monsieur Hamm is very ill. His organs are shutting down. He has begun to hemorrhage internally. It is very difficult to find a vein in which to insert his IV tubes. The members of his family are coming around to say good-bye. Unless you are a good friend, I would suggest you maintain a respectful distance. As far as Mrs. Epp goes, if she does not go into labour soon, we will have to induce her. I have discussed over the phone, with some of my colleagues in Winnipeg, the possibility of transferring her to one of the larger prenatal wards in the city. She is very uncomfortable. Okay, Hosea? Is that what you wanted to know? You know, this information is generally regarded as confidential. Are you happy?"

"Yes. Thank-you, Dr. François."

"Don't mention it."

Hosea put out his hand to shake the doctor's. He truly was grateful. That was exactly what he needed to

apart. I'm afraid one of the babies is not in position. I'm only getting two pulses. A C-section may be necessary."

In a second, Dr. François was gone. Hosea watched him and Nurse Barnes run down the hall, their white coats flying behind them like twin pillow cases on a washline. Hosea wanted to run after them, run with them. For one semi-unconscious moment Hosea envied the uncooperative baby, the one who was stuck, the one who would have the gentle, capable hands of Dr. François guiding him, or her? towards the light, out and up. Towards safety, towards home, towards his mother and his father. Such tenderness, such concern. For something so small as a baby, one of three, a triplet. Hosea's mind almost capsized as he began to imagine the younger Dr. François as his own father, as the cowboy on the range, as the leader of the country, as the . . . Cut it out, Hosea, said Hosea to himself. Dr.

Bon-François is busy, so are the nurses, I'll have a quick peek at old Leander before I go. Thank God for my rubbers, thought Hosea, as he padded softly down the hall, away from the commotion in Mrs. Epp's room.

Hosea peered around the door of room 3. He jumped when his eyes met Leander Hamm's. They were open wide and staring directly at Hosea.

"Mr. Hamm?" whispered Hosea.

"Susie? Susie?" Leander Hamm's eyes didn't leave Hosea's face. Hosea stood, frozen, in the doorway. He knew that Susie had been the name of Leander's wife, long gone now.

"No . . ." whispered Hosea.

"Cut the crap, Suse. Take me . . . with you," Leander Hamm managed to say. He had always been a cantankerous man. He preferred horses to people.

"I can't. I —"

And then Leander Hamm let out a howl that terrified Hosea.

"Shhh, shh . . ." said Hosea. He was worried that the doctor would come running. He would be so angry with Hosea if he saw him in Mr. Hamm's room.

"Okay, I'll take you with me . . . dear. Let's go right now. But please be quiet." And Hosea went over to Leander Hamm and took his hand. He thought of taking Mr. Hamm's pulse, the way the doctor had taken his. He stared at his thumb and tapered forefinger holding Leander Hamm's tiny wrist. Hosea couldn't believe that this narrow piece of bone had held down wild horses, broken savage stallions, held off the

90

powerful hindquarters of a bucking bronc intent on squashing him between the stable boards. But Leander Hamm tightened his grip and, with more surprising strength, pulled Hosea to him so that Hosea's face was touching his. Hosea wasn't quite sure where Leander Hamm wanted to go, or how they'd get there. He just wanted the old man to simmer down.

"Susie, Susie," said Leander Hamm. He moved his

No, no, my darling . . . my love," said Hosea. But it didn't matter. Leander Hamm had released his grip on Hosea's hand. He had released his grip on all of it. Man's life's a vapour. Leander Hamm was dead.

About thirty-five years earlier, when Leander Hamm was only sixty years old, and Hosea was an awkward teenager, Leander had meant to tell Hosea that he thought he knew something about his father. That old story about the Funk girl being handed a baby one night by a man on a horse didn't wash with him. Leander knew that was the official story, and he'd done enough stupid things in his day that he wasn't about to blow the whistle on somebody else, but, gee whiz, you couldn't lead Leander Hamm down the garden path that easily. Besides, he had seen them together in the field. And years later, he had felt something for Hosea, loping around town, so eager to please. He wanted to mention to Hosea that he had been there, at the dance in Whithers, when the man on the horse had left the hall and met Euphemia in the canola field. Leander had noticed that the stranger had left his hat behind, and he ran out to tell him. But when he saw young Euphemia and the cowboy together in the field, he turned around and quickly walked back to the dance hall. "Two kids in heat," he'd muttered to himself at the time.

The cowboy never came back for his hat. It was a Biltmore, a good hat. Leander decided to keep it for himself. Now, he wasn't sure, of course, that this cowboy was Hosea's dad. But he knew, like everybody else in the area did, that Euphemia was no tramp, that she came from a pretty good family and wouldn't have been the kind of girl to sleep with every Tom, Dick, and Harry. So chances were it was the cowboy. He seemed like a healthy boy to Leander, but of course Leander Hamm was partial to anybody who was partial to horses. The only thing that had confused him over the years was how nervous Hosea could be the son of that confident cowboy. But it happens. Anyway, the fact that Euphemia had gone out back with this stranger didn't upset Leander. The stranger was a good boy. They had talked for a few minutes. Was he from Alberta or was he an American, maybe Montana? Leander couldn't remember. And he hadn't gotten around to telling the story to Hosea when he'd thought about it, and then the thought was gone.

He had taken the hat. After all, the cowboy had left and never returned. And who better to wear a quality Biltmore than Leander Hamm? In fact, he had worn that hat every day since he'd acquired it. He never saw a dentist or a doctor but twice a year he'd brought that hat into the city to have it steamed and blocked. Horses had trampled on it, shat on it, his kids had misplaced it, his grandchildren had mocked it, his wife had thrown it in the garbage half a dozen times, and not one, but two, cats had had kittens in it. Just about nightly Leander

back and returned the hat to Leander it had a strange smell and Leander was pissed off.

Instead of leaving his hat at home when he went to church, he decided to leave himself at home with his hat while his wife, Susie, went to church alone. That was that.

And so, on the day that Leander's son Lawrence had taken him to the Charlie Orson Memorial Hospital, he had been wearing the hat. And, when the nurse had told him that she would put all his belongings, including the hat, into the hospital safe while he was a patient there, Leander had managed to grab the hat and say, "Oh no, you don't, Florence Nightingale, I've had that hat longer 'n dogs have been lickin' their balls."

Lawrence had smiled sweetly at the nurse. "That's really not too much to ask, is it?" he'd said. Without a word, the nurse tossed the hat over Leander's shrunken body, to Lawrence, and stalked out.

"You don't throw it, either, it's a Biltmore, you goddamn . . . Nazi!" Leander had yelled after her.

Leander had wanted to wear it, of course, but Lawrence had convinced him that it would be better if he hung it on the IV contraption. That way Leander would be able to see it and to reach out and touch it, but it wouldn't get flattened in bed.

And this was where the hat was hanging when Leander died. Hosea saw it and thought it was a very nice hat. It was a Biltmore, he noted. It felt like flour but was as tough as a pig's hide. He wanted it. Oh God, what would the doctor think if he saw him, first going into Leander's room, then killing him in a convoluted way, and now stealing his hat? He wanted that hat. He didn't know why, but he had to have it. The doctor was busy with Mrs. Epp and the babies. Hosea reached out and grabbed it. Thankfully, Leander's eyes were closed and his hands forever still. Sorry, said Hosea to Leander. And he left with his hat.

CHAPTER
SIX

down the street to see if anybody else was coming. Not
very many people were. Smallest town and everything.
He reminded Knute of the dog who lived in the
apartment block across from hers in the city. He would
hang out his fourth floor window, front legs on the
windowsill, and if he saw somebody wave he'd sort of
wave back. Once Knute saw him on a leash going for a
walk with his owner and he looked sheepish, like, Okay,
yes, now you know, I'm a dog, that's all there is to it.

Knute opened the window and stuck her head out.

"Hey!" she said to the dog. He looked up and
nodded in a dog way but then returned to business.
Somebody was coming down the street. Knute hadn't
done any of the things Hosea had asked her to do,
except get the mail.

She sat on the windowsill and smoked and looked
outside.

"Uh, hello," she heard someone say.

"Can I help you?" she muttered and quickly butted her cigarette against the windowsill and threw it down to the street. She turned around and there was Hosea, wearing a hat. He looked vaguely stricken.

"Oh hell-o," she said. "It's you. Sorry. I hope you don't mind me smoking in here." Hosea put up his hand like a cop saying stop and shook his head. Knute wasn't sure he was shaking his head no, he didn't mind, or no, she shouldn't smoke.

"Any luck?" he said. Again, Knute wasn't sure what he meant exactly, so she said, "No. No luck. But I got your mail."

"Oh. Thank-you," said Hosea.

"No problem." Knute thought Hosea's hat looked good on him. It looked like it must have been a longtime favourite of his.

"So. Thanks again," said Hosea. "Um, I think you'll work out well. Did you, uh, have any problems?"

"No, nope, no problems," said Knute. And she thought how Hosea must be wondering because first she didn't have any luck and now she didn't have any problems, so what exactly did she have?

"Well, then, you may as well go home," said Hosea. "Thanks very much for your help. Well, not your help," he said, "I mean your services, your time. How does two hundred and fifty dollars a week sound? For, oh, a few hours a day, if that's, if that suits you."

"Two hundred and fifty bucks?" Knute said. "That's great. That's fine."

"Because, like I say," said Hosea, "if you need more or if you think it's not enough, just tell me."

96

"Fine, yeah, I will, but it sounds okay to me. It sounds good."

"Say hi to Tom," said Hosea. He sat in his chair and smoothed out the surface of his desk. "I should really drop in again soon. We had a very nice visit the last time I did."

"Yeah," Knute said. "You should." She smiled. Hosea smiled.

"See ya. See ya . . . Knutie. Knute."

She smiled as if to say whatever, call me whatever. "See ya," she said again.

The dog was still sitting there. Dusk was falling in around him. The sky was the colour of raw meat. Knute walked past the dog.

"Hey, you desperado," she said, "what are you waiting for?" No reply. She wondered if Summer Feelin' would like a dog. But no, not with all of Dory's redecorating. She kept walking. Past Darlene's Unisex Salon, past Jim and Brenda's Floral Boutique, past the Style-Rite, past Kowalski Back Hoe Services and Catering, past Willie Wiebe's Western Wear, past the only set of lights in town.

Hosea's hands were shaking. He opened his top right drawer and took out the orange Hilroy scribbler. His memory of what had just happened was, what was that colour, a dusty rose, a throbbing dusty rose? It took him to the doorway of Leander's room, but not beyond. Thank God for my rubbers, he had thought. The babies, a problem with one of them. Go back, Hosea, he had told himself. Go back into the room. You stole the hat. You killed a man and stole his hat. No, I didn't, thought Hosea. I didn't kill him. He just died and I happened to be there. Shouldn't you have told someone? Should I have? Yes, I should have. I know it. But then the doctor would have been angry with me. But this man died! I know, but surely someone will notice very soon. But the hat. Nobody saw me go in and nobody saw me go out, so nobody will know that I took his hat. And that makes it okay? People might think I killed him for his hat. Why did I take the hat? It's a beautiful hat. Because I'm no good. I stole the hat of a dead man. I can't be any good. That's right, that's right. You're no cowboy, Hosea Funk. You're a horse's ass. So I am. So I am.

Hosea sat still in his chair. His head hurt. He opened his scribbler and turned to the Dead column and carefully entered the name Leander Hamm, and the date March 23, 1996. Then he put the scribbler back into the drawer and took out the letter from the Prime Minister and read it twice. He also took out the newspaper photo that showed the Prime Minister sleeping on a plane to Geneva. It was Hosea's favourite. He had a full photo album of newspaper clippings and pictures of the Prime Minister. Shaking hands, singing the national anthem, talking into a reporter's microphone, speaking in the House of Commons,

98

kissing his beautiful wife, playing with his grandchildren, unveiling some monument or another, riding away in a chauffeur-driven limousine. But the one of the Prime Minister sleeping was his favourite. It was the only one of them all in which Hosea could see himself.

"Three babies," Hosea whispered to himself. Three babies. If the third survives. Hmmmm. That's three more people in Algren, one less, Leander Hamm, that

phoned Lorna at his place. No answer. Where was she. There was nowhere for her to go in Algren. And she had said she'd be staying a couple of days. "Damn Damn *damn*," said Hosea, and began to wonder if he was supposed to know anything.

Where was Lorna, anyway? He decided to go home and find out. As he was getting into his car, Combine Jo walked by and looked hard at him, as if she had seen that hat somewhere before, but where?

"La dee dah, Mr. Mayor with the fancy hat," she said. "Going to a party?"

"No," said Hosea. "No, I'm not. I'm going home."

"Ha ha," said Combine Jo. "I'm kidding, Hose, it's a nice hat, suits you. You should wear it on July first if buddy boy in Ottawa comes to town. You know, you look like . . . Oscar Wilde. Hey, didja hear my kid, Max, is coming home? Pretty good, eh?"

"Is it?" said Hosea.

And Combine Jo said, "Well, I think it is."

"Yes, well . . . good," said Hosea. He knew that Max had left town when Knute was pregnant with his child. So many cowboys, thought Hosea. He also knew all about Combine Jo and her craziness and the cause of it and it was no wonder Max flew the coop. He wondered if Knute and Summer Feelin' knew Max was coming back. Then again, maybe he wasn't coming back. Maybe Combine Jo was just talking. But then again, maybe it was true. "Oh, Jo?" he called out to her as she meandered down the sidewalk.

"Yes, m'dear?" she yelled without looking over her shoulder.

"Is he coming back for good? Like, uh, to live here?" he said.

"That's how it's lookin', sweetie. That's how the odds are stackin' up," she said, and she saluted the old black dog as she passed the Wagon Wheel Café.

"Three babies and Max," whispered Hosea to himself as he drove the two blocks back home. Three babies and Max. But Leander's gone, he thought and glanced at himself and his hat in the rearview mirror. Four more residents of Algren, minus one, equals three. And no potentially dead or dying at the moment either, thought Hosea. He drummed his fingers on top of the steering wheel and told himself not to worry, not to worry. He parked the car in the garage and went into his house through the kitchen door. He hoped Lorna was there, in bed where he had left her. He would put his cold hands on her warm thighs and she would say —

100

"Hosea! You're too early!" screeched Lorna. She had flour all over her face and hair and the kitchen smelled wonderful.

"Oops," said Hosea. "I am?"

"Yes, you are, and where did you get that hat? You know, it actually looks good on you! But what the hell are you doing home so early?" She'd said *urr-lee*.

Hosea stopped for a brief second to reflect on that just, You're early! Three babies and Max and no potentially dead other than Leander and now Lorna's hinting at his home being hers, too, which would mean three babies, Max, and Lorna, as new residents of Algren, which would be next to impossible to level off before July first, the day the Prime Minister, his father, the man his mother had said, on her deathbed, was his father, had promised to come and see him — well, see Algren. All of Algren. Well, he had promised to see Canada's smallest town and Hosea hoped that would be Algren. But. Grrr.

"I'm home early because . . . I love you. And what are you doing?"

"I'm baking, Hose, what does it look like?" Lorna was dragging one finger down a page of a recipe book and moving her lips.

"What are you baking?" asked Hosea.

"I'm baking cinnamon buns, Hosea. The smell of cinnamon buns, for a guy, is an aphrodisiac more powerful than all the perfumes on the market, did you know that?"

Oh, Lorna, thought Hosea. I don't need an aphrodisiac with you. Just the mention of your name and I melt. I . . . melt.

"No, I didn't know that," said Hosea. "Well, good. That should help."

Lorna turned around and put one hand on her hip and the other held the recipe book with her middle finger stuck in at the right place.

"What do you mean that will *help*, Hosea?" she said. "Help with what?"

"With us?" he said, knowing, just knowing it was all wrong.

"What do we need help with, exactly?" asked Lorna.

"Um . . . I don't know. I mean, with nothing. We're fine. Right?"

"What are you trying to say, I don't make you hot anymore? You need a fucking cinnamon bun to get turned on?"

"No! You said it. I didn't say that. You said cinnamon buns were more of an aphro —"

"I know what the fuck I said, okay, Hosea?"

"Okay. Let's go back to it then. Say it again. Please? Please?"

"God, you're hopeless, Hosea. Okay, did you know that cinnamon buns are a more powerful aphrodisiac than all the perfumes in the world?" Lorna spoke in a bored singsong voice and moved her head back and forth as if she were reciting something. Hosea was ready now.

"To hell with all the perfumes and all the cinnamon buns in the world, baby," he said. "I don't need any aphrodisiac but you!"

Lorna was laughing now with her hands on her hips and saying, "Yeah, yeah. Not gonna happen. My timer's going off in about four minutes."

sitting on the edge of the bed with her feet on the floor and her hands stretched out on her thighs. Summer Feelin' lifted each of Knute's fingers painfully high, while she talked, and let them drop. From the pinkie on Knute's left hand to the pinkie on her right and back again.

"Is Joey a girl or a boy?" she asked. Joey was the neighbour's yappy dog. Knute hated that dog but Summer Feelin' thought he was cute.

"A boy," said Knute.

"What if he's not?" S.F. asked.

"Then he's a girl."

S.F. stared at Knute, gravely, for a few seconds.

"Do you know what I'm gonna use this stuff for when it gets goopy like nail polish?" She pointed to a container of old liquid blush Dory had given her.

"Uh . . ." Knute said, pretending to rack her brain. "Nail polish?"

"Right, Mom, how'd you know?" said S.F., climbing onto Knute's lap. Knute could feel S.F. starting to quake inside. Soon her head would be back and her arms would be flapping. What's so exciting? Knute wondered. Joey? Nail polish?

"Is he coming back just to see me?" S.F. asked. She shook. Knute knew who S.F. meant. She'd been wondering the same thing. No, she thought to herself, he's run out of money and probably has some type of venereal disease that requires antibiotics and that's why he's coming back.

"Yes, my darling," she said and wrapped her arms around S.F. "You're the main reason he's coming back."

"I knew it," said S.F. Knute fell over like a tree and her head hit Summer Feelin's pillow. She couldn't stop it from happening any longer. She closed her eyes and remembered Max. His hair, his smile, the way he talked, the way he smoked, the way he became maudlin when he drank too much wine, how he hardly ever took anything seriously, the passionate promises he made, how he took care of Combine Jo, how he hardly ever lost his temper, his hands, his stupid jokes, his laugh, his voice, his letters that stopped coming.

"Mom, Mom, don't sleep."

"I'm not sleeping, S.F."

"What are you doing?"

"I'm resting."

"Don't rest."

"Summer Feelin'," Knute said. "Do you think it's kind of selfish of Max just to come and go whenever he

104

pleases? Do you wonder why he hasn't come to see you at all and you're already four years old?"

"I dunno," S.F. said. She shrugged.

Knute sat up and S.F. pulled her off the bed. It was time to make another heart-smart low-fat, low-sodium, low-cholesterol, low-excitement meal, probably of chicken breasts and rice.

"Oh, Knutie?" Dory called from some cubbyhole she

The guy with the hat. Yes. But he was very old. It's a blessing, really."

"Well then!" Knute yelled. "Bless us each and every one and pass the whiskey."

"I just thought you might be interested!" said Dory. "For Pete's sake!"

"Hey, Mom!" Knute yelled. "Why don't you crawl out of that hole and come and hang out in the kitchen with us while I make supper."

"I'll be right there," Dory yelled back. "Put the coffee on!"

"Will do," said Knute, chasing S.F. into the kitchen with wild eyes and singing into the back of her neck, quietly, "He's dead, he's dead, he's given up his bed, he's said all that he's said, away his life has sped, his body's left his head, give us his daily bread," and Summer Feelin' had to laugh in spite of herself. Thank God, thought Knute.

★ ★ ★

Lorna was on her way home. Everything had gone quite well, thought Hosea, very well really, except for the end when she had said, "Oh, Hosea, you know I think about living with you, having a nice easy life together, you know, just . . . being together."

Nice? Easy? Could life be that way, Hosea thought, nice and easy?

Could it? And the two of them together? Obviously she meant in Algren. How could the mayor of the smallest town up and move to the big city? Well, he couldn't, thought Hosea. And after she'd said what she'd said, Hosea had pawed his chest a few times, and said, "Oh you." "Oh *you?*" Lorna had said. "Oh *you?* That's all you can say, Hosea? Oh *you?*" But he hadn't meant it that way. He hadn't meant it to sound like Oh you, you're such a silly kid. But oh you, oh you, oh YOU, my Lorna, my love. Hosea understood how Lorna might have misunderstood. He'd mumbled it into his tugging hand and looked down when he'd said it and had wanted to carry her back to his car, to his house, their house, to their bed, to bring the exercise bike out into the open and have Lorna's sexy, lively colourful stuff all over the place, instead of sad things like Euphemia's tablecloths and ancient jars of Dippity-Do, and forget about his stupid plan and live in honesty, the two of them, day to day, with July first coming and going like just another hot summer memory and not a looming deadline.

God knows how long it would be before Lorna came for another visit, or called to invite him over there,

106

which was always exciting to think about but when he actually got there, to the city, to her apartment, to the cafés and bars and theatres and universities and health food stores and bookstores, he always felt like an idiot, like a big goofy farmboy on a school field trip, riding a big orange bus that said Algren Municipality Elementary School, and Lorna saying "Hi, hi there,

remembered running into a little grocery store and asking to use the telephone and the guy said, "No, no, sorry no." Then, when he got back to his burning car, some kids in the neighbourhood had pelted him with hard, wet snowballs, laughing and yelling at him, "Let it burn! Let it burn!" No, he much preferred to have Lorna in his little house in Algren, baking cinnamon buns, just the two of them. And then, oh stupid me, he thought, that's just what Lorna had said she wanted, too, and he'd said, "Oh you," which she decided he meant as Oh you, that's a crazy romantic notion that really has no place in our lives, when he'd meant the opposite, and wanted the very same thing, but how could he tell her Algren didn't have room for her? She would have to be counted and he didn't have enough dying people to level it off. How could someone tell somebody else something like that? Could Lorna wait until after July first? Hosea shook his head slowly. She would have to, oh please.

Hosea had tried to get her attention but the bus just drove away under a sky the colour of glue and Lorna stared straight ahead. Hosea picked up a piece of hard snow and chucked it at her window and smiled and waved, but she had looked at him with one of those withering looks, a look that said, Chucking hard pieces of snow against my section of bus window will not thaw my frozen heart.

Hosea walked over to the chunk of snow, the one he had chucked at Lorna's window, and looked at it. The snow around it was dusty from the exhaust fumes of the bus. Hosea gently kicked the chunk of snow towards the sidewalk. He walked up to it and kicked it again, a little harder, to get over the ridge of snow that lined the sidewalk. Up and over, there it went. Hosea continued kicking the chunk of snow towards home. It was getting smaller and smaller. He hoped he could get it home before it disappeared. Gentle kicks, but long distances. Scoop it from underneath with the top of your foot. That was the trick. He shouldn't be doing this, he thought. What if somebody saw him, the mayor of Algren, kicking a piece of snow down the sidewalk? Well, it wasn't far to his house, and besides he'd done it as a boy, with Tom. They'd pick their chunks, inspecting them closely to make sure they were pretty much exactly the same size and weight, and then home they'd go. When they got home, if their chunks of snow hadn't disappeared or been kicked so far they got lost, they'd play hockey with one of them until it did disappear and then, for a big laugh, they'd continue to play with it. It wasn't there but they'd play with it anyway, taking slapshots, scoring goals, having it dropped by imaginary referees at centre ice, skating like crazy down the ice to catch the rebound off their sticks. Often, they would argue about goals, the puck being offside, illegal penalty shots, all that stuff, and they'd

down in the snow and stomped on it once for all she was worth and then picked the flattish thing up and tossed it over to them. They'd used it for a while, and Euphemia stood washing dishes looking out at them in the back lane and smiling, and then they'd gone to the front of the house, to the street, where Euphemia wasn't as sure to watch them, and went back to their imaginary puck.

It was Sunday. Algren was dead. Hosea slowly made his way home. As he walked past the back of the Wagon Wheel Café, Mrs. Cherniski, the owner of the café, poked her head out of the kitchen and said, "Hey, Hosea!" Hosea's head snapped up like a fish on a line, but not before he made a mental note of where his chunk of ice had stopped.

"Hello, Mrs. Cherniski, how goes the battle?" said Hosea.

"So that is you, I was wondering," said Mrs. Cherniski, "with that hat and everything. Looks like old Leander gave you his hat before he passed on. Nice of him. But I'd have it cleaned, if I was you."

"Yes, I should, I suppose," said Hosea, thinking that all its filth and wear was what he loved about it.

"Well," said Mrs. Cherniski, "I'll tell you something. If you don't get rid of that damn black dog out there, the one hanging around the front of my shop, I'll shoot the damn thing myself, not a word of a lie."

"Oh no," said Hosea, "don't do that. I'll find out who owns that dog and make sure they keep him on a line from now on."

"Well good, you better," said Mrs. Cherniski. "Last night I had thirty people in my store, you know the Whryahha clan up for the son's wedding, a private booking. I was serving roast beef and lobster bisque and damned if that dog isn't sitting outside right there on the sidewalk, his rear end twitching in the wind. Then, dammit, he's hunkering down in front of all the Whryahha's in their Sunday best, and I see he's having a shit right there on the path."

Hosea adjusted his hat and glanced at his chunk of ice. He shook his head in mock alarm for Mrs. Cherniski's sake and said, "Hmmmph, that's not very good."

"No it isn't," said Mrs. Cherniski. "A tableful of those Whryahhas just up and left, they couldn't finish their meals and they weren't about to pay for them, having to eat while a mangy mutt craps away right there in front of them. I damn well lost close to two hundred

110

dollars last night, not to mention my reputation. Thank God I'm the only café in town, but Jesus, Hosea, you have to do something about that dog."

"You're absolutely right, Mrs. Cherniski. I'll see to it pronto. In the meantime, you might want to try shooing it away, maybe a little kick."

"A little kick, my ass," muttered Mrs. Cherniski. "I'll ~~knock the goddamn~~ thing right between the —" but she

and if he ever found the money for paint. Bright ~~would be nice,~~ maybe with a huge decal of a white horse that would wind itself around the tower's entire circular top. He looked at the boarded-up feed mill and thought of turning it into a type of make-work project for the youth of Algren during the summer months. Perhaps they could turn it into a junior summer stock theatre for tourists passing through, on their way west to Vancouver, or east to Toronto. A quaint prairie play, maybe Lawrence Hamm could donate an old thresher that they could paint and put in the front of the theatre as a symbolic monument to a bucolic past. Now Hosea's mind began to spin.

He passed a couple of kids walking down the street. Their jackets were open and they were wearing rubber boots. "Hello there," he said, "beautiful spring day, isn't it?" The kids smiled and said, "Hi." They knew who he was but they didn't respond to his comment about the beautiful day. As a rule, thought Hosea, and he must remember this in the future, kids do not respond to comments about the weather. He stole a glance over his shoulder, making sure the kids weren't looking back at him, and then quickly retrieved his chunk of ice from the gutter of the road. He had overkicked. Suddenly Hosea wondered to himself what Euphemia had done all day when he was away in school.

"Penny for your thoughts," she'd say to him when he came home from school, and he'd smile and make something up and she'd give him a nickel or a dime but he never asked her what she was thinking about.

One day Hosea came home early because he had an earache, and he found Euphemia doing a handstand on a kitchen chair, gripping the nubby edge of it with her fingers and bicycling her legs around and around up in the air above her head. When she noticed him staring at her, she slowly brought her legs down to the floor and put the chair back beside the table. Then she'd laughed. "You know how it is, Hosea," she'd said. No, he didn't. He had not been amused. He was uncomfortable and alarmed. Why was his mother doing handstands on the kitchen chair? Had she lost her mind? Was she planning to run away and join the circus? Was she a freak? A Buddhist?

He had not been too impressed with that display of athleticism, yet later that evening he tried to do the same thing and could not. Therefore, he surmised at the time, it wasn't something someone could just do on command, and so she must spend her days practising

112

this sort of thing. This is what she must do while I'm in school, he'd concluded. His question answered. But why?

You know how it is, Hosea, she'd said. Now, as Hosea walked along kicking his piece of snow, he understood. Handstands on kitchen chairs, chunks of ice we can't

... disappear until we're home. That's how it is at a

Funk family had told anyone about Euphemia being Hosea's real mother, not even Minty with her big, flapping, eleven-year-old mouth. Even if one of her little brothers had paid attention to the whole brouhaha the night the truth was revealed and then, innocently, mentioned to one of their friends' mothers, "You know what, my sister Phemie is Hosie's real mom," the friend's mother would have said sweetly, "that's right, dear, she is, of course she is, now run along and play."

Euphemia's father had made arrangements for Euphemia to live in the house on First Street rent free. The owner of the house, in exchange, was given a few acres of land by Euphemia's father. Euphemia's father farmed the land but anything reaped from those acres was sold and the money given to the owner of the house.

Just about everybody in Algren, except Leander Hamm — but he didn't really give it much thought —

was under the impression that Euphemia had taken it upon herself to raise this child, Hosea. She was an unmarried so-called mother of a mystery boy. She had committed no sin, of course, because the boy wasn't hers biologically, they thought. The people of Algren were moved by her generosity and her devotion to the boy. It was a simple story with a familiar heroine, one of their own. A mysterious man on a horse gives Euphemia Funk a newborn baby when she's outside using the biffy, and Euphemia, a trooper from the start, accepts her lot, smiles at her fate, and raises the boy. Not only does she raise the boy, she raises him to be the mayor of Algren and the man responsible for its claim to fame, a fame that overshadows that unfortunate cockroach story laid out in the encyclopedia, a fame that makes the Prime Minister and the entire nation take note, a fame that comes with being the smallest town in the country.

But at the beginning, when Hosea was a little boy, the townspeople had no idea he would become their mayor. All they knew was that Euphemia Funk, a girl with so much going for her, had sacrificed it all to raise a child alone. And, furthermore, she didn't seem to mind.

The local churches brought her meals two or three times a week, the wealthier folks in town brought her their ironing and had her do their Christmas baking and sew their curtains and babysit their kids when they went to the city for a night out. Euphemia was almost always paid extravagantly for these jobs and was always promised more work in the future. Euphemia's neighbours would shovel her walk and trim her hedges and clean her eavestrough and mow her lawn in the summertime. Tom's mom gave Hosea all of Tom's old clothes and some new ones, and baked Hosea's favourite meal, Pork Diablo, whenever he stayed for supper.

At first, when Euphemia's parents and brothers and sisters would come to visit, her father would stay

nothing had happened. He missed Hosea more than he thought he would, and a very small and non-verbal part of him admired Euphemia for her spunk and her amazing lie that wasn't really a lie. But he would not set foot in that house. After all, he could make a statement, too. Let Euphemia's mother and Minty and the boys traipse in like they were going to a Sunday school picnic and not the quarters of an unmarried mother and her bastard son, arms full of cookies and sweetmeat pies and strong coffee, table games and crokinole, good cheer and hugs and kisses. He would sit in his truck. Until one day Tom's mother who lived right across the street came by and poked her head into Mr. Funk's cab.

"Have you got an aversion to family gatherings, Mr. Funk? Or are you afraid someone will steal your truck if you leave it alone for a minute? You know, I could have my boy Thomas watch it for you, ha ha ha. Like New

York City. You know, where you pay a little boy from the ghetto a nickel to make sure nobody nicks your automobile, or strips the hubcaps —"

"I was just going in," Mr. Funk growled. "Thank-you for your consideration."

From that day forward, Mr. Funk dutifully entered Euphemia's house along with his wife and the kids and set himself up in the dining room as the king of crokinole. He taught the kids, including Hosea and Tom, the combination shot, the straight-to-the-gonads shot, the right-between-the-eyes shot, and the triple lutz. It was the perfect appointment for him. He could avoid conversation and, at the same time, could release his frustration and self-righteous indignation each and every time he curled his middle finger to his thumb and let fire another crokinole rock.

Euphemia and Minty and Mrs. Funk drank coffee in the kitchen and talked and laughed and the words "oh well," "one more cup," "what's the rush" were always punctuated with the vicious crack of a crokinole piece from the next room.

Well, thought Hosea as he walked along kicking his piece of ice, she must have done more than handstands on kitchen chairs. He was just about home now and Lorna's face came pushing and shoving into his thoughts and the picture of Euphemia upside down churning her long thin legs in the air was gone. Hello, Lorna, I'm sorry, Hosea said to the image of her face in his mind. His piece of ice had made it and just before he went into his house he gave it one last kick up and over his little fence into his neighbour's yard.

"Hey, Hosea, didja hear?" He whirled around to face his other neighbour, Jeannie, who had appeared on her front steps from out of nowhere.

"What's that, Jeannie?"

"Veronica Epp," she said. "She's had her triplets."

"Oh?" said Hosea.

open to have the third? Jeannie shook her head and stared at the ground.

"No. No, I can't," said Hosea.

"Who could?" muttered Jeannie, still staring at the ground and shaking her head. Hosea was about to say Well, can't be easy or something like that and go inside but Jeannie wasn't finished. "They were going to rush her to the city, but, you know, they didn't. No time."

"Ah," said Hosea. "Well."

"So Veronica says seeing as how she went to so much work to have these three babies, she should at least be able to name one of them. Makes sense to me, right, but you know Gord her husband always does the naming, he's that kind of a guy. And he likes names like Ed and Chuck and Dirk and Todd, you know, names that sound like farts. So Gord says, Well, maybe one of them. I heard all this from Rita, you know Rita from the labour pool, she works with Dory, Tom's wife?"

"Hmmmm," said Hosea.

"So he says, Well, maybe one of them, right? And she says, Then again, maybe I should name them all, seeing as I'm the one who says their names the most, like all day every day and I like to say names I like, if I'm going to say them over and over again, she says to Gord, right, according to Rita. And Gord says, No way, you can name one, the one with the slow start because he'll probably turn out to be a mama's boy, anyway. Okay, so this makes Veronica really mad, right, and she says What do you mean by that? And he says Well, you know, kids with lung problems, wheezing and clinging and skinny, the slow starter had some lung problems, the doctor says. But that's all taken care of, she says, and she's really mad, right, and tells Gord to leave the hospital."

"Right," said Hosea.

"In the meantime, she names all three of the boys, fills out the forms for vital stats and gives them to the nurse to mail to the city and get this, Hosea, their names are . . . are you ready?"

"Uh, yeah," said Hosea.

"Their names are, now let's see if I remember, their names are Finbar, you know after that saint of lost souls or whatever he is, Callemachus, after I don't know who, somebody Greek, and Indigo. Like the colour, you know, of jeans?"

Hosea was quiet for a moment. Jeannie was staring at him with her mouth open in one of those frozen poses of suspended laughter and shock where the one suspended waits for the other to twig and then they

118

both collapse in hysterics. Hosea didn't understand this type of gesture, however, and said, "Um, is there more?" His hand moved to his chest and he managed to tug at his jacket with his Thinsulate gloves.

"No, Hosea, that's it. I thought it was funny. You know, Gord will freak when he hears their names, of course he'll probably illegally rename them or something or refuse to call them by name at all, but good-bye.

"Say," said Jeannie, "hold on, where'd you get that hat? Isn't that whatsisname's, the —"

Hosea let the door slam behind him.

Hosea hung up his jacket and laid his gloves and Leander's old hat on the bench in the hallway. He heard the fridge heave and shudder. The kitchen lights flickered for a second while the fridge sucked every available bit of energy in the house. Hosea looked inside his fridge. Half an onion, dry and curled at the edges, a tub of expired sour cream, and the leftovers of the last meal he had shared with Lorna. There's something wrong with my fridge, he thought. All this energy for a rotting onion and love's leftovers. The phone rang. Lorna, thought Hosea. He picked up the phone and said hello.

"Jeannie here," said Jeannie. "One more thing. Apparently the Epps aren't thrilled with Dr. François.

They say Veronica should have been transferred to the city and they're just lucky all three boys survived. So, are you there?"

"Yes," said Hosea.

"So anyway, Rita told me they might sue and Dr. François is getting riled by the whole thing, because the point is, of course, that the boys are all okay. He says even if he had transferred her, the problems she was having would have occurred in the city, too, and the procedure would have been exactly the same. So . . . anyway."

"Okay, then, thanks," said Hosea.

"Hey, by the way," said Jeannie, "when do you find out about Baert's visit? Is he coming?"

"Yes," said Hosea, giving his middle finger to the receiver. "Well, maybe. I don't know at this point. Good-bye." And he hung up the phone. Well, he thought to himself. Hmmm . . . if Dr. François is getting riled he just might leave Algren. He's always hated it here, after all. That would be one less, let's see, that might work . . . and Hosea went through the numbers dance in his head. But how could the hospital function without a doctor? Well maybe it could, just until after the Prime Minister's visit, thought Hosea. Obviously he had work to do. Tomorrow he would have to drive out to Johnny Dranger's farm and tell him he was outside the town limits, again. He would call Lorna and beg her to forgive him for his stupid remarks and maybe he could even explain what it was he was trying to do. That he had a good reason for not asking her to move in with him, and that very soon, in the fall, after the Prime Minister's visit, it would all be different. And he'd have to ask Knute to do something about that black dog. And check into renovating that old feed mill, and painting the water tower. And he'd have to ask her if she'd heard from Max. Fair enough. He could relax. He poured himself a glass of wine and put on his new Emmylou Harris tape. He sat down on the couch and looked around his house. He looked at his tapered

had a sip of the wine. He remembered his exercise bike, hidden behind the furnace. What was it that mattered most in a man's life? He just didn't know. And he didn't know how to find out and he didn't know if ever he did find out he would know what it was he was finding out. Hosea had another sip of wine from his glass. Now his hand was on his forehead. Okay, Hosea, he thought, time to pull your wagons in a circle, time to cut bait, time to, whatever, something, for Christ's sake, the tears were streaming down his face now as Emmylou's voice, pure and high, settled in around him, sweet as mother's milk.

CHAPTER
SEVEN

The TV in Tom and Dory's room droned on, accompanying Tom and Dory's prodigious snoring routine. Summer Feelin' creaked in her bed and sighed, dreaming of who knew what, and the moon outside was portentous. Knute opened her window for the first time that spring. The screens were still stored for the winter so she could stick her head right out into the darkness. Everything was wet and shiny. The snow fell like chunks of warm cake. She lay down on her narrow bed and fell asleep.

"Hey," Max whispered, "hey, Knute? Knutie? Are you there? It's me."

He had his head in her room, sticking through the open window like a bear trying to get his face into somebody's tent. But Knute couldn't see him in the dark, she could only hear him. Then she felt his hand kind of batting at her blanket down around her feet and he was saying quietly, "Oh God, I hope it's you, Knutie, and not Tom. Knute. Knute. I am an asshole, I know it. Talk to me, please? Knutie, my ribs are breaking on this windowsill, say something to me. C'mon, Knutie, just say hello or something, or fuck off, Max, whatever you feel like. C'mon, Knutie. My ass is getting soaked out here, you know it's raining, Knute? Spring is here. I'm here. What are you, dead? Talk to me . . ."

Knute hadn't actually been conscious for most of that. She thought she was dreaming and she was finding the whole thing funny. Until he said, "Spring is here. I'm here," and it dawned on her and she was awake. And then she didn't know what to say. She lay

"In the next room."

"Really? In the next room?" was all Max said for a long time. And they listened to each other breathe for a minute or two.

"Why don't you come out here?" he said, and he batted at the blanket again. Knute sighed heavily.

"I guess she's sleeping?" whispered Max. Knute didn't know what to say. "Knute?" said Max. "Will you come out and talk to me?"

"Okay, hang on," said Knute. "It's raining?"

"Yeah," said Max.

"Okay, hang on."

And then there they were, outside in the rain, standing and staring at each other, not really knowing what to say or how to act. Smiling, then frowning, then smiling again, looking off into the distance, looking at each other, wiping rain off their faces. Finally, Max asked,

"What's she like, Knutie?" and Knute started to cry, she couldn't help it, and he, the favourite fuckster from afar, just stood and from time to time put his hand out towards her without touching her.

Finally he put his arm around her shoulder and she said something like "Don't you fucking put your arm around me."

And he said, "Fine," and dropped it, lit a cigarette and stood there, looking off towards the neighbours'.

"Here," he said. He gave her his lit cigarette and then lit another one for himself. Then they kind of blurted out at the same time, Knute with "You're such a fuck-up," and him with "I know, I know." Then more staring off and smoking.

"Well, Knute, it's been really nice chatting with you."

"Fuck off."

"Hey."

"What."

"Knute?"

"What."

"You're gonna let me see her, aren't you?"

"Oh, well . . ." Knute said, and Max smiled. "Actually, no," Knute continued, "no I'm not, never, well, maybe in four years, you kept her waiting, now it's her turn to keep you waiting."

"Hey, good one. I could wait longer, you know, five, six, twenty-five years, it's up to you, I'll just wait. Starting now. Okay. I'm waiting. You just let me know, give me a sign. I'm here. I'm waiting." Max leaned up against the brick next to the front door and stood there, arms folded, looking down at his wet boots.

"Okay," said Knute, "you wait right here. I'm going in to call the cops."

"All right," said Max, and he tipped an imaginary hat. "Buenas noches." A few minutes later Knute came back outside.

"Well?" said Max.

"There aren't any cops in Algren."

"C'mon, Knutie, let me see her, just let me have one

Dinesen armed and living alone in the savannah or wherever. Blow his head off and nobody would ever know. She wasn't a member of Shining Path. She wasn't Camille Paglia. She let him in and they tiptoed, in their huge combat boots, down the hall to Summer Feelin's room. Max kneeled at S.F.'s bed and stared at her for about ten minutes, like he was at a viewing in a funeral home. The reverent Max. Knute sat at the kitchen table praying Tom and Dory wouldn't wake up.

"I think you should go now," Knute whispered to Max after the ten minutes or so were up. He stood up then but he didn't leave. He swallowed. Knute didn't want to look at him because she thought he might be crying. She hoped he was. Then he said, "So you think . . . you know you think she's warm enough and . . ." He kept his eyes on S.F. and didn't look at Knute.

"Yeah," she said, "I think she'll live through the night." Max smiled.

Outside they shared another cigarette. "I quit for a while," he said.

"Yeah?" said Knute. "That's good." Then Max was grinning, then laughing. "What are you laughing at?" Knute asked.

"Summer Feeling," he said, and he was laughing and coughing, rain falling all over his face, "Oh excuse me, Feelin'. Fee-Lin. Oh God, Knute, you kill me," he said.

Knute sat in the living room and stared out the window for a while after he had left. The rain had stopped. She watched the moon move towards the other end of Algren, somewhere over Hosea Funk's house, probably, or it could have been the other side of the world for all she knew. "Summer Feelin'," she said a few times. "Summer Feelin', Summer Feelin'." Pretty stupid, she thought, shaking her head. She couldn't stop grinning.

All right, I'm up. I'm up. I'm up! I'll fight Tyson. I'll fight Ali, I'll fight, that's it, I'm fighting, thought Hosea. Cassius Clay. I could change my name, he thought. Hosea Ali. Mohammed Funk. Mo Funk. Hosea sighed. Lorna, he thought. Lorna Funk. Lorna Funk, Lorna Funk. He was alone. "Listen to me," he said out loud. The telephone rang. "I got it," said Hosea. The phone quit after one ring. Hosea sighed again. And got up to make some coffee.

First thing that morning, after exercising, he was off to see Johnny Dranger. He would just tell it like it was. Lay it on the table. Let Johnny know he was out again. I'm sorry, Johnny, he'd say. There's been yet another mix-up at the top. They say your farm is outside the town limits of Algren. Johnny wouldn't be happy about it, he knew. Johnny had one passion in life. Putting out fires. He had worked himself up to assistant chief of the Algren volunteer fire department, and was hankering after the number one position. It was his dream. But he couldn't be a volunteer — let alone fire chief — with the Algren fire department if he didn't live within the

living right in Algren and a couple of women, including Jeannie, Hosea's next-door neighbour, wanting to be put on the roster. I like to help out where I can, she'd told Hosea. Occasionally, there'd be a major house fire — once there was a tragedy involving some drunken teenagers — but mostly it was putting out burning outhouses, overheated cars, kitchen fires, and stubble fires. That was Johnny Dranger's specialty. He had it in for stubble burners. But, thought Hosea, the farmers around here don't start burning their stubble until harvest time, and by then he could be back in. I'll make it up to him, thought Hosea, I'll crown him fire chief of Algren after July first, and he'll be in charge just in time to get those darn stubble burners.

Hosea drove down First Street, turned onto Main Street, crossed over the tracks, and began driving down the service road that ran alongside the dike that surrounded Algren. The dike was supposed to protect

Algren from the raging flood-waters of the Rat River. The Rat River, thought Hosea. My ancestors landed in Halifax, hopped on a train going west, then crept up the Rat River and settled in Algren, Manitoba. My mother's dead, my father is the Prime Minister of the country, I think, and I am the mayor of Canada's smallest town and the spurned lover of the bold and beautiful Lorna Garden.

Hosea peered around the countryside. Dirt everywhere and grey snow, dog shit, ugly cows, puffs of steam coming out of their snouts and their rear ends, the smell of wet hay, and the sky that brilliant blue, the colour of toilet bowl cleanser. Hosea heard a screech, a voice. "Hosea, stop, stop!" Mrs. Cherniski the café owner was running down her long driveway wearing what looked like Shaquille O'Neal's basketball shoes and waving a rake around her head. "Get him, Hosea, get that motherfucking dog away from my Pat, goddamn it if he . . . that's it, he's mounting her, Hosea, get him, get him . . ."

Hosea scrambled out of his car and stood there for a minute, straightening his hat, trying to figure out what was going on. "Stop him, Hosea, for Christ's sake!" Mrs. Cherniski had slowed down by now and had her hand on her chest. The last part of her command to Hosea seemed to be swallowed up by tears and rage. She threw her rake as far as she could, spluttering and moaning, "Stop him, oh God, please stop him," and then crumpled into a heap on her driveway.

Hosea stood, frozen to the spot. Was she dead? A heart attack? For a split second he thought of his plan.

Wouldn't that be a stroke of luck, after all, if Mrs. Cherniski was dead? He glanced at the dogs and ran over to Mrs. Cherniski who, by this point, was sitting on the driveway cross-legged and catatonic, shaking her head and muttering, "Bill Quinn, his name is Bill Quinn."

"What's that, Mrs. Cherniski?" said Hosea. "Who's Bill Quinn?"

bad blood coursing through his veins. That dog's the devil's best friend, loyal to the end . . ." Mrs. Cherniski stared straight ahead and spoke in a monotone. "I should have known when I saw him hanging around my café, driving my customers away with his disgusting antics. I should have known he'd be after my Pat next."

"How do you know his name?" asked Hosea.

"I know," said Mrs. Cherniski. "I just know."

"But," said Hosea. "I don't mean to upset you further, Mrs. Cherniski, but isn't it sort of a natural thing for dogs to do, especially now that spring is here?" Hosea couldn't help but steal another peek at the dogs. He turned back to look at Mrs. Cherniski but she was asleep or dead, not moving, anyway — laid out flat now on the wet driveway, basketball shoes pointing up to Polaris, up towards the brilliant blue sky.

Okay, what? thought Hosea. What do I do? "Mrs. Cherniski?" he said, without touching her. "Mrs.

129

Cherniski?" Nothing. Not a peep. She can't be dead, thought Hosea. Just because of . . . of Bill Quinn? Hosea got up and began to run. He ran up the driveway and across the yard and into Mrs. Cherniski's house. The TV was on and the room smelled like vanilla. He found the phone in the hallway and called the hospital.

"Charlie Orson Memorial Hospital, how may I direct your call?"

"What?" said Hosea. Is this a joke? he thought.

"How may I help you? Hello? Hello?"

"It's Hosea Funk."

"Oh God, Hosea, not you again. Now what? Do you want to know what we're serving for lunch? Or maybe —"

"No, no, Dr. Bon — sorry, François — it's Mrs. Cherniski. You know, the woman who owns the Wagon Wheel."

"Yes? What about her?"

"She's lying in her driveway," said Hosea. "I don't know if she's dead or alive. She just collapsed. There's this dog and —"

"Wait. In her driveway?"

"Yes."

"At her house or at the Wagon Wheel?"

"House."

"Okay, I'll be right there. Go back to her and loosen her clothing and see if you can get her to talk to you. You could try doing artificial respiration. I'll be there in three minutes."

Five minutes later Dr. François and Nurse Barnes and Lawrence Hamm, who happened to be the volunteer driver, had Mrs. Cherniski strapped to a gurney and ready to be loaded into the back of the ambulance. The doctor had found her pulse but it was weak and her breathing was irregular and shallow. Thankfully, Hosea had thrown his hat into his car before Lawrence Hamm had driven up. Surely he

ambulance. "Yes," whispered Hosea under his breath, and then, "no, no."

What kind of a . . . Hosea thought. Well, say she died, say Mrs. Cherniski didn't make it, at least she'd be rid of that Bill Quinn character. But then again, he didn't want to wish death upon her, not really, that is. Maybe she won't die but she'll be incapable of looking after herself and she'll have to move in with her daughter in the city. Even if just until July first. By then she'll be fit as a fiddle and she'll be able to come back to Algren and work in the café. Hosea looked over at the dogs. Pat was snapping at some flying thing and Bill Quinn was lying in a puddle, asleep. Bill Quinn, thought Hosea. In a strange and stupid way he admired Bill Quinn.

This is ridiculous, he thought. Bill Quinn has got to go. And I have to get to Johnny Dranger's place and give him the news. Three babies and Max, if he gets here, that's four in; Leander dead and Johnny Dranger put outside town limits, that's two out. Two more out and we're even-steven. If Mrs. Cherniski dies, just one. And Bill Quinn doesn't count, thought Hosea. He tugged at his chest and gazed up at the sky. He'd stay on course. Things would fall into place. He'd see to it. "Prime Minister Baert," he rehearsed, "I'm your son, Hosea Funk, Euphemia's boy. Welcome to Algren, Canada's smallest town."

Bill Quinn, roused by Hosea's voice, lifted his head and stared at Hosea. One watery brown eye closed for a split second and then opened again. But Hosea missed it. He was a million miles away and it didn't matter how many dirty dogs winked at him from wet ditches. He wasn't kidding about his plan. It was on.

"Catch a falling star and put it in your pocket," Hosea sang as he drove up Johnny's driveway. He'd put his hat back on. "Save it for a rainy day." He looked up and noticed that the sky had changed. From the colour of toilet bowl cleanser to the colour of dust. Johnny will know what's up before I even open my mouth, thought Hosea. And it was true. Before Hosea could properly park the Impala in the tiny driveway, Johnny was out of the house and trotting towards him. "So!" he shouted at Hosea from about twenty yards away. "Don't tell me, I'm out. Or am I in? Was I out or am I out now? In or out? Out or in? What's it gonna be this time, Your Excellency?"

Hosea smiled and got out of his car. He was about to shake his head and say, "I'm sorry, John, there's been

132

another mix-up at the top" when Johnny began to shake his head and clear his throat. "I'm sorry, John," said Johnny, "there's been another mix-up at the top." Hosea tried to speak again but Johnny spoke first. "I don't get it, Hosea, who's the Mickey Mouse at the top? And at the top of what? The idiot list? I feel like a Fisher-Price farmer with a Fisher-Price barn and animals. Some moron kid plops me onto the little

removed his quickly and put it inside his car. He still hadn't figured out a way of explaining to people why he was wearing dead Leander Hamm's hat.

"No, I know you're not, John," said Hosea. "You're not a toy." Hosea didn't know what else to say. Johnny stood there glaring at him.

"But I'm out, right?" he said. "Out again, isn't that so, Hosea? Isn't that what you're trying to tell me?"

"It's just that this particular piece of land is, well, has always been, a real trouble spot. It goes back a long way, and the province is still trying to figure out just where it belongs." Hosea's hand went to his chest.

"That's bullshit, Hosea, and you know it. You just haven't got enough to do, that's the real problem."

"Enough to do?" said Hosea. "Enough to do?"

Just then it started to pour.

"Look, Hosea," said John, "why don't you come in for a cup of coffee and I'll tell you what's wrong with this country. Guess there's no way you could put me right *out* of the country, eh, Hosea? Why quit at the municipal level? I've always wanted to live in a hot place, Myanmar, say. Or Burma, or is that the same thing? Anyway, why don't you get your pooh-bah at the top to make a really big mistake and move me and my toy barn and silo and tractor and little horses and cows all the way over to Myanmar?" Hosea looked at Johnny. He noticed Johnny had a strange way of speaking. What should have been the last word of a sentence seemed to become the first word of the sentence after it. Like, I'll tell you what's wrong with this. Country guess there's no way you could —

"I'm just kidding, Hose. C'mon in. You're not allergic to cats, are you?"

"No. No, I'm not," said Hosea. I'm just kidding, Hose. C'mon. In you're not allergic to cats, are you? Hosea repeated in his mind. Maybe he was asthmatic. Maybe it was a breathing problem. Hosea was intrigued with the way that Johnny spoke. Why hadn't he noticed it before?

"Good. I've been having problems with those damn. Cockroaches ever since Yusef. Died Tiny's not a roach eater so. I'm trying cats."

By this time they were inside and Johnny had pointed to a kitchen chair. Hosea sat on it. Johnny went over to the counter to make some coffee.

"You mean the Algren cockroach?" Hosea asked.

"The one and only," said Johnny. "Are there. Others, I mean around here?"

134

"I don't know," said Hosea. His shoulders slumped and he felt depressed. "I guess there could be," he said.

"Yeah," said Johnny, "there could be."

"Johnny," said Hosea. "I know you want to be the fire chief. I'm sorry, I . . ."

John turned around. "Hosea," he said. "I'm a farmer and a widower since the age of. Nineteen I've learned not to rely on. Anything, not my cows, not my horses,

of a plan but what that plan is I cannot begin to imagine. Hosea, in, out, what difference does it make. Anymore, I'm here in the same. Place so I can't be the fire. Chief I'll keep putting out fires just the. Same it's what I have to do doesn't. Matter what anyone calls me, chief or. Johnny I'm gonna put out fires and if some government pantywaist tells me I can't, that won't matter to me. Either a man's gotta do what a man's gotta. Do do you understand what I'm talking about, Hosea?"

"Yes," said Hosea. "Yes, I do."

"Okay," said Johnny.

"I didn't know you were ever married, John," said Hosea.

"Well, I was."

"To who?"

"Whom, you mean. To Caroline Russo."

Hosea thought for a second. "Caroline Russo?" he said. "But she was the girl who died in that house fire years ago, wasn't she? She was our age?" And then Hosea stopped. "Oh, I'm sorry, Johnny. Caroline Russo? I had no idea. Nobody knew you two were married. I'm sorry, Johnny."

"Thanks, it's. Okay it was a long time ago."

Hosea and Johnny were quiet. Both men had sips of their coffee. Hosea remembered Caroline Russo. She was wild. She was very funny.

"We took the train to the city and got married at City Hall I," said Johnny. He smiled at some memory. "Guess we eloped."

"Oh," said Hosea. He smiled too. "She was a beautiful girl."

"Oh yeah," said Johnny. He smiled again. So did Hosea. "So I put out fires."

"Yeah," said Hosea. "Yup." They smiled at each other again. There was no reason to say anything more about it. It was a neighbour's stubble fire that started it. The fire just got out of control and spread. The kids in the house were drunk and didn't have a chance. Hosea knew that Caroline Russo was five months pregnant when she died in the fire. Everybody did. Well, everybody did after the coroner's report. Nobody knew before that. Except Johnny, I guess, thought Hosea. And Hosea knew that Johnny had been one of the lucky ones. He had gone outside to piss or puke, that detail wasn't ever really clear, and then had passed out in the yard behind the house. But nobody knew Caroline was pregnant with Johnny's baby. Nobody knew they had married.

"I wanted to tell. People but I didn't at the. Beginning and then it just sort of got too late to," said Johnny. "I'm sorry."

"You don't have to be sorry, Johnny," said Hosea.

"Well, I may not have to be sorry about it, Hose, but I am sorry about. It I'm as sorry as they come."

hold him in his arms and protect him from harm, never got to show him off and call him son and sweetheart. Hosea's head hurt. He would put Johnny back. Somehow. And before July first. Maybe tomorrow. He knew Johnny would just laugh if he said, Oh, by the way you're back in. He'd have to do it soon, though. And he'd have to get Johnny the job of fire chief of Algren. He was the only man for the job. It was his destiny. And I, thought Hosea, am not God. He took a deep breath.

"So," said Johnny, "more coffee?"

"You were going to tell me what's wrong with this country," said Hosea.

"Right," said John. "Remember Yusef, my. Lab, the garbage eater?"

"Big, black . . ." said Hosea.

"Yeah," said John. "He died in the fall, sudden. Death from lead poisoning." He smiled.

"Lead poisoning?" said Hosea.

"I shot him," said John.

Hosea smiled and nodded. "Why?"

"Cancer of the. Throat I gave him two Big Macs, his favourite, put the rifle to his head and . . . Bam Yusef's. Gone didn't even know what hit. Him far as he knew he was eating a Big Mac with special sauce, box and everything." John shook his head and had a sip of his coffee. "He was a good dog, Yusef."

"Mmmmm," said Hosea. He had a sip of his coffee.

"So a couple of months before Yusef died I got Tiny, another black lab, as a. Replacement they became really good. Friends I hoped Tiny would kill cockroaches the way Yusef. Had but no. Dice Tiny's all right. Not like Yusef, mind you, but Tiny's got a head on his shoulders and his heart's in the right place."

Where had Yusef's head and heart been? thought Hosea. He had another sip and said, "Well, that's good."

"After Yusef died I buried him out. Back it was a hell of a job because the ground was beginning to freeze, but I got him in there and I said good-bye."

But what's wrong with this country? thought Hosea. "That's too bad," he said. His thoughts turned to Caroline Russo. He remembered her orange lunch box. She had called the colour eldorado nights or eldorado sunset or something like that.

"So about a week ago, when we had the first big thaw, I'm riding in the truck with Tiny and I smell something weird and I look over at him and he's got blood and hair hanging off his. Snout sure enough we

138

get home, I go out back, and I see that Tiny's been digging at Yusef's grave and then I get closer and I see that he's actually dug him right up and I see that parts of Yusef have been eaten."

"He's been eating Yusef?" asked Hosea.

"Yeah! And then I thought back to the day I buried. Yusef had Tiny been hanging around? Watching I knew he was shook up about Yusef. Dying they were good

He rubbed his hands on his thighs and began to laugh.

CHAPTER
EIGHT

Max and Knute had worked out a sort of arrangement. He looked after Summer Feelin' from quarter to ten in the morning 'til quarter after two in the afternoon. Those were the hours that Knute worked for Hosea. Although calling it work was a bit of an exaggeration. Mostly it just gave her a break from Tom and Dory and Summer Feelin'. Tom was having more chest pain lately and was feeling depressed. He had quit practising his juggling. He had quit going to the garage to read his veterinarian journals. Dory was worried about him but at the same time she was restless and annoyed. The wallpaper was coming down in sheets all over the house and she'd bought herself a new hammer. Summer Feelin' was giddy with excitement over Max's return and was doing a lot of shaking and flapping. Max and Knute hadn't really talked much about anything. They'd had coffee at the Wagon Wheel together but it was just like always. It was fun at first but then Knute would get a thought in her head and she'd start getting more and more pissed off. The more pissed off she got, the more he joked around. He joked and she glared. And then she got tired of being the sullen, injured one and she said, "Fuck this noise," and left. She really wanted to hurt him the same way he had hurt her, but she didn't know how to. The rest of the time, whenever Max and Knute were together, Summer Feelin' was with them and then, of course, everything was kind of strained. Summer Feelin' and Max adored each other and Knute hung around saying things like "Watch her head" or "She should eat lunch first." Tom and Dory were wondering if Max was going to give Knute regular

paper? Still looking for someone to publish your jottings?" And Dory had given Tom a look and said, "It's called poetry, Tom." And he had said, "Oh really," and walked away.

Once Max had asked Dory if all kids flapped as much as Summer Feelin' did and she had said, "Oh, well, that's just something she does."

He had said, "What do you mean that's just something she does? Shouldn't it be checked out or something? Has she seen a doctor about it? She looks like a hummingbird, man, she could lift off anytime." Then Dory had become irritated.

"Max," she said, "Knutie has been taking very good care of Summer Feelin' with no help from you. Of course she's been checked out. She's fine. And nobody appreciates you, of all people, second-guessing Knute's efforts." She paused and then she said, "You can just keep your mouth shut, Buster."

Max and Knute looked at her. Buster? Knute thought to herself, Dory's mad.

"Really, Knute, he has no right to come in here and question your ability to parent, I mean . . ."

And Knute had said, "I know, I know."

And Max had said, "Sorry, Dory, you're right. It was just all that fluttering and flapping, you know, I was expecting a back door to open up on her and a battalion of soldiers to jump out with flak jackets and camouflage, with somebody giving her hand signals for lift-off —"

"Oh shut up," Dory had said and then, "Excuse me," as she stalked out of the room with her hammer and a pail of plaster.

Just then Summer Feelin' came running into the room. Max said, "Hey, Summer Feelin', it's a beautiful day for collecting bottles. Get your rubber boots on and we'll hit the ditches around the dike. They're full of 'em." This idea got Summer Feelin' flapping and Max started beating his chest to make helicopter noises and saying things like "incoming," "over," "prepare troops for landing," "all clear." Knute looked at Max. At his mouth and his hands, his boots, his narrow hips.

Knute said good-bye to no one in particular and left for work. There was a lot to do. Hosea said he wanted to concentrate on painting the water tower. "Red, with a white horse running right around it," he said. And something about turning the old feed mill into a theatre for young people. Neither of these ideas seemed feasible to Knute. Maybe a red water tower, okay, but how would they get a huge white horse painted on the top of it? "Why a horse?" she'd said. "Why not just the name Algren?"

"No," Hosea said, "it should be a horse, a white horse." She told him that if they painted a horse right around the top of it, it would look like the horse was chasing its butt, like a dog with worms. Then she mentioned that even though the feed mill might make a great theatre, the youth of Algren seemed more

that black dog. This she could handle, she thought. No problem. She could find some farmer outside town, maybe in Whithers, who would want a dog, or she'd just take it into the city, to the Humane Society, and let them find a home for it.

"By the way," Hosea said, "his name's Bill Quinn."

"Bill Quinn?" said Knute. "You mean, he has a first and a last name? Bill Quinn? If he has a name, doesn't he have an owner?"

"Nope," Hosea said. "No, he doesn't. He's his own dog."

"Oh, Bill's a lone wolf, eh?"

"Yes, he is," said Hosea.

Knute was about to say, "Friend of yours?" But Hosea wasn't finished.

"Knute?" he'd said, just before walking out the door, "Please don't let him get hurt. Just get him out of town in one piece."

Knute said she'd do what she could and then sat for a minute and looked out the window on to Main Street. She saw Combine Jo sitting cross-legged on the hood of her car and looking at a magazine. She was wearing a fishing hat with hooks in it. God, she thought, that woman is S.F.'s grandmother. Knute looked the other way down Main Street and there were Marilyn and Josh! She opened the window and stuck her head out. "Marilyn! Hello!" she yelled. "What are you doing here?" Before she could answer Combine Jo yelled up at Knute.

"Hey, Knutie! I'm looking at my Canadian Tire book here, and kids' bikes are cheap! Do you think Summer Feelin' would want one? Does she ride a two-wheeler yet, or a trike? Max could teach her how to ride a two-wheeler, or we could get a two-wheeler and put the, what do you call 'em, training wheels on it. What do you think? Why don't you come down here and have a look! There is one in here with a very sharp racing stripe, and it's purple, did you know purple is S.F.'s favourite colour? And a basket would be nice, too, don't you think?"

Combine Jo pushed her fishing hat back on her head and peered up at Knute's window. She pointed to her catalogue and yelled, "It's all in here, in here!" Marilyn and Josh, by this time, were standing beside Jo's car, looking at her and up at Knute and back at Jo, and Marilyn was grinning.

"Hello," said Combine Jo.

"Marilyn!" Knute yelled from the window. "This is Jo, Max's mom, and Jo, this is Marilyn, my friend, and

144

her son, Josh." Knute felt like throwing herself out the window onto the pavement below.

"Is he here?" asked Marilyn.

"Is who here?" Knute yelled.

"Max!" she said.

"Yes, he is," said Jo. "He's got S.F. at home with him right now, or they're somewhere around, who

training wheels if you want. And, uh, thanks."

"Hear that?" said Jo to Marilyn. "That's the sound of ice breaking. Have a good time, you two," Jo said to Marilyn. "Knutie needs a friend, you know. We all do from time to time."

"That's true," said Marilyn, smiling, and disappeared into the building.

"Hey!" Jo yelled up to the window. "Knutie! Why don't you bring your friend's kid over to my house and Max can look after both of 'em? It would be good for S.F. to have a playmate for a change and then you two gals can have a real good talk, maybe a drink, Hosea wouldn't mind if you called it a day. Tell him I told you to punch out."

Knute felt like saying to Jo, "Would you shut the fuck up, please?" But instead she said, "Yeah maybe, maybe," and slammed the window shut.

Marilyn and Josh came into the office. Marilyn and Knute, both laughing by then, gave each other a big hug. "How's it going, buddy?" said Knute to Josh.

"Fine," he said. "Can I play with Summer Feelin'?"

Marilyn and Knute looked at each other. "Why didn't you tell me he was here?" Marilyn asked. "I can't believe you didn't tell me."

"I don't know," said Knute. "Because I know you would have told me to ignore him totally, or kill him, or have mad passionate et cetera, et cetera [Josh was in the room] with him, and none of those things has happened. It's all been just, you know, ordinary, really. I thought I'd be letting you down."

"Ordinary?" said Marilyn. "Well, that is too bad. But you could have told me, anyway. I need to know these things. We're best friends! You should have told me."

"I know, I know," Knute said.

"So that's Combine Jo, eh?" said Marilyn.

"Yeah." Knute rolled her eyes.

"She's cool," said Marilyn.

"Cool? Combine Jo? You gotta be kidding. She's nuts."

"Well," said Marilyn, "she wants to buy S.F. a bike, that's cool. She's nice."

"God, Marilyn, you have no idea. She's a drunk. She's crazy."

"Well," said Marilyn. "I would be, too, if I was Max's mom and if I lived in this weird town and everybody was pissed off at me for something I did a hundred years ago."

146

"I'm not pissed off at her for what she did way back then, I'm pissed off at her for telling Max to leave me when I was pregnant," said Knute.

"Well," said Marilyn. "I hate to tell you this, beautiful dreamer, but she didn't put a gun to his head."

"Oh, don't be so sure," Knute said. "Anyway, you're here. Why didn't you tell me you were coming? I need to know these things. We're best friends."

"Here we are," said Knute, smiling.

"When can I play with Summer Feelin'?" Josh asked. Knute looked over at Marilyn.

"Do you want to bring him over to Max's?"

"Sure, what the heck. I'm dying to meet him, actually. Has he changed?"

"No."

"Too bad."

"I guess."

"You're still hot for him, I can tell. Aren't you, Knute?"

Before Knute could say anything, Marilyn said, "What about this guy, this mayor dude, is he cute?"

"Cute?" Knute said. "He's old."

"So?"

"I don't think he's cute. Well, maybe. Naah. And he's got some kind of a girlfriend, her last name's Garden."

"Garden?" said Marilyn. "Weird name. Garden of Eden, forbidden fruit. What's his name? Hosea? Strange biblical setup if you ask me. Can I meet him?"

"Maybe, he's all over the place, usually. I don't know what he does most of the time."

"He could be dealing drugs," said Marilyn.

"I doubt it."

"Oh yeah," said Marilyn, "drugs to farmers. They're a very stressed-out bunch of people."

"He wants me to get rid of a dog, actually. Bill Quinn. Do you want to help me?"

"Excuse me?"

"Bill Quinn's gotta go."

"The dog?"

"Yeah."

"Sure, I'll help. How old exactly is he, Knute? Eighty, ninety?"

"Bill Quinn?"

"Hosea."

"No, no, around fifty, I think."

"Oh, pfft," said Marilyn. "That's nothing."

Knute and Marilyn liked Combine Jo's idea about the talk and the drink. While Knute was leaving a note for Hosea telling him her friend was in town and they were off to see what they could do about Bill Quinn, Marilyn opened one of his drawers and pulled out an old orange Hilroy scribbler. "Look at this. Remember these?" she said.

"Marilyn!" said Knute. "Don't go snooping around in his drawers. Put that thing back."

"Wow," said Marilyn. "Hosea's really on the cutting edge, isn't he? He doesn't even have an electric typewriter."

"Let's go," said Knute. "C'mon, Josh. S.F. will be very happy to see you." And they left.

"Bye-bye!" said Combine Jo. "You girls enjoy yourselves. And don't worry about your boy there, he'll be fine with Max. Hell, I might go home myself in a embankment with a crazy old drunk woman. Great. "Okay, Jo, just make sure it has training wheels on it. It needs training wheels."

"Righto!" said Jo. She ripped out the page from the catalogue and smiled. "Have a good time, ladies," she said, and waved them away.

"Did you see her looking at us?" said Marilyn.

"What do you mean?"

"The way she was looking at us. Wistfully like. I bet she'd like to join us for a drink. Does she have any friends, Knute, or what?"

"Oh, I don't know. Probably. Somewhere."

They walked along Main Street towards the dike road and the hatchery and Max's place. They took turns giving Josh a piggyback ride.

"You know, it really smells bad in this town," said Marilyn.

149

"Well, it's spring," said Knute, "that's all the fertilizer thawing, you know, shit on the fields."

"Oh. Real shit?"

"Yeah. Well, not human shit — animal."

"But real shit, not processed or packaged or anything?"

"Right. Raw animal shit. It might be liquidized or something, I don't know. Because they spray it on. You know, like hose it on."

"For fertilizer, eh?"

"Yup. It's the best thing. Crops, crops, crops. This high."

"Wow. But what about afterwards? You know, when we eat them, the crops. Fecal residue."

"We can't tell."

"Really? We're eating animal shit and we don't know it?"

"Well, we know it, I guess, we just don't think about it."

"But that doesn't make sense. It shouldn't stink now. There should be no fertilizer on the fields now because it would have been cut down with the crops, you know, reaped, in the fall. Wouldn't the farmers wait until spring has really sprung to put fresh shit on the fields? Like just before they plant or sow or whatever it's called?"

"Seed," said Knute. "And it's not reaped, it's harvested."

"Seed, yeah," said Marilyn.

"I don't know when they do it," said Knute.

150

"Well, spring, obviously, Knute, that's when crops are planted. That's when they need to be fertilized."

"I don't know, they could be perennials. Maybe they just come up at the same time every year. Like tulips."

"I don't think so," said Marilyn.

"I don't know," said Knute.

Over at Combine Jo's, Marilyn wandered around the

Joshua's allergic to dairy products, she finally managed to say. Knute told Max that Joshua was there to play with S.F. and she and Marilyn were going out. They'd be back around three. Max gave them a bottle of fine wine from Combine Jo's stash and half a pack of cigarettes, and suggested they go out to Johnny Dranger's rotting pile of hay bales, sit on top of it, and get hammered. They'd be able to see for miles and miles, he said. It was covered with orange plastic and sagging in the middle so if they got cold, he added, they could just hunker down in the centre and be protected from the wind.

Good idea, thought Knute, but how the hell did he know about Johnny Dranger's pile of hay?

"I go there to write," he said, grinning. Knute and Marilyn left and as soon as they were out of the house they looked at each other and said, "Yeah, right." Then Marilyn started laughing and telling Knute that Max was foxy, shorter than she had expected, nice eyes, all the stuff Knute already knew. Write, my ass, she thought. "Hang on," she said to Marilyn. She went back to the house and a few minutes later came back with another bottle — Jack Daniel's — and Marilyn said, "What about that dog? Bill Whatshisname, how're we gonna get rid of a dog from on top of a pile of hay?"

"Screw Bill Quinn," Knute said. "Let's go."

CHAPTER
NINE

clothes. He fixed his fridge and cleaned out the grout from behind the taps on the bathroom and kitchen sinks. He had planned to remove all of Euphemia's *Reader's Digest* condensed books from the small pantry in the basement. That's when he found out someone in his house had been drinking rye whiskey, and lots of it. Boxes and boxes of empty bottles had been stored, or hidden, behind the boxes of *Reader's Digests*.

Hosea had sat down on the cold cement floor. His eyes followed a crack that led to the drain hole. He remembered Tom telling him not to pee in it because he'd heard of some guy in Chicago or somewhere who had peed in his drain hole and had hit some electrical current that had travelled up the length of his stream of urine and then zap, his penis had been electrocuted and had turned black and shrivelled up right then and there. He must have been bullshitting me, thought

Hosea. He sat there and no other thoughts came to mind other than the one he had been fighting off for the last minute or two.

She was drunk when she told me the Prime Minister was my father.

No, he thought, she couldn't have been. She was on her deathbed. She couldn't walk to the pantry in the basement to get a bottle, let alone lift her head to drink from it. "Her heart simply gave out on her, Hosea," the doctor had said after she died. Her heart or her liver? She wasn't very old. Had anybody known? Had the doctor known? Why was she drinking herself to death?

He had stared at the bottles for half an hour. He had never seen her drink, never seen her drunk. Had he just not known? She had always seemed content and in control. Did she drink only at night while he slept? During the day while he was at school? Is that what she did all day? Is that why she laughed and shrugged her shoulders at just about everything? Is that why she bought so many bags of scotch mints? Is that why she did handstands on the kitchen chairs?

Oh, Lord, it doesn't matter, Hosea told himself, and smiled. He thought about tempting fate and pissing in the drain hole. Who can blame her, after all? he thought. She was alone.

Is there something bad 'bout a lady drinking all alone in a room? A letter in your handwriting . . . hmmmm, he couldn't remember what the next words were.

Rye whiskey, thought Hosea. Had he picked fresh roses from Euphemia's garden that day after school for

154

somebody who had never been there? Rye whiskey roses for a rye whiskey man. Well, thought Hosea, I'm real, anyway. "Mother," he said out loud, "was your life unbearable?" A letter in your handwriting and the scent of your perfume, I'm sorry, darling, so sorry, darling, I just assumed . . . is that how it went? Hosea hummed a little out of tune. "I'm sorry," he whispered. "I am."

He would tell Lorna about his plan. He would tell

somehow prescient, significant, romantic, and well, just right.

On that same day that he had been cleaning, Hosea had found out from Jeannie that Tom was not doing well. Nor, for that matter, was Dory. Jeannie had said both were depressed and miserable and trying to fool themselves for the sake of their daughter and granddaughter. There was more but Hosea had suddenly feigned back pain and staggered into his house explaining to Jeannie that he needed some Tylenol and an ice pack.

Hosea sat in his clean house and wondered about his old buddy Tom. Expansive, humble, tolerant Tom. Feeling bad. And worse, depressed. Well, thought Hosea. He needs a friend and that friend is me.

Hosea looked outside and noticed Euphemia's rose bush blooming for the first time that spring. A dozen roses in a bottle of rye whiskey, thought Hosea. That would cheer him up. Hosea put on his windbreaker and Leander's hat and went outside and picked some roses and stuffed them inside one of Euphemia's empty whiskey bottles.

"Hosea! Roses! C'mon in!" Dory opened the door and took the bottle of roses. "Thank-you," she said. "That's very sweet of you, Hose." Hosea thought she looked like she'd been crying.

"Well, you're welcome," he said. "You know, I looked out the window and there they were. They're for Tom, too."

"Of course," said Dory, "of course they are." Had she sighed just then? wondered Hosea. "He's in the bedroom, Hose, if you want to say hello. He's not feeling well enough to get out of bed. Just walk in. Here, bring him these." She handed him the bottle of roses and said, "I'm leaving for a while. You keep him company. He's had his pills, he won't eat, and I'll be back in half an hour. Good-bye." She smiled. "If he wakes up and wonders where I am," she said, "tell him I'll be back in half an hour. He likes to know."

Hosea sat on top of Tom and Dory's laundry hamper and stared at Tom. He was sleeping. God, thought Hosea, he looks grey. What's wrong with him?

He did look grey. He looked like Euphemia did weeks before she died. Oh no, thought Hosea. He put the roses on the bedside table, next to several jars of pills, a glass of water, Tom's reading glasses, and a *Maclean's* magazine.

156

"Tom?" whispered Hosea. Nothing. "Tom?" he whispered louder. He picked up the whiskey bottle with the roses and held it to Tom's open mouth. He couldn't see any condensation on the bottle. Very gently, Hosea put his fingers on Tom's chest. For a second or two he couldn't feel anything moving. He panicked. But then he felt a little something. Tom was breathing. It was okay. Hosea glanced over at the magazine. He picked it

thought Hosea. Could there be more children in the

there? Are we a little club? A big club? Hosea thought of the PM's beautiful wife at home in Ottawa. How would she feel about this photograph? Did she care? Was she willing to put up with a bit of hanky-panky just to be the PM's wife? Was she sad? Angry? Was she heartbroken? Had Euphemia been heartbroken? Perhaps he should send the Prime Minister's Office a bill for the cost of thousands of bottles of rye whiskey. Her heart simply gave out on her, the doctor had said. Is being kissed and stroked, impregnated and left, by this man John Baert, a recipe for sorrow? Had he that much charisma, power, and sway? Could a man who broke women's hearts, led the country, inspired thousands, drank martinis with world leaders, and skied at the age of seventy really be my father? thought Hosea. Can the mind work when the heart is broken? Had Euphemia been telling the truth?

"Hosea," said Tom. "Hi." Hosea dropped the magazine and cleared his throat.

"Tom," he said. "Hi. How's it going?" He smiled at his old friend and Tom smiled back.

"Not so good. Did you bring those flowers?"

"Yup. They're roses. First batch this spring."

"They're beautiful, Hosea. Thank-you."

"You're welcome."

"Did you polish off that whiskey to make a vase?" Tom smiled.

"No, no," said Hosea. He tugged on the front of his wind-breaker. "No."

Tom smiled. "I'm just kidding, Hosea," he said.

Hosea grinned. "Dory will be back in half an hour," he said.

"That's good."

"So . . ." said Hosea.

Tom smiled. His eyes were red and his hair was greasy. He needed to shave.

"It's quite nice outside these days," said Hosea. "Spring is here to stay, I'm quite sure."

Hosea remembered the two of them singing in school and getting sent home early. It was how they avoided the big boys.

Tom lay there, staring at the window.

"Knute's doing a terrific job. She's uh . . . a good worker."

Tom looked at Hosea and nodded his head.

"Say, Tom," said Hosea. "Would you mind if I borrowed your *Maclean's* for a day or two?"

"Just take it, Hose," said Tom. "Keep it."

Then the two men sat and lay in silence. Hosea shifted the roses around once or twice. He smoothed his trousers. He smiled at Tom and Tom smiled back. Then Tom fell asleep again. Hosea sat there for a minute or two, staring first at Tom and then at the picture of the Prime Minister. He wanted to hug Tom or at least talk about the old days. He would have liked to tell Tom about Lorna. He wondered how Tom talked

scribbler from his drawer and entered Tom's name in the Dying and Potentially Dead column. Tom's voice in his head saying, Somebody die? And Hosea looking around saying, No, why? 'Cause, said Tom, your flag's flying at half mast. That was more than forty years ago but Hosea still looked down at his zipper every time he thought about it.

He pulled his chair up to the window and stared outside until all the shops on Main Street were closed and the kids hanging around Norm's had gone home and the sky was the colour of fresh liquid manure.

"Okay," said Hosea the next morning. "Okay. Places to go, people to see. Lorna can go to hell. No, I don't mean that, I take it back," he said.

One time he had said, "places to go, people to see" to Lorna and she had said, "Don't ever say that to me again. I hate things like that."

"Me too!" he'd said. But hadn't meant it. He liked them, actually. Maybe later in the day he'd call Lorna and say, Hey, sweetheart, how about reconsidering me? You're a moron, she'd say. I know, I know, what's up, Lorna? he'd say. And she'd say, I don't know, stuff, and slowly they'd get back on track the way they always did.

He had to find out how Mrs. Cherniski was, see if it was true that Dr. François was thinking about leaving town, confirm that Max was back in town, and find out if Knute had done anything about that darn dog, Bill Quinn. Oh, and he had to put Johnny Dranger back in town limits so he could be crowned fire chief of Algren. Fair enough, thought Hosea.

Hosea straightened the framed picture of Lorna he had sitting on his couch, and then kissed it lightly. Soon, he thought, I'll carry you over the threshold. We'll ride off into the sunset, you and me. "I want to grow old with you, Lorna Garden," he said out loud. "Will you marry me?" Or, he thought, would she prefer, Marry me! It was hard to know. Hosea wondered how Tom had asked Dory to marry him. Or had Dory asked Tom? Or had they mutually, silently agreed to marry at precisely the same moment, opened their mouths, out of the blue, and said, "Yes!" in unison, knowing exactly what the other was saying yes to and falling into each other's arms, laughing, knowing, happy.

Probably, thought Hosea. Very likely.

He went out to his car and had a look at the tires. Years ago he'd attended a convention of mayors and town reeves in Sudbury, Ontario, and one of the

160

conventioneers had warned him that hostile townspeople do things to their mayors like slash their tires and throw eggs at their houses. Since then he checked his tires every time he drove. Each time he found them intact and full of air, Hosea congratulated himself on the fine job he was doing keeping everybody in Algren happy — at least happy enough not to slash his tires. He took off his hat and put it on top of the car so he could bend

was her name. Summer Time. Summer Feelin', that was it. He and Max were stopped side by side at Algren's only traffic light. "Hello there," said Hosea through his open window. Max was wearing dark sunglasses and singing, and banging on the dashboard from time to time. Hosea thought he might also be pretending to play a guitar. An imaginary electric guitar hanging down low, on his hips. His fingers were moving very quickly and his left hand slid wildly up and down the neck of the imaginary guitar. His right hand yanked at imaginary strings like somebody trying to start a lawn mower.

Summer Feelin' was laughing and waving her hands around like a symphony conductor, but she noticed Hosea and smiled.

"Your dad likes to rock," said Hosea, smiling back at S.F.

"It's my grandma's car," said S.F. in response.

Hosea knew that but he said, "Oh, I see," and smiled again. Max's song was over and he looked at Hosea.

"Hey, hi," he said. "How are you?" Hosea nodded and smiled.

"Pretty good," Hosea said. "Welcome back to Algren."

"Thanks," said Max, grinning. "Taking your hat for a ride?" Hosea smiled and wondered what Max meant. The light had turned green and Hosea was moving ahead, slowly, through the intersection. He didn't hear Max yell, "Hey, your hat's on top of the car!" As he drove down Main Street, Hosea looked right into the sun and breathed deeply.

He turned his own tape deck up loud and sang along with Emmylou. He got to the chorus and said, "Guitar" along with Emmylou to her band mate.

Hosea parked his car in the hospital parking lot and glanced at himself in the rearview mirror. Where was his hat? Damn, he thought, and Lorna says I look good in it. He got out of the car and began to laugh. "I am such an idiot," he muttered. He grabbed the hat from the top of the car and put it on his head. So, he thought to himself, I drive down Main Street singing and crying, with a hat on top of my car. He scratched his forehead and shook his leg a bit to realign his parts. "I could be senile," he said out loud.

Hosea walked through the front doors of the hospital. There was nobody around. He walked over to the front desk and peered at the posted list of patients. He was looking for the name Cherniski.

162

"Hello, Hosea, making your rounds?"

"Oh, oh, hello, Dr. Bonsoir." Hosea tugged viciously at his windbreaker and then stopped abruptly and stroked the brim of his hat. "How are you?" he said.

"Fine. Just fine. Call me Dr. Trèsbien, Hosea. How are you? How's the chest pain?"

"Oh, it's gone. It was nothing. Something I ate."

"Hmmm. So, Hosea, mind if I ask you a question?"

"Yes, but how did you know her dog was in trouble? How is it that you just showed up at that exact moment when her dog needed rescuing?"

"Well, I don't know. Chance, I suppose. Coincidence? I was on my way to Johnny Dranger's."

"I see. Is he a friend of yours?"

"In a way. Yes."

"Hmmm . . ." said Dr. François.

"How is she?" said Hosea.

"Hard to say at this point."

Hosea told himself not to ask another single question. Why was the doctor acting this way? He stared hard at his shoes and tried to stop himself from opening his mouth. He put his hands in his pockets and felt the hard edge of his hips. He looked up and saw the doctor glance at his watch and then at something behind the desk.

163

"Do you think she'll make it?" he blurted out and cursed himself inside. The doctor stared at Hosea. He opened his mouth and closed it. He smiled.

"What would you say if I told you I was thinking of leaving Algren?" said the doctor. He began to pace back and forth, his hands behind his back.

"Leaving Algren," said Hosea. "But why?"

"For a better paying job in the States."

"The States! Why would you want to go to the States?"

"More money, like I said. And other reasons. Genvieve won't leave Montreal to live in a place like this."

"But what about us? We need you!"

"Well, don't worry, Hosea. I won't leave until you have another doctor. You organize a hiring committee, put an ad in papers across the country, and see how it goes. I'm sorry, Hosea, I need to live in a bigger place. I need to move on."

"It's because of the Epps, isn't it?"

"What about them?"

"Talking about suing you over the baby with the breathing problem."

"No, no, Hosea. That was unavoidable. Any doctor has to be prepared for potential lawsuits and disgruntled patients. That's not the problem. I'm a young man! I need a change! I want to practise in a large hospital and experience as much as I can. That's all."

Dr. François looked at Hosea. Hosea didn't know what to say. He needed to get rid of a few more people,

164

but if the doctor left he'd have to replace him. He couldn't expect the Charlie Orson Memorial Hospital to function without a doctor. At least not for any length of time. Could he get away with not hiring a doctor just for, say, a month or two? Until after July first? The doctor put his hand on Hosea's shoulder. "Don't worry so much, Hosea. You'll kill yourself with worry."

"I hope you change your mind," said Hosea quietly.

bursting through the front doors of the hospital. Two of them were helping Johnny Dranger walk and yelling at the doctor.

"He's not breathing hardly at all, Doc!" said one. "You gotta do something quick!"

The doctor was calm. He helped the men lay Johnny down on a stretcher in the hallway. By now Nurse Barnes had showed up and was already administering oxygen to Johnny.

"What happened to his inhaler?" the doctor asked the men. They all shrugged.

"We don't know," said one of them.

"Was he putting out fires again?" asked the doctor.

"Looks like," said one of the men. "He told us he'd just come from Whithers, some house fire he was helping on, his face was all full of ash and grit. He ordered a coffee, over at the Wagon Wheel, then started in on his coughing fit. Knocked his cup right off the table, and the gal over there, filling in for Cherniski, started yelling at him to get a grip. He started turning blue and he tried to talk but nothing came out, so the boys here and I stuck him in the back of the truck and brought him here. He's looking better, I can see."

Hosea stood beside Johnny, looking down at him and smiling. Johnny still couldn't talk but his colour was coming back and his breathing had settled down. "I'm putting you back in, John," whispered Hosea. Johnny blinked up at Hosea.

"Excuse me, Hosea," said the doctor. "I'll have to ask you to stand back a bit. He'll be fine in a while. He'll be out of here in an hour or two. Until the next time." The doctor was muttering, "An asthmatic firefighter, I don't understand . . ."

Hosea turned and walked towards the door. "Hey, Hosea," said one of the men. "Isn't that Leander Hamm's hat you got on? He gave it to you?" Hosea froze on the spot but the man went on. "Looks pretty good on you, Hosea, looks sharp. Doesn't it, Mel?" he said to the other man.

"Sure does," said Mel. "That's a bronc-bustin' hat you got there, Hosea, you know that? You could be a cowboy if you got yourself a horse."

Hosea smiled and said, "Well, maybe some day." But the men weren't listening. They were already making plans to get back to the Wagon Wheel and finish off their coffees, maybe find out more about the new gal taking over for Cherniski.

Hosea got into his car and backed out of his spot. He drove slowly down Main Street, nodding at the few people strolling along the sidewalk. Suddenly a dog stepped off the curb and sauntered across the street. Hosea slammed on his brakes and swore out loud. That damn Knute! She was supposed to get rid of that dog! Immediately Hosea felt bad about his outburst. He rolled down his window. "Uh, Bill Quinn?" he said. "Get off the road! Shoo! C'mon now, get going!" Bill Quinn turned his head to look at Hosea and then

at the spot where the tire had just been, put his leg down and continued to cross the street. He found a square of sunlight and lay down in it. With his legs stretched out in front of him and behind him he took up the entire width of the sidewalk.

Hosea watched as a woman and her child gingerly stepped over the dog. The child bent down and scratched Bill Quinn between the ears. Bill Quinn licked the boy's face and the woman smiled. Hosea shook his head.

Well, thought Hosea, I'm really no further ahead than when I started. I've got three new babies and Max on my hands and nobody gone except Leander. I'm no further ahead. Hosea remembered raking leaves for Euphemia. As soon as he'd finished a patch of the lawn, the wind would blow and more leaves would fall from the trees directly onto his freshly raked patch. "C'mon in, Hosea," Euphemia would yell from the doorway, "don't worry about every single leaf." But he had worried about every single leaf. He'd stay outside until ten or eleven at night trying to rake up every leaf, trying to beat the wind. Sometimes Tom would help out for a while but eventually he'd get bored and wander off. "I'm going to bed, Hose," Euphemia would eventually call out into the darkness, "wherever you are, good night."

Hosea parked his car on the street in front of his office and got out. He said, "Hello, Peej," to a small stooped man who stood on the sidewalk gazing up at the sky. "Have you got seeding weather, Peej, or not?" Hosea smiled. "Let's hope," said Peej.

"Well, take 'er easy, Peej." A vicious jerk of Peej's chin by way of saying good-bye and Hosea had safely entered his office building.

He peered out the window of his office. He watched a couple getting out of their grey Subaru and going in to the Wagon Wheel. The woman glanced at Bill Quinn lying on the sidewalk and smiled. He thumped his fingers against the windowsill to a familiar tune. Waterloo, he thumped, my Waterloo. The couple took a table next to the large window in the front of the café. Hosea watched as the man removed the woman's coat and then disappeared into the café, looking for a place to hang it. You'll have to hang it over the back of a chair, it's the Wagon Wheel you're sitting in, not the Ritz, thought Hosea. He stared at the woman and wondered if she was married to the man or was she his sister, his daughter? He thought of Lorna. The woman sat at the table, her legs crossed and sticking out to the side, and picked up a menu. She looked up at Hosea. Hosea looked up at the sky, to the right and to the left as if he'd just heard an airplane, and then quickly moved away from his window.

He noticed a note lying on his desk and picked it up.

Hi, Hosea, I let myself in with the key you gave me

still in town, but I'm working on it. And I'll be buying the flowers later today with the money from that account. That's where I'm going now. Oh yeah, Lorna called. See ya, Knute.

P.S. Are you still interested in turning the old fred mill into a theatre because Jeannie, you know, your neighbour? said she's thinking about buying it and turning it into an aerobics/laundromat kind of place. She said she'd talk to you.

I'm sure she did, thought Hosea. "When?" said Hosea out loud. When, Knute? When did Lorna call, what did she say, how did she sound? Was she at work, at home? Why hadn't Knute just let the answering machine go? It would have been more helpful. At least he could have heard her voice. Hosea stood up and walked over to the window. He watched the couple for

169

a while. The woman didn't look up at him again. A warm wind touched him. Knute's note fluttered off the desk and onto the floor. "You!" he shouted at Bill Quinn. The dog lifted one ear. "Get out of my town! Get the heck out of Algren!" Bill Quinn let his ear drop, yawned, and tried to get comfortable again. Combine Jo, who had been standing on the street with her back to Hosea, peering into the window of Willie Wiebe's Western Wear, turned around and looked up at him.

"Who the hell are you yelling at, Hosea? It's a little undignified, don't you think?" She was grinning. "Have you lost your mind, Hosea? Why the hell don't you come on out of your little tower and enjoy the sunshine. Summer's just around the corner! Did I mention S.F. and me are gonna be riding our bikes over on the dike? Hey, Hosea, you gotta bike?"

Hosea shook his head. "I was, uh, talking to Bill Quinn, to the dog," he said. "To that black dog there on the sidewalk."

"Oh him," shouted Combine Jo. "He looks harmless. Hey, wait a second, did you say his name is Bill Quinn? You mean from the original Bill Quinn? Is that one of his? Oh boy." Combine Jo shook her head.

"What do you mean, 'oh boy'?" shouted Hosea. "What's the story with the Quinns?"

"Oh, they're just wild, Hosea. They can't be trained. They can't be taught a thing. They do as they please. A few generations must have lived in Whithers or who knows where, 'cause you obviously missed out on it. Just ask Cherniski! She'll tell you all about it!"

170

Combine Jo shook her head. "Christ," she said. She looked amused. "I guess they're back. Yell all you want, Hosea, that dog ain't gonna budge." She turned back to the display window of Wiebe's with a little wave over her shoulder. Hosea lifted his hand.

The phone rang.

"Lorna," said Hosea as he picked up the phone.

I've missed you, too," she said.

Hosea had been about to say I've been better.

"Yeah," he said. "How are you?" he asked again.

"I'm okay. Pretty good. Hosea, there's something we need to talk about."

"Yeah," he said. He wondered what it could be. "Yeah," he said again. "We should talk."

"Could I come out on the bus tonight?"

"Oh," said Hosea. "Of course you can, of course you can. I'll be there to pick you up. I love you. I'm sorry I'm such an idiot. I'm sorry I didn't call sooner. Lorna, I'm just really sorry."

She sighed. "You keep telling me that, Hosea, and nothing ever changes."

Hosea whispered, "I know. I'm sorry."

"Will you quit saying you're fucking sorry!" she said.

"Okay," said Hosea. "Yes I will, I love you."

"And stop saying that, too!" said Lorna.

"Why?" asked Hosea. "Why should I stop saying I love you when I do?"

"Because it makes me sad, Hosea, that's why. Because I wonder."

"Okay," said Hosea.

"Is that all you can say? Okay? So what does that mean, Hosea, that your love for me *is* a sad thing, that you don't even know if you mean it or not?"

Hosea put his hand on his forehead. "Tell me," she said again, softly. Was she crying?

"I have a plan, Lorna," he said. "It's a, well, it's just a plan. And if you'll just come here tonight I'll tell you everything and then you'll understand. My love for you is not a sad thing, Lorna. Please don't think it is."

"Just pick me up at seven, Hosea," she said. "And you know, whatever." She hung up.

Hosea closed his eyes. He could feel the warm wind blowing through his open window. He could smell the dust left over from last fall and he could hear Combine Jo laughing down on the street. He thought how much happier Leander Hamm's corpse would be now that the earth was drying up and the snow had gone. My blood, he thought. I'd sell my blood to buy her chocolate donuts. That had been the first line of a poem he'd written on a scrap of paper the day he had decided to become a poet. He'd changed it around a million times trying to get something to rhyme with donuts and then with blood. Nothing. Except flood, and that had seemed futile. Euphemia had found the scrap of paper in his pocket and had laughed out loud for twenty minutes, and then had broken her leg. Hosea had been

172

in the basement and had seen a spider, and because he was frustrated with his poem had screamed at the top of his lungs, "SPIDER!" Euphemia had come running and falling down the stairs, saying, "Where where where's the fire" and her leg made a snapping noise and her femur poked off in the wrong direction, and Hosea had been quite happy about it. Even while Euphemia lay writhing on the basement floor, he had

tell her the truth about his plan and she would understand. She would know why he wanted to see his father. She loved him and she would know. He would take the Prime Minister by the arm and they would stroll off a ways from the crowd, down Main Street towards where the sidewalk ends, and then up Town Line Road in the direction of the dike, and Hosea would smile and say, Mr. Prime Minister, do you remember meeting a girl named Euphemia Funk years ago right here in this town? Well, I'm her son. He would smile and look into the PM's face. And yours, he'd say. He wanted to show the Prime Minister his town, Canada's smallest, the place of his conception, his birth, and his whole life. He wanted the Prime Minister to see it and to like it and to think well of Euphemia and the place where she was from and the son that she had raised. Lorna would understand. It was simple.

Hosea nodded his head and smoothed the shiny surface of his desk with his hand. He reached for the top drawer and then decided against opening it. He would find Knute and the two of them would plant the flowers along Main Street. He would help her. And then he would go to the bus depot and pick up Lorna and show her the flowers and take her home.

CHAPTER
TEN

"No. Not really, no," said Dory. She and Knute were in the kitchen drinking coffee and watching the sun go down. Dory leaned towards the open window, over the sink, and the warm breeze blew the hair off her forehead. Beyond Tom and Dory's big backyard was a field, plowed and ready for seeding, pitch-black and chunky, with a faint line of bushes towards the very end, and the giant orange sun was slipping down behind those bushes, round as a poker chip, and the purple sky covered everything. That was the view.

"You know what, Knutie?" said Dory. "Tom and I have lived here all our lives. In this town, every single day of our lives."

"Do you think that's what's making Dad so sad?" asked Knute. Dory looked at her and smiled.

"No, Knute," she said. "It's just the opposite. He loves this place, it's all he's known. He's afraid to say good-bye. He's afraid to leave it behind. He's afraid, Knutie."

"But he's been given a second chance," said Knute. "He's still alive."

"It's more mysterious than that," said Dory. "He wants his old life. He's not a stupid man. For him to get up and cheerfully make the most of each day, at this point . . . he would feel like a fool." Dory shook her head. Then she said, "He would be admitting to himself that life has suddenly become very short, very precious, that soon he'll no longer exist, that it'll be over. Of course he knew that, we know that, we say it, but to really, really know it, to be certain of it, is more than he can be right now. His bed is safe. Sleep is easy." Then she said again, "He's not a stupid man."

The sun had gone down right before their eyes. "Did you notice it disappear?" Dory asked Knute.

"Well, I noticed it was gone," said Knute. She put their coffee cups in the dishwasher and then stood with her hands on her hips and looked at Dory. "I'm going out," she said. "Don't worry about Summer Feelin', she won't wake up." Dory reached out her arms and put her hands over Knute's.

"I'm not worried," she said. "I think I can take care of one little girl well enough on my own."

"Yeah, well," said Knute, smiling, "I suppose you've managed before, more or less."

"What do you mean *you suppose*? What do you mean *more or less*?" Dory said, grabbing the tea towel from the fridge door and swatting Knute with it. "More or less," she growled. "My foot, more or less. Ingrate!

Get out of here!" She snapped Knute with the towel. "Hey," she said, "where are you off to?"

"Oh," said Knute, grinning. "A little paperwork at the office."

"Really? I'm impressed."

"Nah," Knute said, "I'm going to check out my flowers. Hosea and I planted millions of them today, all along Main Street. And they're all red and white. We

can all be proud of Algren, Canada's smallest town. Well, Dory, I, uh, I, uh, I, uh, really better get going. You know how it is, places to go, people to see."

"Yes yes, Mayor Funk," said Dory. "Onward and upward. Don't let me stand in the way of progress. Carpe diem."

"Okey, dokey," said Knute. "And give my regards to Tom. And, uh, thanks for the coffee, Dory, you always did make a fine cup of coffee."

Dory shook her head. "Oh you," she said. "Go already." She was looking at the wall where the mirror used to be, before Combine Jo broke it. Hosea Funk, she sighed. Lord love him, what a funny man.

Knute walked out of the house and down the driveway. The night was warm and very dark. She felt like crying. She hadn't done a good job of helping Dory with Tom, and it was already June. She hadn't helped him get better or lightened Dory's load. He'd taken to his bed and Knute was concerned that Dory might be thinking of joining him. How much longer could she renovate one medium-sized house? Knute cut behind the feed mill and around by the bank and the post office and walked towards the flowers. She could smell them, they were beautiful, and they shone under the only streetlight. Something small and black jumped out from the middle of the flower bed and disappeared. Then another followed, and another. She bent over to see what they were and was almost hit in the face with another one. The Algren cockroach! The bastards were eating her flowers! She stood up and frowned at the flower bed and then picked up a few pebbles from the road and threw them into the flowers. About twenty of the cockroaches flew up and took off in different directions. She picked up another handful of gravel and threw it in the flowers and was about to do it again when she heard a voice say "Hey!" and she nearly fell over from fright.

"You're gonna kill them if you do that." She turned around and saw Max coming toward her, stepping into the white glow of the streetlight.

"Good," she said. "Damn it, I just planted these things this afternoon."

"And now you want to kill them?" asked Max.

"I don't want to kill the flowers, I want to kill the cockroaches. Look at them. They're eating the flowers."

"They're not eating the flowers, they're copulating in the fresh dirt you used for planting. They don't eat flowers. The Algren cockroach is conceived in dirt. They love dirt."

178

She picked up another handful of gravel and threw it at the flowers.

"And stop doing that, you'll just hurt the flowers."

Knute sighed.

"So this is your work, eh?" said Max.

"Part of it," said Knute.

"Do you enjoy it?" he said. He leaned against the streetlight and folded his arms.

"What do you mean *other women*, Knute?" he said. "Other than who?" They grinned at each other. Two little shapes moved towards them in the dark, making clicking noises on the pavement.

"Hey," said Knute, as the shapes came closer, "it's Bill Quinn."

"And a friend," said Max. He moved his foot out of the way so the dogs could pass.

"I'm supposed to get rid of him," said Knute. "He gave Mrs. Cherniski a heart attack."

"You're doing a great job," said Max.

"Yeah, well, you would know." Knute looked at her flowers and up at the sky. It would be nice if it rained. She knew Max was looking at her watching the sky. She knew he was leaning against the streetlight smoking a cigarette with nothing to do and nowhere to do it. She picked up another handful of gravel to throw at the cockroaches in her flower bed, and Max said softly, "Is there a place we can go?"

"Um . . ." she said quietly, "there's . . ."

"You know what I mean," he said, looking at his big boots, blowing smoke at them, and waiting for Knute to rescue him.

She still had Hosea's office key in her back pocket. She could feel the outline of it through her jeans. "Well," she said, "I don't know." Max looked up and opened his mouth but didn't say anything. He put his hands up in front of him, palms outward, as if to ward off an assault. He smiled.

"I can ask," he whispered. Knute reached out and took his hand. He closed his eyes for a second or two and put his arms around her. They stood that way for a while in the dark, on the deserted main street of their hometown. He smelled like hay and cigarette smoke and the back of his neck was as soft as Summer Feelin's. He pulled his T-shirt out of his jeans and put Knute's hands on his bare back.

She moved his hand to her back pocket and he took out the key and said, "Where's the door for this thing?"

"Right here," said Knute. "We're leaning against it. It's my office." She smiled.

"Your office," Max breathed. "You have an office?"

"It's Hosea's office." Max had already opened the door and was pulling Knute up the stairs.

They made love on the top of Hosea's shiny desk, and on the floor, and when they were finished they lay there naked, smoking cigarettes and talking. "I love you," said Max. And she said, "You don't really know me anymore." And he said, "Well, there's that." And they laughed and acted casual about everything and tried not to make any promises or plans. They could never go back to where they'd been. And nothing seemed to be waiting for them down the road. So they were free. It was a sad kind of freedom but at least they knew it. They didn't say it but they both knew Summer Feelin' was the best thing either of them

away from his eyes.

"Remember that time you cut my hair outside that bar?" he said. "Remember that grey sweater dress you had on?" They took turns kissing each other gently and touching each other and then they went back to leaning on the windowsill and looking out. Neither of them wanted to go home.

"So, let's see, what's new . . . hmmmm," said Hosea. He had picked Lorna up from the bus depot and now they were sitting at his kitchen table drinking herbal tea and trying to get to a spot in their conversation where they could feel natural with each other. "Well," Hosea cleared his throat, "Max is back in town."

"Max?" said Lorna.

"Knute's old boyfriend," said Hosea. "Summer Feelin's dad."

"Oh yeah," said Lorna. "You told me about Knute and Summer Feelin'. What a great name, Summer Feelin'."

Hosea smiled.

"It's okay," he said.

"It's a great name," said Lorna again.

"Okay," said Hosea. "She's a sweet kid, too."

"Yeah?" said Lorna. "It's nice for her to have her dad back, I guess."

Hosea nodded. "They get along," he said. "He takes care of her while Knute works in the office."

Lorna nodded and sipped her tea. "Hmmm," said Lorna, looking at her watch. "It's June sixth today, D-Day."

"Is that right?" said Hosea. Oh my God, he thought.

Lorna shrugged.

"Yeah," he said, "I guess it is."

He stared at Lorna while she fiddled with her watch. He was trying to work up the nerve to tell her his plan. *Isthmus* rhymes with *Christmas,* he told himself. Her eyes, two oceans of blue, and a skinny isthmus of a nose running in-between. Her mouth, the Bermuda Triangle, no, that's wrong. Dehumanize your audience. Hosea could hear the voice of Mr. Flett, his old speech arts teacher. Pretend your audience is a brick fence, a body of water, an ancient land mass. And then say what you have to say. A field of wheat won't think you're ridiculous. A small continent won't get up and leave. Tell her right now, Hosea told himself, tell her. You love her, you need her, you deserve her, tell her right now or kill yourself.

"Lorna!" he said loudly, scaring himself and making her jump.

"What?" said Lorna. "Are you nuts? I'm not deaf."

"We should do that talking now, the talking we talked about before," said Hosea, "on the phone."

"Okay," said Lorna, taking a big breath. "You're right." She smiled. "It's very weird."

Hosea was confused. What was weird? What did she

her hands, put her lips against his forehead, and whispered ". . . is that I'm pregnant."

Mr. Flett had never mentioned the possibility of a land mass getting pregnant. Pregnant. Pregnant. Lorna's lips were still fastened to his forehead. He could stick out his tongue and lick her neck if he wanted to. He put his arms around her and said, "That's amazing, Lorna. That's amazing."

She sat back down in her chair, folded her arms, and said, "I know it is." She looked at Hosea. "Please smile," she said, "oh, please smile."

"I am," said Hosea, frowning, "I am."

Lorna laughed. "Are you happy?" she asked. He was happy, he was thrilled. It had never occurred to him that he could make a woman pregnant, especially not a beautiful woman he really loved and wanted to live with for the rest of his life. He was happy, all right.

"Yes, Lorna, I'm happy," he said, smiling. Trying to smile. "I'm happy." And then he added, "Are you?"

Lorna nodded. "I think so," she said. "I'm pretty sure I am."

"Amazing," he said.

"The doctor told me it's the size of my thumbnail," said Lorna.

"Really, wow," said Hosea. "Let me see your thumb." She held it up and he looked at it closely. He pulled her thumb to his lips and kissed it.

"But the thing is," she said, holding out her thumb, "the thing is, Hosea, it's got to be different."

"How do you mean?" Hosea stopped kissing her thumb and held her hand in his lap.

"I'm just not gonna fool around anymore, Hosea. I'm too old for that and so are you. I'm not gonna date you like a teenager or have some kind of long-distance love affair with you when I'm pregnant with your kid. Forget it."

"Okay," said Hosea, "I know. I know what you mean, and things will change. You're going to move in with me and we'll be happy, we'll be a family, we'll all live together right here in Algren. We have a school, there's a park, okay? Okay, Lorna?" Hosea smiled and opened his eyes wide.

"Today, Hosea," said Lorna. "As of today I'm living here. If you can't make that commitment, knowing we're having a baby, and everything else — you know we're not kids, you know we're not getting any younger — then I don't know. Then I just don't know. Basically, I think, it would just be over. I'm not gonna raise a kid with you if you can't make one commitment. Then I might not even have it."

Hosea let go of Lorna's hand and reached for the front of his shirt.

"Don't," said Lorna. "Don't do that. Just deal with this, okay? I don't mean for this to be an ultimatum, Hosea, I hate ultimatums, but it's just at that point where we have to, where you have to, make a decision.

were you? What did you want to talk about."

"I just need you to trust me," said Hosea.

"You need me to trust you?" said Lorna.

"Yes," he whispered.

"No," said Lorna. "You need to trust me, you need to trust yourself. I do trust you. Why the hell do you think I'm here right now? Why the hell do you think I keep coming back to you time after time? Why are you so afraid of living with me? Because it might not work out? Because I'll become more real to you? Because you'll not have a reason to feel sorry for yourself, all alone? Why? I don't understand, Hosea. Is there somebody else? Are you seeing somebody else?"

"God, no," said Hosea. "I have a plan, and it's very important to me, and if you just wait for three weeks, it'll be over, and my life, my whole life, will be yours, and the baby's. Please understand, Lorna, please don't leave me . . ."

"Tell me what your plan is," said Lorna. "Tell me what it is, and we'll see." She moved behind Hosea and stroked his hair and rubbed his back. "Tell me," she said. "C'mon, Hosea."

Hosea turned around to face her and he put his hands on her waist. "I want to see my father," he said. "I want to see what he looks like. I want to talk to him. I want to see if I'm like him at all. I want him to see my town."

"Hosea," said Lorna, "who is your father?"

Hosea cleared his throat. "John Baert, I think. My mother told me that, anyway."

"You don't mean the Prime Minister, do you?" Lorna smiled.

Hosea nodded. "Yeah," he said. "That's the one."

Max and Knute said good-bye on the street with a high-five in slow motion, their hands clasped together for a couple of seconds reaching for the sky and everything else unattainable, and then they smiled at each other and went their separate ways.

When Knute got home, Dory was still up. She had her SoHo T-shirt on and Tom's sweats and she was steaming the wallpaper in the dining room with a kettle and tearing at it with a plastic scraper.

"Mom," Knute whispered. "What are you doing? It's the middle of the night."

"Yes, Knutie," she said, "I made that observation myself. What does it look like I'm doing?" She hadn't taken her eyes off the wallpaper.

186

"You're gonna take out the whole wall, not just the paper, if you keep banging at it like that," said Knute.

"Thank-you for that," Dory said. "It might be a good idea."

"Well," Knute yawned, "this is kind of strange. Why don't you go to bed and finish it in the morning? Or I could help you after work tomorrow."

"Where were you?" asked Dory, her eyes still fixed

"Oh, Mom," said Knute. "It's not that big a deal." Dory nodded and blinked a few times. "It's really not."

"I don't . . ." Dory began.

"I know," said Knute. "Don't worry." Dory looked at her and smiled, sadly, and wiped the sweat off her nose with the bottom of her T-shirt.

"Do you remember Candace Wheeler?" she asked.

"Candace Wheeler," said Knute. "Candace Wheeler. No, I don't. Why?" Knute already knew it would be something terrible, maybe a pitchfork through her cheek or flesh-eating disease.

"She had to have a C-section in the city," said Dory.

"That's too bad," said Knute, thinking it could have been a lot worse. She wanted to go to bed. She wanted to dream of Max and their nowhere relationship before the sun rose and ruined everything.

"The baby was totally, you know, totally . . . stressed out," Dory continued.

Knute smiled. "Stressed out?"

"Well, whatever," Dory said. "Under stress, I guess is what it was, or duress. Apparently Candace's pelvis wouldn't open up far enough for the baby to go through, but they only discovered this after eighteen hours of hard labour. So Candace was just about dead from the pain, and then suddenly they decide to do the C-section. They thought they had given her enough anesthetic, but because they were in such a hurry to save the baby, they made a mistake with the levels and she wasn't entirely, you know, frozen, you know, the area, and so she could feel the knife cutting her open. She was only slightly numb. She was far too weak to object, though, and, oh, Knute, it was awful. A large flap of skin, the stomach skin, was pushed aside, sort of draped up over her breasts and then it took two doctors to pry her rib cage open far enough to get the baby out. And she's feeling all of th —"

"Mom," Knute said. "Please stop." Dory began to cry, and moved her finger through the condensation on the kettle and shook her head. "It's okay," said Knute. She sat down on the floor next to Dory and put her arms around her. Dory put her head on Knute's shoulder and wept.

"Oh, Knutie," she sobbed, "I don't know what to do. I don't know how to make him live. I don't know how to make him talk."

"It's okay, Mom." Knute stroked Dory's hair the way Dory used to stroke hers when she was sad or sick.

"He doesn't talk to me, Knute. He just lies there."

188

"I know." Knute nodded her head. She didn't know what to say.

"I don't want him to die, sweetheart," said Dory. She had stopped sobbing but tears were still streaming down her cheeks.

"I know," Knute said again. She kissed her mother's forehead.

"But sometimes I do," said Dory.

be patient and let him get up when he's ready or if I should tell him I'll leave if he doesn't try, at least, but that's so cruel and I don't want to leave him. How could I? I just don't know. And it's not his fault. But he could at least sit down for meals or go on a little drive with me or just talk to me. Uncle Jack called earlier this evening and I couldn't stop crying on the phone. You know how much Jack's always loved Tom. He said he'd try to talk to him, but I don't know . . ."

Knute didn't know, either. "Maybe . . ."

"He can't think straight, Knute, and it's getting worse. The neurologist thinks that he's had a series of small strokes, not big enough for anybody to really notice, except he knows it and he can't do things, you know, like he used to. He can't read anymore. When he said he was reading his journals in the garage while I worked, he wasn't, you know, he just pretended to. His handwriting is illegible. His short-term memory is gone. Sometimes he forgets where he is, he gets dizzy. He can't drive. And, Knute, he's not affectionate like he used to be, he's not funny, with the jokes and laughing, he's just not the same guy . . ."

Knute closed her eyes and leaned her head against the damp wall.

"I'm sorry," Dory said. "I don't want to upset you. I just needed to talk to someone. I don't know what to do. I want you to be happy, and now with Max back, I don't know what's going to happen, will he leave you again? Pregnant? Will he break Summer Feelin's heart, too, this time? How many times is this going to happen?"

"Mom," said Knute, "I'm not going to get pregnant. Don't worry. Max and I aren't even in a relationship. I can't help it if he leaves again, but Summer Feelin' is better off knowing him, having seen him, and having had fun with him. She'll miss him but she'll be fine. If he leaves again, I'm sure he'll be back to see her. He won't be able to stay away for long. He's crazy about her. His mom lives here, I'm here for the time being, and this is his town. Don't worry about me and Summer Feelin' on top of everything else. Let's just go to sleep and in the morning I want to hear about Dad and you and we'll talk about it, and figure out what we can do, how we can live with it. It's gonna be okay."

Dory began to cry again.

"I love you, Mom," said Knute. "I love you very much."

Dory whispered, "I know you do, Knutie," and stared at her ravaged wall.

Later, after Dory was asleep, Knute went to the garage and looked at Tom's veterinarian journals. She skimmed over an article on ringworm and one on pregnant-mare urine, and then went inside the house and had a quick peek at Summer Feelin'. Her mouth was open, and her arms and legs were spread apart like a starfish. Knute moved her right arm and leg to make some room and then curled up beside her. "The sun's

stretched out her right arm and leg again, on top of Knute.

"So, let me get this straight," said Lorna. "You think Baert is your dad, but you're not sure. Euphemia told you on her deathbed, and you believe she was lucid enough to know what she was talking about. That was three years ago. Since then you haven't called him or even tried to get —"

Hosea interrupted. "Well, Lorna," he said, "I can't just call up the Prime Minister and say, Hey, I'm your son, you know, about fifty some years ago you rode through this small prairie town on a horse and —"

"Okay, okay," said Lorna. "Fine, I understand. So then you get a letter from the Prime Minister saying he's going to visit Canada's smallest town on July first as a way of showing the country he's interested in, well, small towns, I guess."

"Right," said Hosea.

"Hmmm," said Lorna. "Interesting publicity stunt."

"It's not a publicity stunt," said Hosea. "It's a way of reaching out to rural Canadians, to show them that he cares."

"Yeah," said Lorna, "about their votes."

"Well even so," said Hosea, "it's my chance."

"Okay," said Lorna. "It's your chance. So, you want to make sure Algren is Canada's smallest town on July first so you get a chance to see your dad, and show him what you've accomplished in your life."

"Well," Hosea smiled. "I guess —"

Lorna interrupted again. "Well, that's basically it, isn't it?" She smiled. "God, you're an idiot, Hose."

"Am I?" he said. "But do you love me?"

"Yeah," she said, "because I'm an idiot, too, and now we'll have a kid who's an idiot, because how could it not be, with two idiot parents like us?"

Hosea smiled and for a second worried that she might be right.

"Okay," she sighed. "Max and three babies. Four too many. Right?"

Hosea nodded. "Right," he said. "Fifteen hundred is the number I need."

"I know," said Lorna. "You told me that. Okay, anybody else pregnant?" she asked.

"Just you," he said.

"I mean anybody else in Algren due to give birth before July first?"

"Not that I know of," said Hosea.

192

"Okay," said Lorna again. She tapped her finger against her forehead.

"Look," said Hosea, "the sun's coming up."

"Hmmm," said Lorna. "You sound surprised. Now, Leander Hamm's dead, so that's one. Three left to get rid of."

"Don't say that," said Hosea.

"Bill Quinn," said Hosea.

"But," said Lorna, "who knows where that'll go? If she makes it, she might go and live with her daughter in the city, which would be good. If she dies . . . well . . . I don't want her to die. I'm just saying if she does, that would work out."

Hosea frowned. "Well . . ." he said, "that's not exactly how I —"

"I know, I know," said Lorna. "Let's just say Cherniski's up in the air. Okay, then there's the doctor. He says he might leave. But only after another doctor's been hired and trained and et cetera et cetera and there's no way that can happen before July first, so don't even think of him as an option. You know, I can't believe I'm doing this."

"I'm sorry," said Hosea. "It's like I can't stop, I can't stop until —"

"Okay," said Lorna, yawning and holding up her hand. "Stop. Then, um, who's this Johnny guy?"

"Johnny Dranger," said Hosea.

"Right," said Lorna. "The guy who could be in or out?"

"Yup," said Hosea. "But he has to be in, because he needs to be the fire chief."

Lorna looked at Hosea for a second. "Needs to be the fire chief?" she asked. "Like he needs to eat and sleep?"

"Exactly," said Hosea. "Just like that. He has to stay in, to be the fire chief. He loves to put out fires. He has to put out fires. I'll explain another time."

Lorna raised her eyebrows and let her head fall to her chest, in a dramatic gesture of defeat and exhaustion. "Make me some coffee," she said. "No wait . . . no caffeine . . ." She had her head resting on her arms, on the table.

Hosea thought of Caroline Russo, pregnant with Johnny's baby, and dying in the fire while Johnny was passed out in the yard. He nodded his head and stroked Lorna's hair. "He needs to put out fires," he murmured softly. "He really does." Hosea understood perfectly. "You see, Lorna, it's like this," he said. "Years ago . . . Lorna?" said Hosea. "Lorna?" Lorna made a purring sound but didn't move. She loves me, thought Hosea. She will help me meet my father, and then she'll have our baby. Carefully, he picked Lorna up from the kitchen chair and carried her to the bed. As he bent over to remove her socks he noticed they didn't match. One was pink and fleecy and had a little ball on it that poked out from behind Lorna's ankle like a spur, and the other one was a kneesock, plain and white. Hosea gently pulled the socks off Lorna's wide feet and laid them over the back of the chair so she would find them when she woke up. He stared at Lorna's bare feet for a minute or two. He considered lifting her T-shirt slightly just to see her stomach and to imagine the thumbnail-sized embryo that was inside it that he had

horse racing round its bulbous top. If he could paint the water tower the colour the sky was right then, the colour of Knute's filters, thought Hosea, then the water tower would become one with the sky and the white horse would look like it was flying through the air. At least at those times of the day when the sky was orange. Like right now, thought Hosea, looking at the time on his VCR. 5:20, it said. Well, that's quite early, thought Hosea. But how else to achieve this effect? When the baby was grown up a bit, thought Hosea, he could choose the colour of sky he liked best and Hosea would find a paint to match, maybe dark blue or pink, and Hosea could pass on his flying horse to his son. Or his daughter. "Or my daughter," said Hosea out loud, smiling. Now close your eyes, honey, and stand over here and look way up and when I say open your eyes you will see a horse flying. But, thought Hosea, for now it will be filter orange. I've got to get on it. I'm running out of time. Will I be guaranteed an orange sky and a flying horse when the Prime Minister is in town? Not necessarily, he thought. But you never know. Hosea banged his scarred palm against the side of the table but felt no pain. Hmph, he thought, it must come and go. He did it again and still nothing, not a twinge, not one jot of tenderness, no pain. Hosea walked over to the bedroom and took off his clothes and lay down next to Lorna. She opened her eyes for a second and put her arm over his chest and her head on his shoulder.

Dory had asked Tom's Uncle Jack to pay him a visit. Uncle Jack lived in the States, just on the other side of the border in Fargo, North Dakota. He was a part-time magician and a full-time auctioneer and even when he wasn't working he spoke really fast, in entire paragraphs, a hundred miles an hour, like the telling of his stories was a timed Olympic event. Tom loved the guy, and Dory was sure that if anyone could jar Tom from his depressive stupor, at least for a minute or two, it would be Uncle Jack.

All right, I'm here, but not for long, you son of a bitch, what gives? Lost your sea legs, Tom? You're down, you're not beat, not yet, listen to me, I had a cancer of the groin not once but twice, not a fuckin' picnic, I'll tell ya, though it hasn't, I repeat, has not affected my performance, the girls'll attest to that much, what are you smiling at, two weeks after the chemotherapy gets rid of that mess in my groin, my prostate explodes in my ass, hadda have it hoovered out through my backdoor, eh? eh? still smiling? I shit you not, my friend, it's true, Doc told me not to ride my horse for four goddamn months, I was on her in a week, scuze me? Less than a week, that's right, four days it was, but then, Jesus Christ, that shit for a horse falls on top of me, breaks fifteen of my ribs, that's all, but what? four? five? still, my pelvis, my arms, both of 'em, and my goddamn tailbone — that's when I quit

woman, she never told me it was her husband, she said, never ever, she said, Partner, partner, I said partner, Dad, she says to me, partner, Tom? What is that? Partner! But never mind, last summer I hooked my eyeball with the end of a bungee cord, pierced the retina, the iris, the cornea, the works, the hook stuck in my eye socket like it was plugged into a wall, the bungee cord dangling there like this, and I'm thinking, though of course I'm in excruciating pain, excuse me, do I look like a source of power, my eye holds no electrical current, under fifty watts in this cash register at all times, please unplug this hook from my eye, somebody, and then wouldn't you know it, the neighbour's cat spies the cord dangling and makes a running leap for it, I can just see it out of my good eye, the one without a hook stuck in the middle of it, and I'm thinking, No way, don't do it, don't do it, don't, but forget about it, he does it, and I'm thinking good-bye, right or left or whatever eye, depends of course on how you're looking at it, good-bye it was nice seeing you or seeing with you as the case may be, because as soon as this damn cat, it's a fat son of a bitch — looks like a small pony, makes contact with the bungee cord he'll yank the entire eye unit out of its hole, and I'll be Mr. One-Eye, Mr. Cyclops, the life of every boring party as I drop the glassy job they give me in the hospital into the punch bowl, and drag my foot around behind me, I'm thinking, you know, of how I can work this unfortunate loss of mine to my advantage when the damn thing falls right out onto the ground, the hook, that is, along with the cord, not my eye, the cat's miffed and leaves, blood squirts from my eye, from the hole where until then the hook had been, blocking the blood from leaving, you know, like a knife in the back, you leave it in until you get to the hospital, so you don't bleed to death, and so there I am, at emergency I didn't have to wait, of course, nobody likes to sit in a waiting room next to some guy projectile bleeding from one eye and trying to read a magazine with his other, Doc slaps a patch over my pierced eye, the slimy tissue grows over the hole, leaving a faint scar, and everybody's happy. Eh, Tom? Tom?

"Jesus Christ, man, a heart attack, not a death sentence . . . Can you not look at me? I'm cracking a beer here and now I am pouring it — ahhhhhhh, good — down my throat. Cold, familiar beer. Want one? . . . Okay, I'll drink it all myself. And when I'm done I'll have fortified myself enough to give you a proper burial because this, this is not a life, pal. All I gotta do is get rid of this bed, pry away the carpet and the floorboards, not to mention the underlay and linoleum, then lower myself a few feet, jackhammer the concrete basement floor, drop you into the dirt, bed 'n' all, and you're in your bloody grave, man, say a few Hail Marys, remember the laughs, hope it doesn't happen to me anytime soon, and Uncle Jack bids a fond farewell to

a groundsheet, fumbling with a bottle of extra-strength Tylenol. "Like Cheerios I eat these," he said to Dory. He turned to Summer Feelin' and said, "You're perfect, you are a perfect little girl."

"She's a perfect little girl," he said to Knute.

And then to Summer Feelin' he said, "I was born the day the *Titanic* sank." Summer Feelin' smiled. "That's right, two disasters in one day," said Uncle Jack. "But never mind, have you got a pumpkin?" Summer Feelin' shook her head. "That's too bad," said Uncle Jack. "If you had a pumpkin I could show you my card trick. Do you know that I can throw an ordinary playing card right through a pumpkin and have the damn thing come out the other side with not one, I shit you not, not one shred of pumpkin flesh hanging from it, and the slit from the card entering and exiting barely visible on either side of the pumpkin?"

"Can you do it with a cantaloupe?" asked Summer Feelin'. Or somebody's head? Knute wondered. "Absolutely not," said Uncle Jack. "It must be a pumpkin. But listen to me, have you got a ten-story building anywhere around here, anywhere in this town?"

"A tall one, you mean a tall, tall building?" said Summer Feelin' standing on her tiptoes and holding her arms up over her head.

"That's right, it's gotta be ten stories, not nine, not eleven, but ten, ten stories tall."

"No, we don't have one of those," said Summer Feelin'.

"Well, that is too bad, that's really a shame, because if you had a ten-story building I could show you another card trick. There are only two men in the whole world who can do this trick, me and my brother, your Uncle Skylar."

Dory cleared her throat. "Jack," she said gently, "Sky's been dead for . . ."

"Never mind," said Uncle Jack, "that's what you think."

Dory shook her head and tried not to laugh, not because she didn't want to offend Uncle Jack, but because she didn't want to encourage him.

"Now listen to me, Hooked on a Feelin' or whatever your —"

"Summer Feelin'!" said Summer Feelin'.

"That's right," said Uncle Jack, "and some aren't. Listen! I can take an ordinary playing card and, on the very first try, with just the right wind conditions, of course, throw that playing card onto the top of a ten-story building. Standing on the ground, me standing on the ground, of course. What do you think of that, Summer-Time Feelin'?"

Summer Feelin' began to flap and hum. "What are you doing?" said Uncle Jack. "What's she doing?" he said to Knute.

"She's excited," said Knute. "Don't worry. She likes

trick, too, no charge. I mean it. Tell Tom to climb out of his coffin and come along, he's seen me do it, I'm better at it than Skylar ever was, or is —"

"Good-bye, Uncle Jack," they all said in unison.

"Find me that building, Knutie!" he yelled just before getting into his car. "I'll do the trick, I promise! Good-bye! A rivederci! So long, Knutie! Keep your knees together . . ." his voice trailed off as he drove away.

CHAPTER
ELEVEN

"Areola is a nice name for a girl," said Hosea. "Don't you think?"

Lorna started to laugh. "Areola?" she spluttered. "God, you kill me —" Lorna was laughing hard. "Hey, Hose," she said, "what do you think — ?"

"Oops, watch your step, my dear."

"Stop telling me to be careful, please. If you don't let me move around normally my body will think I'm dead and reject the baby. I'll end up aborting, Hosea, if you keep —"

"Well, every name means something, doesn't it?"

"Areola Garden Funk, lovely. Sure. I love it. Can we walk a little faster, Hosea?"

"I never walk, you know, never, beats me why, I just —"

"Well, you're fat and lazy, that's why, I'm only pregnant, I can walk."

"I prefer Funk Garden . . . isn't that a band?"

"No, you're thinking of Sound Garden."

"Am I? Hey, wait a second . . ."

"Look," said Hosea. "Shit. Shit, shit."

"What's wrong?" asked Lorna, looking around, pushing her sunglasses to the top of her head for a better view.

"Over there! Behind the Wagon Wheel. It's Mrs. Cherniski, oh shit, that means she's back, she's okay. She's already working, for Christ's sake, some kind of feeble heart attack that must have been —"

"Hosea!" said Lorna, trying to unscramble her sunglasses from her hair. "I promised you I wouldn't laugh, I promised you I wouldn't move to Algren until

. . . I just thought if Cherniski had gone to live with her daughter in the city, then —"

"Oh, bullshit, you just wanted her gone. Even if she'd croaked, you wouldn't have minded."

"Lorna, that is not true, and don't get all mad at me, it's bad for the baby, and it's —"

"Now listen to you, Hosea. In one breath you're pissed off that Cherniski's heart attack didn't kill her, in the next you're all concerned for the baby and admonishing me for, well, for basically reacting the way any normal person would to your bizarre plan, getting your father —"

"Hello, Mrs. Cherniski," said Hosea, looking at Lorna and casually slicing his index finger across his throat in an attempt to shut her up. "It's good to see you up and around, and back at work so soon, my God, you're a lucky woman."

Mrs. Cherniski glared at Hosea like she'd just been hit with a pitch, and was preparing to storm the mound. "Lucky? Lucky, my foot," she said. "Lucky to be back slaving over a hot stove for a bunch of greasy, gap-toothed men in overalls and rubber boots who wouldn't know a decent meal from a poke in the eye . . ." Mrs. Cherniski heaved a black garbage bag into the giant bin outside the Wagon Wheel and stomped back inside.

"I'll tell you what, though, Hosea," she yelled through the screen door. "Lucky is that my daughter is coming to Algren to help me out. She's moving here, the whole kit and caboodle, and I'm gonna get myself some long overdue help from that girl. By the way, I hope to heck you've managed to get rid of that bastard Bill Quinn, you know he was the one who put me in the hospital, and if I see his scrawny butt ever again you're the one who'll be in the hospital, Hosea Funk."

Hosea smiled and nodded. "Uh, when? When is she, are they, coming?"

"Can't hear you, Hosea! What'd you say?"

Hosea's hand flew to the front of his shirt. "I said when? When —"

Lorna grabbed Hosea by the arm and hissed, "Forget it, Hosea, don't be so obvious, just let it go . . . say good-bye."

"But . . ." said Hosea.

"Good-bye, Mrs. Cherniski," said Lorna cheerfully, "don't work too hard!"

Hosea and Lorna walked around to the front of the Wagon Wheel and nearly tripped over Bill Quinn, who

204

was strolling down the sidewalk, tick tick tick, with his overgrown toenails clicking on the concrete and a new goatee-ish tuft of mangled hair on his chin and his soft wet eyes ringed by dark circles as if he'd spent all night smoking Gitanes in a waterfront speakeasy.

"Dammit," said Hosea, "it's Bill Quinn." Hosea lunged for the dog and missed while Lorna put her hands to her face like Munch's model in *The Scream*,

worry. She crouched down and touched his shoulder.

"All right, up you go now, old man," said Lorna.

"Hey! Whatcha doin', Hose?" said Combine Jo, who had just pulled up next to the sidewalk Hosea was lying on. "Listening for hoofbeats? Are we in for a raid? Whoah, girl," she said, as she turned off the ignition. "How much time do we have, Sheriff Funk?"

Hosea cleared his throat. "Actually, I was trying to catch Bill Quinn, but he got away and I tripped over him." Lorna and Combine Jo exchanged grins.

"Hah!" said Combine Jo, "serves you right, padre, nobody catches a Quinn. Hello, Lorna, nice seeing you, you oughtta hang a sign around Mr. Loverboy here's neck saying so and so many accident-free days — you wouldn't get past eight or nine. You know he's a magnet for trouble, Cherniski will attest to that, strange things happen when he's around, ask the doc, when Hosea goes to the hospital the Earth moves. People die, babies are born . . ."

"Oh, Jo, that's not true," said Hosea, stretching his mouth into the shape of a smile, more painful than vaginal tearing during childbirth, he thought, remembering the lurid chapter of the pregnant woman book he was currently reading. Not true at all, heh, heh, stretch those lips, push the teeth to the fore and chuckle confidently, now he felt his mouth was at least forty centimetres dilated, don't forget to breathe and —

"She's gone, Hosea," said Lorna. "Are you okay?"

"I'm fine," said Hosea, massaging his cheeks, returning them to their original position, expecting to taste blood and pass out at any moment. "Just fine. Shall we?" he said. Hosea and Lorna walked slowly to the bus depot. Hosea didn't want to say good-bye. He hated saying good-bye. Lorna was sighing in that way people do after laughing, shaking her head, "Ooohhhh God, Hosea," wiping at her eyes, emitting a few remaining snorts and guffaws. Hosea nodded his head and grimaced amicably. "Ha ha," he said, "go ahead and laugh. It's good for the baby."

"Good-bye, Hosea," said Lorna, dropping her sunglasses and her bus ticket and holding her arms out for a hug.

"Oops, I'll get those," said Hosea. "Good-bye, Lorna, don't take your love to town."

"Excuse me?" said Lorna, starting to laugh all over again. "Okay, Hosea, I won't . . . don't you take your love to town, either . . ." And then she was gone, laughing, dropping her sunglasses, waving good-bye.

206

Hosea popped a Frisk into his mouth and stood watching while the bus disappeared. He headed back to the Wagon Wheel, hoping, as he always did, for an answer to his question. Man's life's a vapour, full of woes . . . Oh, Mrs. Cherniski, he rehearsed in his mind, you know how I like to pay a visit to new residents of Algren, just to make them feel welcome and all that, so I'm just wondering . . . (Hosea cocked his head in an

you've breached the conditions of your probation, Hosea, and now you must be punished. Hosea practised his delivery one more time, "Oh, Mrs. Cherniski . . . just to make them feel welcome and all that." He saw Lawrence Hamm pulling up to the feed mill in his silver pickup and immediately Hosea felt the top of his head, was it there? No, thank God, no hat . . . he'd left it at home. Well, thought Hosea, that will have to do. He nodded at Lawrence across the street, had a quick look around for Bill Quinn, and opened the front door of the Wagon Wheel Café.

In the evenings after Summer Feelin' went to bed, Max and Knute would sit on top of Johnny Dranger's pile of hay and smoke and talk and make love. It seemed like maybe they could be a real couple again. They talked about their childhoods. They were okay, pretty good. Knute's was better. Max told her that he felt his mother

207

loved him. That she loved a lot of things, a lot of people, and that hers was a hard way to go, a potentially disastrous way of living. Knute listened to him talk a lot about Combine Jo. She had got used to hating her, so she didn't know what to say. Knute talked a bit about Tom and Dory, and Max shook his head. "I wonder what he wants," he said about Tom. They talked about what Summer Feelin' got from Max and what she got from Knute. They laughed a lot. The purple sky and warm breeze and the smell of dirt and fresh seed inspired them. Even if they couldn't quite see a future together they could remember a past, and that was enough to build on. Dusk on the prairie in June, that's where they were. Enough light to see what's in your face, too much darkness to see what lies beyond.

"It's good to be back," said Max. "I missed you, Nudie. And I love being a dad, although it is weird . . ."

"That would explain all those hundreds of letters and long-distance phone calls," said Knute. They were lying on top of their pile of hay, in Johnny's field.

"Yeah," he said. "Okay, I didn't call or write or whatever, but I was fucked up. So you can't resent the fact, or you can, whatever, but you can't be justifiably pissed that I had a brain problem and left when I was told to. And as for Summer Feelin', I was scared to death of finding out about her. That was a major deal for me and don't you think for a second I didn't care about her. I figured I was doing her and you a favour by just disappearing. Okay, it's a cliché, whatever, and you probably don't believe me, but it's true. I didn't have a

208

fucking clue what to do about her or you or myself or anything."

"Well," said Knute, "didn't your mother tell you to leave so you wouldn't get stuck being a father at your age, and with some girl who you maybe weren't totally sure about and you just said, 'Yes, Mother, good idea, Mother . . .'"

I was mad that we couldn't just deal with it openly, I was pissed off that I couldn't express doubt about having a baby without being thought of as a total shit . . . So, whatever, for some stupid reason, I guess I was just scared, or confused, or whatever, I said my mother had encouraged me to leave, which, in hindsight, made me look like a total fucking spineless little kid, Mommy told me to leave, et cetera, et cetera, and made you hate me, and my mother, who really is just a harmless drunk, not a bad one, and she can't figure out why you hate her, except that she assumed you'd hate me, for leaving, and . . . you know, hate her by proxy. I don't know, whatever, it was a lie and I had a major brain problem. Okay? I'm sorry."

"It's okay," said Knute. "Okay?" She took Max's hand.

Max took a deep breath. "Fine," he said.

Knute looked at his face. She tried to see it the way Combine Jo would have. She tried to look at it with love only. And concern.

They lay there quietly for a long time and watched the purple fade from the sky. They saw some lights go on in town and saw Johnny Dranger's yard light go on and they heard his dog bark a couple of times and the slam of a car door and Johnny yelling at the dog. If they hadn't lived in Algren most of their lives they would have smelled the liquid fertilizer on the fields. They were used to the smell of shit.

Max lay next to Knute, propped up on his elbows. His smooth white butt, surrounded by the brownish straw of the bales, shone like a giant egg in a dark nest. "Why didn't you tan your bum in the South of France?" Knute asked him.

"Shut up," said Max, laughing.

She gave him a big push with her foot and she heard him yell and then he disappeared entirely and there was a dull thud. Max had fallen overboard into the field. "Oh my God, are you okay?" she shrieked, scrambling to put her clothes on and peer over the side at the same time.

"Fucking hell," said Max, "I think I broke my leg. You're gonna have to go get Johnny, Knute, for fuck's sakes . . ."

Knute landed on the ground beside him and leaned over to have a look.

"Did you bring my clothes?" he asked.

"No," said Knute, "sorry."

"Oh fuck, oh God, my leg is fucking killing me . . ."

"I'll go get Johnny!" she yelled, already running through the field towards Johnny's little house.

"Hurry, I'm dying!" Max yelled. "I'll rot in this fucking field!"

Johnny brought them to the hospital in his truck. Max lay stretched out on the seat with his head on Johnny's

the doctor to show up. By then it was around midnight, and the only person on duty was Nurse Barnes, who shook her head when Knute told her what had happened to Max. "I see," she said. "I see." It didn't look like she saw. If she had seen she would have been nodding her head, not shaking it. "Can you put any weight on it?" she asked Max.

"No!" he said. Johnny laughed at that point and so did Knute. Max was lying on a gurney in the reception area, dressed in his gunny sack and staring up at the ceiling. "What the hell is so hilarious over there?" he said. He cursed under his breath. "Can I smoke in here?"

Nurse Barnes said, "No, I'm sorry." And she added, "I'm afraid Dr. François is having some car trouble, it may be a few minutes before he arrives." So Johnny wheeled Max outside and they all had a cigarette on the front steps of the hospital. Nurse Barnes passed by the open front door pushing an X-ray machine or microwave oven or something and said, "Johnny, I'm surprised at you, with your asthma."

Johnny shrugged and Max said, "What the hell does that mean?"

"Sorry," Knute said to Johnny, "for dragging you around like this. Sorry Max is naked. It was a very warm evening, you know, and . . ." She was smiling and Johnny nodded.

"Sorry?" yelled Max. "Why the hell are you saying sorry to *him*? I'm the one you booted off the bales. I'm the one with the fucking broken leg here!"

"And I'm sorry, Johnny," said Knute, "that Max isn't more grateful . . ."

"You guys are so lucky," said Johnny out of the blue. He was staring at the moon. "You really are —"

Max interrupted him. "Lucky!" he said. "Lucky? Jesus, Johnny, are you warped?"

"Shut up, Max," said Knute.

"Or what? You'll break my other leg? . . . Johnny," he said, "are you there?"

"Yeah," said Johnny.

Nurse Barnes poked her head outside and waved her hand in front of her face. "Smoky," she said. Max said "fuck off" in a very low voice, and then Nurse Barnes said, "The doctor's here now, c'mon back inside."

"I'll race you to the front desk," said Max, and Johnny wheeled him back inside.

The next morning Combine Jo drove Max over to Tom and Dory's place. Summer Feelin' saw them drive up and went running out to help Max with his crutches. She was looking forward to drawing all over his cast with her markers. Combine Jo made sure Max made it to the front door and then gave him a reassuring pat on the back. She picked up Summer Feelin' and kissed her. "See you later, aviator," she said to S.F. who grinned and shook her head. "See you later, hot potater?"

screamed. "Where's the alligator?

By now S.F. was flapping wildly with delight. "Over there!" She pointed to a spot behind Combine Jo, who jumped to the side. "No, no, over there!" S.F. said, and Combine Jo screamed and jumped again.

"Hey, Jo," said Knute. Jo stopped jumping and put S.F. back down on the ground.

"Yes, ma'am?" she said, laughing and out of breath.

"Do you want to come in for a cup of coffee?"

"Oh no," she said. "Thanks anyway, Knuter, but I have some shopping to do, and a few errands to run, another time, though, eh?" She smiled and looked at S.F. "See you soon, you big balloon. Bye, Knute, see ya, Max! Dory!" she yelled into the house. "Give my regards to Tom!" Max had already hobbled into the kitchen and was sitting at the table with Dory, reading the morning paper.

Dory said, "Will do, Jo."

And Max said, "Don't forget, king-size! Not lights! And thanks," he added.

This was the situation. Dory and Knute had had a long talk about Tom, about Max, about Summer Feelin' and about themselves. They agreed that the most frustrating thing was that they didn't know what to do. That is, they didn't know how to make Tom happy, how to get him out of his bed. The doctors said there wasn't much they could do, either. If a grown man decides to stay in bed for the rest of his life, what can you do? His headaches and his confusion and memory loss and depression, all of that was real. And his heart was weaker than it had been before his heart attack, but not strong enough yet to have open-heart surgery. He had been diagnosed as clinically depressed by his psychiatrist, but he had refused to talk to the doctor about his life, his family, his hopes, his dreams, the world, his sadness, anything. Then he had refused to go altogether. So Dory had started going to his appointments instead and discussing her life with Tom. Tom was on medication for all of his illnesses but nothing seemed to change. His medication had been increased, decreased, changed entirely, stopped altogether, and then prescribed again. The doctors said he should be able to do some light work, go for walks, travel, socialize with friends, stuff like that, without too much discomfort, or none at all. Staying in bed, they said, was not going to make him well. But what do you do when a grown man takes to his bed and won't budge? Tom was lying at the bottom of his own mysterious black hole and they could do nothing to help. All they could

214

do was wait for him to make a decision on his own, or for his sadness to lift. "Can you die from being sad?" S.F. had asked. And what could Knute say?

In the meantime, Dory would get on with her life. She decided that she would stop with the home renovations for a while, and go back to work full time at the labour pool, and join a support group in the city for people like her — women who love men who love beds,

reminded the old name and Dory wasn't happy about it. She wanted to be happy about it, but she wasn't. "I need some time to process this," she'd told Knute. She was still worried that Max would disappear any time and leave Knute and S.F. heartbroken once again. But Max and Knute were fine. They were in love, still, and having fun. They had plans for the future, to move to the city, to find work, and to raise their daughter together. "People can change, Dory," Knute said. "People can grow up."

"Yes, Knutie," Dory said, "that's true."

But for now, Knute still had her job with Hosea, Dory was back at the labour pool and Max, they had decided, would look after S.F. at Tom and Dory's place so that Tom would have some company while Dory and Knute were gone. Neither Max nor Tom was looking forward to spending their days together. When Dory had casually mentioned the plan to Tom, he spoke for the first time in days. He rolled over and said, "Preposterous. That boy has the constitution of an Oxo cube. Not to mention the resolve. Put him in a situation requiring responsibility and he'll dissolve at once. He's unfit to look after himself, let alone a child and an old man who happens to hate his guts."

Dory had said, "Tom, Max is not a boy, the child is his own and they get along beautifully, and you are not an old man, although you're acting like one. And, furthermore, since when do you use the expression to hate someone's guts? Really, Tom. People change, people grow up. If you haven't noticed, I'm not a big fan of Max's, either, but right now he's all we have, so get used to it."

Or that's how Dory told it, anyway. She was proud of her firm response to Tom's indignation. She would have loved him to have gone on about it, to argue and rant, to jump up and down on the bed, to refuse to have Max in the house, to have said anything more at all, but he didn't. He rolled over and didn't say another word. When Knute told Max about the plan he responded, initially, with laughter. "Tom hates me," he said.

"We all do, Max," said Knute, "you're a parasite."

"I know, I know," he said. "But, Knute, it'll be pure hell, I have to take care of him? *And* Summer Feelin'?"

"Yes," said Knute. "That's correct."

And now he had a broken leg, too. But that was the situation. Dory and Knute were confident they would manage somehow.

That morning, before Max showed up with his cast and crutches, Knute called Marilyn. She told her all about the night before and they had a good laugh. Then she told her all about Tom. "Are we young or old, do you think, Marilyn?" she asked.

"Oh, for fuck's sake, Knutie," said Marilyn. "We're young, sort of. Young enough. Tell me what you said when S.F. asked if you can die from sadness."

"I didn't say anything," said Knute. "I didn't know

can't die from sadness' would be a terribly clinical thing to say, Marilyn. To say, 'Well, technically, the heart stops beating, the brain stops sending signals, the internal organs shut down and that's how a person dies. End of story,' she'd grow up to be a cynic. I just think it's more mysterious than that. I think you can die from sadness."

"Well," said Marilyn, "it's like a passive form of suicide, just letting go, checking out. Though I still think it takes more than one botched response to your kid to turn her into a cynic."

"Okay," said Knute, "whatever. It's not his fault. It's not a lack of willpower."

"I know," said Marilyn. "Drugs might help Tom, but then again they might not."

"They don't," said Knute. "They don't seem to, anyway. And you know, this sadness . . . as far as I

217

know, Tom's had a happy life, except for his heart attack and now the mental lapses . . ."

"Well, that's enough, isn't it?" asked Marilyn. "Sometimes it's just the fucking sadness in the world, from the beginning of time, and no end to it in sight that begins to eat away at some people. A lot of people, I think. But a lot of people do things about it, like drink too much, or work too hard, or sleep around too much . . ."

"Tom just floats on it," said Knute, "and it takes him out to sea. He gets lost."

"How do you get him back?" asked Marilyn.

"I don't know . . ."

Knute had to go to work, and Marilyn had to answer the door so they said good-bye. Marilyn said it would be a while before they could all get together again because Josh had the chicken pox and she had met a nice guy who was fixing the street in front of her place, so maybe her social life would pick up. But they agreed to talk again soon.

CHAPTER
TWELVE

her head vigorously. Then she pointed to the flowers
and laughed. She looks so much like Tom, thought
Hosea. She really does. For a second or two Hosea
thought about his own child residing within Lorna's
womb and he wondered, would he or she look like him?
He watched Knute say good-bye to the other woman
and light up a cigarette. She smokes too much, he
thought. She'll end up having a heart attack like Tom.
But then Hosea remembered that Tom had never
smoked, except for a couple of cigarettes one summer
night up on the dike when he was a kid, because Peej
had forced him to. Actually Peej had tried to force
Hosea to smoke the cigarettes, but Tom had told Peej
that Hosea was asthmatic and could die if he inhaled.
"Here," Tom had said, "gimme those damn things, I'll
smoke 'em myself."

Hosea opened his office window and wedged a fat
felt-tipped marker under it to keep it up. He tried to

make out the emblem on the front of Knute's baseball cap. He thought it was the Brooklyn Dodgers. Tom's cap, he thought. That's Tom's old cap.

Peej had always wanted to fight Hosea. He knew he would win and he knew Hosea wouldn't tell Euphemia, and even if she found out she'd probably just shrug it off or make a joke. And Hosea had no father to defend him.

Hosea remembered watching the baseball game from the relative safety of the dike. He'd known Peej was there waiting for him. Hosea rode his bike around and around the dike. All the boys playing baseball could see him up on the dike and from time to time one of them would wave. Peej wasn't going to go up there to fight Hosea because he wanted an audience. He wanted Hosea to come down to the field where all the boys were. Finally Tom couldn't stand it any longer and he threw his baseball glove in the grass and walked over to where Peej stood. "C'mon, you stupid piece of shit, I'll fight you."

This made Peej laugh. "Go back to your little game, you jam tart, you're not the girl I'm looking for." Tom looked up at the dike. Hosea had stopped riding and stood straddling his bike, watching.

"C'mon," said Tom, "you big chickenshit. Fight me. If I win, you leave Hosea alone. You never touch him, ever."

Peej laughed. "Okay," he said. "And if I win?" Tom flew at him. He didn't have an answer for that question. He just knew he had to win.

220

Tom didn't really know how to fight. He didn't know how to punch and kick and ward off blows, hook and jab, all that stuff. In fact, he fought like a girl. He clawed P.J.'s face with his fingernails. He pulled P.J.'s hair until his head snapped back and his tongue stuck out and that's when he bit half of it off and spit it back into P.J.'s face. And that's when P.J. went down and the fight was over. Tom was sobbing and trembling and he

Knute was watering the petunias along Main Street, having a cigarette and keeping a lookout for the painters from Whithers. She had hired them to paint the water tower and put the horse decal on it and they had guaranteed the job would be finished by July first, when the Prime Minister might be coming for a visit. They were coming with a few truckloads of paint called eldorado, a kind of filter-orange, Hosea had said, a colour that would blend with the fiery hues of the sunrise and make it look like the white horse was racing through the sky and not plastered onto the side of a water tower. Whatever, she had thought to herself when Hosea told her that. She figured it must have been his girlfriend Lorna's idea. Anyway, she was watering the flowers when Hosea opened his window and called out, "Hey, Knutie, who was that woman you were just talking to? I haven't seen her around town before!"

"It's Iris!" she yelled back. "Iris Cherniski! She's moved here to help her mom at the Wagon Wheel!" And then Hosea slammed his window shut, just like that — end of conversation.

Hosea put his head on his desk. Well, he thought, she's here. Those damn Cherniski women don't waste any time, do they? Now I've got Max, the triplets, and Iris Cherniski, that's five over fifteen hundred. Hosea opened his top drawer and pulled out his orange Hilroy scribbler. Under the column New Citizens of Algren, he added the name Iris Cherniski. He put his scribbler back in the top drawer and closed it. Then he opened the middle drawer and pulled out the tattered copy of the letter from the Prime Minister, promising to visit Canada's smallest town on July first. It has to be, thought Hosea, it just has to be. He thought of the boxes of empty bottles in his basement and of Euphemia's dying words, "Your father is John Baert, the Prime Minister." He didn't want to think about it. He re-folded the letter and put it back into the middle drawer. Wait a second, he thought. Today's my birthday! Today's my friggin' birthday. He knew he'd have to remind Lorna. She often had trouble remembering her own. God, I'm ancient, he thought. People will think I'm my baby's grandfather. Hosea flipped his hands over and checked for liver spots and any type of trembling. Had his left hand quivered? He decided to go home and make himself some lunch. He would call Lorna and have a quick nap, and on his way back to the office he would check on the painters and also on the

222

progress of the carpenters who were busy transforming the old feed mill into a theatre. Then he would talk to Knute about Bill Quinn, and also drive out to the Welcome to Algren, Canada's Smallest Town sign, and think about how to jazz it up.

Hosea drove home and pulled into his driveway. He imagined himself reaching over and unbuckling the ~~securely~~ fastened around his

and was almost in his house when Jeannie appeared from between their houses. Hosea was afraid she'd bring up the subject of turning the feed mill into an aerobics/laundromat and he was about to tell her he already had plans for it, but he didn't get the chance. "Oh, Hosea," said Jeannie, "thank God I caught you, is this a bad time?"

"Uh," said Hosea, "for what?" He knew for what, and yes, he thought, it was a bad time. Every time was a bad time as far as Jeannie was concerned.

"Well, I'll just be a second," she said. "Listen to this. Veronica, you know, Veronica Epp? With all the kids? She's leaving her husband. Apparently, he's being a jerk and not helping out with the triplets at all, he says they're probably not his, excuse me? Not his? I don't think so. It's not like Veronica has any time to have affairs on the side. But he says triplets don't run in his family, and they don't run in hers, so in whose do they run? Veronica says, Well for Pete's sake, they don't really run in most families. So anyway, she's had enough. She's leaving. And she's taking the triplets with her. She was going to take all the kids, but they don't want to go, you know, they're older and all that, and Gord's nice to them because he can see the resemblance, et cetera, et cetera, so —"

"Wait!" said Hosea. "Veronica's leaving? With the triplets? You mean all three of them?"

"Well, yes, Hosea, all three of them," she said. "Triplets, three, get it?"

"I can't believe it," said Hosea, "that's fabulous, well not fabulous, I mean, as in good, I mean, you know, fabulous, as in like a fable, it's so strange, can it be true? That kind of fabulous . . ." Hosea's hand flew to his shirt.

Jeannie shook her head. "Well, I don't know, Gord may be a jerk, but he was probably more help than she realized. It won't be easy for her to be alone with three babies, not to mention being separated from her other kids, and who knows what strange ideas Gord will put in their heads about their mother and their three baby brothers?"

"So," said Hosea, "where is she moving to?" A quick horrible thought came to him. Maybe she was moving into the next block, in with her sister who lived in Algren, in which case it would make no difference to the number of citizens, she'd still be in the same town.

"Winnipeg," said Jeannie. "She's moving into public housing in Winnipeg and she's gonna go on welfare until she can get her act together. Right at the beginning she'll be at her sister's. They call it a trial separation, you know, they're not getting a divorce or anything, but as far as I'm concerned, those trial separations never work, that's it, it's over, people don't get back together again, they just call it a trial separation 'cause it's not so, you know, conclusive, and, of course, for the sake of the kids, who probably don't

 for her parents, who

Jeanne.

"Yeah, sometime on the weekend. She's fed up."

"Oh, you know what?" said Hosea. "I think I hear my phone ringing. I'd better go." Hosea had heard all that he needed to hear. This was wonderful news. And on his birthday! Four people leaving, that would leave only one person too many for Canada's smallest town. There was some hope, there was a chance Hosea's dream might come true. He threw Leander's hat down on the sofa and rushed to the phone to call Lorna.

"Do you know anything about the Algren cockroach?" Knute asked Tom. No answer. "Do you know anything about petunias?" No answer. "Do you know anything about polite conversation?"

"Plenty," said Tom. "Too much."

"Then tell me about the Algren cockroach," said Knute. No answer. She sat down on the bed next to

225

him. "Did you know that cockroaches are responsible for producing 85 percent of the world's methane gas?"

"No," said Tom, sadly, "I didn't."

"Well, it's true, it's their flatulence that does it. Have you ever delivered a two-headed calf?"

"No."

"A two-headed horse?"

"No."

"A two-headed anything?" No answer. She sat and stared at her hands. She yanked a few bits of material dangling from her cutoffs and rolled them into a ball and flicked it to the floor.

"Do you miss being a vet?" she asked.

"No," he said. Silence for a while. S.F. was playing in her room and Knute could hear her softly singing. She looked at the sky through the window. It would be a very hot day. It was time to leave for work. She got up and Tom said, "I never loved being a vet."

"No?" said Knute.

"I wanted to take care of people," said Tom. "I would have liked to have become a doctor."

"Really? Why didn't you?"

Tom sighed and smiled at her. "I was afraid I'd make a mistake." They heard S.F. running down the hall and yelling, "Daddy's here, Daddy's here!"

"Well," said Knute, "S.F. needs a lot of attention and Max has a broken leg . . ."

Tom smiled. "Think that'll keep him from running away again?" he asked.

Knute reached around to feel her cigarettes in her back pocket.

"Gotta go," she said.

"Hey, Knutie," said Tom, "how's Hosea doing?"

"Fine, fine," Knute said. "He's kind of strange, he's okay."

Tom smiled. "Say hi to him, will you?"

Knute nodded. "You were afraid to make a mistake because . . . why?"

Tom sighed again.

. . .

"But then again, you might have saved somebody's life. Or made it better."

Tom was quiet.

"You know," he said finally, "horses gather in clusters when they know it's going to rain. Isn't that smart? So if you want to know when it's going to rain, go for a drive in the country and look at the horses. They always know." He closed his eyes and smiled. Knute could hear Dory giving instructions to Max. ". . . and a chicken casserole in the freezer if you're interested . . . and his tablets are on the kitchen table, S.F. likes to bring them to him in an egg cup . . ."

"Tablets?" said Max.

"Pills," said S.F. "Tablets are pills."

"Okay," said Max, "fine. Do you know how many he gets and how many times, all that?"

"She knows," said Dory. "If he doesn't wake up or respond when she goes in, she just leaves them on the bedside table. He takes them eventually. Or so we think, anyway . . . is that a skirt you're wearing?"

Knute looked at Tom. Did he listen to their conversations all day? Did he care? His eyes were closed and his feet stuck out from beneath his blanket. They were big, strong-looking feet with blue veins all over them and they looked ridiculous poking out from under the soft, yellow cover.

"Yeah, it's a skirt," Knute heard Max say. "I'm not going to cut my jeans to get them over this stupid cast, and I refuse, on principle, to wear sweat pants or baggy shorts, so for now I'm wearing dresses. They're cooler." Knute heard Dory and S.F. begin to laugh and she left Tom to join them. Sure enough, Max had a skirt on and a wide leather belt. The skirt was a green suede mini with pockets that had outer stitching on them. He had one big black boot on, with a hockey sock, a baseball cap on backwards that said And? on the front of it, and no shirt. She noticed a few scratches on his shoulder that she had probably given him. His cast was covered with S.F.'s drawings of hearts and flowers and crooked houses with smoke coming out of their chimneys. She had painted the toenails poking out of the cast a light pink. "It's one of my mom's," he explained to us. "It was too big, of course, so I just cinched it here with this tool belt, like this, and . . . what do you think?" S.F. nodded her head and said, "It's cute," and Dory said, "Nice legs."

smiled. He was on his way to Gord and Fereida

Epp's place. On the way he'd survey his town and note the progress Knute was making with the flowers, the painters were making with the water tower, and the renovation people with the old feed mill.

It was a beautiful hot mid-June day and Hosea was wearing shorts for the first time that year. He also had on a tomato-red T-shirt with white letters spelling Canada, a woven belt he'd bought at a Native American craft shop in Denver when he'd been trying to impress Lorna at the auctioneers' convention, white tube socks, and his L.A. Gear runners. And, of course, his hat, Leander's hat, which was the same shade of beige as his shorts. He looked down at himself, for a second, while driving, and thought he might look like Indiana Jones's dad. Oh well, he didn't care. Things were good, only one person too many in his town, a woman who loved him, an almost guaranteed visit from the man who must be his father, a bun in the oven — sorry, he thought, a baby on the way — and, to top it off, he'd lost six and a half pounds.

He drove down First Street and turned left onto Main, towards the feed mill. On the sunny side of the street he saw Knute, who had been taking care of the flowers, suddenly drench herself with the water in her watering can, and the doctor standing beside her wearing cycling shorts and a tight T-shirt and laughing. Hosea smiled. Nothing wrong with that, he thought. He watched as Knute shook her head and sprayed water all over the doctor.

Hosea wiped his brow and rubbed his sweaty hand on his shorts. "Gad, it's hat," he said out loud like an American in a sauna somewhere in Texas. Knutie and Bonsoir can't be having a, a thing, can they? he thought to himself, remembering the young men in the city Lorna hugged and cracked jokes with. If I wasn't so old, he thought, if I wasn't Indiana Jones's pappy, I'd understand. Hosea quickly tugged at his shirt front and dropped his shoulders in an attempt to appear relaxed. No, can't be, he thought. He knew Max and Knute were a happy couple these days . . . he'd been hoping Max would leave town again, mysteriously disappear like before, in fact he was sure it would happen, and now . . . it wasn't happening. But of course he was happy for Max and Knute and Summer Feelin', he just, dammit, he just needed Max to leave. He needed somebody to leave, anybody really, he had thought Max would be the natural choice. But S.F. loves him, she knows him now, how could he hope Max would disappear . . . "Fucking hell!" said Hosea. He looked down at the neatly ironed crease in his shorts and his pale legs and thought about the Prime Minister, about Lorna, Euphemia, his own unborn child, and what a doofus he was. To hope that a child's father would disappear so that he, an adult, a responsible mayor and soon-to-be father, could have one afternoon with his own dad, alleged dad, not even . . . "Oh for fuck's

life-saving mountain trek. Hosea slowed down and drove up beside the doctor and the dog.

"Hello there," he said. "I've been trying to get rid of that dog for weeks now, and here he is again . . ."

"Ah, Hosea," said the doctor, ignoring his comments, "I've been wanting to talk to you." Hosea stopped his car and the doctor came over and leaned in through Hosea's open window. "Oh, nice belt," said the doctor. Hosea was about to say, "Thanks, it's a Native American blah blah blah," but the doctor said, "So, this is the thing. I've had an offer from a big hospital in Indianapolis, it's a teaching hospital with a good reputation, it's in a great neighbourhood, it's altogether a great offer, and the money, of course, is much better, not that that's your fault or anybody's, it's just fact."

Hosea cleared his throat and nodded, "And?" he said. He smiled and glanced for a second at Bill Quinn, who was lying on the hot sidewalk licking his balls. Bill Quinn lifted his head for a moment, winked at Hosea, and then resumed his position, head bowed and bobbing, back leg sticking straight up in the air.

"And," said the doctor, "I don't know what to do."

"Hmmm," said Hosea. "I can understand that." Leave! he thought to himself, Go to Indianapolis! Take Bill Quinn with you!

"I kind of like Algren," said the doctor. "Especially now that summer is here, it's an easy place to live, you know, an easy place to practise. I wish I could take on a few more challenges professionally, but then again, that may be overrated. I think people like me here, maybe —"

"Oh no, for sure, Doctor," said Hosea. "They like you for sure. I know I do . . ." and he really did, he always had. He admired the doctor's easy ways and his unfailing professionalism and dedication. And they will in Indianapolis, too, he thought sadly, and happily at the same time. This could be the one. The one to leave and make Algren's population a perfect fifteen hundred. He could easily get another doctor immediately after July first, or so he hoped. The doctor and Hosea smiled at each other like a couple of kids.

"Thanks, Hosea," said the doctor. "I like you, too." He patted Hosea on the shoulder and Hosea smoothed down the front of his Canada T-shirt. He nodded.

"Good," he said. He looked down at his white tube socks and back up at the doctor's smiling face. "Good," he said again, awkwardly patting the hand the doctor had rested on Hosea's shoulder for the time being. Is this a French thing? he thought. He might kiss me.

"So, anyway," said the doctor, much to Hosea's relief, "I don't know what to do." A few drops of water fell from the doctor's hair onto Hosea's lap. How soon would this happen? thought Hosea, trying to remember what highway you take from Algren to Indianapolis. "At least," the doctor continued, "I didn't know what to do

"Genvieve called and told me she'd be willing to move here if she could set up a darkroom and do her photography. I told her I had this offer to go to Indianapolis and she said if I did I could just, how do you say that, get out of her life . . ."

Of course she did, thought Hosea, hating all women for a split second and feeling intensely ashamed of himself. "Well," he said, "does she want you to move back to Montreal?" The doctor shook his head and more drops of water fell onto Hosea's shorts.

"No, no," said the doctor. "That's the thing. Now she wants to get out of Montreal, she's tried of all this yes, no, yes, no business, so she's decided to marry me and move to Algren." The doctor was beaming. Hosea willed himself to smile back.

"That's great," he said meekly. "Wonderful. Wonderful news." Hosea shook his head slowly as if to indicate the wonder of life and all its sudden glory.

"Well," he cleared his throat, "I'm very happy that you'll be staying in Algren. Your services have been . . . impeccable. And I'm really looking forward to meeting Genvieve." Hosea stuck his hand out the window. "Put her there, Doc. Congratulations."

The doctor put both his hands over Hosea's and said warmly, "Thank-you, Mayor Funk." Bill Quinn had stopped licking his balls and was fast asleep in the middle of the sidewalk. Hosea heard the faraway sound of a child laughing and a mother calling, "Come here right now and put your sun hat on. I mean it. Come here right now."

"Well," said the doctor, "I'd better be getting to work. Care to join me on my rounds today, Hosea? I know how much you enjoy visiting the hospital —"

"No, no," said Hosea, smiling. "I'll leave it to you. Say, when is your girlfriend coming?" He glanced at Bill Quinn. Had that damn dog cocked his ear just then? Was he listening to everything Hosea said? Hosea wiped his brow. I may need medication, he thought.

"Oh, in the fall," said the doctor. "She had some loose ends to tie up over there, you know . . ."

"In the fall," Hosea repeated. Thank the Good Lord Jesus Christ Almighty, amen, he thought. "Well," he said, "in the fall. Lovely. That's lovely."

The doctor nodded. "I'm happy," he said. "I love her." Hosea was about to say, me too, but said instead, "I'm sure you do."

The doctor whistled at Bill Quinn and said, "C'mon, boy, I'll give you some leftover tuna casserole from the cafeteria . . . See ya, Hosea." Bill Quinn leapt from the

234

sidewalk, had a quick piss on one of Hosea's tires, and left with the doctor. Hosea stayed where he was and looked at the position of his hands on the steering wheel. Ten to two, he thought. He remembered that stupid joke Tom had told him: "Hey, Hose, when's it time for you to use a rubber? Ten to two, get it? Get it? The arms on the clock are the girl's legs, get it?" Hosea had hated that joke. He hadn't got it at first but when

see that sun hat lying on the ground you're coming in for the rest of the day. And I mean it."

Hosea drove away slowly from the curb. He felt his pulse and wondered if his heart was racing. "Relax, Hosea," he said out loud. "Calm yourself." He turned onto Second Street towards the water tower. *That's it, sweetheart,* he heard the voice of Euphemia, *that's it. Find a peaceful place inside yourself and go there, Hosie, don't worry anymore.*

When Hosea was about five or six, he had insisted that Euphemia warm up his bed for him while he was in the tub, having a bath. *Is it ready?* he'd screech from the bathroom, *is it ready?* Warm as toast, Hosea, she'd yell from his bed, make a beeline for it! And Hosea would leap from the tub, grab a towel and run for his preheated bed. At just the right moment Euphemia would lift the blanket and Hosea would dive in. Ladies and gentlemen, we have a new record, Euphemia would always say and make up a time less than the one before. Hank Williams would be singing in the living room and Euphemia would read a *Reader's Digest* or a novel and Hosea would curl up next to her and fall asleep.

Well, thought Hosea as he drove down Second Street, that was a peaceful place. He tugged on his shirt and cleared his throat.

He drove into the tiny parking lot at the base of the water tower and got out of his car. That's a beautiful thing, he thought to himself. The workers at the top waved down at him from their scaffolding and gave him the thumbs-up sign. Not one of them was wearing a shirt. Hosea cleared his throat again and returned the gesture. "Nice," he yelled up at the men.

"What's that?" one of them yelled back.

"Nice!" said Hosea. "Nice work!"

"Okay," said the guy at the top, and went back to his painting. It was perfect, thought Hosea. It was exactly the colour of the sky at five o'clock on a June morning, the colour of Knutie's cigarette filters, and now all it needed was the giant decal of the flying white horse and it would be complete. A week to go, he thought, and the paint needs two days to dry completely, hopefully it won't rain, the painters will be done painting today, they promised, which means the decal goes on on Thursday and then . . . then it's time, thought Hosea, then it's the day. He remembered a recent Associated Press photograph of the Prime Minister avoiding a scrum of reporters and holding his briefcase high over his head, the way a soldier holds his gun up in the air when he wades through a stream. It looked like a backgammon game, thought Hosea. In fact, all those politicians look like they're hurrying to important backgammon tournaments all over the country. Hosea thought about his own briefcase and frowned. He wondered for a split second if he could get _____ his old backgammon game

water tower _____

himself to make that call to Lorna as soon ___ home.

The Epps lived on the edge of town in an old house with a few modern additions built on. They had hay bales around the old part for insulation, and a swimming pool in the backyard. Their cars were rusted-out beaters and their farming equipment was brand new. Their silo had had skulls and crossbones spray-painted on it by one of their teenage sons, and a homemade wooden sign that dangled from their mailbox said Welcome to the Epps.

Hosea drove up the driveway and parked in front of the two-car garage. He hoped Gord wouldn't be home. He and Gord had never really spoken to each other. They knew each other, of course, like everybody in Algren, but they'd never had much to say to one another. Hosea wasn't sure if he could entirely believe what Jeannie had said about Gord accusing Veronica of having an affair, and him not being the father of the triplets, and all that stuff, but he could believe that Gord wasn't much of a help around the house because he spent most of his spare time in the Wagon Wheel drinking coffee and chatting with the boys. Hosea got out of his car and straightened his hat. Where was everyone? he thought. Where were all the kids? Hosea walked to the front door and rang the bell. He peered in through one of the glass panes and saw Gord lying on the couch in the living room, apparently asleep. He saw a baby swing set up in the living room, next to a giant TV that was on, but no babies, no Veronica, just Gord. Hosea looked at Gord asleep on the couch. His bare stomach hung over the couch like a pillow-case half full of Halloween treats, and one arm covered his head and face. Gord's work boots were placed neatly beside the couch. Hosea could see tiny streaks of sweat on the back of Gord's neck. He decided to go home and call Lorna about the backgammon briefcase. If Veronica hadn't already left with the triplets, she would by the weekend. Or so Jeannie had said, anyway. Hosea had just about reached his car, when the Epps' front door swung open and there was Gord. "What's up, Funk?" he said, looking tired and pissed off. "What's the problem?"

"Oh," said Hosea, "Gord, hi, I hope I didn't wake you up, there's no problem, it's just —"

"How'd you know I was sleepin'?" asked Gord.

"Oh," said Hosea again, "well, I, uh, I could see you through the window on the door, you were sleeping on the couch —"

"I wasn't sleeping on the couch, I was lying on the couch. Thinking," said Gord.

"Okay," said Hosea nodding his head. "I hope I didn't, I hope you weren't, um —"

"She's gone, Hosea," said Gord. "I don't know what to do about it. I wish I did." Gord sat down on the front step and stared off towards the road. "And here it is," he said sadly, "a beautiful day."

these diapers, these Huggies, expensive and that perry natal care stuff like the doctor said, you know, and I was trying to keep all the other kids from mauling the babies and giving her a break and, well, I thought I was, we were, okay, it was hell, but we were okay, we were managing."

Hosea walked over to where Gord was sitting. He put his hand on Gord's shoulder and kept it there for a while, the way the doctor had. "I'm sorry, Gord," he said again.

"When the kids come home from school, I have to tell 'em," said Gord. "Veronica said and tell 'em why, just before she left. But fuck me if I know why . . . we were doing okay . . . I don't know what to tell 'em."

"She might come back," said Hosea. "She probably just needs a break."

"I was givin' her breaks," said Gord. "I was. I was trying to. We needed a break together, that's what we

239

needed. Go somewhere, drink champagne, go on a tour or something. That place we went to once. We needed a break together, that's for sure." Hosea took his hand off Gord's shoulder. One Veronica, three babies, that makes four gone. Hurray, hurray, Hosea thought bitterly. And one broken man. Right here, right beside me.

"It'll just take a little time to get used to, probably," said Hosea.

"I don't want to get used to it," said Gord. "I want her back. I want my babies back, too." Gord shook his head and stared off at the road some more. "I never thought this would happen," he said. "Not in a million years." Hosea stared at the road too and tried not to cry. He wanted to leave the Epps' sad farm and call Lorna and tell her how much he loved her. He hadn't made Veronica go away and take the babies. No, he hadn't. Gord had. Or maybe he hadn't. Who knows why Veronica left? He wished she'd come back, for Gord's sake. There was still a week left. Maybe a different family would leave before July first, all together and for a good reason.

"When I see that school bus come down the road with my kids in it, all happy and innocent, I'm gonna cry," said Gord. "I'm just gonna sit here and cry and my older boys are gonna despise me and the little ones will just be scared of me crying. And I don't even know what happened. And even if I did, it's too late. I waited too long and now I'm screwed."

"Why don't you call her at her sister's?" said Hosea.

"Ah, so I guess Jeannie told you where she went, eh?" said Gord.

"Do you want me to call her?" said Hosea. He didn't have a clue what he would say, but he'd call if Gord wanted him to. "Gord?" said Hosea. Gord put his hands over his face and shook his head.

"I can't talk to her, Hosea," he said through his tears. "I don't know what to say. I've never known what to say

stuff, and then —" Gord cried. Hosea sat down Gord and put his arm around his shoulders. Finally Gord spoke again. "I just love her, I want her back. And the babies, too." Hosea nodded and both men stared off at the long road and the empty sky above it. After a while Gord said, "Do you listen to Lightnin' Hopkins ever?"

And Hosea said, "Country's my thing, really."

Gord nodded and then said, "You know what the names of my babies are?"

"What are they?" said Hosea, vaguely remembering.

Gord took a breath. "Indigo," he said, "and Callemachus, and Finbar. He's the one with a little lung problem, Finbar is. But the doctor said it would heal." Gord looked at Hosea. "Do you like those names at all?" he asked.

"Yeah," said Hosea, "you know, I do. I really do. They're names of, well, of distinction."

Gord stared at the road. "The bus is comin'," he said. "I can hear it."

"I guess I'd better be going," said Hosea.

"Yup," said Gord, getting to his feet. "That's an Impala?" he asked, pointing to Hosea's car.

"That's right," said Hosea.

Gord nodded. "Nice lines," he said. "Good mileage?"

"Pretty good," said Hosea. "I don't go very far."

Gord opened his front door. "Well," he said, "that bus is comin'."

"Bye, Gord," said Hosea. Gord nodded and walked into his house.

What the hell is this? thought Knute. She'd gone up to Hosea's office to call Max and see how things were going and she saw a note addressed to her on Hosea's desk.

Dear Knutie, here's twenty dollars to buy yourself a regular pair of shorts and some nice sandals, for the festivities on the first. Hope you don't mind. Regards, Hosea Funk.

Nice sandals? She didn't think so. She didn't think Baert would care what she wore, that is if he even showed up. She flipped the note over and wrote *Will Do, Cheers, K.* and pocketed the twenty. She could wear some of Dory's regular shorts on the Big Day and buy Summer Feelin' some new ones. She called home but it was busy. She stared out the window for a while

242

and watched three guys and two women renovating the old feed mill into a theatre. Hosea thought he'd get Jeannie or someone to organize a production of *Arsenic and Old Lace* or *The Music Man* and get it running over the summer. Right now the only thing that would make anybody think it was a theatre and not a feed mill was a huge sign that read Future Home of the Feed Mill Summer Theatre of Algren. Which reminded her,

the city?"

"No, I'm at work, in Hosea's office."

"You're working in the office now?"

"No, I'm calling from the office. I have to go and paint a sign."

"The one in the ditch? The smallest town in the world?"

"In Canada. Yeah."

Marilyn laughed and said, "Well, you still have the job, that's a record, isn't it?"

"Yeah. I think so. I think it is, actually."

"How's the domestic situation?" she asked.

"Weird. How's yours?"

"Stupid."

"I figured. So, hey, do you and Josh want to come out here for Canada Day? There'll be a little midway and fireworks, Baert might even show up."

"What? The Prime Minister? Really?"

"Yeah, that's the plan. It was in the paper a while ago. He promised to visit Canada's smallest town on the first. And we might be it. I have to wear nice sandals."

Marilyn was laughing. "Herod's idea?" she asked.

"Hosea's. Yeah. I know, I know."

"You know, I'd like to meet the Prime Minister, I've got a couple of questions for him. What's he gonna do, operate the ferris wheel? He's pretty ancient, isn't he?"

"He'll just walk around, I guess, and check things out, make a speech. You know, the usual."

They talked for a while and Marilyn told Knute she'd try to make it out on the first, and then Knute had to go and paint the sign. On the way to the ditch she decided to stop in at home and see how things were going. Everything was quiet when she got there. She looked around thinking maybe Max and S.F. would jump out at any second and scare the shit out of her. She looked into Tom's bedroom and he appeared to be fast asleep. Then she heard some murmuring coming from the basement and she snuck down the stairs as quietly as she could.

"Yeah," she heard Max say. "I miss you, too. Yeah. Yeah. No, not really."

He was on the phone. Who does he miss? she wondered. And then she knew. He missed a woman. Some woman she didn't know. Some woman he had met in Europe or somewhere. She sat on the bottom stair looking at his bare back and listening to him talking to this woman. "No," he said, "I'm not, either. Yeah, I still do. I love you, too. What? Yeah, sometimes.

Summer Feelin'. I know. My old girlfriend. She has blond hair, yeah, she's four. Five? No, she's four."

Yeah, she's fucking four, Knute thought to herself. Get it straight, asshole.

"Yeah, I broke it," Max said. "Oh, I fell. Nah."

"Tell her how you fell!" Knute yelled and she ran for the phone and grabbed it from him and threw it against

of thing. That sort of very typical thing. She yanked the cord out of the wall and then threw the phone at Max, both of them screaming the whole time. He ducked and the phone knocked over a lamp and the bulb shattered all over the rug. "Where the hell is S.F.?" she yelled. By now she was sobbing and yelling, "I thought I could trust you!" And mixed in with "Where's S.F.?" and "Who was that?" and "I can't fucking believe it." Then back to "I thought I could fucking trust you!" Over and over. Max was trying to get to her, to hold her and calm her down, but his cast hooked onto the phone cord and he fell into the broken light bulb, and he cut his back and started to bleed, and just lay there, saying, "Calm the fuck down, Jesus Christ, calm the fuck down, please. She's playing in the back, she's playing in the backyard with Madison. Shut the fuck up and let me talk to you."

Knute could hear Tom yelling from his bed, "What in the Sam Hill is going on down there? What broke?!"

And then she left. She ran out of the house and out of the town and past the sign she was supposed to be painting and she just kept running down the highway.

"Hello, sweetheart," said Hosea from his desk. He saw Knute's note and smiled. "How are you?"

"Oh, you know, fat," said Lorna over the phone. "And green."

"Fat and green?" asked Hosea.

"Pretty much, yeah. I'm hideous."

"No, you're not."

"I feel hideous," said Lorna. "How are you?"

"Well, I'm fat, too," said Hosea. "Fat and white. I'm wearing shorts."

"Well, it's hot enough," said Lorna.

"What are you wearing?" asked Hosea.

"Nothing," said Lorna.

Hosea smiled. "Really?"

"No," said Lorna, "I'm wearing shorts, too, with a panel."

"A panel?" asked Hosea.

"Stretchy stuff in the front, maternity shorts."

"Oh," said Hosea, "I should get a pair."

Lorna laughed. "I don't really need them yet, I'm just trying them out. How's the plan?"

Hosea cleared his throat. "Remember when I told you that Veronica Epp had left with her triplets?"

"Yeah," said Lorna.

"That's actually a shitty thing," said Hosea.

"But it brings it down to one person, doesn't it?" she asked.

"Yeah, but it's shitty for Gord and her other children."

"I guess it would be," said Lorna. "But, you know, it might be good for Veronica. Anyway, Hosea, it's not your fault, you know."

"You're laughing, aren't you?" asked Hosea.

"No, of course not."

"Lorna!" said Hosea.

"Well, okay, I am, but c'mon, Hosea, what do you expect?"

Hosea thought for a second. "I don't know," he said. He wanted to beg Lorna never to leave him. He wanted her to promise she would never leave him sitting heartbroken on the front step. He wanted her to promise she would never take their baby away from him. "The water tower looks great, though," he said. "It's perfect."

"Is the horse on yet?" asked Lorna.

"Almost. Hey," he said, remembering the favour he needed to ask of Lorna. "Do you think you could buy one of those backgammon-type briefcases for me and bring it out when you come on the thirtieth?"

All right, okay, thought Hosea as he popped an Emmylou Harris tape into his car deck. That's taken care of. They'd made arrangements that Lorna would come out on the thirtieth with a bag of clothes and the backgammon briefcase, and after the first they'd move the rest of her stuff into Hosea's place. Their place. "Huhhhhhhh," said Hosea, expelling a giant breath of relief. One more's gotta go. Just one more. I'm happy, thought Hosea. He thought of Gord on his front step. Am I happy or am I sad? he thought. I don't know which to choose.

He pressed play on his tape deck. Then he changed his mind and pushed the eject button.

Knute ran until she was too tired to run, and then she walked. She thought maybe she'd walk to Winnipeg, to Marilyn's, or maybe all the way down the Trans-Canada Highway to Vancouver. She walked into the ditch and up to a barbed-wire fence surrounding a field. She lifted the top wire and climbed through the fence and then she walked to a little tuft of bluish long grass in the middle of the dirt and lay down.

Caroline Russo, thought Hosea. Caroline Russo was pregnant with Johnny's baby. Wild Caroline Russo with the eldorado-coloured lunch kit and the leather flask full of Dr. Pepper. If she and the baby were still alive, they'd be the kind of family that would sail around the world on a homemade boat, and let the kids go naked, and Johnny would have a beard . . . they'd laugh a lot

. . . Hosea pulled into Johnny's driveway. Johnny was standing there in his doorway smiling and holding two bottles of beer, like he'd been expecting Hosea. "Am I out?" he asked Hosea.

Hosea smiled. "No, no," he said. "You're still in. Soon you'll be Algren's new fire chief."

"Hmmmm," said Johnny.

"'Cause I'm leaving this place day after tomorrow."

"For how long?" asked Hosea.

"For good. I don't want to die here."

"But you're not that old," said Hosea.

"I know," said Johnny. "I don't want to die here, you know, I don't want to live here like I'm dead. I don't mind dying here, I just don't want to *die* here, do you know what I mean?"

"I think so," said Hosea. "I didn't know you hated it here."

"I don't," said Johnny. "I don't hate. It it's fine."

"You might not find another place you like any better," said Hosea.

"That's true," said Johnny. "But I can have a look around anyway and. Besides, I can just keep. Moving I don't have to stay put in one. Place there's no reason for me to. Oh, don't look so. Sad, Hose, it's a good.

249

Thing I'm excited about moving. On I'm looking forward to it."

"But what are you going to do while you move around?" asked Hosea. "What about your farm?"

"I'm gonna put out fires," said Johnny. "There are fires burning out of control all over the. World I'll get fed, and put up in some place, and I'll just fight fires all over, until I've had. Enough or until my lungs give out." Hosea stared at Johnny. "And there'll be other things to do, too, Hosea, don't. Worry can I tell you something?"

"Yeah," said Hosea. "Of course."

"I want to sleep with women," said Johnny. "Women from all. Over I want to have. Sex, you know? Just a lot of good, happy. Sex I'm tired of Caroline's memory hanging over. Me I want to remember her, but I don't want it to stop me from doing stuff anymore."

Hosea cleared his throat and looked at Johnny gravely. "Do you really think you'll be happy just moving around and screwing all sorts of women?" At that point both Johnny and Hosea began to laugh.

"Yeah," said Johnny, "I really do." Hosea was shaking with laughter now and Johnny could barely speak. "Yeah," he managed to say, "I think I will be very happy doing that for a while." Hosea was laughing too hard to say anything but he lifted his beer up to Johnny's, against the pink sky, and they clanked their bottles together, and he thought he heard Johnny say, "To Caroline." Or maybe he had said something else entirely and Hosea had only imagined that Johnny had said her name.

★   ★   ★

Eventually Knute woke up and decided to go home. First she sat in that blue tuft and examined the grass marks on her bare legs and then she wondered is it better to try to understand life or is it better not to? Which makes you happier? She remembered a book of Dory's that said the mystery of life is one with the ░░░░░░░░░░░░░░ thought. Yeah, okay, makes sense.

CHAPTER
FOURTEEN

"Are you drunk?" asked Lorna.

"Maybe," said Hosea. "I was drinking beer with Johnny. In the sun. A lot of beer, I don't know how many, but a lot. Good beer, though, very good beer. We had a good time, just sitting there at his little picnic table and —"

"Hey, Hosea!" shouted Lorna over the phone. "Snap out of it. I get the picture."

"Okay," said Hosea. He was writing the name Johnny Dranger in the Soon To Be Leaving Algren column and Veronica Epp and three babies in the Moved Away column. "Okay," he said again to Lorna. He slapped a hand over his right eye and tried to focus on the page. "I wanted to tell you what we were doing."

"You were drinking beer in the sun, you already told me that. Call me when you're sober, Hose, and please don't make a habit of getting hammered with losers like Johnny Dranger. You're going to be a father soon."

"That's right," said Hosea, slurring his words.

"Man, that beer should have been mine," Lorna continued. "I wouldn't mind having a cold beer, it's so fucking hot, and I'm so itchy, do you think one would hurt? Hosea? Hosea!"

"We were celebrating, Lorna," said Hosea. He'd put his head down on the desk and had the phone resting on the side of his head so he could still hear her. His eyes were closed. His hands dangled down by the floor. "I'm so happy. Everything's just . . . so good. I've got fifteen hundred. I've got it right."

. . . Lorna. "How?"

. . . . nts to meet

the wo. . . .

other end. His lips slid into a . . . you love me?" he whispered, and the phone fell on his head and onto the desk, and Hosea was sound asleep.

Knute went home. The sky was a beautiful shade of blue, dark and soft and warm, and she could hear people talking in their houses because all the windows were open, and she could smell barbecues, and maybe a bit of rain on its way, and she could hear a lawn mower off in the distance and a car with no muffler tearing down deserted Main Street, looking for a race, and the crickets were starting up but sounded a bit rusty, and in front of her house, on the road, was a small woollen mitten covered in dust. It was S.F.'s so she picked it up and took it in.

Dory and Summer Feelin' were playing Junior Monopoly and eating ice cream. They didn't think anything was wrong. "Hi, Mommy!" said S.F.

"Oh, Knute," said Dory, "Max said you'd be late. There's some pizza left on the counter if you're hungry."

She gave S.F. a kiss and said thanks to Dory. Then she walked into Tom's room. He knew she was coming. He was awake and was wearing his glasses. Knute closed the door quietly and sat on the edge of his bed and began to cry. "I didn't tell them," said Tom. "They don't know what happened."

"Do you?" she asked.

"Yes," he said.

"How do you know?"

"Max told me."

"He told you? Max came in here and talked to you?"

"No. I got up and went down and helped him clean up the glass and I put some hydrogen peroxide on his cuts. S.F. played outside the whole time with the neighbour kids."

"So," said Knute, "aren't you going to tell me you told me so, about Max being the same old Max?"

"He was talking to a girl. A little girl. He had a job taking care of her in London, her and her baby brother, and he was calling her to tell her he wouldn't be back. When he left he had told her he might be, and now he just wanted to tell her the truth."

Knute looked at Tom. "He told you that?" she said. "And you believe it?"

"Yes, I do. He called her back after you had, well, interrupted him, and he apologized, and then he told her what he wanted to tell her."

"That he wasn't coming back," said Knute.

"Right," said Tom. "That he wasn't coming back."

"Because he wants to stay here?"

"Yes."

"So where is he?"

"I don't know."

"Was he going home?"

"No, Combine Jo called here looking for him."

"Oh, God," Knute said, and put her head in her

"You know, Knutie," said Tom, closing his eyes. "If you have fun with the guy . . ." Tom took a deep breath ". . . I hate advice," he said. "But why don't — if you have what you want — Why don't —"

"Knutie!" Dory yelled from the kitchen. "It's Jo on the phone. She's wondering if you have any idea where Max could be."

Hosea woke up from his nap with a stiff neck and a dry mouth. The room was much darker than it had been. He put the phone back where it belonged and put his notebook in the drawer. "I've got my fifteen hundred," he whispered. "I've got the smallest town." He sat at his desk with his hands folded in his lap and wondered, Was I coming or going? Well, he thought. I'm here now so I must be going. He stood up and walked to the open window and stared out at Main Street. It was completely deserted except for two small girls. They sat on the curb in the yellow light under the streetlight, playing a clapping game, and taking time out for sips from a Coke they were sharing. "Con-cen-tray-shun," Hosea heard them chanting, "Concentration must begin-keep-in-rhyth-UM!" One of the girls slapped her thighs at the wrong time and both of them put their heads back and roared with laughter. "Okay, start again. Start again," one girl said. "Okay, okay, hang on, okay, no, wait, okay," said the other, and began to laugh again.

Hosea didn't feel like going home. Tom, he thought. I'll visit Tom. He was about to leave a note reminding Knute to spray the petunias with cockroach killer one more time, before July first, but then remembered that he'd be seeing her at Tom's. Or, if she was out, he could leave the message there and she'd get it in the morning. Hosea left his office and his car, which he could barely remember parking, and set off for Tom and Dory's. "Hello," he said as he passed the girls on the curb. "Lovely summer evening, isn't it?" The girl who'd been having a hard time concentrating was trying not to laugh, and nodded her head, and the other one said, "Mm hmmm." She made a face at Hosea as soon as he had passed, and both girls burst into laughter yet again.

"C'mon, Summer Feelin'," said Knute, "we're going to find Max. Hurry up, let's go."

"Is he lost?" she asked.

"We'll see," said Knute. "You can go barefoot, c'mon. We're taking the car."

256

Dory stood up from the table. "What's going on?" she asked.

"Ask Tom," Knute said. "He knows."

"Tom knows?" asked Dory, as Knute and S.F. ran out the door.

"Ask him!" Knute yelled. "Wake him up!"

_____ the door. "Is

having a little, w___ .
in, then. Go and talk to him. My goodness, ___
here." Dory shook her head and peered off into the night. "Do you want a beer?" she asked suddenly.

"Oh no," said Hosea. "No thank-you. Well, all right," he said, and thought, hair o' the dog, after all.

"Go on in," said Dory, "I'll bring you one. The only reason why I have a beer to offer you is because of Max. He's looking after S.F. and Tom, while Knutie and I are off at work."

"Well," said Hosea, "that's a nice arrangement."

Dory frowned and stared off into the darkness again. "Go on in," she said. "I'll be right there."

"Um, I could just get it myself, Dory," said Hosea. "I know where the fridge is."

"Fine," said Dory. "Help yourself."

"Sure thing," said Hosea. "Thank-you." He went to the fridge and got himself a beer and then went over and knocked on Tom's door. No answer.

"For heaven's sake, Hosea, just walk in," Dory yelled. "He won't answer. Just go in."

Well, thought Hosea. Dory's acting very strangely. "Thanks, okay," he called out.

Hosea sat down on the laundry hamper and crossed and uncrossed his legs. He put his beer on the dresser next to the laundry hamper, and cleared his throat and tugged at his Canada T-shirt. All he could see of Tom was the back of his ruffled head poking out from under the blanket. *Whooooo*, Hosea kind of breathed out loud. It was a hot day all right. Hosea stared at the back of Tom's head, willing it to swivel around and face him. Hosea could hear the crickets and the hum of the refrigerator. Dory must have stepped outside to have a good long look at the dark sky, he thought. "So," said Hosea, "what's new?" He stared at the back of Tom's head and said to himself, Move, move, your damn head. Look at me. He drank some of his beer and did a mental tally of the number of beers he had had that day. This was his eighth. And last, he told himself. He thought briefly of Lorna, and of the baby-to-be, and of his father, the Prime Minister. And then he thought of Euphemia. "So," he said again, "how are you feeling, Tom?" He finished off his bottle of beer and longed for another. I'll just get one, he thought. He wanted to talk about his fifteen hundred, his smallest town, so badly, he wanted to tell someone about it. He got up and went to the kitchen for another beer. Nine, he thought. No more. He went back to Tom's room and sat down on the laundry hamper again. Tom's head was in the same position. Nice head, he felt like saying. Needs combing.

258

Hosea leaned over so his head was close to Tom's. He could hear Tom breathing. He reached over and put his hand on Tom's chest. Up and down, up and down, good sign. Like a baby, thought Hosea. Well. "So, Tom," he said, "something is happening. To me. Something good." He leaned over and pulled gently on Tom's _____ "Something good, Tom," he whispered. Hosea _____ _____ he said. "You _____

_____ asleep, then, thought Hosea. _____ say. Hosea had a sip of his beer. "And he's coming to visit me on July first," he said. Hosea told Tom all about the smallest town contest and about all the comings and goings of the people of Algren, about the triplets and Veronica Epp, about Leander Hamm, and Iris Cherniski, about the doctor's girlfriend, and Max, and Johnny Dranger, about Lorna, and the baby, and how, finally, Algren had fifteen hundred people exactly, which was just the right number to make it the smallest town, and on and on. "So," he said, "I'm going to meet my dad, Tom. I'll see him for the first time, and I'll tell him who I am, and I'll show him my town."

Tom's head didn't move. "What do you think of that, Tom?" said Hosea. "What the hell do you think of that, Tom!" he said. "This is my dream, you bastard, now what the hell do you think? Aren't you my fucking friend, Tom?"

259

Still, Tom's head didn't move. "I'm sorry, Tom," said Hosea. "I'm sorry for yelling. I need a friend, Tom, that's all, really. I'm sorry," he said. "Okay? I'm sorry." Hosea pulled on Tom's blanket again, and then got up and left.

Knute knew exactly where to find Max, except that when she and S.F. got to that place he wasn't there. If he wasn't at the hay bales and he wasn't at Jo's and he had a cast on his leg and no car, then where was he? Bill Quinn was at the bales, though, looking kind of lost, so Summer Feelin' coaxed him into the car and they took him with them. "You know," Knute said to her, "I'm supposed to be getting rid of that dog."

"Why?" S.F. asked. She asked why a few times, but Knute didn't really hear her because she was so worried that Max had left for good, again. And she was so mad because why couldn't she just get mad and yell and run away for a couple of hours, without having to worry about him leaving, too, on top of everything else? Why couldn't they be a normal couple? Get mad, get misunderstood, act stupidly, know the other's not going to run away, come home, make up, have fun, you know, until the next shitty time comes up, and they'd just ride that wave then.

"Why, Mom?" asked Summer Feelin'.

"Why what?" said Knute. She was driving around the four streets of Algren now, around and around, trying to come up with a plan.

"Why do you have to get rid of him?"

"I don't know," said Knute. "Well, because Hosea asked me to."

"So?" said S.F. She had begun to flap and Bill Quinn sat there on the back seat staring at her. Knute looked at him in the rearview mirror.

"I'm going to crawl over and sit with Bill Quinn," ~~said~~ ... ~~added~~ "I don't know."

"No!"

Bill Quinn looked out the window ~~pointedly~~ was pretending not to hear the conversation. Then S.F. started up with "Why not? Why not? Please, please, please."

"Okay, you can," said Knute. This was just fucked, she thought to herself. Where the hell was that jerk?

"Yippeeeee!" yelled S.F. "You're my dog!" She put her arms around him and he barked and licked her face. "You're so cute, Bill Quinn," she said, rubbing her nose against his.

All right, Knute thought to herself, maybe he's at Jo's. Maybe she's drunk and he's hiding out in his room, pissed off at the world, or just at me, really, and it's a big house, maybe she doesn't even know he's there. Whatever, I'll try it.

She sped up near the dike road and S.F. toppled over onto the dog. "Put your seatbelt on," said Knute. She just wanted to say sorry and get back on track, and not lose him. Just because he was the one who went away for four years didn't mean that she couldn't say sorry every once in a while.

Then she saw Hosea. He was up on the dike, walking in the dark, all alone, like some kind of sentry who hadn't heard the war was over. She slowed down and stopped on the road, below him. "Hey," she yelled through her open window "Hi, Hosea!"

He stopped and looked at her and waved. Then he came down from the dike and walked over to the car. Shit, she thought, Bill Quinn.

"Hello, Knutie," he said, "is that Summer . . ." His voice trailed off.

"Feelin'," said Knute.

"That's it. Summer Feelin'," he said. "Hello there, Summer Feelin'. You've got a dog?"

"It's Bill Quinn," said Knute. It was dark and she knew there was a chance Hosea wouldn't recognize him, but Hosea had a look on his face, a faraway look, and it didn't seem right, for some reason, to lie to him.

"Is it?" he said. He shook his head and smiled. "They come," he said, "and they go."

"I'm trying to find Max," said Knute. "Have you seen him?"

"No, I haven't," said Hosea. "Not recently. Why? Where'd he go?"

"Well, I don't know exactly, that's why I'm trying to find him."

"You don't think he's left . . ." Hosea glanced at S.F., who was busy playing with Bill Quinn ". . . left Algren?"

262

"No," said Knute, "I don't think so. I'm going to check at his house. Jo hasn't seen him, but you know . . . he might be there."

Hosea looked like a ghost in the moonlight. His face was as white as the letters spelling Canada on his red shirt. "What if he's gone?" he said. Knute looked back ~~~~~ Feelin'. She didn't want to get into this with

~~~~~ ~~~~~ 1 "

sitting right there, ~~~~

"Don't worry, Hosea," she said. It ~~ find him. He's got a broken leg." She started driving away slowly. "Okay, see ya, Hosea, see ya at work tomorrow. Don't worry!" she yelled out the window, "I'll find him!"

Hosea walked home and sat on his front steps for a while. He could see part of the white horse decal on the water tower, sort of shimmering in the black sky and he looked forward to seeing the whole thing against the filter-orange sky of early morning. "I hope you find him," he said out loud, remembering S.F.'s smiling face in the back seat. It was a pure thought, a simple wish, with no strings attached. He truly did not care about his fifteen hundred at this point. He hoped on every star and flying horse in the universe that S.F. would find her dad. He thought of calling Lorna to tell her that everything was, once again, up in the air. Max was missing. He'd yelled at his buddy Tom, and made a fool of himself. Why would he want to tell Lorna that? he asked himself. He went inside and lay down on his bed and wept.

When Knute and S.F. got to Jo's house, Jo came lumbering out to the driveway and said, "No, he's not here, Knutie, I don't know where he is." It was really late by then, after midnight, and Knute told S.F. to lie down on the back seat with Bill Quinn, and try to go to sleep. She got out of the car and lit a cigarette and Jo said, "What happened, anyway? Why'd he take off?" So Knute leaned against the car and told her exactly what had happened, and she said, "Oh for Christ's sake, Knutie, he loves you, it's so fucking simple. Let it be! He hasn't run away from you. It's the goddamn guilt that's killing him."

"Oh," said Knute, "he's running away from the guilt of running away?"

"Yeah," said Jo, "and all the work in front of him trying to rebuild your trust, which he wants, and S.F.'s, and all that very difficult shit. And believe me, it's difficult. He hasn't run away from you!"

"Okay," Knute said. "Then where do I find him?"

"How the hell should I know?" said Jo. "Wouldn't I have found him myself if I knew? The poor kid has a broken leg, after all, he can't have gone far."

"If he was walking," said Knute.

"Right," said Jo, "and I'm sure he was. His private helicopter is in the shop and it's his chauffeur's day off. Don't be ridiculous, Knute. Even if he'd have tried hitchhiking to God knows where, do you honestly think anybody would pick up a guy in a cast and a skirt and a ballcap? No shirt, no suitcase? Trust me, he walked."

Knute threw her cigarette down and ground it out with the heel of her boot.

"Listen," said Jo, "why don't we have a drink and then I'll come looking with you?"

... Let's go."

been driving

about her habit of blasting down Main Street combine and sharing a drink with her dead husband over at the cemetery. "That combine thing, Jo, do you ever . . . ?"

Jo looked at her and sighed. "I don't do it anymore," she said. Knute nodded and they kept driving. "You know," said Jo, sitting in the front with Knute, and resting her arm on the windowsill, "when Max was nine I took him to Cooperstown."

"Oh yeah?" said Knute. "What's that?" She thought Jo had been too drunk and fat to get out of the house all those years. That's how the story had gone, anyway. She wondered how much she really knew about her little town and the people living in it.

"Cooperstown," she said. "Cooperstown, New York. The Baseball Hall of Fame is there."

"Oh," said Knute, "keep looking out your side." S.F. and Bill Quinn were fast asleep in the back seat.

"Max was so excited," continued Jo. "He'd say, oh, four days 'til we get there, and then, you know, two days, one day, six hours, three hours, like that. And, you know, we had driven for days and days and finally we got there, to Cooperstown, and Max didn't want to go to the museum! We had gone all that way for him, you know, he loved baseball and this was a dream come true for him, the livin' end, and then he balked. The little fucker, I thought then. What's going on? So I said 'Okay then, let's have something to eat' and he chose a restaurant a little way down the street from the hall of fame, so we could just sort of see the flagpost that was in front of it, but not the actual building. And then he just farted around in that damn café for an hour and a half, making up excuses not to go to the g.d. hall of fame! So, you know, we took a little trolley ride around the town, it's a really pretty little place, just up this windy road from Woodstock, actually. Anyway, a fun little trolley ride packed with other tourists and some local people. And finally I thought, Okay, we have to go to that hall of fame now. We just have to. So I told Max, 'Okay, we're getting off this trolley at the next stop and we are going into that hall of fame. End of story. You know, the damn thing's gonna close for the day before we get in.' So we get off and we walk up to the front steps of the building and Max stops. He just stops and stands there staring at it. And I take his hand, you know, c'mon, c'mon. But he stands there and he starts to cry. Now I'm totally fed up, but, you know, a little concerned, and I say, 'Max sweetheart, what is the

266

problem here?' And he says, 'If I go in now, it'll soon all be over, like a dream. And I don't want it to end.'"

Jo shook her head and laughed. "Crazy little fucker, eh?"

"Well," asked Knute, "did you eventually go in?"

"Oh yeah," she said. "We did."

"Was it . . . did it work out okay?"

"No," said Jo. "No, I don't think he did. He was perfectly content, as I recall."

"I thought you never left the house when you were, uh, when Max was little."

"That's just another lie, Knutie," said Jo. "Don't believe everything you hear."

"Well," Jo said a little later, "we're not finding him, are we?" She passed Knute her bottle of bourbon.

"Maybe he's in Cooperstown," said Knute. Jo laughed and yawned.

"Are you okay to drive, Knutie?" she asked. "Not too sleepy?" She put her head back and shifted her large body around on the seat.

"I'm fine," Knute answered.

"I'll just have a quick catnap, then, if you don't mind," said Jo, and closed her eyes.

267

Knute was worried. She was already circling back the way she'd come and if she hadn't seen him on the way out of town, she didn't know why she should expect to see him on the way in. Besides, he wouldn't necessarily be on the road, he might have walked into somebody's field and fallen asleep or gone into an open silo, a barn, anything. She passed the Hamms' farm on the left. It had a giant yard light on that lit up the entire area for what seemed like miles. A million moths and bugs flew around the light and a couple of dogs were walking around in the yard. No lights were on in the house. Then Knute had an idea! She stepped on the gas and drove straight into town and out the other side, back onto the dike road and headed for Johnny Dranger's house.

She peeled into the driveway, pulled right up to Johnny's front door and left Jo, S.F., and Bill Quinn asleep in the car. She could hear music coming from the house and laughter and low voices and she knew she had her man. She just walked right in and said, "Hello, Max, hello, Johnny, what's up?" They both stood there, smiling and staring at her, and instead of yelling she smiled and stared back. Johnny said, "Have a seat, Knute."

"You're mad at me, aren't you, Knutie?" said Max.

"Nah," she said, "I'm here to apologize." Johnny disappeared into the kitchen then and Knutie whispered, "But why do you keep running away?"

"You ran away, Knute, this time. I didn't."

"You ran away after I ran away," she said.

268

"No I didn't," said Max. "I stayed at your place until Dory came home, like I was supposed to, then I offered to take S.F. back to my house but she said no, she was gonna make pizza with Dory, so fine, no problem, then I left and —"

"And didn't tell anybody where you were going," interrupted Knute.

said Max. "I'm an adult,

understand how I ———

happened before."

"Yeah," said Max. "Okay, whatever, I'm not going to argue anymore, I have too fucking much at stake now, okay? You want me to understand all this stuff about you, fine, why don't you try to understand some stuff about me?"

Knute didn't say anything then. What was there to say? Then she thought of something. "Okay," she said. Silence.

"Well, thank-you," said Max. He smiled.

"You're welcome." Silence. "How's your leg?"

"Fine, thank-you," said Max. "How's yours?" Knute smiled. Silence.

"I know about the phone call," she said.

"I assumed," said Max. "Tom told you?"

"Yeah." Silence.

"I have something to ask you, Knute," said Max.

"Do you think you and S.F. would like to live here with me? You know, just try it out, see how it goes, we could fight on a more regular basis, you know . . ."

It was the first time Knute had seen Max looking unsure of himself.

"What do you mean?" she asked. "Where?"

Max took a cigarette out of his pack and lit it. "Right here," he said, blowing out smoke.

Knute pointed to the kitchen. "With Johnny?" she whispered.

"No, no, he's leaving," said Max. "That's the thing. And he's offered me his place. Us his place. If you want it."

"Well, sure," said Knute, "okay," and then they laughed for a while thinking of themselves as farmers and Johnny came back into the living room with some snacks. Eventually Knute remembered that S.F. and Jo and Bill Quinn were sleeping in the car. Johnny threw them out at four in the morning, said he had to pack. Knute drove Max and Jo home. Bill Quinn went with them. And then S.F. woke up and said she was going with the dog, so that night she slept over at Max's. And Knute went home alone.

CHAPTER
FIFTEEN

Dear Knutie, S.F. will ▓▓▓▓
for the day. Tom says he doesn't mind ▓▓▓
alone for the afternoon while we're at work. And
Hosea called, would like you to pick up more
cockroach spray and give the petunias one more
squirt on your way into the office.
Love, D.

P.S. I know about yesterday, so relax. And what's
this about S.F. having a dog? I'm having a few
people from Friends of Houdini over tonight.

She had written something else about someone in town
stepping on a rusty nail and having a strange reaction
to the tetanus shot, but she had crossed most of it out,
and written "Oh never mind" underneath.

Knute peeked into Tom's room and asked him if
there was anything he needed before she left. He shook
his head and smiled. She told him about Max and her

271

and S.F. moving into Johnny's house and looking after his farm, and he gave her the thumbs-up sign and said, "That's great." He seemed short of breath and she asked him if he was okay and he nodded. She kissed him good-bye and left for work.

When Knute got to the office Hosea was there and he said, "Did you find him?"

"Yup," answered Knute. "At Johnny's house." And then she told him about the plan to move in with Max and he, too, was very happy about it.

"How's Tom doing today?" he asked, and Knute said she didn't know.

"It's hard to know anything about him these days," she said. Hosea told her that they had the smallest town, they had fifteen hundred people, as soon as Johnny left, anyway. The count would happen in the next day or two and that would be that. The Prime Minister would be coming to Algren on July first.

"Well then," said Knute, "all is well."

"Quite," said Hosea, formally, and kind of sadly, and Knute put up her hand for him to slap, you know, high-five, but he said, "Oh, you're going?" And he waved back.

Which was one of the funnier things that had happened to Knute in a while.

Hosea sat at his desk and felt the warm midday sun on his back. As randomly as I was conceived, he thought, as randomly as I was named, as randomly as . . . he heard a horn honking under his window and he got up and walked over to have a look. "Hey, Hosea!" shouted

272

Johnny Dranger. "I'm leaving! I'm gone!" Hosea waved and yelled, "Good luck! Come back alive! And send me a postcard from time to time!"

"I will!" yelled Johnny. "So long!" And he was gone.

The phone rang and Hosea hoped it would be Lorna. "Hello?" he said.

"May I speak to Mayor Hosea Funk, please?" said ⸻ on the other end of the line.

"Yeah, yes, I know that," said ⸻, "thanks."

"One of our census people will be in your town tomorrow to do an official, uh, count, and who shall we tell her will be the person to contact when she arrives?"

"Oh," said Hosea, "that could be me."

"Yourself?" said the woman.

"Yes," said Hosea. He coughed. "Yes, myself."

"Very good then," said the woman. "And the address of your office being?"

"Office being?" said Hosea.

"Yes," said the woman.

"Oh," said Hosea, "okay." And he gave her the address.

"Our counter should be there at ten o'clock, Mayor Funk, is that convenient for you? Mayor Funk? Hello, Mayor Funk? Mayor Funk!"

"Oh yes," said Hosea. "Sure thing. Thank-you."

Hosea hung up the phone and two seconds later heard the scream of Algren's one and only ambulance as it ripped through the torpor of the day. Before Hosea could make it to the window, the ambulance had passed and the street was, once again, as dead as a ghost town.

Hosea ran out of his office and towards the hospital. The siren had stopped and Hosea could hear birds singing and an airplane flying directly behind him, maybe it was a crop duster, why was it following him? And a stampede of horses. Or was it his heart? One kid stopped playing in his yard and looked up at the strange sight of Hosea Funk sprinting down the sidewalk like an escaped parolee, and a couple of women visiting outside stared at him and shook their heads. "That Hosea Funk," one said, but Hosea, by that time, was nearing the hospital, and then he was there, running up the stairs, then through the front door, towards the emergency room, and shouting, "No! No! No!"

Tom lay on the stretcher surrounded by machines and cords. Dr. François was pounding on his chest and checking levels on one of the machines. Nurse Barnes was injecting Tom with something and another nurse was standing next to the doctor, watching a machine and opening up a small package. A third nurse was on the phone to another hospital and Hosea heard her say, ". . . massive cardiac . . ." and then some numbers. Then the doctor speaking to the nurse beside him, softly, and . . . Tom, just lying there. The doctor turned around and saw Hosea standing in the doorway and said, "For God's sake . . ." and turned back to Tom. After a few seconds, the doctor said to Hosea, "Find Dory," and then he and the nurses surrounded Tom, and Tom disappeared inside them.

Twenty minutes later, Dory and Knute stood in the waiting room, waiting for the news. The doctor was _____ _____ ___ there was no way he could _____ __ fact.

would ___ __
"He wouldn't have made it to ___ __ ___ answered. He told them that Tom had called the hospital himself before he had the heart attack, saying he was feeling very strange, and when they got to him he had been dead, for that minute.

So, there they were. Tom was on a lot of morphine and lay there with his eyes closed, but Dory and Knute squeezed his hands and kissed him and said good-bye. They were in shock, complete shock. Hosea came in for about a minute, that's all the doctor would allow him, and he touched Tom's arm and looked at Tom. "I'm so sorry," he said. "I'm so sorry." Then he was asked to leave the room.

But then things got weird. Tom wasn't dying. Knute and Dory could tell Dr. François was getting sort of nervous because he probably figured he should have transferred him to Winnipeg after all. Not that the doctor wanted Tom to die, he just seemed a little

275

confused. So Tom remained alive and eventually Knute even left to get some coffee for herself and Dory. The doctor came in and by then a few doctors had come from other towns, and one from Winnipeg, and they huddled around Tom, speaking in hushed tones, telling Knute and Dory that they had to admit they were puzzled. That the heart had sustained so much damage, they didn't know how it was capable of functioning. Knute and Dory were still so overwhelmed that they just nodded and stared at Tom and, well, just waited.

Hosea tried to make himself comfortable in the waiting room. The doctor gave him updates on Tom's condition, but mostly Tom was just still alive. "Still alive?" Hosea would ask, and the doctor would nod and go back into Tom's room. At one point Dory came out and asked Hosea if he would sit with Tom while she went to the cafeteria to get some more coffee. Knute had left to get Max and Summer Feelin' and bring them to the hospital. Hosea sat down next to Tom. Suddenly, without opening his eyes, Tom whispered, "What time is the count?" Hosea, startled, grabbed at the front of his shirt and cleared his throat. He looked at Tom, and said, "What? What did you say, Tom?"

Tom, exhausted by the effort he had made to speak, began again. "What . . . time . . ." He took a deep breath, and then was quiet for a long time.

Hosea held his hand and squeezed. ". . . Is the count?" he whispered in Tom's ear. Tom nodded once.

"At ten o'clock tomorrow morning," said Hosea. "They called me today from Ottawa . . . but how did you know . . . how do you know about the count?" Tom didn't say anything. He'd heard it all the other night, every word, thought Hosea. He knows the Prime Minister is my father. He knows what's going on.

"Tom," he whispered, "you don't —"

Just then the doctor came into the room with Dory and said to Hosea, "Okay, Hose, let's not tire him out," and Hosea nodded and went back to the waiting room.

room, Max took S.F. home and

doctors and nurses walked in and out quietly, adjusting levels, writing down information, and Hosea curled up as best he could on a sweaty vinyl couch in the lobby of the hospital, where he spent the night alone and dreaming.

He was dead. Right after he died, he said, "I don't want to be put into a box and buried in the dirt," so they pumped him full of helium and tied a steel cable to his ankle and cranked him up into the sky so he could float around the world and check things out, without getting lost, and losing Algren. He checked out a Mexican circus and New York City and lost tribes and a few hundred wars and a housing project in New Orleans. And then he felt a gentle touch, a hand on his shoulder. He had a short-wave radio with him, propped up on his stomach, and he lay on his back and floated for a while over mountains somewhere in the world and listened to police calls on his radio, and then Knutie's voice on the other end saying, "We need you here in Algren, we're bringing you back," and the cable jerked on his ankle and the short-wave radio fell off his stomach and they started cranking him back down to earth. Iris Cherniski was squirting a little WD-40 into the crank machine and saying, "That's it, that's it, easy does it," and Max was there with a microphone and holding S.F. in his arms, saying, "Perfect two-point landing, ladies and gentlemen, thank you for flying with CorpseAir, we hope you enjoyed your flight." And there were Peej and Euphemia playing concentration on the curb, smiling shyly at each other and ignoring Hosea entirely, and then there was John Baert, standing beside Euphemia, asking if he could play, and Hosea tried to undo the steel cable from his ankle and go over there, "Those're my folks," he said to Max. "I gotta get this thing off. Today's the day. Help me get this thing off."

"But, Hosea," said his Aunt Minty, who had just showed up, "you're still pumped full of helium, if we take it off you'll float away."

"Then empty me!" yelled Hosea. "C'mon, help me, Minty!"

"Oh, Hosie," said Euphemia, finally looking up, "relax, sweetheart, you're dead." She smiled sweetly at Peej and John Baert and said, "He's so dead . . ."

"Tough shit!" yelled Hosea. "So are you, get this damn thing off me!"

And Minty said, "Well, we could take the head off and let some of the pressure out, but I don't know . . ." and she disappeared, and in her place was Lorna. She put her hand out to Hosea to touch him and she said, "You're so round, you're so bloated, like me, look," and Dory brought coffee out for everyone and Hosea could hear Dory say, "I like my stories happy, the sadness comes creeping out of the cracks in the story like blood, happy stories are the saddest." And then it began to snow and Max said, "Excellent, Dory! Excellent!"

"Hello?" she said. "Uncle Jack?" Hosea smiled back and nodded. He pointed to Tom's room, but Knute had turned her back to him and was talking to Uncle Jack. Hosea went into Tom's room and stood beside him. He wanted to tell Tom he didn't have to stay alive if he didn't want to, if it was too hard, but he knew he couldn't say these words out loud, not with Dory there, not with the way things were. That is, the way life was, the way life was that precluded us from saying things like that out loud. And besides, what he meant was that Tom didn't have to do this for him, for his cockeyed plan to see his father. But instead, he leaned over and whispered, "Tom, I'm going to my office now." He'd wanted to say something more, something poignant and earth-shattering, words that conveyed the love he felt for Tom, and the gratitude. Instead he said, "So long, Tom," and turned to go. But then he heard Tom's voice. "Time," he said, not moving his lips so it sounded like *tie*. Hosea stopped and looked at Tom. "Tie," he said again.

"Time?" said Hosea. "Well, uh, the time is 9:45, Tom." He cleared his throat and looked over at Dory who was waking up in the other bed. "It's 9:45," he said again.

"Okay, thanks," said Dory. "My goodness, I slept too long. How is he?" Hosea was about to answer her, then noticed that she was talking to the doctor who had come into the room and was standing behind him, writing something again, and so he mumbled a garbled good-bye and left Dory and the doctor to discuss Tom's condition.

Hosea walked out into the beautiful day to meet his census taker, and do the count. The counter's name was Anita and she told Hosea she had a sister who was also an official counter and was doing a count somewhere in Nova Scotia as they spoke. "A contender," she said. The two of them walked the dusty streets of Algren, knocking on doors, getting information from the neighbours of people who weren't home, and referring to Hosea's notebook. Anita raised her eyebrows when she saw the orange Hilroy scribbler and said, "Geez, Mr. Funk, you want this bad, don't you?"

You don't know the half of it, lady, were words that came to Hosea's mind, but he smiled and said, "Well, we'd all love to see the Prime Minister come to Algren. It would be a special day for all of us."

"Well, then," said Anita, "let's hope this one's a promise he keeps." She laughed and said, "I'm kidding."

And Hosea laughed, too, and said, "Good one."

That evening it was on the news. Algren was the winner with an uncanny fifteen hundred exactly. How did it happen? It doesn't matter, it did. It was the last item on the news, the feel-good piece to put people to bed with, to leave them with the impression that not all was as bad as it seemed.

Tom died that night, too. His last words were,

was sure he'd told her he loved her.

At 5 a.m. on July first, anyone floating over Algren would have been impressed. All along Main Street, Canadian flags in the form of red and white petunias sparkled with dew and reflected the sun, which was beginning to rise. The new Algren Feed Mill Summer Theatre, at least the outside of it, really looked like a theatre, and over at the edge of town a white horse flew through the sky. For a few minutes, anyway, until the colour of the sky changed and the water tower became visible and the horse was revealed as a decal. But it was an interesting few minutes of optical illusion, and why not? Surrounding the little town were fields of yellow and blue so that if you were floating over you could pretend you were on a sandy beach in Rio. Nobody was out and about in Algren at that time except a black dog who stood next to a farmhouse on the edge of town,

281

jumping up from time to time and snapping at a few bugs, and a little girl who sat on the front step of that farmhouse, stretching and yawning and laughing at the dog, and waiting for her mom and dad to get out of bed.

Hosea didn't hear the phone ring because he was fast asleep, too, with his arms around Lorna and his face buried in her hair. He slept until the sun was well up and so bright that the white horse on the water tower was all but obliterated by its rays. Later in the day he returned the phone message from Ottawa with one of his own.

"Hosea Funk here, not to worry, things come up, maybe next year. Please wish him a Happy Canada Day from the mayor of Algren."

OUTWITTING HOUSEWORK

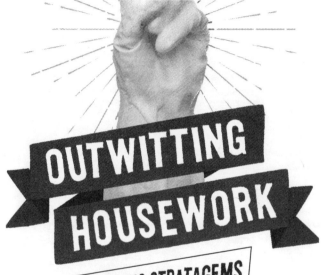

OUTWITTING HOUSEWORK

101 CUNNING STRATAGEMS
to Reduce Your Housework
to a Minimum

BARTY PHILLIPS

Michael O'Mara Books Limited

First published in Great Britain in 2018
by Michael O'Mara Books Limited
9 Lion Yard
Tremadoc Road
London SW4 7NQ

A CIP catalogue record for this book is available from the British
Library.

Papers used by Michael O'Mara Books Limited are natural, recyclable
products made from wood grown in sustainable forests. The
manufacturing processes conform to the environmental regulations of
the country of origin.

ISBN 978-1-78243-914-1 in paperback print format
ISBN 978-1-78243-926-4 in ebook format

1 2 3 4 5 6 7 8 9 10

www.mombooks.com

Designed and typeset by K.DESIGN, Winscombe, Somerset
Illustrations by Andrew Pinder

Printed and bound by CPI Group (UK) Ltd, Croydon, CR0 4YY

To my sister –
arch outwitter of housework

CONTENTS

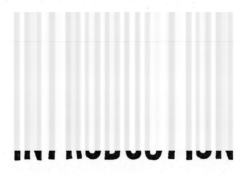

INTRODUCTION

There's no getting away from it – if you have a home, it will need some housework. But you can avoid much of it by using low cunning to forestall incipient chaos, gathering dust, ingrained stains and pet hairs nestling on your best black trousers.

You sometimes hear people boast about staying in a hotel that was so clean 'you could eat your dinner off the bathroom floor'. Luckily, I have never wanted to eat my dinner off any floor in my home, but I still want everything underfoot (and everywhere else for that matter) to look attractive and feel clean. 'How clean?' is the question, and that will depend on you and whether you have only yourself to please or if you are living with other people whose requirements are rather different from your own; a partner who is irritated by your crumbs on the tablecloth, say, or a child who carelessly scatters packet-loads of cereal everywhere at breakfast time.

In general, the tidier the home, the easier it is to keep housework at bay. But with the best will in the world, you are not going to prevent the cat from shedding hairs on the sofa, or your nearest and dearest walking in with muddy boots or scattering mobiles, games consoles or half-eaten wraps under every cushion. Your best hope for outwitting housework nowadays is to relax about it. If you don't have to scrub and polish, don't. If a cleaning product requires to be left for a length of time after you've applied it, leave it; go away, forget about it, do something nice, listen to some music, dance in front of the mirror. The product will quietly get on with its work and all you have to do is forget about it until it has done its job.

At least these days we don't have to cope with that thing our ancestors used to call 'spring cleaning' in which not only did every piece of furniture have to be removed to the middle of the room and covered with dust sheets, so that the surfaces under and behind them could be scrubbed, but the curtains had to be changed

My copy of *Every Woman's Enquire Within: A Complete Library of Household Knowledge for all Home-loving Women* published in 1940 by George Newnes minutely details how this should be done, including 'advance preparation' (such as turning out all the drawers in every chest and cleaning their contents), then polishing the furniture, removing dust with a vacuum cleaner 'if you have one' – otherwise 'a brush must be used instead'. Oh, and, of course, you had to get the chimney swept, too.

With modern surfaces and finishes, modern vacuum and carpet cleaners, grease-busting cloths, and no coal-burning fires to leave soot and smuts over everything, the most noticeable spring-cleaning job necessary for us today is getting rid of the smears and splatters on window panes highlighted by the first rays of the new year's sun.

As a person who feels there are more interesting things to do in the world than housework blitzes, I have spent a lifetime trying to find ways of avoiding any need for spring cleaning by keeping a clean, tidy and efficient home while using up the least possible time and energy. And in this book I'd like to share some of these discoveries with you. It is by no means a comprehensive how-to-do-everything book, but I hope it will offer schemes and strategies to outwit the chaos and grime lurking in every home and waiting to pounce. I don't advocate striving for perfection, which inevitably leads to disappointment and a feeling of failure, but for comfort and a vague sense of control, saving time and energy and allowing yourself the occasional luxury of lounging in tidy comfort on the sofa to watch a complete evening of your favourite TV.

CONTROLLING
TECHNOLOGY

Technology, we are told, has revolutionized our lives and made the stresses of housework more or less a thing of the past. Unfortunately, the very technology itself often seems to require rather more effort and time than the ordinary cleaning and dusting that preceded it. Tempting though it may be to buy the latest, shiniest and most advertised equipment, my advice is – get what's right for you. If you spend your time on your smartphone, then remote-controlled electronic devices that will draw your living-room curtains at the press of a button may be the ideal thing. But if you are baffled by the digital controls of your central heating, you certainly won't want a remote-controlled washing machine or robo vac. So, when buying your equipment don't let your advisers drag you kicking and screaming into the twenty-first century unless you are going to understand and enjoy it. Many houseworkers still prefer simple knobs to digital controls, and digital controls can themselves be simple or complicated. If you are a technophobe, go for the simplest of programming devices that will be quick to master.

Outwitting your equipment

It's easy to be seduced by bulky and attractive packaging and become rather distracted from the actual object you're buying and its suitability for you and your home. Machines come in sizes varying from petite to giant, and big is often not best. One Christmas, for example, a friend of mine was given a wonderful Rolls Royce-grade toaster. It was coated in shiny silver metal, had four slots, a special programme for muffins and sophisticated timing technology. She lives on her own and only eats toast very occasionally. She has been trying ever since to give it back to the

squeegee for window cleaning, the short handle will not let me reach the top of my windows. But a large bucket is just no good for me, as I can't lift it when it's full. On their own, these things sound very trivial, but if you consider that they will be used regularly, it's important that they work for you.

For a large family, robust is almost certainly better than digitally advanced. An uncomplicated object that doesn't come in many parts will get much more use than one that takes hours to master and assemble. I once attended a London trade exhibition of white goods. One of the machines on show was a wonderfully simple washing machine that just tumbled the clothes and had two knobs: off/on and a timer. I asked the rep where you could get this desirable machine. 'Oh!' he said, 'I'm afraid it's not available in this country; it's for the Third World.' I felt bereft – on my readers' behalf as well as my own. I now have a machine with eight programmes of which I probably use two.

Get your vacuum cleaner onside

If you live in a large and open space, such as a loft apartment, and have miles of carpet and not too much furniture to get in the way, why not get a professional-quality upright vacuum, which will last for decades and get the job done efficiently and quickly (though it may be a mite noisier than other vacuums). A commercial machine is likely to be longer lasting and more effective than a domestic one and may be a good buy for larger homes and families, depending on their interests and activities. It will generally be made of more robust materials and will have fewer little pretty bits to fall off. Also, it will usually be bigger, heavier and more expensive than domestic machines. A wide-track vacuum cleaner would be useful in an open, unobstructed space because you'd cover more floor area with each pacing of the room.

A wet-and-dry vacuum cleaner might be good for a family of teenagers. These machines will suck up anything from sawdust and nails to a flood caused by overflowing bath water. Instead of a vacuum bag,

switching over every time you change the function of the machine. You also have to remember to empty the liquid compartment promptly into a bucket every time you use it, otherwise it will become stagnant and begin to smell horrible. As usual with dual-function equipment, the use and maintenance are more complicated than with mono-use machines.

There are some things such a machine will do that, with luck, you won't need, clever though they may be. For example, some can suck out solid-fuel ash from a fireplace, gulp up flooding from burst pipes, unblock the sink (what's wrong with a plunger?) and clear away snow and dead leaves outside the house.

Large commercial wet-and-dry vacuums seem to do the job best, but they are nothing if not heavy and they also make a fearful noise, so are best in a workshop or large building like a school. Medium ones are more compact and still give a good performance, so might be the thing for a large family in a big house

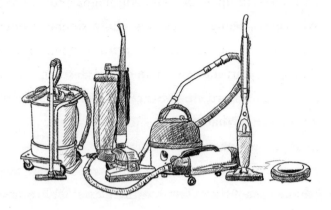

where there's lots going on. The small and mini ones are less worthwhile unless you live in a very small space or just want to use them for sucking up crumbs, though it may be quicker to mop up small spills with a dustpan or a cloth.

In a small flat, a wall-hung cordless vacuum will take up less room and do a satisfactory job. Between these are dozens and dozens of makes of vacuum cleaner. Choose one with the minimum necessary attachments and don't keep those jumbled in a cardboard box under the stairs where they will be impossible to get at. If you are a clean tidy person, or someone who spends a lot of time at the gym or on the town, rather

push it backwards and forwards. One of their big advantages is that they are so quiet compared with their vacuuming cousins.

If you can, do your shopping research online – you can see pictures, get measurements, find reviews of everything, but don't buy anything expensive until you've had the chance to try it out for yourself. Whatever you choose must be easy to maintain (having no bag can be an advantage). Anything with a rotary brush will collect animal hairs, though these are sometimes tricky to clear of the inevitable long hairs that wind themselves tightly round the spindle.

How about a robo vac?

For technophiles, this is a fun way to get a rather boring chore done. In fact, a robo vac is rather like having a household pet: it will roam around your home snuffling out dust and crumbs, but without the need for affection or constant feeding. Most are about the size of a large round hat box, in black or possibly white. They are small enough to be given kennel space under the bed and will do a satisfactory job provided you live in an already fairly neat and tidy home without too many obstructions.

Some go round on their own seemingly at random (though of course they are actually mapping the space all the time). You can choose from such things as auto, manual, spot, point clean, turbo and dust sensor. Turbo is the most powerfully made and picks up most dirt and dust. Some have remote controls so you can direct them from your desk or sofa, but the more controls they have, the more expensive they become. Some have sweeper brushes that stick out from the side and sweep in dust to be sucked up, while others suck up dirt from underneath. With some you have to charge and replace the battery pack, which can be fiddly. The cheapest and simplest may just have three buttons, S, M and L, indicating a small, medium or large room, so not too much programming is required, but they only deal with hard floors and short-pile

better things to do than check on the housework, thank you.

Control your household detergents

Specialized cleaning agents full of chemicals abound. You can spend a fortune buying a different one for each household job and it is very tempting to buy too many. Believe me, you do not need them all. What

you need for everyday house cleaning is to deal with grease, hard-water deposits and dust, and perhaps a bit of mould – that's about it. Three cleaning agents in squirty bottles would be enough to clean the whole of your home. You don't need one preparation for tiles, another for glass, another for your desk and another for worktops.

There are some basic ingredients that make up household cleaners.

Acids and alkalis

Acids and alkalis make up a large part of most chemical cleaners. *Acids* dissolve in water and produce a sour solution, although many acids are far too poisonous to try and taste. They are used to remove blood, oil and food deposits, and the most commonly used in commercial products is phosphoric acid. *Alkalis* (ammonia, caustic soda and other soda compounds) are also soluble in water. Caustic detergents are predominantly alkaline and often contain sodium hydroxide. Alkalis neutralize acids, will rot animal and vegetable substances such as wool, silk and rayon, and will change colours in many dyes.

cleaning products could be cheaper bought in bulk from your local janitorial/cleaning supplier, but although buying in bulk may seem a good saving, decanting items or even storing large containers may be more trouble than it's worth.

Of the hundreds of cleaning preparations on the market you will need only a few:

1. An all-purpose neutral cleaner, which can be used for almost any type of cleaning and will be safe on nearly all surfaces.

2. A disinfectant cleaner for wherever you feel you need something that will kill germs; for example, for wiping a worktop after preparing meat or poultry or in or near the lavatory in the bathroom.

3. A heavy-duty, grease-busting cleaner for build-ups of grease, particularly in the kitchen. This will

have a high percentage of mild acid in it to break down deposits of grease (look on the label for a pH of around 7).

4. A window cleaner – although this will be optional if you follow my advice on using natural cleaners (see page 158).

I also keep a foam spot carpet and upholstery cleaner for spilled disasters. Oh, and if you have antique or traditional polished wood furniture, some furniture polish. You shouldn't need a cleaner for the oven because you will sensibly have bought a self-cleaner, so a basic four should be perfectly adequate unless you want to double up on an all-purpose cleaner and keep one in the kitchen and one in the bathroom for convenience.

Of course, you will save time and effort if you wipe surfaces down automatically after use: a quick pass round the basin and taps with a damp cloth every time you wash your hands, and equally over the worktops and drainer when you tidy up in the kitchen after cooking, will keep the amount of cleaning you have to do to a minimum. This regular wiping takes

In fact, acids and alkalis do not have to be bought in the form of patented products. If you want to be green and use safer and less toxic substances for your cleaning, lemons and household vinegar are acid and bicarbonate of soda is alkaline. All of these are used every day in cooking and it is pleasantly surprising how much of your cleaning can be done with just these three items. Being edible, they are also very safe to use.

You can remove bathroom hard-water scale with vinegar, which, mixed with a mild washing-up liquid and water, can also be used for cleaning windows. Lemon juice is great for cleaning the interior of your microwave. And baking soda, otherwise known as bicarbonate of soda or soda bicarbonate, is a weak alkali that has numerous uses round the house. For example, it's good for cleaning the fridge interior, and a little pot of bicarbonate in the back of the fridge will absorb nasty smells. (I know there shouldn't be any nasty smells in the fridge, but do you really always remember to cover that little bit of left-over tuna?) It can also be used to clean worktops, stainless steel sinks, and even baked-on food on oven dishes. Use it dry, sprinkled on pet baskets or musty-smelling

furiously scrub. If you add a handful to liquid laundry
detergent it will help balance the pH level and will get

clothes cleaner. It's good for smelly trainers (sprinkled dry, left for half an hour, and then shaken out). If you have to wait too long for your rubbish collection, place a spoonful in the bottom of your food caddy or rubbish bin to stop them getting stinky.

What sort of cloths?

This may not sound like a terribly important part of your equipment, but cloth technology is much advanced these days and there are so many different choices with or without 'built-in' disinfectant – cotton, terry cotton, linen, cellulose, long-lasting or disposable, fabric or sponge – and it can be hard to choose. What you don't want is something like the traditional old 'washing rag' made out of an old vest too worn to absorb much of anything.

You can buy cloths impregnated with disinfectant for use in the kitchen. However useful these may be, they are no substitute for actually keeping the cooking and sink areas dry and clean, and if you do that, you don't need a disinfectant cloth anyway. The

So what sort of cloths should we be using then? Among the best is the microfibre family (or E-cloths). The magic material they are made of cleans easily and thoroughly without any chemicals at all. You can use them with plain water on nearly every surface in the home, including walls, windowsills, floors, carpets, window panes and hobs. There are different textures: finer for glass, rougher for worktops or floors. They come in different colours, so you could colour code, using a red one for the floor and a blue one for the worktops and sink. You only use them with water, no need for detergents or cleaners of any kind, and they are still said to 'remove 99 per cent of bacteria including E. coli and listeria'. All you have to do is rinse them out when done and let them dry. You can occasionally send them through a washing machine programme (albeit without adding fabric softener, as this reduces their effectiveness), and they are supposed to survive

300 washes – in other words they are practically indestructible.

With all sponges and cloths, rinse them through, wash off any debris and squeeze well after every use. If they start to smell, chuck them out immediately.

Just a quick word about tea towels: these need to be absorbent without leaving linty bits. The best fabric for drying, especially glass, is 100 per cent linen, which will leave no lint, but a good-quality cotton will do a decent job, too. They should be washed frequently and, if possible, don't use them for wiping the worktop or the bottoms of pans. Beware when buying online as some turn out to be quite a lot smaller than the standard (which is around 62 × 46 cm/24 × 18 in) and those extra centimetres make all the difference to their drying capacity.

Foil your washing machine

All-singing all-dancing washing machines are available at large cost but you can get cheap machines that do a good job. The question is: how do you know which is

several shirts and T-shirts and a towel or two without squashing them up, but if you live on your own, a smaller machine will probably be more sensible.

The energy rating is another key feature, especially with rising fuel costs. The machine should have a label showing its energy rating. The most economical is shown in a green strip (A+++) and the most electricity-greedy in red (D) (similar labels can be found on dishwashers and fridge/freezers – all new machines since 2014 will be A, A+). This label may include water consumption, especially important if you are on a water meter, and rated capacity, which shows how much washing the machine will efficiently take.

Sensor technology can recognize the size of the load and adjust the water, energy and time to give the most energy-efficient washes, and some cheaper machines benefit from this technology. Spin-drying efficiency is hugely important if you want things to dry quickly – the fastest spin speed will fling off a large part of the water, and one capable of 800 or more revs a minute will get most clothes dry enough to iron.

You should also find out how noisy the machine is, both when washing and spinning. A good spin-dry programme might mean you don't need a tumble dryer, which is good if you are short of space or not

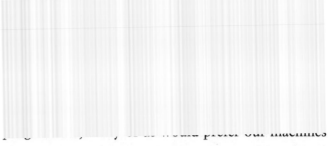

to be less complicated and most of us would like to have at least one programme that takes half an hour or less.

Of course, having made your choices and installed your machine, you can foil its wiles by taking the trouble to read (and understand) the instructions in the manual. But, occasionally, these should be taken with a pinch of salt. For example, you can almost certainly use slightly less detergent than is recommended and it will do a perfectly satisfactory job. In fact, using the recommended amount may result in some detergent being left in the clothes even after rinsing, so you might have to do another rinse because left-over detergent attracts dirt. The manual will indicate which temperature is right for a particular programme, although if you choose a cool temperature detergent you may not want to use that programme.

Outwitting the instruction manual

We all do the laundry so often, we don't realize that we are not making the best of our machines. But there are several things you can do that will make your wash load more efficient. For example, selecting the right water temperature every time you do a wash makes a big difference. Cool water is good for delicate fabrics, for clothes that might shrink or for dark colours that tend to bleed. And, of course, reducing the cost of heating the water is not to be sneezed at.

Hot-water programmes are for cotton and linen – things like towels and bedlinen, white shirts, filthy work clothes, and oil and grease splodges (not all in the same load though, obviously).

There are some things the instruction manual may not tell you: for instance, if you don't want synthetic clothes to cling to your body after washing, give them twenty minutes of cold tumbling at the end of a drying cycle to reduce

will

drying time? A tumble

an expensive if efficient way of drying clothes. Fold clothes (if completely dry) the moment you take them from the tumble dryer and they should need little or no ironing.

Whenever possible use low-temperature washes, economy washes and half-load programmes to save water and electricity. Buy sufficient clothes that you often change, like vests and knickers and socks, so that you can save up the dirty ones and wash them all at once. But don't overload your machine and don't try to squeeze the equivalent of two loads into one. Clothes need space to move around if you want them to actually get clean.

Don't forget about the pre-soak cycle. This programme agitates the contents and may even dispense detergent before starting the main wash. It is a good way of getting very dirty clothes clean without having to use a very hot wash or to go through the programme twice.

Wash synthetic fabrics every time you wear them. They can be really hard to get clean if you let them become stained or very grubby. The same goes for silk because strong deodorants and perspiration can weaken the fibres.

Know your laundry detergents

There's also the all-perplexing decision about what detergent to use. Here, manufacturers have cunningly produced so many – with so many different ingredients and said to do so many different things – that you have a whole new mind-numbing decision-making process ahead of you. They start off with acids and alkalis, like household detergents, but often have a whole lot of added ingredients to make things look more pristine.

Detergent manufacturers try to keep their individual magic formulas secret, especially from other manufacturers, and each is a cocktail of exotic ingredients whose aim is to remove stains and dirt from clothes and impart a fresh clean look to fabrics.

...how many ingredients ... in everyday over-the-counter detergents, so let's look at them. All laundry detergents will contain some or all of the following:

Surfactants: These are the active cleaning agents that disperse dirt that doesn't normally dissolve in water.

Builders: These are alkaline and boost the effectiveness of the surfactants.

Alkalis: These raise the pH of the water, which helps break up oily and acidic dirt. They form an emulsion, and the oily or soluble particles remain in the emulsion and don't creep back onto the fabric. The most commonly used alkalis are caustic soda and potassium hydroxide. The strongest ones are dangerous if swallowed and can damage fabrics and leave clothes feeling rough to the skin.

Enzymes: These are biological molecules that speed up chemical reactions and help to remove stains. They include proteases (which help break down blood, egg and gravy), amylases for starches, and lipases for fats and grease. They are a natural phenomenon (found, for example, in yeast). They enable us to use a lower water temperature and less detergent. Some people may be sensitive to enzymes, in which case use a non-bio detergent.

Oxygen bleaches (sodium percarbonate or hydrogen peroxide) can be used on coloureds without damaging the colour.

Sanitizers: These include chemicals such as chlorine, phenol and quaternary ammonium compounds and are used to reduce the number of bacteria and other organisms.

separating in the container, and *foam regulators* to stop the machine from foaming at the mouth. They also have *corrosion inhibitors* to prevent the chemicals damaging the machine.

Lastly, there are probably *colourants* and *dyes*. They don't make the clothes any cleaner, they just make them look cleaner, and they too may cause skin irritation. Each of the ingredients may involve several different chemicals, so you have a cocktail of things that may pollute the environment and exacerbate skin allergies and asthma. Of course, some manufacturers offer simpler detergents that will not irritate the skin and that have gentler ingredients.

Powdered detergents work well in general and may be less expensive than liquids, but they don't always dissolve properly in cold water and will then leave white residues on fabrics. Liquid detergents come in a wealth of cartons and recipes and are available in pods, which means you don't have to measure them, just throw them in with the wash. Then there are 'laundry balls' – containing various ingredients such as ceramic balls, magnetic material or just a coloured liquid and/or detergent, which some people claim to be effective. Although most detergents will work in cold water, it's best to choose one actually formulated for this if you intend to use that wash option often.

You could try making your own detergent, using soap, borax and washing soda – much better for the environment, but probably not so good at getting rid of obstinate, very dirty stains. And I imagine few of us are blessed with the leisure time to experiment.

Beat your dishwasher

Dishwashers line up in showrooms or websites looking so shiny, neat and efficient. But which one is best for you? If you are not a great cook and eat out most of the time, you will not need an enormous family dishwasher. If you enjoy cooking for family or friends, check that it will take large pots and pans and serving dishes. A

... amount of
... by hand. It has been done!

Assuming you have opted for a dishwasher, as with washing machines, energy efficiency and speed are among the first things to check when choosing your machine. All are rated according to energy use, like washing machines. An eco-programme will use less energy and less water. Try out different programmes and use the coolest setting that will produce an acceptable result – and if you are interested in the state of the environment, use detergents that are biodegradable and free of phosphates.

How well a dishwasher washes will depend to some extent on how you have prepared what's going in – whether you've scraped off all excess food or allowed it to dry on to the plates and cutlery. Loading correctly is important and I quite understand people who won't let anybody else load up their dishwasher – badly placed items can obstruct the jets of water or the revolving spray arm, or block the detergent dispenser outlet.

Then there's the issue of whether to opt for a heat-dry or an air-dry machine. The heat-dry cycle pumps very hot air through the interior and a small extractor fan pulls the moisture out through vents. An air-dry machine cycles air at room temperature, so no extra heating is required. Heat drying obviously uses more energy than air drying, so is more expensive to run, but after an air-dry cycle the dishes may have a vague film over them or moisture spots, meaning

important if you live in an upstairs apartment and don't want to ruin your neighbour's life).

Having chosen the dishwasher of your dreams, you will save much trouble and strife if you treat it well. Whichever option you go for, the dishwasher should be as near to the sink as possible. Always use the recommended brand of detergent and rinse aid. There is a temptation to use too much detergent, especially in soft-water areas or if your machine has a built-in water softener – in which case remember to refill with water softener regularly.

You may have noticed something called 'detergent bloom', which discolours the blades of stainless steel knives leaving a sort of greyish-blue finish, spoiling their beautiful looks. The mixture of hot water and detergent chemicals can produce discolouration in stainless steel cutlery, producing this blue tarnish. Some companies advise against mixing different metal items, such as chromed steel, stainless steel and silver plate in dishwashers, as the variety of metals can cause chemical reactions that result in this blue bloom. It can also be caused by using too much rinse aid.

Running the dishwasher half empty is an expensive mistake. Double quantities of cutlery and crockery will allow you still to have something to eat off and drink out of while the dishwasher's filling up. But, equally, if you think you can use the dishwasher as a sort of storage compartment once everything's clean, think again. You need to empty the thing as soon as the drying cycle is complete, otherwise smears will ensue, apart from the fact that the clean things will inevitably get mixed up with the next load and will probably unnecessarily go through a second wash. Oh, and you should clean the filter and the spray arms after every use – it doesn't take a moment to remove and rinse them through and will eliminate clogging-up trouble later on.

We must all have opened up the dishwasher to find a malformed plastic dish that melted during the hot process. Things to avoid trying to wash in the machine are heat-sensitive plastics, wooden bowls, insulated ware, glass with a metal trim, delicate china or cut

There are times when you will have to do a bit of washing up by hand anyway. All those things you can't dishwash, like the china you inherited from your grandparents, but also, sometimes, a few mugs or plates if people turn up unexpectedly and there's nothing clean to drink out of because it's all locked away in the dishwasher.

There are, of course, many people reading this who will not have a dishwasher, sometimes through necessity (cost or lack of space) and sometimes through choice. Perhaps, like me, you are eccentric enough to actually prefer doing the washing up yourself. I think I must be one of the few people in the world who rather enjoys it. It's fine by me as long as I can do it at leisure at midnight or after breakfast if I feel like it.

So, for those doing the dishwashing by hand, a plastic bowl in the sink uses less water, makes washing up less clattery, is less hard on delicate objects and is

home orderly when the vacuum cleaner hose is held together with parcel tape, the broom handle keeps popping out of the broom head and the lavatory brush is so worn it just scratches the U-bend. I can't tell you which you will need most because it will depend on whether you live in a stately mansion, a country cottage or a block of flats. The wise householder will choose only the things necessary, but they will be the best or most effective.

So here are some ideas for your *batterie de ménage*. I would suggest you choose as few as possible to cover all your home's requirements, and make sure they are good at their job, easy to store and fun to use.

Broom, and a dustpan and brush

Every home needs these whatever other technological home aids there are. I remember how proud I was at the age of eighteen when I bought a small red plastic dustpan set – it might have been a brand-new sports car, I was so delighted.

wheezing or howling of an electrically driven machine and there's very little to go wrong with them.

Vacuum cleaner

Here you have the gamut of electric cleaners: drag along, push along, upright, trundling, cordless, wet-and-dry, or of course robo (see page 21).

Floor mop

For tiny rooms and hard floors. Choose one with an oblong folding head that holds a changeable sponge, just right for a tiny studio flat or small kitchen. I don't mean an Old English Sheepdog mop with a tousled head that needs to be squeezed out in a bucket and then has to be dried somewhere. A sponge mop is much less care intensive.

Bucket

This will always come in useful, for rinsing out mops and cloths if nothing else.

Squeegee

This is a rubber strip on a handle. It is by far the best thing for cleaning windows and do keep one in the shower so users can (you hope) give the cubicle a quick wipe-down when they've finished.

Cobweb brush

Thinking of areas above the floor now, sooner or later you will want to get at those little nests of spiders' webs that gather in the taller corners of the room, not to mention the dust that gathers on tops of picture frames and door ledges. You can sweep them with a broom, but that's a bit like taking a sledgehammer to a tintack. Long-handled cobweb brushes are made for the job, but some of the telescopic ones leave their woolly heads nodding about foolishly on the extended handle, which makes the thing infuriatingly difficult to control.

Cloths

These are essential, of course (see page 30). Although microfibre cloths are good for most things, you might want something softer, like a duster, for delicate decorative items and a separate one for shoe cleaning,

Lavatory brush

This is another of the essentials. Robust is what you need, plenty of tough bristles on the outside and softer ones on the inside. This brush is supposed to be used regularly and often, so make sure you choose one that will last and that will get into the U-bend and other hidden places.

So that's the main basic hardware and software in your *batterie de ménage*. When choosing, remember to check that there's somewhere for everything to go. There's no point carting home an upright vac if there's no cupboard space to store it. My granddaughter, who can only afford to live near her work in London by sharing a flat with five other people, swears by a small, handheld vacuum cleaner because there's nowhere in the flat for a larger one. It will suck up a pile of dust after sweeping, run over worktops, tabletops, skirting boards, deals with stairs and can be hung on the wall when she's finished. In fact, in a small home, the more cleaning equipment you can hang up the better, rather like in a well-organized garden shed. So, wherever possible, hang items up rather than letting them sit on the floor, gathering the dust they are supposed to be removing.

WHAT TO DO

- Give up the idea of a tame robo vac and with the money you've saved treat yourself to that expensive facial you've had your eye on for ages.

- Use crumpled newspaper instead of a cloth to finish off your window cleaning – it may leave printing ink on your fingers but it gets all the smears off the glass.

- Keep a bowl of lemons in the kitchen. You can use them to clean your microwave, freshen up the sink, wipe over the chopping board, and if you still have some over, you can slice and freeze them for your next G&T.

...enormous family-sized washing machine and dryer just because it's on sale, which you then won't be able to get up the stairs into your tiny studio flat.

- Waste your best traditional balsamic vinegar of Modena on cleaning your windows – save it for a delicious salad dressing or drizzled onto strawberries and ice cream. Ordinary malt vinegar will clean windows better and costs much less.

2

OUTWITTING UNWANTED CREATURES

You may think it's just you and your family living in your house – but you would be wrong. Creatures are a fact of life and often benefit from living with humans, so whether you like it or not, over time your home will be host to all sorts of uninvited visitors. Some will want to make your home their own and just a few will come as lodgers for a season before leaving again of their own accord. They may be harmless, irritating, annoying or downright dangerous, depending on their particular lifecycle and habits. In any case, if left to their own devices they will multiply and can become

you'll want to find a way to eliminate a particular infestation altogether. In my time I have had to deal with mice, rats, flies, clothes moths, wasps, hornets, mosquitoes, ants, spiders, silverfish, stray cats, fleas and woodworm. It's easy to ignore small scuttling movements in corners or the sense of something flitting about in a cupboard, but the quicker you can identify a creature the quicker you can tackle the problem.

Local authorities vary in their ability or willingness to help control certain creatures. You will often be referred to a local pest control company and will have to pay the going rate for their lethal skills.

Scampering visitors

Mice and rats

I once lived in a flat where I had a wire plate rack sitting on the worktop. I came into the kitchen one morning and was enchanted to find a mouse, bold as brass, peeping at me from behind the bars. But one mouse will soon produce more mice and, once it becomes a colony rather than just an individual, it will become a nuisance and be smelly, as they often leave little torpedo-shaped droppings all over shelves, worktops and food cupboards. These little rodents, with their bright apple-pip eyes, tiny pink paws and naked tails can leave their paw marks in the butter, chew through

_ᵤ ....ᵢₗ out by blocking up noles where pipes lead outside, but mice can extrude themselves through the tiniest of spaces. They may be coming through from the roof space, especially in terraced houses where they can run from house to house and multiply happily in attics. It's often impossible to tell exactly where they are coming from.

So, it's sometimes necessary to put deterrents in place. The kindest of these are plug-in ultrasonic mice deterrents; long-life battery-operated sonic rat and mouse repellents; natural peppermint scent repellents, such as 'Mouse Oil' and others of the same kind. I've not tried these natural scent repellents myself and I wonder if they would deal with a bad infestation.

The best deterrent in the first instance may be a young and enthusiastic cat, though if your cat is old and lazy that may not be enough. I once found my old tortoiseshell cat sitting comfortably in front of the fireplace and right next to her was a mouse. I could only suppose the mouse had been around for a while and had become, in the cat's estimation, part of the family.

Your next option is to use mousetraps. The traditional kind, a spring-loaded bar of metal which snaps onto any mouse that tries to take the bait (usually a piece of strong old Cheddar) is a fairly brutal solution and these are quite difficult to set without snapping your thumb. They do work, but are perhaps less effective on wise old mice, so it's hard to get rid of a whole colony that way.

If you don't like the idea of killing in this rather medieval way there are other traps, including something called a kill-gate trap, which locks the mouse inside a tunnel and snaps it dead once inside. These types of traps are a better idea if you have young children or pets in the house, but they're still very brutal traps – the killing is just less visible.

Some traps will capture mice alive, leaving you to dispose of them as you wish or to deposit them elsewhere. But what are you going to do with them – pop them through your neighbour's letterbox? Or take them to the nearest park, where they will die, because they are house mice, not field mice?

rormulated for mice and
follow the directions on
the packet. You
may have to
persevere for
several weeks.

Keep the poison well away from food, children and pets. And don't forget where you have put it or that it is lurking there. Other mouse poisons, intended only for professional use, are available on the internet, but they can be very dangerous, so please don't buy them.

In the end, you may be reduced to calling in a pest control service. Such companies may offer medical-sounding treatments like 'emergency same-day treatment', 'three-treatment package' or 'inspection with endoscope cameras'. This can be expensive but will probably cure the problem provided you have found a way to stop more mice moving in. Some companies include a 'mouse-proofing service' which should prevent re-infestation.

The urban myth that you are never more than six feet away from a rat is just that, a myth. All the same there are an awful lot of rats around and the chances are you may find one in your home at some stage in your life. Not only are rats much larger members of the rodent family and therefore more intimidating prospects than mice, but they can also pose a serious health hazard. They will be encouraged if they find food lying around and the wherewithal to make nests. They like old rags, paper, open dustbins and compost heaps with a large proportion of kitchen and food waste. I have known rats to make a nest in an old pouffe turned out into the garage.

Some rats are developing immunity to poisons, so if you think you have a rat, the most sensible thing is to go straight to your local council or health authority and get them to deal with the problem – the service may be free. Otherwise call in a local pest control company.

Flies

There are two varieties of fly in particular that can harass the home owner; house flies and fruit flies. House flies can spread dozens of different diseases to humans and animals, so anything you can do to keep their numbers down is worthwhile. They breed on garbage and rotting meat, so always keep all food well covered and make sure dustbins have well-fitting lids. Keep dustbins clean and disinfected, preferably using bin-liners, and keep food caddies lined with biodegradable liners and their lids properly closed. Don't forget this applies to pet areas, too, which should be kept as meticulously clean as human and child areas.

There are various ways of killing house flies. The most basic is the simple fly-swat, good at dealing with the odd obstinate fly that won't leave you alone, but not so good at coping with many flies all at once. Fly-papers, though old-fashioned, still exist and are surprisingly effective, although they do look unattractive and the feeble buzzing of flies not immediately killed can be disturbing. Aerosol contact sprays catch the fly in flight, but remember not to be over-enthusiastic or to spray them near food or people. Slow-release vaporizers should last six months without doing harm to other living things, although you shouldn't leave them in rooms where there are old people or children.

Fruit flies are smaller than houseflies and usually more of a summer problem. They are basically alcoholics and go for fruit that has started to ferment. They also like beer, wine and other alcoholic drinks. They can multiply very fast and can rise in a disconcerting cloud when you lean over the fruit bowl. Prevention, as always, is better than cure, so throw away overripe fruit and thoroughly clean areas where they are collecting. I'm always surprised how quickly they disperse when they can't get at their favourite foods. There are also, of course, the bigger blowflies such as bluebottles and greenbottles. They behave in much the same way as house flies and should be dealt with in the same way.

...wn colour. The females lay between 30 and 200 eggs, which glue themselves to the surfaces of fabrics and hatch into tiny white caterpillars. These begin to feed straightaway on any natural fibres, wool and silk being favourites, though they like cotton and natural furs, too, and will target clothes, carpets, curtains and collections of textiles. They will also munch on synthetic fibres, but only if blended with wool or other natural fibres. They prefer dirty fabrics, especially if they are sweaty or have had organic drinks spilled on them. If there's nothing better to feast on they will put up with feathers, or go to the food cupboard and lay into the flour and biscuits. They are happiest in warm places and in the dark, so check in clothes cupboards but also the edges of fitted carpets. Tell-tale signs are roundish jagged holes in fabrics about the size of a little fingernail, sometimes so close together they seem to have become a sort of lace.

Moths are unlikely to attack clothes that are in frequent use. The things to keep an eye on are

woollens and cottons, curtains, blankets, duvets and eiderdowns being stored for the summer. Clothes wrapped or zipped into air-tight polythene (plastic carrier bags folded over at the top work well) are normally safe provided the moths can't find a way in.

In cupboards you can hang clothes-moth traps treated with artificial pheromones that fool the

... some are highly flammable, so I wouldn't recommend them. Lavender oil, orange peel, turpentine, camphor and black pepper can all be used in drawers or hung in wardrobes to deter moths. However, delicious though they may smell, if you have a bad infestation, they will not be effective in getting rid of the little pests.

The moment you find a moth hole or actually see a moth flitting softly about, you need to act quickly. Brushing vigorously in bright light can dislodge the eggs and larvae, though you'll inevitably miss a few. If your freezer is big enough, you can try freezing a piece of fabric for several days at a temperature below −8°; or take affected clothes to be dry cleaned, which will kill any moth larvae. Vacuuming carpets will also pick up a number of larvae, but none of these things are likely to get rid of every larva and those that are left will reproduce to turn into another infestation later on. If you have a bad infestation it's probably best to resort to an aerosol moth killer. Follow the instructions exactly and leave the room for a few hours after spraying – what's toxic to a moth is probably not very good for us either.

Wasps and hornets

Wasps, hornets and bees normally make their nests outdoors and very seldom cause much trouble indoors. But occasionally they may find a useful crevice under tiles or in a roof space and then you may encounter rather more of them in your house than you are comfortable with. Bats, too, like to roost in sheltered spaces under eaves or in the roof space of a garage. In most cases there is no danger, but if you are allergic to stings or phobic about bats, you might like to know what you can do about such visitors.

Wasps can become aggressive, especially in late summer, and can be extremely annoying. To deter them, keep meats and sweet things covered when eating meals and make sure pet foods are not left lying around uneaten. The queen wasp hibernates in winter and emerges to build a beautifully constructed new nest in spring, made of wood pulp moulded to a shell with many rooms inside. As said, these are usually built outdoors but occasionally they may

choose a loft space or garage. If you see many wasps leaving and entering your home, there may be a nest somewhere, but it is best to leave it untouched until the end of summer when all the wasps die except the new queens, who will go off to hibernate. Old nests are not reused (although the new queen might choose to build a new one next to the old one).

If they are becoming a nuisance, you can scatter an insecticidal dust at the entrance to the nest after dark. You could use an insecticidal spray for flying insects, but take care how you use these toxins. Always follow the instructions carefully or get in a local professional pest control company. But remember that wasps are useful pollinators and garden pest predators (they love greenflies), so if you can bear it, let them be.

Hornets look like giant wasps, which is in fact what they are. The local farmers in France, where hornets are common, used to love warning us holidaymakers about them by saying proudly, 'Eight hornet stings can kill a cow.' Their life cycle is similar to the wasp's; they are attracted to the same sort of food and also to outside house lights in the evening. If they do get inside, they are inclined to blunder about bumping into things. Deal with them in the same way as wasps and try not to get stung. And if you want to enjoy a warm evening's aperitifs on the terrace, don't switch on the outside bulkhead lights – that really attracts them. It's better to light a few candles instead, preferably citronella.

Bees

A bee colony can sometimes get too big, and then a swarm will detach itself and find somewhere else to go, usually in a tree, though occasionally in a chimney or loft space instead. This offers rather a different

...... and eat the honey and take it back to their own nests or hives, and it will kill them, too. Bees are essential pollinators for a large part of the world's crop foods and they are in a sad state of decline at present, partly because of the use of pesticides. So, the advice is to leave them to get on with things. They are not likely to sting unless attacked – they have more important things to do, such as making honey for a start. If you are really worried, get in touch with your local bee-keeping association, which may have someone who can collect the swarm. Pest control companies will not destroy bees' nests, and you shouldn't attempt this either.

Bats

Bats are another matter entirely. There are eighteen species of bats in Britain alone (300 worldwide) and they are protected. Whereas they were once very common, loss of habitat is affecting them, and chemical timber treatments and insecticides can poison them. They are the only mammals that can fly, and many roost in attics, garages or outhouse roof spaces for the summer. They pose no danger and it is illegal to disturb a roost unless you are a licensed bat worker. They are not rodents and will not nibble or gnaw at wires or insulation (what they like to eat are insects, including mosquitoes). Their droppings are dry and crumble to dust so there are no known health risks. Most are only seasonal visitors anyway and are unlikely to demand your hospitality all year round.

Mosquitoes

Mosquitoes breed in water and warmth. In my London garden they breed in a tiny pond made out of a flexible plastic bucket I buried in the ground. This is surrounded by ferns and a frog lives in it throughout the summer. However, the frog is obviously unable to eat as many mosquitoes as are breeding there because, towards dusk, the mosquitoes, out for blood, get into the house if the windows are left open and do a bit of night biting.

Preventing them from breeding in the first place is the best thing to do, although it is very difficult to eliminate all breeding sites, since they don't mind

...more than a
...ean is a good start, because
prefer stagnant water to clean water. You can keep a pond aerated with a moving-water feature such as a little fountain to keep mosquitoes away. Make sure rainwater gutters are cleared out, rainwater butts tightly covered, and don't forget to change the water in your bird bath.

Since mosquitoes search for your blood by smell, a good way to confuse them is with some other strong smell such as citronella or camphor. You can get citronella candles, and camphor balls (moth balls) can be placed in bowls of water and in the corners of a room. These are strong smelling, flammable, toxic when eaten, and should not be applied to broken or damaged skin, so it's probably best to stick with the citronella.

Apart from all the usual coils (made of a dried paste of pyrethrum powder burned slowly to produce a mosquito repellent smoke) and sprays and ultrasonic repellents, there is a natural biological product that will kill mosquito larvae. It's called *Bacillus thuringiensis israeliensis* and is sold as 'bits' or 'dunks', which turn into crystals. The larvae eat it and die, but once they have become pupae it no longer works, so you have to catch them early. It's not cheap but it does seem to be effective – it is also not toxic to other animals and will quickly biodegrade.

Creeping, jumping and scuttling visitors

Ants

Ants will sometimes send a few scouts into your home from outside and, after foraging around for a while, if they find enough interesting food will set up a supply chain of workers to carry it back to their nest. They can get themselves into seemingly impossible spaces such as jam jars and honey pots with their lids on, and although a nuisance rather than a danger it's best to keep them where they belong – out of doors. I have tried obsessively stamping on all antish comings and goings until they give up, but this takes stamina, time

their larvae. It takes some days to kill a large nest, but it is supposedly safe to use if placed where it can't be reached by children and pets. Alternatively, use an insecticidal dusting powder.

But I prefer to keep them out rather than kill them. One way is to follow their route march to the point of entry into the house and block up the hole with sealant or cotton wool soaked in paraffin, which should deter without killing them. (Paraffin is, of course, flammable, so try not to leave the bottle open on the kitchen table.) Scattering the entry point with curry paste, salt, pepper or talcum powder is also supposed to put them off.

Meanwhile, seal up all ant-food sources, screw on all jam-jar tops tightly, and wipe down work surfaces with half-and-half vinegar and water to destroy all the pheromones left by the ants.

And, if you happen to be a gardener, remember that ants are co-gardeners and on your side, so destroying a nest is counter-productive. Ants disperse seeds, aerate the soil and redistribute nutrients while also patrolling flowers and buds and attacking greenfly.

Spiders

If I stay up late at night I'm often joined by a spider with enormously long legs who lopes from one side of the room to the other, usually towards the fireplace. Where she stays during the day I have no idea, but I find her fascinating and quite companionable. Spiders are not interested in your food; they like instead to catch flies and small insects. The silk they create for their webs is tougher weight for weight than steel and is being researched as a potential material for artificial joints, so it's a real pity to kill them. You will never get rid of all spiders anyway – new ones will always find a way in – but you can keep them under control by vacuuming and dusting regularly, especially round skirting boards, window sills and the corners of ceilings where they like to weave their webs. Also fill in any cracks or gaps in walls, windows and doors. If you find an individual spider and are not completely phobic, catch it under a glass, slip a piece of card underneath it and take it outside.

Oh, and if you find a spider in the bath, it will not have crawled up the pipe and come through the plug hole, it will simply have fallen in and won't like the situation any more than you do. Either catch it and take it outside or hang a towel over the side of the bath so the spider can crawl up and get free.

Cockroaches

It may not be much consolation, but cockroaches are an ancient species that have always lived among humans. In some countries they seem to be a fact of life for many people. I remember once on a trip to New York, while sleeping on a friend's floor, feeling the roaches run over my face during the night and nobody (except me) was the least bit perturbed. They look like rather flat beetles, are dark brown to black in colour and about a thumbnail long. They are considered a health hazard because they will feed on just about anything and enjoy dining in drains and rubbish bins, thus spreading such things as salmonella and *E. coli*, which cause gastroenteritis and dysentery. They may even cause allergic reactions in some people, including asthmatics.

They tend to be more of a menace in apartment blocks and other large-scale buildings, where they can get from neighbouring properties via holes in walls, service pipes, air-conditioning conduits, drains, light fittings, refuse areas, boiler areas and so forth. Cockroaches are quick to breed, and where there is a large infestation it is very likely that neighbours and surrounding properties will have a problem, too.

Each female cockroach will lay several egg capsules in her lifetime, each containing up to forty eggs, so control of these creatures is important. Cockroaches

are darkness,
and areas containing food – fresh
or, even better, rotting.

Take a torch and look behind cupboards, refrigerators and cookers to find the creatures and their egg cases. You may find dead ones, egg capsules, faeces (which look like ground coffee) and some alive and scuttling about. In a bad infestation there is a recognizable and unpleasant smell, best described as oily and musty.

The best advice is to prevent an infestation in the first place by blocking up absolutely any hole or crevice through which the creatures could enter your home, and by eliminating any place where they could hide, such as wall panelling. Keep food in sealed containers, clean up food-preparation and cooking areas, especially where they get greasy, clear up after every meal and don't leave food out overnight. It also helps to keep surfaces and work areas as dry, clean and ordered as possible.

If you do think you have the beginning of an infestation, get in touch with your local authority straightaway. This is not something to try and sort out yourself and the quicker it is tackled the better.

If you have to get in a private pest control company, make sure you get three quotes and check that the price is for eradication of the pest; otherwise you might be charged per visit, which could become horrendously expensive.

Silverfish

These small, wingless creatures are among the oldest insects in the world. They are not much bigger than an ant, with long antennae and three bristles at the back. They are silvery blue in colour and seem to glide along the floor quite fast with a sort of undulating motion rather like a fish, hence the name. In spite of being related to cockroaches they are not a risk to health. They like dark, damp places and a cool atmosphere, so the bathroom is the place you are most likely to find them though they will also venture into laundry areas, kitchens and basements. Their favourite diet consists of starch, cellulose, sugar, glue, paper, hair, carpets, cotton, viscose and dandruff.

..........., warmth and light will help. Keeping lids on shampoo and bath products is also helpful as these often contain carbohydrates and are therefore tempting.

Wiping walls and floors with a solution of bleach and water may help if you find the odd silverfish roaming about, but if you have an infestation you may want to use an insecticidal spray.

Fleas

If you find a flea in your home it has probably arrived nestled in the fur of your dog or cat. Having arrived, it will lay its eggs on your pet and these may roll off and end up in the pet basket or the carpet, soon developing into adult fleas. The thing is, they can lie low for months waiting for a meal to arrive in the form of an animal or human and then emerge with a vengeance to feast on blood. When friends of mine were away one summer, they emailed to ask me to fetch something from their flat. By the time I had crossed their living room floor, to my horror my bare legs were black with a coating of fleas that had simply been waiting patiently for the vibration of someone's footsteps to pounce.

You do need cunning to deal with fleas. Look for signs such as your dog or cat scratching madly with a pained expression on its face or an itchy bite (often three or so in a row), because they will bite humans too. Flea faeces look like flakes of coarsely ground black pepper and you may find them when stroking or grooming your pet or shaking out its bedding. You may even spot a flea itself, scuttling about in partings in your animal's fur.

If you suspect there are fleas, take your animal to a vet rather than buy products over the counter or online; cats, in particular, are sensitive to the chemicals used in some flea collars and other anti-flea accessories and it's best to get professional advice as to what's safe.

Once protected, your loved one will be less likely to be attacked again, but to avoid flea problems you should shake out pet baskets and bedding regularly (out of doors if possible) and vacuum carpets, upholstery, nooks, crannies and areas where your pet

... the fleas you
... eggs – you need to get rid of
..., too, with a household flea spray.

Bedbugs

The thought of creatures hiding near your bed and coming out at night to nibble you for your blood is excruciating. But bedbugs are not attracted to dirt and don't spread diseases as roaches do. They can easily be brought into your home in holiday luggage or second-hand clothing, bedding and furniture. If you find you have bites on your skin, tiny black spots (bed bug faeces) or blood spots on your mattress and a musty smell in the bedroom then it's time to act. Bed bugs are difficult to get rid of. They can hide in tiny spaces, in or under the mattress, behind mirrors, in the headboard, or in cracks in the wall. So, contact your local authority, who can use special insecticides or steam or freezing processes. There are things you can do, too, to help, such as vacuuming up any bugs you can see and sealing them up before binning them;

wash infested clothes and bedclothes at 60°C or put them in a dryer at a hot setting for thirty minutes. Throw away any heavily infested objects and use plastic mattress covers that encase the whole mattress, which will prevent any more bugs getting in or out.

Boring visitors

Woodworm

If you find small pin-head holes in wooden furniture or beams in your home, especially if there are tiny piles of fine sawdust near them, you may have a woodworm problem. This is usually more likely to happen in older houses where the framework is wood. Woodworms are not worms, they are wood-boring beetles. If they do get into your home they can eventually cause structural damage. They can also attack skirting boards, floorboards, joists and wooden furniture. They can be brought into your home already ensconced in furniture bought in second-hand emporiums, car boot sales or yard sales. So, if you love Victoriana and Retro or other traditional

... interior and ... through the holes as adults. On ... whole they prefer damp conditions, so a bit of warmth and good ventilation may well keep them away. There are treatments you can apply. Sticky fly traps hung in an upstairs loft space can catch adult beetles as they emerge from a woodworm hole; a technologically sophisticated ultraviolet insect killer will also catch them, especially in summer, which is when they emerge. You can try a contact insecticide, which will involve painting or spraying the infested area with a fluid, filling the holes and coating the surface – this will kill the insects before they can emerge and breed again. If you think you have too many to deal with yourself, you can, of course, enlist the help of a pest control company.

Deathwatch beetle

This creature is very similar to woodworm but larger. It prefers old oak timbers that have previously been infiltrated by fungal decay because of damp. It will lay its eggs at the ends of rafters affected by roof or gutter leaks. The larval stage can take up to thirteen years. The creature's name comes from the fact that the adult beetle makes a clicking noise by banging its head against the wood to attract a mate, thought to forecast an approaching death. Happily, you are not likely to be bothered by deathwatch beetle at home, unless you live in a converted church full of old timber.

Stray visitors

Stray cats

This may sound a bit far-fetched, but stray cats can have several reasons for wanting to visit your home. For a start they may want to consort with your own cat or they may feel hungry or lonely or simply curious and use the cat flap or any window left open or ajar to get in. When my neighbours next door went on holiday for two weeks, they did not realize that a young tortoiseshell cat had crept into their flat. They duly locked up and left for sunnier shores. Two weeks later my neighbours returned home to find the cat asleep on

cat flap of the kind that only your cat's collar will open. Other cats will then bash their noses against the closed flap should they try to enter. And never encourage cats you don't want with offers of titbits and tickles behind the ears.

Stray foxes

This may sound even more unlikely because foxes are wild animals and belong out of doors, but they are curious and will investigate any open door or window or even cat flap if they think there's nobody around. They are, however, wary of people and will usually run away to avoid them. If you do find a fox in your home, the best thing is to move calmly and quietly, open windows and outside doors, and let the fox find its own way out, which it will do if it doesn't lose its head and panic.

What about deterrents? Well, there are plenty of ideas, from scarecrows to coffee grounds, prickly barriers, threatening smells like lion turds and sonic screeches, but on the whole, these don't work for very long, if at all. Large animal turds are available from some zoos or online as deterrents or as compost. They are prepared and in packets and therefore dry and quite hygienic. In the long run, I suspect they are more use as a rather expensive form of compost for the garden, but you can always try them as a deterrent.

If you have a really prickly shrub in your garden, you could try blocking a possible entry point using

there. But they soon discovered how to dislodge these and provide a space for lounging. So you will probably always have to be keeping one step ahead, trying new and ever-more ingenious deterrents. At least in urban areas the fox population is thought to have reached a status quo and won't get any larger.

WHAT TO DO

- Welcome and observe any bat making a roost in your attic or loft for the summer. Find out about bats online. They are fascinating creatures, not unhygienic and will do you no harm.

- As part of your housework strategy, spend bonding time grooming your pet, whether Persian, German Shepherd, mongrel or moggie. This will be beautifully relaxing as well as a way of making sure they are not flea-ridden.

WHAT NOT TO DO

- Imagine a bees' nest in your porch or chimney is a threat. Bees are only interested in collecting pollen and making honey; they are far too busy to be thinking about you. They are important to the ecosystem and in serious decline.

- Encourage the local macho cat into your home. Though he may be charming and sweet as pie to you and your offer of goodies, he may be a bullying brute to your own cat when you are not looking.

OUTWITTING FAMILY AND PETS

One person's clean and tidy home is another person's hovel. You can be the neatest, most organized person in the world, but how do you get your nearest and dearest to follow your example? Or perhaps you are quite haphazard but live with someone whose standards are rocket high? Either way, low cunning and unabashed manipulation will be called for to achieve an acceptable state of order and cleanliness for everybody. Impossible ambition as it may seem, this means getting everyone to accept an active role and contribute to keeping the place under control. It doesn't matter if you live in a high-rise apartment with five other people or a house full of children or a cottage with a couple of cats and a Jack Russell, or even if it's just you – you will need some rules, some discipline and some chaos-avoiding ideas.

Outsmarting trampling feet

The very first thing is to invest in the householder's best friend – a good doormat. After all, not only is the entrance where people will get their first impressions of your home – a tremendously important consideration – but all the floors will need much less cleaning if you provide an efficient trap for dust and dirt where people come in. Otherwise mud, dust, old leaves, insects and general outside muck will be brought in with the pram, the dog, boots and wheeled shopping trolleys and then spread throughout the house. In fact, most of the grime in your home is brought in from outside and can amount to several vacuum bags a month, so any way you can catch it at source will save a whole lot of extra work. I guess the higher up you live the less this will happen since stairs and the lift will take a fair amount of muck, but shoes do carry the outside

You can keep a broom or a hand vacuum by the door and frantically sweep or suck up rubbish as it comes in, but that simply doesn't make sense for a busy person and there are better things to do with one's time, so a really effective, good-sized doormat is the answer. Make it as large as the floor space will permit. As is so often the case, mats designed for commercial use are frequently a better answer than those designed for the home. Most doormats designed for domestic use are not much bigger than a tea towel and you will be spending half the money on a cheery design of welcoming hedgehogs or a message saying 'Home Sweet Home'. What you actually need is a mat measuring around 120 × 90 cm (47 × 35½ in), which will fit most entrance spaces and allows plenty of room to wipe boots and shoes, buggy and trolley wheels. The mat needs to be seriously absorbent, so that it will contain all this muck until you have time to vacuum or wash it.

There are innumerable doormat materials, including both natural and manmade fibres, and they vary enormously in their ability to absorb dust and detritus. Natural materials include coir, sisal and jute, which do absorb dirt but are not very good at taking up moisture and are inclined to shed bits, which rather cancels out their ability to keep things to themselves. Absorbent cotton can be excellent but wet cotton is heavy, making

. Some are woven,
...ers have a pile, and both are surprisingly effective in trapping and holding dirt.

The best mats are machine-washable and lightweight, and seem to be pretty indestructible. They are often rubber backed and have a flat rubber edge, which means you don't trip over them and they don't slip around on the floor. You frequently see them in entrances to shops and stores as well as in offices. The colours chosen by businesses are usually dull and sober, the most commonly seen being a muddy grey, presumably because this is least likely to show the dirt. But if you investigate you will find there are some cheerful bright colours, such as deep sky blue as well as green and yellow and a geranium red.

Such mats go under labels like 'barrier mats', 'dirt trapper mats' and 'water trapper mats'. They have a longish pile that the dirt sinks into and stays hidden in until you are ready to shake, vacuum or wash.

To make this mat's life easier, you can add an outdoor mat as a first line of defence. Mats made of black rubber are made up of linked pieces acting rather like boot scrapers and allowing muddy bits to fall through the gaps onto the ground ready to be swept up. And let's not forget boot scrapers themselves, which can be so useful on the garden side of a house or on very wet days, when you can scrape the worst off your boots before you get inside.

The helpless and the potentially helpful

As individuals, your family are, of course, so lovely, so clever, so talented, so loving and so completely, infuriatingly messy! As a group they can be divided into the helpless and the potentially helpful (adults and children alike). Theoretically, everybody sharing a home should expect to share in the housework. In practice, it usually needs somebody to see that this happens and it may seem the easiest option to just get on with it yourself – but if you can get your family or housemates to help out, life will be easier and more pleasant in the long run.

...when you can

...work. It's almost impossible

...any time to yourself to read a book, let alone do anything practical aside from feeding, nappy changing, soothing, up-winding and starting all over again. Toddlers need to be watched every moment as they try to crawl down the stairs, pull the TV apart, investigate electric sockets, fall down, have tantrums and want to do things they are not able to do yet. So, apart from learning to be much more relaxed about the state of your home and enjoying this fascinating (and short-lived) baby stage to its full, what can you do? A good start is to make a pact with a neighbour or friend with a child of the same age. They can take yours for one or two mornings a week and you can do the same for them. With luck, a quick session of vacuuming, and a quick tidy-up, will leave you time to do half an hour's yoga or have a bath.

When they're at the youngest stage you can carry your baby in a sling while you do the vacuuming and other tasks, provided it doesn't give you backache.

They may be soothed by the constant gentle movement, though I hope you have a quiet machine.

Alternatively, young children often like to watch you doing things, especially if they have an activity toy attached to their chair so they can be busy while you are. It's even more fun being slightly higher up than usual so they can feel on top of things, so to speak, and have a wider view. From about six to eighteen months a baby-bouncer is great for this, especially if hung over the kitchen table so the baby can bounce on its surface and get a really good bird's-eye view of all the action.

Needless to say, household animals, like babies, will not be a help to you in the house. What's more, they will shed fur and forget to wipe their paws, so raw cunning is required to make them conform to some pet training. Persuade your dogs to choose only one place which is theirs to relax in; either their own dog bed or a particular chair. Some people think dogs have to have a dog crate, and that can indeed be a place of refuge for some animals, but I have known a dog that hated the very idea of an enclosed space, in which case an open dog bed is a much better idea. If

them. Cats ... and won't necessarily do what you ask. You will just have to hope you have one that likes its own place and isn't going to go around the house playing musical chairs.

From the moment children are able to walk and reliably hold things, they can become potentially helpful. Whether they are actually helpful is largely

up to you. First of all, don't ever treat housework as if it were a boring chore. Make it a game for younger boys and girls and a privilege to be allowed to do it. Don't ask too much and do praise, praise, praise them. Show them how to do things so they feel they have skills they can be proud of. Annoyed shouts of 'What did I say about putting your socks away?' are not going to get anybody on your side. And above all, don't differentiate between what's suitable for boys and for girls: anything that has to be done in the home should be shared by everybody equally. It's easier to achieve this when the children are young, and, once established, helpful habits should die hard.

You might expect young children to make their beds in the morning, something that really shouldn't be too difficult since they only need to spread out the duvet and puff up the pillows. When I was ten we had to make our own beds with sheets and blankets, all with hospital corners. I was rather good at it and immensely proud of mine. Other ways for young children to help are, for example, to water house plants (but only fairly long-suffering ones that will put up with too much water sometimes and too little

thing young children can learn. They may not be very good at it, but they might as well get used to the skills needed to wield a broom and use a dustpan and brush. They can also help to clear the table after a meal, and that applies to takeaways, too, which tend to leave an amazing amount of left-over ketchup and splatters on the tablecloth.

As children grow older they can be encouraged to take more responsibility for certain tasks. This is fine up to the terrible teens, but then the real problem is that their minds are concentrated with ferocity on themselves, their place in the world, their sex, their appearance and what other people think of them. What's housework compared to all that? I suppose the more technological-minded teenager might be persuaded to vacuum from time to time, especially if you have a robo vac, but the novelty may soon wear off. Perhaps they could carry rubbish bins out on the appropriate day – try emphasizing how strong and capable they are.

Anyway, until then, there are lots of ways kids can make the houseworker's life easier – for a start, whoever does not do the cooking for a meal can lay the table, clear away afterwards and stack the dishwasher. None of these things need take longer than about five minutes, so it's not asking a lot, but, added to the cooking, it can be a chore. And certainly everybody should feel responsible for mopping up and putting the top back on the toothpaste after using the bathroom, for putting away their own coats and boots, and for not leaving their laptops and telephones underneath the sofa cushions.

This is not forgetting that you may be the lucky one with a child who longs for order at least as much as you do and will automatically tidy and clean up after her- or himself. They do exist. Or that you yourself can learn to be much more relaxed about how 'worked' the house should be, as I have been ever since my youngest came home from school one day, having dropped in at a friend's house for tea, where he had had to take off his shoes in the hall and where nothing was out of place. He glanced around at our kitchen with its piles of magazines and books

and unpaid bills and said, 'I like this house. There's always something interesting to look at.' Even today I comfort myself with his words and go back to my coffee and vampire novel with a guiltless heart.

If all else fails, as it well may, you could keep a really big lost-property basket in which to put everything left lying around during the day – all the tiny Lego pieces, the headsets, the mobile phones and mini laptops, the odd sock, hair grips, homework notebooks, house keys. That would become the first port of call when things get lost.

Challenging your inner hoarder

Most of us are hoarders and most of us have far more belongings than we either need or want. But we don't know that. We are trapped into thinking everything has a value, whether sentimental or because 'it might come in useful one day'. There are, of course, always some meaningful belongings which are loved by us for various reasons. These are the most difficult to get rid of, and if they can earn their living, why get rid of them? My mother's Victorian rosewood gate-legged table is where I work these days – it's by no means as practical as a purpose-designed desk, but it has outwitted me – I like it too much. But I have happily passed on a big laundry hamper my mother gave me as a wedding present because, much as I love it, there

... usefulness of things; we often use it

as an excuse not to make the ultimate decision to throw things out. So the space under the stairs becomes a chaotic jumble of old cardboard boxes – which obviously have huge potential: for returning unwanted goods, storing garden equipment and so forth. The floor of the wardrobe turns into a jumble of tried-and-discarded clothes that you are never going to wear, and the kitchen gets stacked high with too many mugs, bowls and jugs you have collected unsuspectingly over the years. And what about all those gadgets in the kitchen drawer: the rude bottle opener and six different pastry brushes? And the out-of-date herb and spice jars?

There's a useful rule I try to follow: if something becomes cracked or chipped, throw it away at once. In a boisterous family, this quickly gets rid of a whole lot of redundancies. The other rule I always strictly obey: never throw away other people's belongings, even if the children have grown out of some of their toys, I always ask before I throw. After all, a complete

...shop or collection. But draw the line at down-at-heel boots, torn books or damaged toys.

Clothes are among the most difficult things to be strict about. Usually we hang on to clothes for entirely sentimental reasons long after they have become unwearable. They crowd out clothes spaces, lie crumpled under beds and lurk on hangers hidden by newer tops. The fact is, if you haven't worn something for a year, the chances are you never will again, so grit your teeth and turn it out, then appreciate the new spaciousness in your cupboard. Old boots and shoes are particularly tricky – how we do love them! They are probably shapeless, scuffed and smelly, but they have been close friends. Those ones you wore at your friend's stag night when the heel fell off, or the ones you wore every day for a year, which seem to have become part of you but whose soles are now like paper? You can't let them get the better of you and they do take up an awful lot of room. They have to go. Sorry.

When you are clearing cupboards, take everything out to begin with – otherwise it's very easy to get disheartened and, after dutifully removing a thing or two, to just shove the whole lot back in again and forget about it. The secret is to do only one drawer or cupboard at a time. Why martyr yourself to decluttering? A little at a time is quite enough; after all, how long has it taken to build up all this stuff? One cupboard drawer will make you feel proud and satisfied; attempting every cupboard in the home will exhaust you, such that you can't even be bothered to open that relaxing bottle of Shiraz.

Now you've decluttered, what are you going to do with all these things? Some of those storage boxes under the stairs could come in useful, but they are probably the wrong size, or too heavy to lift when full, so not a lot of use. You could have a car boot sale – that can be entertaining – but you will certainly not be guaranteed to get rid of everything that way. Anything left over can go into the rubbish, but may not fit in, and that just becomes another problem. Probably the easiest thing is to take it all down to your local charity shop or second-hand emporium.

...ners. Anyway, what makes us cling on to that old half-eaten jar of stale chutney and that one sardine still in its tin? Believe me, they are never going to come in useful. The trouble is they get pushed right to the back when the new shopping arrives and then may not be unearthed for weeks. A fridge relieved of all those little ends of butter in greasy wrappings, withered old lettuces, flabby carrots and half-finished pasta sauce in the unreachable inner caverns is much more efficient and less guilt-inducing.

Master storage solutions

No matter how earnestly you declutter your home, if you are human, there will still be 'things' in everyday use lying about that make housework deeply frustrating. You can't vacuum thoroughly if the floor is covered in discarded trainers, toys, remote controls and footballs, and cleaning work surfaces becomes almost impossible if they are littered with opened and unopened letters, pens, paper, games consoles, tablets and dog leads.

The more people of various ages and interests you have living with you, the more varied and space consuming their paraphernalia will be. I don't know how you can stop this happening altogether. People may be as thoughtful and neat as Disney princesses

...takeaway pizza app.

A good start is to review the home storage situation. The only hope you will ever have of a clear run at the housework is to make sure you have enough storage designed to actually be used, so it has to be conveniently arranged and conveniently placed. On the understanding that you have already decluttered, this shouldn't be too difficult, but it does need some clear thinking and probably a few checklists as well.

In a large house it's not difficult to create conventional or eccentric storage spaces; for example, enormous antique mahogany wardrobes or modern wall-to-wall mirrored cupboards, window seats (good for toys), or fitted cupboards under the stairs and umbrella and coat stands in the hall.

In a smaller home it may be much trickier to find storage solutions. In particular, modern blocks of flats are often blessed with surprisingly tiny spaces and sometimes no integral cupboards or shelves at all. Here you have to use all your wit and cunning to work out where you can provide a place for everything.

And the place to start is to categorize the things you own and that belong together that you want to store.

Clothes and equipment

Obviously, storage is most likely to get used if it is conveniently placed. For example, the things you use when going out or coming in, such as outdoor footwear, coats, scarves, umbrellas, should be near the front door, not just so that you won't be dragging dirt into the rest of the home, but equally so that you will be able to hang them up the moment you set foot through the door and also to find them when you want to go out. Storing sports equipment could be tricky in a small space and the same applies to dog leads, whistles, bouncy balls, woolly jackets and pooper scoopers. If you have a back door with an entrance passage and room for cupboards or boot holders that might be a good depository, but if you have just a small hall and only one door, the answer is probably lots of hooks (see page 119) to hang things from, rather than the dusty overused spaces under beds.

..., and CDs and DVDs have become redundant and therefore pose no problem for the houseworker. In reality, plenty of households have stacks of them piled chaotically on top of one another; a magnet for dust, which is then scattered all over the floor when you are searching for the one you want. There are all sorts of ingenious space-saving and convenient solutions readily available on the market for these items. Choose one big enough to hold your complete collection and keep it conveniently next to your TV/CD player.

Books

In spite of modern technology's attempt to take the place of books, I know few people who have no books in their home and many whose homes are full to bursting with them. Apart from the universal paperback, publishers are producing collections of beautifully designed and produced editions as collectors' pieces to be carefully housed and maintained. Badly organized books look sloppy, get damaged, and, above all, get in the way of doing the housework. Which of us is going to do a quick run-over with a duster if we have to move several piles of books before we can begin?

So the first cunning move has to be to provide enough shelving or bookcases for the books we do have. It's best to have them upright so you can easily identify them with adjustable shelves to accommodate different sizes of books. Then you can begin to think about how to keep them in good condition. Apart from jumbles of books making dusting around the home difficult, dust is not good for the books themselves; it is gritty, scratchy and can damage the pages and the binding. Early twentieth-century household manuals used to advise taking each book out and slapping its pages together to chase out the dust, but that is actually not a good idea. Books are delicate souls and don't like being beaten up. It's best to use a non-scratchy duster and run it between the books and the next shelf up. If you've organized the space very tightly, you may have to take each book out briefly.

If you want to make a feature of them, give the shelves pride of place in your living room; otherwise,

...... can house them. A friend of mine has framed a large double-door that opens between reception rooms with bookcases running up on either

side, and a shelf for displaying ceramic jugs running along the top of the door frame. It looks attractive and interesting and saves a huge amount of space. One advantage of an adjustable shelf-and-bracket kit is that you can fit the spaces to the books you have; different types of books can go onto a dedicated shelf specially designed for them.

Kitchen storage

Of course, in the kitchen, for convenience, cups should be near the kettle, the refrigerator next to a food-preparation area, the plate rack next to the sink, cupboards (for plates and so forth) as near as possible to the dining table. Admittedly, many modern kitchens are so tiny it doesn't really matter where you put these things; you'll probably be able to reach them all from the middle of the room anyway. But it does help in a larger kitchen to make ergonomic sense of the storage spaces.

I know that open shelves in a kitchen will attract dust, but I am eccentric enough to like open shelves, on which I can see my favourite objects all the time, so I have a built-in kitchen dresser with shelves of bowls, and a collection of decorative tins. Another advantage of this is that there are fewer cupboard doors, which can often make a room feel enclosed and claustrophobic. This is a very personal choice and would not suit everyone, but I enjoy it. Because most of the items stored there are in everyday use, they get washed, anyway, as a matter of course.

Hooks

The fewer things you have on the floor, whether clothes, toys or furniture, the easier your housework is going to be. Hooks and pegs are very much underused as a way of getting things off the floor and, incidentally, of encouraging your loved ones to actually put their stuff away instead of casting it to the ground. Rows of cup hooks under shelves in the bedroom can carry numerous necklaces and bangles, while showing them off prettily, like a miniature shop display. Extra large cup hooks can hold delicate silk scarves and keep them off the floor of the clothes cupboard. They are great for storing decorative shopping bags, too.

In entrance halls or lobbies, where space may be at a premium and where you are desperately trying to encourage everybody to leave their outdoor clothes and paraphernalia, a long row of hooks – not the timid four-hook variety usually on offer, but one as long as the wall will take – can change your life. With luck, each coat, hat, scarf and parka can have its own hook so won't create a pregnant 'stomach' of piled-up coats sticking out from the wall and taking up all the space. You could make your own from a plank of wood and choose your own generously sized hooks.

There is also the original Shaker idea of hanging up any furniture that was not being used at one time. Chairs were designed to be hung on pegs on the wall, making not just moving about but sweeping less of a task. This may not seem the most practical idea in small spaces in today's homes, but it seems too good to dismiss completely. There are folding stools and chairs available on the market which can be fixed on hooks and lie absolutely flat against the wall, so if you entertain a lot but don't want the place littered with seating when there are no guests, the hanging idea is worth a second thought.

example, what do
about Christmas decorations that are variously
sized, strangely shaped, often delicate and breakable?
You only use them once a year, so the best idea is to
find suitable storage boxes – lightweight cardboard or
plastic – or even robust carrier bags that can be stored
under a bed, on top of a cupboard or on a tall shelf.
Otherwise they will be stuffed into a drawer, or several
drawers, and the chances of finding them all again is
remote. Christmas lights are among the trickiest to
store. Try to remember to keep their original boxes
– it may take time squeezing all the wiring back into
the box but what came out must be able to go back
in, and it will keep the lights protected.

Jewellery

There's another perennial problem, especially when
it comes to dusting: jewellery. What do you do with
all those tiny brooches left to you by your great aunt,
and the dozens of hair combs and grips you absolutely
can't do without, and the chokers and gold chains and

beaded strings and all those rings you will wear one day but not all at once? Undecorated wooden boxes are great for storing these, although you'll probably need more than one; wooden sewing boxes that concertina open can also be excellent as long as you have the width of space to get them open. The best ones are undecorated so you can paint or cover them with your own glue-on bits and pieces (they make very welcome presents for birthdays, too).

Tools

Household tools are always a problem unless you are lucky enough to have a workroom/garage or have room for a separate work space. But every home does need its basic supply of hammer and nails, pliers, screwdriver, saw, plumbing tape, adhesives, radiator key, picture hooks and whatnot. The traditional canvas tool bag is a flexible holder for a very small and rudimentary kit designed originally for carrying the things needed for a particular job. It could be the answer for a householder who actually seldom uses tools and doesn't much like doing so. A better solution for a serious kit is a metal toolbox with

...ere will always

...such tools, carpet tape, paint brushes, cup

hooks and other maintenance objects and keeping the

together in their own box is a good idea.

Paperwork

Another snag for the houseworker is the amount of
paperwork that arrives through the post (in spite of
emails and social networking). Even after you have
recycled all the spam post, begging letters, money-
making schemes and promises of enormous raffle
prizes, not to mention never-to-be-repeated offers of
double glazing and/or solar roofs, you will still be
left with bills that need to be paid, reminders to have
your eyes tested, notifications of school term dates
and countless messages you feel you have to keep
because you would like to reply one day. There are
also cuttings taken from magazines that you think you
will follow up, paint samples for when you get around
to redecorating, and countless other ephemeral items
that cannot be thrown away, all conspiring against

the neatness and tidiness of your home.

This is where storage used for offices can be truly effective at home. And one of the most useful is the humble box file, which can come in really handy for filing and categorizing various types of paper storage. Lined up on a shelf, clearly labelled and colour coordinated, they can look really efficient, as though you are in control, and you *will be* a lot more in control than you were before you got them. Also, you can now clear and dust the newly available space on the kitchen table.

All this cunning storage is no excuse to stop decluttering. I'm afraid you're still going to have to bag-up, chuck out, give away or burn, as you accumulate, because no amount of storage will absorb your everyday acquisitions.

Just because you love your pets to bits does not mean you have to let them walk all over you or bring a wet day's detritus indoors or shed their hairs all over the place. Dogs are particularly good at having a good shake on a wet day just as they come indoors. Luckily, if you've followed my advice, your generous and absorbent doormat will protect the floor and carpet to some extent, and if you keep an old terry towel just inside the front door you'll have at least half a chance of giving the dog's coat a good wipe before he or she spatters the walls with mud.

Unfortunately, the front door is not the only place a pet will have the opportunity to shed hairs and fur. If the animal is willing to be faithful to its own bed, so much the better; you have done a good job of helping your own cause. All you need do is shake out and wash the bedding fairly regularly and you'll have saved yourself hours of de-hairing work. Although I am sure such good behaviour is possible to cultivate, I have to admit it is expecting rather a lot. After all, if you have a pet, you want to stroke it and groom it and sit it on your knee and pull its ears and rub its tummy. Immediately you do so, your clothes will be covered in hairs, and if your dog is a long-haired Maltese terrier or your cat is white and Persian, you'll have your work cut out to make yourself presentable. What's more, try as you may to get an animal to stick to its own bed, typically they prefer a comfortable

't have to put the whole lot away every
omes to visit.

ome in every shape, size and vulnerability,
s important. To start with the smallest,
ways endless collections of tiny figures,
ard animals, to soldiers, astronauts and
from electronic games, that get collected,
played with – and lost. One large biscuit
tin (or perhaps several, depending on the
of the collection) can sometimes be enough
hese.

useful storage categories are bricks, anything
eels, electronic toys, dolls and clothes, books,
ard and card games. Once you have roughly
ized them (you can't be too precise because

from a sofa or chair there is a good
view of everything going on, including who's visiting
and what's cooking. Inevitably, people sit on the dog
hairs before they realize what they've done. Once
you've accepted this as inevitable, you can cover the
chair with a blanket or throw, which can be taken up
when a human rather than animal wants to sit down.

So, whatever you do, you will have animal hairs and
fur to deal with. There are all sorts of cunning devices
designed to pick up pet hairs quickly and efficiently.
For example, there are small, handheld tools that will
brush, comb and trim as they de-fur, or handheld
vacuums specially designed to pick up loose hairs.
To be honest, lots of pets I have known would never
let themselves be seen anywhere near such electronic
gadgets, so you'll have to groom in the old-fashioned
way with a brush and comb, or use 'grooming and de-
shedding' gloves. For hairs on upholstery and clothes,
there are simple rollers that use sticky paper to run
over the fabric. At a pinch, you can use strips of sticky
tape (postal, carpet or plumber's), which will pick up

hairs pretty well but are not as convenient as a roller. There are also rubber brushes that are supposed to miraculously pick up hairs from fabrics and furniture. For want of any of these, dampened rubber gloves should do the job.

The great toy challenge

The moment a modern baby is born, it acquires countless belongings. Apart from essential equipment such as the cot, the bath, the buggy, the car seat,

th
nec
gran
some
is a w
furry b
centres.
as in the
be admired
above peopl
will continue
become more v
home completel

Throwing toys
impossible, becaus
feelings, the child b
and they all have sen
is the only option – o
control when and how

Probably the best wa
crew of toys is to buy a s
stackable boxes. This make
one or two for a particula

means you don
time a friend o
Since toys c
categorizing
there are al
from farmy
characters
exchanged
or sweetie
diversity
to store
Other
with wh
and bo
catego

... to make this system work, of course, you do need to help the child to put everything away in its right box when play is over. But it will save an awful lot of trouble later on.

Your teenager's room

Aargh! It's so hard to know what to do about this. Very few teenagers in this world really love order and like to be neat and tidy or arrange their possessions so they look attractive. If we're honest, most of us were not like that as teenagers either. Teenager's rooms are simply big refuse tips with sweaty socks and tights and bus passes hidden under mountains of tried-on and discarded clothes, makeup, bath products and the ubiquitous iPad or tablet. You can hit your head against a rock by trying to insist on some order and responsibility, or you can bite the bullet and accept that this will continue until after college and just keep

the door closed and never, ever look in. The best you can do is tell your offspring that the room is theirs and the responsibility is theirs, and provide plenty of cupboard space, hanging space, drawer space, a bedside table with compartments, and a good mirror (in which all this chaos will be reflected – but teenagers are really only aware of the chaos in themselves, so won't see that).

It will all pass in time – good luck!

hedgehog or owl design, perhaps, or dachshund or squirrel – rather than a mundane one, and you will be much more likely to get your children to wipe their boots before they come indoors.

- Clear out the overloaded chest of drawers in the spare room; give the chest away and replace it with an upright piano or digital keyboard that everyone in the family can enjoy. A set of earphones would be an optional extra but one welcomed by your neighbours.

WHAT NOT TO DO

- If you use duvets, and most people do these days, *please* don't bother with a top sheet as well as a duvet cover – it's just a way of getting all tangled up in the middle of the night and of having to do unnecessary extra washing.

- Go down to the charity shop and buy back the things you donated the week before.

4

OUTWITTING HOUSEHOLD GRIME

In the face of the plethora of grimy substances that surround us, from environmental pollutants, to sticky things, greasy things, mud, bodily wastes, crayon marks, food crumbs and hard-water scale, keeping our home feeling clean feels like a constant battle.

So, how best to keep your home clean while doing as little housework as possible? First, don't imagine you have to keep everything spotless all the time. No amount of bright shiny cleaning equipment will eliminate the need for housework. And never feel guilty if something needs doing and you haven't done it – being a martyr doesn't necessarily get things done. There's nothing so guaranteed to prevent you

easier (see page 106). In a similar vein, it's also very useful to clean up as you go along. This may sound obvious, but not all of us do it and it's incredibly effective. If you have ten minutes before you have to catch your bus, you can put away five pairs of shoes, or clean the sink, or fold up a cardboard box and put it in the recycle bin. It takes practically no time to run a cloth round the bath or basin or shake out a couple of rugs; you'd hardly notice yourself doing it.

My third ruse: just do it – little and often. Don't feel you have to give up doing something pleasurable to slave over all the greasy cooking areas at a time or to vacuum the floors. I'm all in favour of doing things bit by bit and only when they become annoying. The dirt on the kitchen floor can accumulate without your noticing it for days, and then suddenly you realize you are noticing it, so you reach for a broom and mop and it's done – you will probably be inspired to do a bit in the hall and bathroom, too. So don't sit around thinking about it – it'll probably take less than ten minutes and nothing need take longer than half an hour. It won't dominate your day at all, then, and your satisfaction will be immense.

It's a bit of a mantra in this book, I know, but when it comes to housework, doing a little but often will lessen the overall workload considerably. A useful benchmark is to keep everything in such a state that if somebody comes to visit you unexpectedly, you can get your home fit to be seen in ten minutes or so. Of course, we all have our own view of what is 'fit to be seen', but unless you are obsessively house proud a quick vacuum or mop, plumping of cushions and smell of percolating coffee should do the trick. Attracting the eye to something interesting such as a beautiful vase of flowers is a great way to ensure people's attention is diverted from less salubrious parts of your home or piles of unfinished projects.

So how can we make the essential tasks as easy as they can be? Why not start with the dirtiest, most challenging, area – the kitchen.

where clean-up-as-you-go-along
⸺ itself in buckets. Food preparation creates
mess. In my early married days, my husband was
the cook and used to produce gourmet meals with

enormous aplomb and unbelievable quantities of used pans, bowls, chef's knives, wooden spoons and food spatters. It was while cleaning up after him that I got the message about always, automatically wiping the work surfaces at every step. Then food doesn't have time to dry on and won't become difficult to remove. Used utensils belong in or near the sink, smears should be wiped routinely, bits of food binned as appropriate. At the end of the session the chaos is much less daunting and quicker to deal with. Afterwards, a quick sweep of the floor will prevent you from treading crumbs and food bits into the surface and drying to an obstinate concrete.

As we looked at in a previous chapter, the three most useful and effective kitchen cleaners you can keep in your armoury are all edible: lemons, vinegar and bicarbonate of soda (see page 28). You can mix up a preparation of edible cleaner more quickly than making a trip to the supermarket or even ordering online, by putting one cup each of vinegar, baking soda and hot water in a jug. Stir it, let it cool, then pour it into a squeezy bottle and label it. Then, when you want to remove fly marks on walls, grubby finger

Lemons

One of the nice things about a lemon is that if you cut it in half you are left with two fit-in-the-palm cleaning pads that can be comfortably gripped for rubbing onto greasy stains on anything from worktops to taps.

Starting with the cooking areas, let's first address the microwave, which can gradually build up splatters of food without you even noticing. If you stand a bowl of water with half a lemon squeezed into it in the centre of the microwave and run the machine for ten minutes or so, the steam will collect on the interior surfaces. Leave for a few minutes before opening the microwave and then you can wipe the surfaces off with a damp cloth or kitchen towel, leaving it pristine and smelling delicious. You can use a similar technique on conventional ovens by filling a third of an oven tray with water and the juice and rinds of two lemons. Cut the lemons in half, squeeze the juice into the water and add the skins of the lemons, too.

Bake at 250° C for about half an hour or, if your oven is really filthy, for forty minutes. Allow the oven to cool, remove the dish and then use a scouring pad, a spatula (not a sharp blade) and a microfibre cloth dipped into the lemon water to wipe off all the excess burned-on grease. Finish off with an old terry towel if you have one, because they are super-absorbent, and throw it away afterwards – or use kitchen roll. I don't need to remind you to let the oven cool down before opening and wiping, do I? The secret here is to go away and do something interesting while you let your lemon preparation work its magic. Apart from avoiding caustic chemicals, the whole point is to make things easier, so don't frantically start scrubbing away at the dried-on grease, but let the solution quietly get on with the job until it's ready. If you haven't cleaned the oven for months (or perhaps years?), you might like to give it another half-hour with more water and two more lemons, or even resort to a chemical cleaner, but it's a good way of dealing with a well-kept oven.

My grandchildren love to cook and produce delicious curries and vegan salads. When they've all gone home again, I am left with a hob that looks like the inside of

_ scouring pad,
_, baking soda and all, you can then leave it for ten minutes before wiping the whole greasy lot away. This works equally well on chopping boards or laminated worktops, especially given the mildly disinfecting quality of lemons.

Vinegar

Also an acid and very similar to lemon juice when it comes to cleaning, this is another cheap and safe edible cleaning ingredient that can be used all around the house. If you have large areas needing a clean, vinegar is probably the cheaper option.

If you have a blocked drain and have tried a plunger with no results, pour half a cup of bicarbonate of soda down the drain, followed by half a cup of vinegar and one cup of very hot water. Wait for ten minutes, then pour down more hot water. After that, if necessary, try plunging again. The waiting, as always, is important, giving you time to go away and think about something else while the mixture works.

A cup of vinegar in the bottom of the dishwasher before use will stop glassware from becoming cloudy, and if your kettle is suffering from hard-water deposits, half fill it with water and add an egg-cupful of vinegar, then boil it up and leave for ten minutes. This should have demolished the hard-water scale and you just need to rinse the kettle out. One word of warning: don't overfill the kettle, because the whole thing is liable to foam when it boils and will come frothing out if it's too full. Vinegar will also remove hard-water scale from taps, shower heads and the

...... you are out, ... scale with an old toothbrush. You may wonder how you are going to get the vinegar to sit in the loo bowl, but once you have soaked a length of toilet roll or some cotton wool in vinegar, it will stick to the limescale nicely while it eats its way through it. As with so many cleaning jobs, have patience, go away and leave it for a few hours, or apply the treatment just before you go to bed and finish it the next morning – then it'll brush off easily. A friend of mine in her thatched cottage in rural Sussex found her shower wasn't allowing any water through at all because of limescale. She put some vinegar in a mug and left the shower head in it for the morning while we went for a walk by the river. By lunchtime the shower was working perfectly – we hardly had to brush it out.

When you've finished with the windows (see page 158), you can pour some vinegar into a plastic spray bottle and spray the shower walls and curtains to prevent mildew. You will also prevent mildew if everybody remembers to leave the curtains drawn across so that they don't form thick pleats and prevent the air getting at them.

Baking soda

This is a mild alkali and can be used on its own or together with lemon juice or vinegar to clean a multitude of objects around the house. It always surprises me how something so bland and edible can be so effective. It will clean really obstinate coffee and tea stains left on cups and mugs – fill them with a mixture of an egg-cupful of baking soda and two egg-cupfuls of warm water and leave overnight. Wash them in warm water next morning. Do the same thing with burned-on food on pans and dishes, though perhaps in a slightly stronger solution, and wash the next day.

Baking soda will also absorb doggy smells from upholstery if you sprinkle a little over the smelly parts, then leave it overnight and vacuum thereafter. Do not rush in and vacuum immediately after you have sprinkled on the baking soda – allow the powder time to absorb the smells. The method can work with

...... to clean out your fridge, keep it from getting smelly by putting an egg-cupful of baking soda tucked in at the back. It will absorb most smells. Unfortunately, if the smell beats the baking soda, cleaning the fridge can't be put off any longer.

Cream of tartar

Finally, there is another edible ingredient used in baking, which also has bleaching qualities. Again, this is a mild acid, a by-product of wine making. Mostly it's used as a raising agent in baking, but it has cleansing uses as well. A paste made of cream of tartar and lemon juice applied with a toothbrush over stained old grout in a bathroom or kitchen splashback and left for a few hours, then wiped with a damp cloth, will brighten the grout up considerably. You can use it in the same way as baking soda for cleaning a coffee pot. Just put three teaspoons of cream of tartar in the pot, add water, heat up, then leave for an hour or so and rinse out.

Floors

A clean and spotless floor will give the impression of cleanliness to the whole house and help to conceal the fact that you haven't done any dusting for a month. If your floorboards shine with a polished look and the carpet is newly vacuumed and as fresh and springy as a puppy's coat, you will have gone a good way to earn your reputation as an outstanding houseworker.

If you have had the very good sense to install a good, absorbent and large doormat (see page 94) you will already have saved yourself a mountain of vacuuming and sweeping.

Crumbs, dust, mud and sand are the things that are most noticeable on floors and carpets and that can do the most damage if left lying around. The odd rubber, bitumen or wax crayon mark doesn't look half as awful as the loose detritus and can be left until you have time to deal with them. A quick vacuum in the five minutes before you go out (and before you have time to decide you can't be bothered) will help to keep things under control. Or a swift sweep round with a

...ard floors

To make things easier, wood floors can be sealed rather than waxed, which protects them from getting scratched or absorbing water and means they won't need buffing up. In fact, you should never wax a sealed floor, and even waxed floors don't need half as much polish as they are often given. Too much wax makes for a slippery floor. Untreated concrete flooring, in a garage or workshop for example, will

continue to produce its own grit and sand, so people going back and forth carry it with them on the soles of their boots. Cleaning it up can be a never-ending process. Special concrete sealants are available, which can eliminate all the dust and prevent hours of work.

The ancient skill of sprinkling a kitchen floor with damp tea leaves and then sweeping them up solved two problems; it provided an answer to what to do with old tea leaves and prevented the dust from escaping into the air. Used tea bags, if still damp, can do the same thing – they are a bit bulkier to sweep up but still help to contain the dust. The floor will look 100 per cent better than it did before, even if you only have time to clean the bits people can see and leave the rest under a rug. I always appreciate the moment in *Snow White* when one of the seven dwarves brushes the sweepings under the rag rug. I don't usually do that, but I have done.

Carpets

If your carpet is new, vacuum it every day for the first few weeks. This will pick up any loose fibres that work their way to the surface. If a piece of carpet

...uuning it fairly

...p to prevent dirt from becoming embedded in it and will also keep the tufts upright. A vacuum cleaner with a brush and a beater is best for tufted-pile carpets, and one without those fitments is best for loop-pile carpets. Vacuum at the right speed: if you're anything like me and always busy, you will rush over the carpet, hardly giving the mouth time to touch the floor. One slow pass over a slightly soiled carpet will be sufficient, but where it gets a lot of tread and grit, try going over it slowly twice. You'll eliminate a lot of dirt and further extra work like that.

Don't try to save time by urging your vacuum cleaner to pick up things it obviously doesn't want to, like drawing pins, paper clips and glass beads. Bend down and pick them up yourself or sweep them up first.

Whichever carpet you have, no vacuum cleaner in its right mind will clean effectively if the bag isn't emptied regularly. My mother used to tell me that the bag should be emptied every time you use it – a counsel of perfection I have never been able to live up to, but it is important to empty the bag before it is completely full. If your vacuum is bagless, then it's just as important to wash the filter regularly. Most filters are really easy to remove, wash and put back when dry. The recommended time seems to be every three months or so.

Every now and again it's a good idea to run over your carpet with a DIY carpet cleaner. Since you probably only need to do this once a year or so, buying one might seem an unnecessary expense for just one household, as well as being rather space consuming, so why not share one with friends or family?

Upholstery

Upholstered chairs and sofas with or without loose covers get a really hard time in most homes. They always look splendid when new, but it doesn't take long for people to spill their coffee and drop their tomato sauce on it; grubby fingers smear the armrests, muddy shoe soles mark the cushions, pet hairs cling

...s every morning

...from time to time giving it a cursory run-over with the upholstery attachment of your vacuum or with a handheld vac, just to keep it all in trim. Pat the cushions and adjust the covers to make it look sprightly. Pet owners, as mentioned earlier, often have a blanket to cover the animal's favourite chair; they can then easily just remove the rug when the chair is needed for an actual person.

The great thing with upholstery is to try and keep it uniformly clean. If it has a slight overall feeling of grubbiness you can run over its arm rests, back and crevices with a damp microfibre cloth to freshen it up. Mop up anything spilled before it has time to settle in, dry out and stain the fabric for good. Turn the cushions from time to time and dry-shampoo chairs with a suitable upholstery shampoo two or three times a year, even if the furniture still looks clean. Try to do this at odd moments fairly frequently; then you won't have to have them laundered or dry cleaned too often.

New upholstery with removable covers should be labelled with an international labelling system that indicates how to clean it. These labels are usually found hidden under the seat cushions. If they are not there, check all the tags found on the furniture (let's hope you didn't cut them off when you brought the furniture home). A tag with a 'W' on it means clean only with an upholstery shampoo or other water-based cleaner; 'S' means clean with a water-free solvent or call in a professional; 'S/W' means clean with either of the above – this is seldom seen on new furniture and it means you'd be best to take it to a dry cleaner. When buying upholstery or when in doubt about how to clean something, it can be worth looking for these tags before you end up using the wrong product and ruining the sofa cover.

Curtains

How on earth do you outwit the wiles of curtains in your home, especially heavy, lined curtains designed to fall in graceful cascades and end in gathers on the

...problem of climbing ... or unloop them and making decisions about how best to deal with them. Of course, you can put this off effectively for a good long time by keeping them generally dust- and splash-free. A good shake once a week or a run-over with a long-handled vacuum tool will keep them fresh. If you are vacuuming, remember the tops of the curtain rails or rods. But there will come a time when you can't hide it from yourself any longer that they need something more radical. Find the label that tells you if they are washable or need dry cleaning. Sometimes the main fabric is washable but the lining isn't. Lightweight muslin or sheer curtains can be washed in a pillowcase or mesh bag and dried easily. Large bulky curtains get very heavy when wet, may not fit into your machine, will need somewhere to hang out to dry, and need to be folded and ironed. If you are determined, wash them in a cool programme with a small amount of laundry detergent, but if you really want the best deal, you will take them to the nearest laundry or dry cleaner and get them dealt with professionally.

Window blinds

It is a truth universally acknowledged that a single professional cleaner can do a better job of laundering curtains and blinds, along with double duvets and pillows, than you can do yourself.

All blinds are a bit unwieldy to wash and dry. Theoretically, you can take down Venetian blinds and wash them in the bath, but to be honest they are cumbersome, have sharp edges and will probably

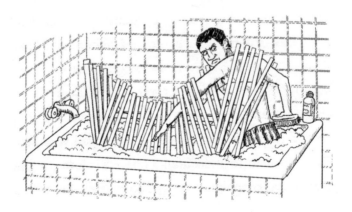

...foam rubber pads
... for this job, but they are almost certainly more trouble than using gloved fingers.

Roller blinds can be rubbed with a dry microfibre cloth when they become too obviously grubby. Some are washable but, again, it's a rather cumbersome procedure, so avoid it if possible. Plastic-coated blinds can be wiped down with a damp microfibre cloth.

Vertical surfaces and coping with heights

On the whole, vertical surfaces such as walls and doors don't get dirty obviously or quickly, apart from a mild coating of grey everyday pollution. If you really want to, you can wipe this film off from time to time with a cobweb brush or dry microfibre cloth. But you should normally only have to wash a wall when you are preparing to redecorate. The dry cloth method works well for painted and papered walls. But if your wallcovering has a raised surface, a dusting brush would be better because, if used gently, it will disperse the dust without damaging the surface.

The most noticeable foreign objects on vertical surfaces are the spiders' webs, with their booty of dead flies, that collect in the corners where the walls meet the ceiling and in the upper corners of window frames. These can multiply in time without being noticed, but once your eye catches them they become horribly obvious, waving gently in the draught and spreading a feeling of guilt and neglect. Again, it's best to deal with these with a dry cloth or brush. Once you start trying to wash them, the dust and fly wings just smear themselves over the wall, making it much more difficult to get clean. Use the cobweb brush for dusting ceiling lights

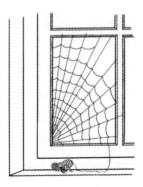

as well, and certainly never try to clean those with water or a damp cloth. You might think of spreading an old sheet underneath to catch the debris, otherwise you'll have to get the vacuum cleaner out unnecessarily.

... ...ic on shiny, flat, pale-coloured surfaces such as window panes, mirrors and white walls, where they defecate and regurgitate, leaving small spots or specks. You often don't notice these until they've built up, but they are easy to remove with a paper towel dipped into a cup of equal parts of vinegar and warm water. This simple method will also remove finger marks from light switches – where do those marks come from? Who'd have thought we all had such grubby fingers?

Light fittings

When light bulbs collect too much dust they stop being effective and become dingy. Fluorescent tubes, for example, are said to lose 40 per cent of their illumination if they get very dirty, which they often do in a kitchen or workshop. But all bulbs will need dusting occasionally or you will wonder why you can't see to peel the potatoes or read your letters. Of course, don't forget to turn the light off before you tamper with it.

Sparkling glass

Windows

You will find an array of aerosol window cleaners to choose from in supermarkets. If you use any of them, remember they are for use on dry glass, so if you have condensation or it's been very rainy, dry the window beforehand. In fact, using vinegar rather than a chemical product for window cleaning is cheap and just as effective. All you need to do is fill a bucket with warm water and add a cupful of vinegar (the size of the cup is not important; we're not talking rocket science here).

Before you start, take a damp cloth and gently brush away any dry debris such as dust particles, bits of dead leaves and old cobwebs, so you have a clear start. These days a squeegee is the tool to use, rather than a selection of cotton cloths and old rags. Squeegees come in many widths; you can get a small one (the sort you'd

…blade is well covered with the water/vinegar mixture; then, starting at the top, draw the blade in horizontal strips along and down the window pane until you reach the bottom. If the window is very dirty (the exterior of a ground-floor window, for example) you may have to repeat

this. After every stroke, wipe the blade dry with the magic secret ingredient – crumpled newspaper – then dip it in the bucket again and continue. When you've covered the whole window from side to side and top to bottom, dry it off with crumpled newspaper and use the newspaper to rub off the last little obstinate spots of dirt or water drips – *et voila!* I know some people dismiss the thought that newspaper works, but I assure you, it does. I don't know whether it's the printing ink or the paper itself, which is absorbent, but it is quick and really effective and the paper can be recycled afterwards.

If you want to give yourself a treat, buy a chamois leather. A chamois is an agile goat-antelope with short hooked horns, and its skin was once used to make a soft, pliable leather for gloves and cleaning cloths. Nowadays, chamois leather is made out of sheepskin or lambskin, but it has the same soft, pliable texture, which is a pleasure to use. It's good for cleaning the squeegee blade while working, and for rubbing off the last of the smears when you've finished. Use it in tandem with the crumpled newspaper, not instead of it.

grubbiness catches your eye, but frost makes the glass more vulnerable and likely to crack and in bright sunlight the water dries too fast, encouraging smears – plus you'll probably be blinded by the light and won't be able to see what you're doing anyway. Whatever you do, don't use any sort of abrasive pad to get rid of obstinate marks. Just allow the vinegar and water to remain on the pane a little bit longer before wiping it off.

Mirrors, acrylics, screens and phones

Efficient though squeegees may be on window glass, they shouldn't be used on *mirrors* that have a silver backing with a copper-paint backing behind that. If water gets between the glass and the backing, the mirror can become discoloured, so put your vinegar-and-water mixture into a squirty bottle, spray the mixture onto a microfibre cloth to just dampen it, and then wipe the glass carefully all over, keeping any dampness clear of the edges.

Other glass-like materials also need careful

treatment. For example, *acrylic* (a transparent thermoplastic also known as Plexiglas or Perspex) is, of course, not glass at all but a form of plastic, and solvents can damage it – and anything abrasive, even dust, can scratch it. It is sometimes used as a substitute for window glass, roof windows, picture or photo frames, TV screens and baths, and should always be cleaned with a special product for cleaning acrylic and nothing else.

Your *computer screen* can gather muck for ages before, one morning, you suddenly catch sight of the smears and rush for the cleaner. You can use a water-and-vinegar solution (50/50 mix) but not tap water, just distilled. Don't use any solution with ammonia, or window-cleaning products that can discolour the monitor. In fact, it's probably best to buy a special solution, spray it on a soft cloth, then rub that over the screen very gently. Don't use kitchen roll, tea towels or facial tissues – believe it or not, they are all too abrasive. Oh, and by the way, you might like to know that crisps and croissant crumbs can be moved from the keyboard very easily with a soft watercolour paint brush.

which may have a special coating on the surface that can be damaged by window-cleaning products. It might be worth checking the instruction manual to see if it recommends a particular cleaner. Good screen cleaners will state that they do not use alcohol or ammonia. Just keep a smooth microfibre cloth for the purpose and use it dry. If your screen is disgustingly dirty, use the cloth very slightly damp and don't press too hard – it's so easy to break a screen. I shouldn't have to point this out, but turn the appliance off before you start cleaning it, just in case of electric shock.

I suppose it should be obvious really that our *phones* are among the dirtiest things we own. We breathe into them all the time and handle them without washing our hands first. At least with mobiles the object is more or less smooth, and easy to wipe, but with landline phones there are handsets and mouthpieces and often more than one person using the thing. Ideally, you should unplug it before cleaning, but as long as you don't get it wet, you shouldn't have to do that. For all types of phone, don't spray water directly onto it but slightly dampen a soft cloth to remove fingerprints, coffee splatters and germs, and use a dry corner of the cloth to remove any dampness. Cotton swabs will get rid of dust and crumbs in any corners.

The furniture that's out to get you

Luckily, dusting is the most important thing for keeping furniture under control. There's no need to make an appointment in your diary, just do it when you notice it. While doing so, it's a good idea occasionally to glance at the bottom rungs and base supports of chairs and tables, which are often forgotten, and to keep an eye on the armrests, which can become grubby all too quickly and may need a damp microfibre cloth rather than just a duster. Your efficient doormat and general vacuuming will minimize the dust anyway, so you shouldn't have to do it too often. But when you do dust, do it first and vacuum afterwards so that the dust when settled on the floor gets picked up by the vacuum cleaner. Feather dusters are brilliant for

...these days has an ...an, hard-to-damage finish that, apart from dusting, only needs an occasional wipe-down with a dry or damp cloth and that's it. But if you have an elderly or antique piece, especially if it's made of wood, it will need a bit more care and attention to keep it looking its best and to prevent damage to its exquisite and expensive surface. If the item is a bit grubby, wipe it with a cloth dipped in a cup of water with a few drops of vinegar added. Then you can concentrate on getting the best finish. Luckily, most advice is, if in doubt, don't interfere, and clean as little as possible.

So, let's have a quick run-down of the most usual types of wood finish and how to treat them.

Painted furniture: Paints used on modern furniture are usually gloss, semi-gloss or latex. They are all hard-wearing and resistant to stains, so the furniture just needs a rub-down with neat washing-up liquid and then a wipe with a clean cloth.

Stained wood: Again, hard-wearing and unpolished, so just needs to be wiped with a damp cloth.

Unsealed wood: This is often found on solid-wood kitchen tables and worktops. Some people like to apply an oil to unsealed wood furniture and others prefer to leave it in its natural state. Either way, apply soapy liquid onto a cloth first, not directly onto the wood, and the surface should never be left wet.

Varnished or lacquered wood: Mostly used on tables and chairs, this should be damp wiped and then buffed up; very occasionally, a coat of spray polish can be used, but it is tempting to apply too much polish too often and then it just accumulates and attracts more dirt and dust.

Veneer: This is simply a very thin layer of wood glued onto a base. It's a fragile finish and needs to be cleaned with care. Damp-dust only, because a thin varnish over the veneer can bubble up if it gets wet. And make sure it is completely dry when you've finished.

...u and involve ...s of thin woods, and possibly ...als. The most important thing is that they should never get wet. Water will lift the intricate little slivers of wood and they will then curl up and be almost impossible to mend. Don't use a duster for dusting; small fibres can get snagged in the inlay and damage the piece, so use a soft-bristled hand brush or a soft watercolour paint brush. You should hardly ever need to add polish.

WHAT TO DO

- If the housework builds up and you can't somehow get around to dealing with it, invite a few friends for coffee. It's remarkable how quickly you will find the energy to clear up before they arrive.

- Next time you're using baking powder, perhaps when making Scotch pancakes, blinis or fluffy American pancakes for Pancake Day, take the opportunity to boil a little extra baking powder in some water in the frying pan to make it squeaky clean afterwards.

WHAT NOT TO DO

- Keep adding more polish to floors or furniture because you like the smell and it makes you feel virtuous; this will just attract more dirt more quickly and build up to a hard gunge. Buffing up with a soft cloth is quite enough.

- Climb onto a chair balanced on a table to replace a light bulb. Wait until you can find a willing assistant at least to hold the chair – or get a sturdy set of steps.

...CKING INTO STAINS

The best way to outwit stains is, of course, never to spill anything. But try telling that to the person whose expansive gesture has just knocked over the bottle of Claret, or whose puppy has just peed all over the new rug, or whose indelible ink is slowly spreading across the oak table.

Even so, there are things you can do to keep stains at bay. An obvious ruse is to wear an apron or overalls while cooking, house painting, cleaning the car, gardening, using permanent markers or inks, or indeed any other dirty job. When changing the toner in a printer or using inks or paints, spread the working area with newspaper or kitchen roll so spillages can be wrapped up and discarded. You can protect upholstery and carpets by spraying on a fabric protector, which will help prevent stains from being absorbed. When opening bottles and jars of any kind, make sure you do it over a smooth, wipeable surface and not over a carpet or tablecloth. When putting on your makeup, take the time to fling an old scarf over your shoulders so you don't get eyeliner or lipstick on your best dress. Use a sealer on concrete, stone, linoleum, wood and cork floors so they won't absorb anything that gets spilled.

In spite of these precautions, of course, accidents do happen and when things get spilled, the important thing is to act quickly. If you act swiftly, the chances are you'll be able to remove the spillage and the stain completely, whereas if you wait until the next day it will have soaked in, dried up and settled down for good. But acting quickly does not mean brandishing the bleach or scrubbing brush in a panic and setting the stain for ever. Modern chemicals, up-to-date scientific knowledge and protective fabric finishes have made stain removal in the twenty-first century easier, but at the same time modern fibres and combinations of

...ᴋₑₛ sense to
... kit handy. This should
...paper tissues (your kitchen roll is best), a small sponge, cotton wool balls, a medicine dropper for powerful solvents, a squirty bottle with a fine-spray nozzle for cold water (or cleaning mixtures), a suede brush if you have a suede coat or shoes, a soft old toothbrush, a clothes brush, a soft shoe brush, your choice of solvents and bleaches, and white vinegar and lemons. Some of these things will be in daily use in your home anyway; the strong solvents should be kept in a locked cupboard that children can't reach.

How you tackle a stain will depend on what the stain is made of and also, crucially, what material it is on. Clothes and other textiles should have a label indicating the fibres used (e.g. '100 per cent cotton' or '75 per cent cotton/25 per cent polyester'), which is helpful when deciding what stain remover to use. If you have a collection of retro clothes, the chances are they will be too old to have such labels, so you'll have to use your common sense. Spillages on flat surfaces, rugs or upholstery should be soaked up immediately, either with salt or kitchen roll. In any case, as with all cleaning, although you have to be quick to deal with stains, patience is the key to success. Don't rush at a spill in a panic with a nail brush. Little, gently and repeated if necessary will give you a much better result.

Getting your priorities right

There are six basic techniques for dealing with stains, each suitable for specific sorts of stain and specific sorts of material. But first of all, there are some basic rules you need to know.

...ff *as you*

...ne or spatula is good for this,

...her with a bowl of warm water and disinfectant. Work from the edges towards the centre so you don't spread the stain. Hold the knife at a low angle so you can pick up the spill smoothly, and if the matter has hardened it may help to pat it with a short-bristle brush.

Don't apply heat in any form when first tackling a stain. Don't, for example, rinse the garment in hot water. Many food stains contain albumen or similar protein, which is fixed by heat, so if you apply heat you'll never get the stains out and may even spread them to a wider area. As one professional cleaner told me, 'I'm always getting people who say, "I've spilled egg on this sheepskin coat but I haven't touched it at all – I just held it over the kettle for a bit." Without realizing it, they've shrunk the leather, cooked the egg and made the mark almost impossible to remove.'

Check the effect of whichever stain remover you're going to use on an inconspicuous piece of the garment – the inside hem is a good place, or an inside seam. This particularly applies to precious or dyed fabrics, or when you are not sure what fibres they are made of. Some treatments may harm one of the fibres in a combination and some may make dyes run or fade.

Don't try to remove the traces of very stubborn stains. It is often better to wear the thing with a shadow of the stain still there than risk ruining the fabric by applying too much solvent or rubbing too fiercely. You can always wear a scarf thrown nonchalantly over your shoulder to conceal the mark.

Six basic techniques

There are six basic techniques for getting stains out of clothes, textiles and furniture: washing in water, absorbing, using solvent, bleaching, lubricating and freezing. These techniques are your essential armoury,

... Never underestimate the value of water for getting rid of stains. Non-greasy stains on washable fabrics should be rinsed immediately with cold water. Cold water is excellent for getting rid of blood stains and urine stains. Non-washable fabrics can still be treated by dabbing just the stained area very gently with cotton wool or clean white paper towel squeezed out in cold water. Don't rub, twist or wring; just press gently, using a clean plug of cotton wool or fresh paper towel from time to time. Don't use water at all on dyed wild silk or moiré, or any fabric that might show a water mark. Take such fabrics to a dry cleaner and explain what's been spilled. Textiles are generally weaker when wet, so treat them gently. Greasy stains on fabrics can be treated by adding detergent to the water. In fact, on sturdy fabrics such as cotton you can use neat washing-up liquid rubbed gently into the grain of the fibres with a very soft toothbrush. You can soak a whole

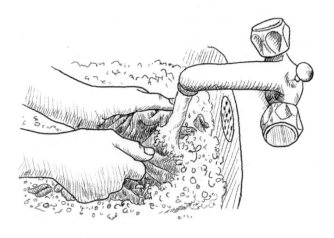

garment in cold water and detergent and leave it for several hours before rinsing it out and then washing as normal.

2. **Absorbing:** Wet things such as wine, fruit juices and urine spilled on carpets or fabrics can often be absorbed completely without any need for rubbing or scrubbing. This method can also be used for greasy particles lodged in fur and other unwashable fabrics. There are various suitable absorbents. Salt, for example, will absorb wine and fruit-juice stains from carpets. Be generous with the salt, as there will have to be enough to absorb the amount that was spilled. The best thing

No salt? Try kitchen roll and tread them gently into the stain, changing them frequently. It's better to use kitchen roll than salt on valuable carpets, the colours of which might be affected by the salt. Good absorbents for non-washable fabrics, used in the days before 'dry cleaning' was invented, but still effective, include bran, Fuller's earth (a light clay that is slightly alkaline) and French chalk. Shake the absorbent gently onto the fabric to be cleaned. Leave for twelve hours or so, then brush gently but thoroughly. You need to remove as much as you can of the absorbent as well as the spill or it will itself attract dirt.

3. **Lubricating:** This is a really useful technique for removing impossible items such as chewing gum from your daughter's long hair and grass stains from tennis shorts, or tar and engine oil. Useful lubricants include glycerine, petroleum jelly (Vaseline), lard and margarine. Rub any of these

onto the substance and work it in well with your fingers, then wash it out or, in the case of chewing gum in someone's hair, stroke it down the hair strands until you can pull it out at the ends.

4. **Using solvents:** There are a number of solvents, such as methylated spirits and white spirit, that will dissolve grease and also remove those obstinate little labels often stuck onto glass which are so difficult to remove. There are also several good proprietary stain removers on the market, most of which contain similar solvents. If using methylated spirits or white spirit or any other neat solvent, dab and blot in succession on fabrics that should not become too wet such as suede or wool (which, by the way, should never be rubbed or it will shrink). If using a proprietary product, follow the manufacturer's instructions. Many solvents are flammable and/or poisonous, so use them with care and common sense, making sure there is a window open and no open flame nearby. Milder solvents include vinegar and lemon juice. For cleaning whites, obviously use white vinegar or you will have to remove the

bleaches to use than the chlorine bleaches usually used in the lavatory. *Hydrogen peroxide* is a safe and mild bleach just made up of oxygen and water. It can be bought in pharmacies (usually for use as a mouthwash or mild oxidizing disinfectant, which tells you how mild it is), and is a useful bleaching stain remover. *Lemons*, too, have a mild bleaching quality and are worth trying when you don't want to use anything too strong. *Chlorine bleach* is a rather harsh form of bleach not recommended for removing stains at home, but *percarbonate* or *oxygen bleach* is used to whiten and brighten laundry and can remove certain stains effectively. It can contain sodium perborate, sodium percarbonate or hydrogen peroxide. This type of bleach is an ingredient of many laundry detergents and is safe for use on most white or coloured washable fabrics. It works more slowly than chlorine bleach, and is less corrosive and damaging to fibres. It is sold as either powder or liquid. Over time, the active chemicals will break down into soda ash or borax, which is environmentally friendly. Oxygen bleach solutions work well to remove stains from carpet and upholstery. Follow the directions on the packet for solution strengths. Mix a solution and blot onto the stained area, trying not to get the surface too wet. Leave the solution to work for at least half an hour and then blot the excess stain with clean white paper towels. Repeat as necessary. It is better to use a weak solution several times than to try to get the stain out in one fell swoop using a stronger solution. When you've finished, give the garment a rinse in cold water, otherwise you may be left with a powdery white residue.

6. **Freezing:** There are just a few items, such as chewing gum, chocolate and candle wax, that harden when dry, and can then be frozen and broken off in bits. After that you may have to use a solvent or washing process to get rid of any colour residue.

Many stain-removing solvents are caustic, poisonous, flammable and give off toxic fumes. Please read the manufacturer's instructions, even if they are in tiny print, and then follow them. Keep all solvents in a locked cupboard out of the reach of children (not decanted into other containers) and clearly labelled. Work in a well-ventilated room, preferably with the window open and away from any naked flame. Never mix one type of cleaner with another unless specified or you may set off your very own home explosion. Don't use ammonia together with chlorine bleach because, together, they can produce a dangerous toxic vapour.

Know your enemies

A stain may be made up of several different substances. Gravy, for example, isn't just greasy but is also made up of blood and colouring. So you may have to flush it out with cold water initially to deal with the blood, then treat it with detergent for the grease, and finally use a solvent if the detergent doesn't work on the colouring. If the fabric is white, you might want to finish off with a mild bleach. On delicate fabrics you could try using a mild bleach such as lemon juice (see page 179). Again, white coffee stains will contain colour from the coffee, which will need detergent, and fat from the milk or cream, which will need a solvent.

Certain fabrics and certain stains are best treated by a professional. For example, anything of historic interest, such as old tapestries and rugs or anything particularly fine or valuable such as silks, wools, moirés and chiffons, can be easily ruined by the wrong treatment.

Sometimes, powdery particles remain trapped between the fibres after the rest of the stain has dissolved and been flushed away. The temptation is to scrape this away with a fingernail before rushing off to work. Leave yourself time to apply neat liquid detergent and gently work the fabric between your fingers. The particles become suspended in the detergent, which

can then be washed away with water, taking th
it. You need patience for this as you'll need to
rinsing three or four times to get rid of all the de
and particles.

A reminder: take your time, don't switch fro
method to another before you've given the first
chance to work.

Chocolate

You might be a budding chocolatier and gloop the chocolate by mistake out of the saucepan onto your shirtfront, or you may sit on a box of chocolates lurking among the sofa cushions. If the chocolate has dried, this is a time when you can use the freezing technique. Either put the whole item into the freezer until it has become brittle and then break the bits of chocolate off. Otherwise, use a bag of ice cubes to rub over the chocolate until it has become frozen enough to break off. In any event, treat the spill as for blood – get out of your clothes and rinse them under the cold tap or soak them in biological detergent solution. Then launder them as usual. If the fabric is non-washable, use a proprietary stain remover. Liquid chocolate or residual stains can be sponged well with a solution of one tablespoon of borax to a pint of water, or you can use an upholstery spotting kit. Any chocolate bits trodden into a carpet should be removed with a blunt knife and then treated with a carpet stain remover.

... ~~~~ ~~~~~~~~~ with clean
tissues.

Mildew

This unpleasant grey or black mould loves damp, warmth and gloom, so it's not surprising that you often get it in the bathroom, settling into a shower cubicle or in the gaps between the bath or basin and the wall. Obviously, then, it's a good idea to wipe down damp surfaces as often as possible and to introduce a flow of fresh air into the room by opening doors and windows and fitting a fan. You can get mildew off plastic shower curtains by laundering them in a gentle cycle together with a couple of bath towels. For gaps round the bath, mix up a solution of chlorine bleach according to the manufacturer's instructions (wear rubber gloves and an apron) and rub small areas of mildew, one at a time, with an old toothbrush. Then rinse and dry. And if you don't want to keep having to do this, get someone to reseal the gap. Mildew can also attach itself to items left in a warm damp cupboard and, if it does, the musty smell is rather unpleasant, but such items can usually be successfully laundered in a hot programme; mouldy leather can simply be wiped over with undiluted antiseptic mouthwash and then wiped dry.

Alcohol

This doesn't just mean drinks; medicines, skin lotions and perfumes may also contain alcohol, which can dissolve many finishes, so when you do spill that sort of thing, treat it at once. When I spilled red wine on a new silk shirt, I took it to the cleaner's the very next day, but the alcohol had already damaged the colour. I should have torn it off my back there and then and run it under the cold tap. You could also soak it in a detergent solution for a few hours before laundering as usual. Any residual stain can be treated with hydrogen peroxide solution (one part hydrogen peroxide to six parts water).

Beetroot

This delicious vegetable really knows how to stain. Rinse in cold water or soak overnight. Try rubbing

try sprinkling some borax on the dampened stain and pour very hot water through it.

Gravy and sauces

Lift off any deposit with the back of a knife. Flush out as much as you can under the cold-water tap, then use a solvent or proprietary stain remover to deal with the grease and finally launder as usual (you may find a good laundering with a squirt of laundry stain remover will do the trick without the use of a solvent). If the stain has dried, soak it in a biological detergent solution for at least half an hour before laundering. Non-washable fabrics should be sponged gently with cold water using the dab and blot technique and making sure not to get the fabric too soggy; then, if necessary, apply a stain remover.

Bird droppings

If you use an outside drying line, the insult of all insults is when a bird drops cherry-stained globules onto your clean sheets. Remove the excess with a blunt knife and then soak the article in a warm biological detergent solution before laundering it again. If the item is non-washable, dab and blot with white vinegar and a clean paper towel. If the droppings are stained with berries (pigeons are particularly good at this), bleach with a hydrogen peroxide solution of one part hydrogen peroxide to six parts of water.

Chewing gum

The only place I know which doesn't suffer from chewing gum blobs all over the pavements is Singapore, where it is an offence to drop it on the ground. At home, however, it can get into a child's hair or onto the carpet and you really do need to get rid of it. You can buy specifically formulated spray-on chewing gum or 'sticky stuff' removers, which will help deal with gum on clothes, rugs and carpets. Follow the manufacturer's instructions. Otherwise, try putting the whole garment in the freezer and,

... until it's frozen ...ugh to break bits off. Treat any residual marks with a solvent such as methylated spirits and then launder the garment as usual. If the gum has nestled into someone's hair, lubricate it with margarine or glycerine and slide it off.

Nail varnish

Absorb as much as you can with tissues before it dries and then dab and blot with acetone or amyl acetate (but not oily nail varnish remover). A word

of warning: acetone will damage acetate or triacetate fabrics, so check the fabric first.

Urine

Whether human or pet urine, if left for too long the stain and smell of this can be difficult to remove. If you catch it at once, rinse through with cold water, then soak for a few hours in cold water or biological detergent solution before laundering as usual. Dried stains should be soaked in biological detergent solution, or use a specially formulated proprietary stain remover. If the fabric is non-washable, sponge it with cold water immediately and blot well. Then sponge with a vinegar solution (one tablespoon of white vinegar to 9 fl. oz – 250 ml – of water). On carpet, squirt a soda siphon onto the mark or sponge with cold water and blot well. Then use carpet shampoo and finally dab and blot with cold water containing a few drops of antiseptic. If the stain has discoloured a cork, linoleum or vinyl floor, make a solution of two tablespoons of vinegar in one pint of water with a few drops of liquid detergent and scrub this into the floor with a soft-bristled brush before

...g a pool of lemon juice on a dog's urine stain that had soaked into a pale-coloured vinyl floor and within two hours the mark had been largely eliminated.

Mustard

Although mustard can be a very bright yellow, it is much easier to deal with than, say, turmeric. Scrape the excess off with the back of a knife. Then rub detergent into the stain or soak detergent solution for a few hours. Afterwards, launder as usual. Treat non-washable fabrics with a proprietary stain remover.

Cod liver oil

Fresh stains from cod liver oil – which is oh so good for you, with its omega-3 fatty acids – can be easily removed. But old stains are practically impossible to get rid of, even with bleach, so either take your oil as capsules or stand on a tiled floor while pouring it into the spoon. If you catch it at once, absorb as much as possible with a paper towel and apply a solvent from the back of the stain. Baby clothes should be sponged with a strong solution of washing-up liquid, rinsed and then washed as usual. If the stains have dried, try methylated spirits or a proprietary stain remover, and for carpets use a carpet stain remover.

Paint

Paint, like most spills, should be treated while still wet or the chances are you will never get it out. Different paints require different actions, so check before you act. *Water-based paints*, including emulsion, acrylics and water-based oils, can be flushed under the cold tap when still wet. Then rub detergent into the stain and leave for a few hours before laundering as usual. Any remaining colour residue can be dabbed and blotted with a proprietary stain remover or a solution of one part methylated spirits to six parts water.

Oil-based paints, including gloss paint and undercoat, should be dabbed with white spirit or paintbrush cleaner and sponged afterwards with cold water. For carpets and upholstery, absorb as much as you can as quickly as you can with kitchen roll and then use a carpet stain remover or upholstery spotting kit.

...that you may find on beaches during a summer holiday, or on a road or street being resurfaced, and they can be very clinging. If they get on shoes, they can transfer themselves onto trousers surprisingly quickly. Some seaside shops now sell a cleaning product, made up of a solvent and detergent, that often seems to work. Failing that, your first move is to try to scrape off as much of the solid stuff as you can by softening it first with a proprietary solvent. Then you can rub a colourless grease, such as lard or petroleum jelly, or a syrupy substance such as glycerine, into the fabric, after which both tar and grease can be laundered out using a strong detergent solution. Often a grey residual stain will remain, which you can try re-treating with solvent or bleaching with hydrogen peroxide or lemon juice.

Engine oil

This is very difficult to remove, as you will have discovered if you've ever had to tamper with the engine of your car. First rub in neat liquid detergent and rinse in cold water. Then flush with a proprietary stain remover. As always, it's best to try this gently several times rather than rush in too energetically and damage the fabric.

Fruit juices

These include fruit drinks and juices from fruits themselves. Hold under the cold tap, rub in liquid detergent, leave for ten minutes or so and then rinse thoroughly in cold water. Wash at as high a temperature as the fabric will take, otherwise use a cool programme with biological detergent. Non-washable fabrics should be sponged with cold water and then blotted dry with clean paper towels. If there is a residual stain, lubricate it with equal parts glycerine and water, leave for an hour and then launder as usual.

For silk, nylon and wool use a proprietary colour remover or stain remover rather than water.

Grass

Grass stains normally only show up badly on whites. If you are a Wimbledon player or get grass on your

... with a laundry stain remover. On trainers and tennis shoes, blot with methylated spirits. For non-washable clothes, you can buy a proprietary stain remover specially formulated for grass stains.

Blood

Blood is one of the dreaded and inevitable stains that occasionally have to be tackled at home. But if you can catch it while it is still wet, it can usually be washed out completely by holding it under the cold tap or soaking it in cold salt water. Don't use hot or even warm water, which will just help to set the stain. Afterwards, launder as usual. If the blood has dried, brush off as much as you can and soak in a warm solution of biological washing powder, or try soaking in a solution of one part hydrogen peroxide to six parts water.

Candle wax

This often ends up on tablecloths at dinner parties, but sometimes also on shirt cuffs when carrying a lighted candle with a shaky hand. This is one time when it's best to be slow – let the wax dry and harden before trying to remove it. If there's space, put the item into the freezer until the wax has hardened enough for you to be able to break it off in bits. If your freezer's full to busting already, try heat instead: sandwich the fabric between two sheets of clean blotting paper or tissue and smooth it with a warm iron. Use the lowest setting and don't melt the fabric. Any wax remaining should be dissolved and flushed away with a dry-cleaning solvent. Any colour left from the wax should be dabbed with methylated spirits and then rinsed.

Grease

This can be anything from butter or margarine and various oils to ingredients in gravy, mayonnaise, ice cream, ketchup and makeup. Remove as much deposit as you can with the back of a knife. Wash at a high temperature if the fabric allows it, using a laundry detergent that includes percarbonate oxygen bleach.

For residual stains, try a professional stain remover or other solvent, or a solution of one part hydrogen peroxide to six parts water.

...paste with cold water. Leave to dry for an hour or so and then brush out gently. Sometimes, grease marks on wool and silk can be absorbed by sandwiching the fabric between tissues and pressing with a cool iron.

Hair dye

Temporary dyes should be easy to rinse out in cold water. For permanent dyes you need to work some liquid detergent into the spill and then launder the fabric as usual. There's no excuse for letting it dry; as a dye it is not supposed to be easily removed once dried. This goes for henna and other vegetable dyes, too.

Adhesives

There are many different glues, and if you spill them or glue the wrong things together, each will need a different treatment. *Household glues* and *model aircraft cement* are cellulose based and can be removed with acetone (but don't use this on acetate fabrics).

Some manufacturers make a solvent for their cements. *Superglues* (cyan acrylics) are activated by moisture and moisture will also undo them. If you stick your eyelids together by mistake (these adhesives do work very fast), hold a damp cloth over the place until it comes unstuck. Soothing words and dampness is what you need. *Epoxy adhesives* consist of glue and a hardener mixed together. They can be removed with methylated spirits, but only before they set. Once hardened they cannot be undone. *PVA* (polyvinyl acetate), also known as wood glue, carpenter's glue and school glue, can be cleaned off with methylated spirits. *Rubber-based adhesives* are used for craftwork; they are quite runny and overflow easily, but spills can be removed by soaking with cold water and rubbing gently. The residue from *sticky labels* and *tape*, which can be horribly obstinate, can be removed with methylated spirits.

Beer

Rinse through with white vinegar and then with water. If that hasn't worked, try biological detergent. If the fabric is washable, wash at a high temperature.

to remove than others. If you use ink for artworks, the chances are you will spill some sooner or later. There are proprietary stain removers for inks that may be worth keeping in your stain-removal kit. And here are some other ideas for you to try, but don't be too optimistic (and wear an artist's smock when working). The first rule for all inks is do not use heat to try and remove them.

Indelible pencil

As the name implies, this is not easy to remove, but in some cases it's not impossible and certainly worth a try. Don't try to use water as that will just spread the stain. Mix up a half-and-half solution of household ammonia and methylated spirits, and dab and blot the stain using a soft cloth or sponge. Be prepared to spend some time on this, and continue gently and patiently until the mark begins to fade (if you are worried about the colours running, use meths on its own). Then rub in a liquid detergent or soak in detergent solution overnight if possible and then launder as usual. If the stain persists, treat it with a solution of one part hydrogen peroxide to six parts water and rinse thoroughly. At this point, you have either removed the stain or you might as well give up. If the fabric is delicate or valuable, take it to a professional dry cleaner. Some people swear by soaking the stain in milk overnight. I have not tried this but it's probably worth a go. Afterwards, use a laundry stain remover to deal with any grease left from the milk.

Ballpoint pen

This is not the disaster it is often thought to be. Most ballpoint inks are soluble in methylated spirits and can be removed if you dab repeatedly with meths. On walls, try using a soft nail brush; gently though.

Felt-tip pen

Don't despair; you can probably get the ink out. You might like to contact the manufacturer, who may have produced or recommend a stain-removal product. Otherwise, lubricate the stain with soap or glycerine, leave it to work for an hour or so,

Coffee and tea

Flush out immediately under the cold tap. Black coffee and tea will probably respond to soaking in hand-hot washing detergent solution followed by a good rinse and a normal wash. Any residual stain can be tackled with a solution of one part hydrogen peroxide

to six parts water. If there is milk involved, soak for a few hours in warm biological washing solution to counteract the fat in the milk, then wash as usual. If the drink has been spilled on a carpet, squirt the stain with a soda siphon if you have one; otherwise treat it with a carpet shampoo.

Makeup

Eye makeup is usually quite easy to remove from sheets and pillowcases, after you've flopped into bed directly from a night out. *Eye shadow* will usually come out in a normal wash with a squirt of laundry stain remover on the stained areas. *Eyebrow pencil* may need treatment with a proprietary stain-removing solvent such as methylated spirits before being laundered. Mascara can be rubbed with neat liquid detergent and then dabbed and blotted with household ammonia solution (one teaspoon of ammonia to a pint of water). *Foundation cream* usually comes out if you wet the fabric and then rub in liquid detergent and rinse thoroughly. If the foundation is a very greasy one, try a proprietary stain remover. Powder should be shaken out immediately first of all and any residue treated like liquid.

...........y spread, remove the excess carefully with the back of a thin knife. Then immediately dab and blot with methylated spirits or a proprietary stain remover. Give yourself time to repeat this several times. Rinse with cold water. Soak in a liquid detergent solution for an hour or two, then rinse and launder as usual. 'Indelible' lipstick can be softened with equal parts of glycerine and water and then rinsed well and washed as usual.

Crayon

If your toddler has created an unofficial mural on the wall with wax crayons, let's hope it's a painted wall. Then you can dab the affected area with a proprietary stain-removing solvent or even just neat vinegar and wipe it off with kitchen roll or a microfibre cloth. If the wall is papered, you have to be a bit gentler or your treatment might damage the paper. Try very gently rubbing the marks with a soft eraser, or pass a damp soft sponge pad very lightly over the surface and pat dry immediately.

Curry

Stains from curry are caused by the spices used in the cooking, especially turmeric. These should be treated immediately, because once they have dried they are really difficult to remove. Scrape off as much as you can with the back of a knife, trying not to spread the stain as you do it. Soften with glycerine solution (equal parts glycerine and water), then soak in biological detergent solution. The residual stain can be treated with juice from a cut lemon. In fact, if the spillage happens in a restaurant, you can ask for a slice of lemon and treat the stain straightaway. Having acted quickly, it's a good idea to follow up by getting the garment professionally dry cleaned.

Mud

Resist the temptation to wipe it off while still wet, which will just drive it further into the fabric. This is one time when you should wait and allow the mud to dry. Then you will be able to brush it all off easily and launder the garment afterwards.

...part hydrogen peroxide to six parts of water. Then soak overnight in a biological detergent solution and launder. On viscose, nylon and polyester fabrics, use household (chlorine) bleach solution (two teaspoons of bleach to half a pint of water) and don't leave for longer than fifteen minutes.

Sauces

See gravy.

Cream, yogurt, crème fraîche

Although ostensibly white, all these things are fatty, so unless you deal with them quickly they will leave marks on fabrics – usually tablecloths and fronts of shirts and tops. Scrape off any excess with the back of a knife and, as soon as you can, rinse the object in cold water or soak it in biological detergent solution, then rinse and launder as usual. For non-washable fabrics, use a proprietary stain remover, and if the stain is greasy, dab it gently and use kitchen roll to take up the solvent.

Shoe polish

Remove deposit with the back of a knife. Use a proprietary stain remover or solvent such as methylated spirits (one part to six parts water), then soak in liquid detergent solution with a few drops of household ammonia added. Launder as usual. On carpets, use carpet stain remover and for upholstery use an upholstery spotting kit. Any residual colour stain can be treated with a mild bleach such as hydrogen peroxide or lemon juice, but check on a hidden part of the fabric first to make sure it won't be damaged.

Tomato juice

See fruit juice.

Wine

If wine is spilled on a carpet, absorb as much as you can immediately with salt (leave it in a heap overnight) or paper towels, trodden but not rubbed into the spill. Be prepared to use a whole roll. This may solve the problem entirely, but if a slight discolouration remains, try dabbing and blotting it with one part

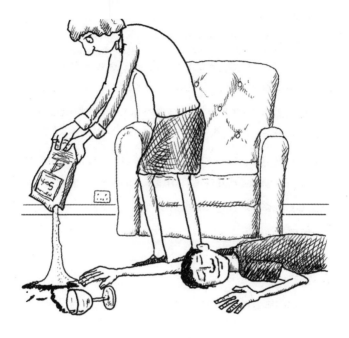

hydrogen peroxide to six parts of water. This applies
to white and red wine; both can stain.

WHAT TO DO

- Cover one of the walls in your child's room with a coat of washable white emulsion paint so that children can legitimately be creative with chalks, paints or crayons without getting into trouble.

- When serving beetroot soup or borscht, make sure to supply enormous red disposable paper napkins and use an oilskin or multi-coloured tablecloth so that inevitable spills can be wiped clean or will disappear into the pattern.

WHAT NOT TO DO

- Don't cover a puppy puddle with a rug and pretend it never happened. It is amazing how quickly something so seemingly innocuous will begin to smell and what a dark colour it can stain a floor or carpet. If you are determined to have a puppy, be prepared to follow it around with an absorbent cloth until it becomes house trained.

- Don't meticulously apply your makeup for your birthday party before getting dressed and then try and pull your best white silk shirt over your head.

CONCLUSIONS

Housework is an integral part of life. I used to think it was very boring and something to struggle through as quickly as possible, but I have since learned to incorporate it into my day as a matter of course and even to take pleasure in it. The important point to take on board is that one should never aim to be wonderworker. The idea is to keep things under just enough control to feel comfortable in your own home and comfortable about inviting visitors in. There's a big difference between a bit of disorder and actually having nowhere to sit down because all the seating is covered in junk or not being able to offer someone a cup of coffee because there isn't a clean cup in the place. Of course, to some extent everyone's idea of cleanliness is individual. You may love a minimalist appearance with few objects on display and everything in its appointed place. Or you may prefer to live in what amounts to an artist's studio, with pens, inks, papers and other paraphernalia strewn all about and lots of different objects in a seeming jumble. There are numerous possibilities in between – the choice is yours. A well-kept home is not supposed to feel like a hotel; it's a personal expression of your own life and personality, so a certain lived-in quality can only be good – we just need to get the measure of that right.

Enjoy your housework and don't be a martyr to it; treat it as a skill, not a chore. Skills are acquired, so make sure you learn how to use the various bits of domestic equipment at your disposal. Once you've acquired these skills, the process becomes automatic and there is something wonderfully encouraging in knowing you do something well. The moment you begin to feel resentful about 'all this housework', take a break, ring a friend, play some music, go for a walk, relax. Then return to it later with a clear head and you'll find yourself doing what needs to be done in no time and with no hard feelings. Apart from

you have headphones on, the vacuum won't matter anyway.

Never apologize for the state of your home and never explain. Your visitor probably won't have noticed, or won't care anyway, and most likely their homes are in the same state. Point out the things that are interesting, such as your latest acquisition of a painting, or the latest painting by your toddler, or the fantastic bouquet you got for your birthday, or the first snowdrops out in the garden. If you have a book or two to swap, that'll take your visitor's mind off the state of the tablecloth. I once visited an interior designer in her home, which was a jewel of interesting ideas and pretty finishes. I would have really enjoyed the visit except that she kept apologizing for dust on the glass tabletop (which I couldn't see) and pictures that were not straight, which seemed perfectly straight to me, so instead of being able to enjoy her very attractive and fashionable home I was forced to keep reassuring her that it was perfectly in order (and in a very much better state than my own home).

So the answer to housework is know how to do it, don't shy away from it, but above all be relaxed about it. As long as it is welcoming, warm, comfortable and clean-ish, you should be very happy with your home.

ACKNOWLEDGEMENTS

Many thanks to: Phil and Jane Glynn; Sue MacIntyre; Deborah Wolton; Rosie Lee Phillips; Charlotte Halliday – all busy people who stopped what they were doing when I approached them, and thought about housework and how they outwit it; and always to my mother, who, when I was young, taught me the many wonderful uses for lemons.

Thanks also to Jane Priestman for her patience and support, James Wills for his encouragement, and Jo Stansall for being a lovely editor.

INDEX